OPPOSING VIEWPOINTS® SERIES

Education

Other Books of Related Interest:

Opposing Viewpoints Series

Charter Schools

At Issue Series

Do Schools Prepare Students for a Global Economy?

Do Students Have Too Much Homework?

High School Dropouts

Standardized Testing

What Is the Role of Technology in Education?

Current Controversies Series

E-books

"Congress shall make no law . . . abridging the freedom of speech, or of the press."

First Amendment to the US Constitution

The basic foundation of our democracy is the First Amendment guarantee of freedom of expression. The Opposing Viewpoints Series is dedicated to the concept of this basic freedom and the idea that it is more important to practice it than to enshrine it.

OPPOSING VIEWPOINTS® SERIES

Education

Noël Merino, Book Editor

GREENHAVEN PRESS
A part of Gale, Cengage Learning

GALE
CENGAGE Learning·

Detroit • New York • San Francisco • New Haven, Conn • Waterville, Maine • London

GALE
CENGAGE Learning

Elizabeth Des Chenes, *Director, Content Strategy*
Cynthia Sanner, *Publisher*
Douglas Dentino, *Manager, New Product*

LIBRARY OF CONGRESS CATALOGING-IN-PUBLICATION DATA

Education / Noël Merino.
      pages cm. -- (Opposing viewpoints)
   Summary: "Opposing Viewpoints: Education: Opposing Viewpoints is the leading source for libraries and classrooms in need of current-issue materials. The viewpoints are selected from a wide range of highly respected sources and publications"-- Provided by publisher.
   Includes bibliographical references and index.
   ISBN 978-0-7377-6434-5 (hardback) -- ISBN 978-0-7377-6433-8 (paperback)
   1. Education--Case studies. I. Merino, Noël II. Gale Research Inc.
   LA21.E29 2014
   370--dc23

                                                     2013030015

Printed in the United States of America
   1 2 3 4 5   18 17 16 15 14

Contents

Chapter 3: Should Religion and Religious Ideas Be Part of Public Education?

Chapter 4: How Should the Education System Be Improved?

Why Consider Opposing Viewpoints?

> *"The only way in which a human being can make some approach to knowing the whole of a subject is by hearing what can be said about it by persons of every variety of opinion and studying all modes in which it can be looked at by every character of mind. No wise man ever acquired his wisdom in any mode but this."*
>
> *John Stuart Mill*

In our media-intensive culture it is not difficult to find differing opinions. Thousands of newspapers and magazines and dozens of radio and television talk shows resound with differing points of view. The difficulty lies in deciding which opinion to agree with and which "experts" seem the most credible. The more inundated we become with differing opinions and claims, the more essential it is to hone critical reading and thinking skills to evaluate these ideas. Opposing Viewpoints books address this problem directly by presenting stimulating debates that can be used to enhance and teach these skills. The varied opinions contained in each book examine many different aspects of a single issue. While examining these conveniently edited opposing views, readers can develop critical thinking skills such as the ability to compare and contrast authors' credibility, facts, argumentation styles, use of persuasive techniques, and other stylistic tools. In short, the Opposing Viewpoints Series is an ideal way to attain the higher-level thinking and reading skills so essential in a culture of diverse and contradictory opinions.

In addition to providing a tool for critical thinking, Opposing Viewpoints books challenge readers to question their own strongly held opinions and assumptions. Most people form their opinions on the basis of upbringing, peer pressure, and personal, cultural, or professional bias. By reading carefully balanced opposing views, readers must directly confront new ideas as well as the opinions of those with whom they disagree. This is not to simplistically argue that everyone who reads opposing views will—or should—change his or her opinion. Instead, the series enhances readers' understanding of their own views by encouraging confrontation with opposing ideas. Careful examination of others' views can lead to the readers' understanding of the logical inconsistencies in their own opinions, perspective on why they hold an opinion, and the consideration of the possibility that their opinion requires further evaluation.

Evaluating Other Opinions

To ensure that this type of examination occurs, Opposing Viewpoints books present all types of opinions. Prominent spokespeople on different sides of each issue as well as well-known professionals from many disciplines challenge the reader. An additional goal of the series is to provide a forum for other, less known, or even unpopular viewpoints. The opinion of an ordinary person who has had to make the decision to cut off life support from a terminally ill relative, for example, may be just as valuable and provide just as much insight as a medical ethicist's professional opinion. The editors have two additional purposes in including these less known views. One, the editors encourage readers to respect others' opinions—even when not enhanced by professional credibility. It is only by reading or listening to and objectively evaluating others' ideas that one can determine whether they are worthy of consideration. Two, the inclusion of such viewpoints encourages the important critical thinking skill of objectively evaluating an author's credentials and bias. This evaluation will illuminate an author's reasons for taking a particular stance on an issue and will aid in readers' evaluation of the author's ideas.

It is our hope that these books will give readers a deeper understanding of the issues debated and an appreciation of the complexity of even seemingly simple issues when good and honest people disagree. This awareness is particularly important in a democratic society such as ours in which people enter into public debate to determine the common good. Those with whom one disagrees should not be regarded as enemies but rather as people whose views deserve careful examination and may shed light on one's own.

Thomas Jefferson once said that "difference of opinion leads to inquiry, and inquiry to truth." Jefferson, a broadly educated man, argued that "if a nation expects to be ignorant and free . . . it expects what never was and never will be." As individuals and as a nation, it is imperative that we consider the opinions of others and examine them with skill and discernment. The Opposing Viewpoints Series is intended to help readers achieve this goal.

David L. Bender and Bruno Leone,
Founders

Introduction

"Separate educational facilities are inherently unequal."

Chief Justice Earl Warren,
Brown v. Board of Education *(1954)*

The public school system in the United States of America is rooted in an attempt to bring equal education to all American children. The first major development in establishing public education focused on providing free schools to the poor in the nineteenth century. The second major development was in the twentieth century and aimed to desegregate schools and provide equal education to all Americans regardless of race. In both movements, the core principle of equal education for all emerged, forming the foundation of the public school system that exists today.

The American public school system has its origins in the nineteenth-century movement by several states to provide public funds for education. Prior to that, education had been a function of the family, church, or private entities that charged tuition. During the early nineteenth century, churches and charity organizations promoted free schooling for the poor. In Massachusetts, state legislators James G. Carter and Horace Mann led efforts to establish a system of public schooling in that state. In 1827, Massachusetts passed The Massachusetts Public School Act requiring towns to provide schools and teachers:

> Each town or district of 50 families must have a teacher of orthography, geography, reading, writing, English grammar, arithmetic and good behavior at least 6 months in a year. If of 100 families, there must be teachers to equal 18 months in a year. If 500 families, must equal 24 months in a year and must add the History of the United States, bookkeeping

by single entry, geometry, surveying, and algebra and must have a Master for Latin and Greek.[1]

In 1837, Massachusetts was the first state to establish a board of education, headed by Mann, establishing statewide standards. The advent of free public schooling was driven by the idea that poverty should not be a barrier to education.

By 1870, all states had free elementary schools and by the end of the nineteenth century, public high schools outnumbered private ones. By 1900, more than half the states had laws requiring school attendance until at least age fourteen. Despite progress in establishing schooling for all, schools in the early twentieth century were segregated by race. The US Supreme Court in 1896 had ruled that states were allowed to pass laws requiring racial segregation:

> Laws permitting, and even requiring, their separation in places where they are liable to be brought into contact do not necessarily imply the inferiority of either race to the other, and have been generally, if not universally, recognized as within the competency of the state legislatures in the exercise of their police power. The most common instance of this is connected with the establishment of separate schools for white and colored children, which has been held to be a valid exercise of the legislative power even by courts of States where the political rights of the colored race have been longest and most earnestly enforced.[2]

Thus, during the first half of the nineteenth century, all American students had access to education, but the schools were segregated by race.

The Civil Rights Movement of the mid-twentieth century brought to light the inequalities of segregation. In 1954 the Supreme Court repudiated its 1896 decision, holding in its landmark unanimous decision of *Brown v. Board of Education* that "in the field of public education, the doctrine of 'separate but equal' has no place. Separate educational facilities are inherently unequal."[3] The decision was not welcomed by all, especially by states in the South, and the process of desegregation was lengthy and violent at times. The decision did firmly establish, however, that all Americans were to be treated equally under the law when it came to education.

Despite the establishment of free public schools and the official abandonment of legal segregation, many public schools in America continue to have wide racial and socioeconomic disparities. A 2012 report by the Civil Rights Project contends that racial segregation in public schools continues over fifty years after the Court's decision in *Brown v. Board of Education*: "In spite of the dramatic suburbanization of nonwhite families, 80% of Latino students and 74% of black students attend majority nonwhite schools (50–100% minority), and 43% of Latinos and 38% of blacks attend intensely segregated schools (those with only 0–10% of white students) across the nation." Furthermore, schools are currently segregated by both race and income: "The typical black or Latino today attends school with almost double the share of low-income students in their schools than the typical white or Asian student."[4] Whether these trends undermine the foundational principles for public education is open to debate, but they do illustrate that despite efforts to bring equal education to all American children regardless of income or race, the demographics of public schools show continued segregation in both these spheres.

The mission to establish free public education for all in America is one that has been fraught with questions about the best way to bring education to a diverse nation of students. Students from all socioeconomic, racial, religious, and cultural backgrounds are served by the public school system. Efforts to meet their educational needs and the desires of their parents in a way that promotes equality inevitably create debate at both the national and local levels, prompting a variety of questions, the following of which appear as chapter titles in the current volume: What Is the State of Education in

America?, Are School-Choice Alternatives a Good Idea?, Should Religion and Religious Ideas Be Part of Public Education?, and How Should the Education System Be Improved?

A variety of answers to these questions regarding the current state of public education in America and the proposals for improving the system for all children are explored in *Opposing Viewpoints: Education*.

Notes

1. Quoted in David A. Copeland, *The Antebellum Era: Primary Documents on Events from 1820 to 1860*. Westport, CT: Greenwood Press, 2003.
2. *Plessy v. Ferguson*, 163 US 537 (1896).
3. *Brown v. Board of Education*, 347 US 483 (1954).
4. Gary Orfield, John Kucsera, and Genevieve Siegel-Hawley, "*E Pluribus* . . . Separation: Deepening Double Segregation for More Students," Civil Rights Project, September 2012. www.civilrightsproject.ucla.edu.

OPPOSING
VIEWPOINTS®
SERIES

CHAPTER 1

What Is the State of Education in America?

Chapter Preface

According to the Gallup polling organization, most Americans are dissatisfied with the quality of education that students receive from kindergarten through grade twelve. A poll in August 2012 showed that 37 percent of Americans were somewhat dissatisfied and 16 percent completely dissatisfied, whereas 36 percent were somewhat satisfied and only 8 percent completely satisfied. When Americans were asked how much confidence they had in the public schools, only 11 percent said they had a great deal of confidence, and 28 percent reported very little confidence. When asked to rate public schools, only 5 percent of Americans said that public schools provide children with an excellent education. Thirty-two percent felt that public school education was good, but 42 percent said it was only fair, and 19 percent thought it was poor. Clearly, Americans differ in their assessment of the state of education in America.

In response to widespread dissatisfaction with education outcomes, Congress passed, and President George W. Bush signed, the No Child Left Behind Act (NCLB) in 2001. Among other requirements, NCLB requires all public schools that receive federal funding to administer yearly standardized tests and to give evidence of adequate yearly progress. The states are able to design their own tests and set their own benchmarks for defining and measuring yearly progress. Allowing the states control over education testing and goals is popular among those who want local control of education policy and less federal involvement; however, critics charge that without national standards, there is no reliable way to assess how students are doing from state to state, nor is there a way to ensure that one state's standards are not vastly lower than another state's standards.

When asked to poll Americans in August 2012 about how NCLB has impacted the education of public school students, the Gallup organization reported that only 16 percent of Americans said that it had made education better, whereas 29 percent thought that it had made public school education worse. When asked whether the federal government should be more involved in education, 39 percent of all adults said yes, and 42 percent of parents of school-aged children said yes. But 36 percent of all adults wanted less government involvement, similar to the 35 percent of parents of school-aged children who said the same. There is certainly a consensus that American public education can be improved, but assessments of problem areas and possible solutions vary widely, as the debate in this chapter shows.

> *"Only 6 percent of U.S. students per-*
> *form at the advanced-proficiency level*
> *in math, a share that lags behind kids*
> *in some 30 other countries."*

American Students Perform Poorly Compared to Students in Other Countries

Amanda Ripley

In the following viewpoint, Amanda Ripley argues that educa-
tion in the United States compares unfavorably with interna-
tional levels. Ripley claims that even when comparing individual
states to other countries, no US state comes out in the top twelve.
Furthermore, she contends that researchers have found that even
among the privileged, American students do not stand out among
international groups. Ripley does aver that the relative success of
education in Massachusetts is providing a template for education
reform across the country.

Amanda Ripley writes for the Atlantic Monthly *and* Time
magazine and is the author of The Smartest Kids in the
World—and How They Got That Way.

As you read, consider the following questions:

1. According to the author, which two US states are ranked in the upper-middle tier when comparing math performance internationally?

2. What is the "diversity excuse" that parents give for America's low education ranking internationally, according to Ripley?

3. According to the author, which three other countries spend more than the United States does on elementary and secondary education?

Imagine for a moment that a rich, innovative company is looking to draft the best and brightest high-school grads from across the globe without regard to geography. Let's say this company's recruiter has a round-the-world plane ticket and just a few weeks to scout for talent. Where should he go?

The Quality of U.S. Education

Our hypothetical recruiter knows there's little sense in judging a nation like the United States by comparing it to, say, Finland. This is a big country, after all, and school quality varies dramatically from state to state. What he really wants to know is, should he visit Finland or Florida? Korea or Connecticut? Uruguay or Utah?

Stanford economist Eric Hanushek and two colleagues recently conducted an experiment to answer just such questions, ranking American states and foreign countries side by side. Like our recruiter, they looked specifically at the best and brightest in each place—the kids most likely to get good jobs in the future—using scores on standardized math tests as a proxy for educational achievement.

We've known for some time how this story ends nationwide: only 6 percent of U.S. students perform at the advanced-proficiency level in math, a share that lags behind kids in some 30 other countries, from the United Kingdom to Taiwan. But what happens when we break down the results? Do any individual U.S. states wind up near the top?

Incredibly, no. Even if we treat each state as its own country, not a single one makes it into the top dozen contenders on the list. The best performer is Massachusetts, ringing in at No. 17. Minnesota also makes it into the upper-middle tier, followed by Vermont, New Jersey, and Washington. And down it goes from there, all the way to Mississippi, whose students—by this measure at least—might as well be attending school in Thailand or Serbia.

Explaining Underperformance

Hanushek, who grew up outside Cleveland and graduated from the Air Force Academy in 1965, has the gentle voice and manner of [children's television personality] Mr. Rogers, but he has spent the past 40 years calmly butchering conventional wisdom on education. In study after study, he has demonstrated that our assumptions about what works are almost always wrong. More money does *not* tend to lead to better results; smaller class sizes do *not* tend to improve learning. "Historically," he says, "reporters call me [when] the editor asks, 'What is the other side of this story?'"

Over the years, as Hanushek has focused more on international comparisons, he has heard a variety of theories as to why U.S. students underperform so egregiously. When he started, the prevailing excuse was that the testing wasn't fair. Other countries were testing a more select group of students, while we were testing everyone. That is no longer true: due to better sampling techniques and other countries' decisions to educate more of their citizens, we're now generally comparing apples to apples.

These days, the theory Hanushek hears most often is what we might call the diversity excuse. When he runs into his neighbors at Palo Alto [California] coffee shops, they lament the condition of public schools overall, but are quick to exempt the schools their own kids attend. "In the litany of excuses, one explanation is always, 'We're a very heterogeneous society—all these immigrants are dragging us down. But *our* kids are doing fine,'" Hanushek says. This latest study was designed, in part, to test the diversity excuse.

To do this, Hanushek, along with Paul Peterson at Harvard and Ludger Woessmann at the University of Munich, looked at the American kids performing at the top of the charts on an international math test. (Math tests are easier to normalize across countries, regardless of language barriers; and math skills tend to better predict future earnings than other skills taught in high school.) Then, to get state-by-state data, they correlated the results of that international test with the results of the National Assessment of Educational Progress exam, which is given to a much larger sample in the U.S. and can be used to draw statewide conclusions.

Testing the Diversity Excuse

The international test Hanushek used for this study—the Programme for International Student Assessment, or PISA—is administered every three years to 15-year-olds in about 60 countries. Some experts love this test; others, like Tom Loveless at the Brookings Institution, criticize it as a poor judge of what schools are teaching. But despite his concerns about PISA, Loveless, who has read an advance version of Hanushek's study, agrees with its primary conclusion. "The United States does not do a good job of educating kids at the top," he says. "There's a long-standing attitude that, 'Well, smart kids can make it on their own. And after all, they're doing well. So why worry about them?'"

Of course, the fact that no U.S. state does very well compared with other rich nations does not necessarily disprove the diversity excuse: parents in Palo Alto could reasonably infer that California's poor ranking (in the bottom third, just

Student Achievement in Advanced Math

This three-page chart shows the percentage of students at an advanced level of math achievement in the fifty states and in countries participating in the 2006 Programme for International Student Assessment (PISA).

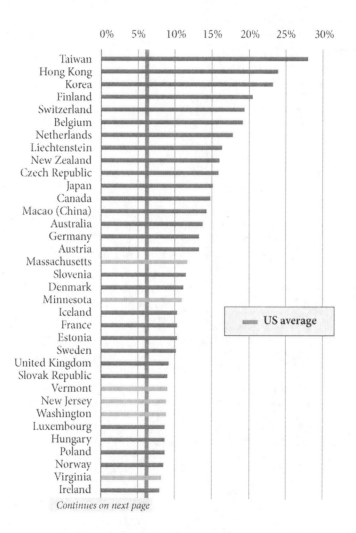

TAKEN FROM: Eric A. Hanushek, Paul E. Peterson, and Ludger Woessmann, "Teaching Math to the Talented," *Education Next*, Winter 2011.

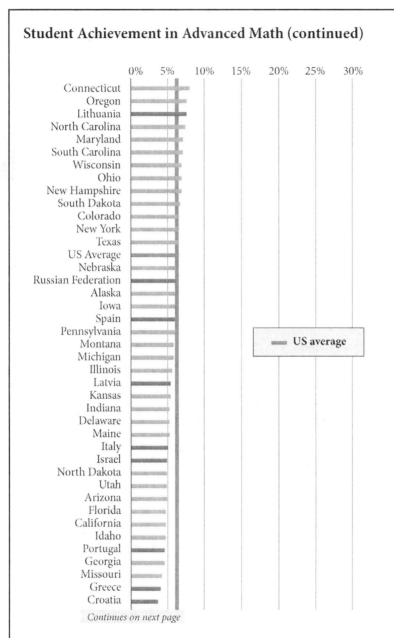

Student Achievement in Advanced Math (continued)

| | 0% | 5% | 10% | 15% | 20% | 25% | 30% |

Connecticut
Oregon
Lithuania
North Carolina
Maryland
South Carolina
Wisconsin
Ohio
New Hampshire
South Dakota
Colorado
New York
Texas
US Average
Nebraska
Russian Federation
Alaska
Iowa
Spain
Pennsylvania
Montana
Michigan
Illinois
Latvia
Kansas
Indiana
Delaware
Maine
Italy
Israel
North Dakota
Utah
Arizona
Florida
California
Idaho
Portugal
Georgia
Missouri
Greece
Croatia

US average

Continues on next page

TAKEN FROM: Eric A. Hanushek, Paul E. Peterson, and Ludger Woessmann, "Teaching Math to the Talented," *Education Next*, Winter 2011.

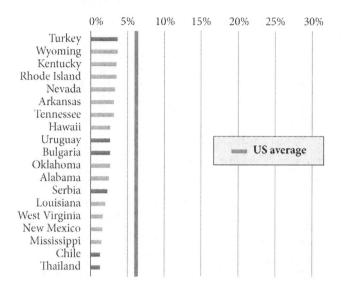

Student Achievement in Advanced Math (continued)

Based on data from the US National Assessment of Educational Progress (NAEP) and from the Organisation for Economic Co-Operation and Development (OECD), which conducts the PISA assessment. Excludes participating countries below 1 percent: Romania, Argentina, Azerbaijan, Mexico, Qatar, Tunisia, Colombia, Indonesia, Jordan, and Kyrgyzstan.

TAKEN FROM: Eric A. Hanushek, Paul E. Peterson, and Ludger Woessmann, "Teaching Math to the Talented," *Education Next*, Winter 2011.

above Portugal and below Italy) is a function of the state's large population of poor and/or immigrant children, and does not reflect their own kids' relatively well-off circumstances.

So Hanushek and his co-authors sliced the data more thinly still. They couldn't control for income, since students don't report their parents' salaries when they take these tests; but they could use reliable proxies. How would our states do if we looked just at the white kids performing at high levels—kids who are not, generally speaking, subject to language barriers or racial discrimination? Or if we looked just at kids with at least one college-educated parent?

As it turned out, even these relatively privileged students do not compete favorably with average students in other well-off countries. On a percentage basis, New York state has fewer high performers among white kids than Poland has among kids overall. In Illinois, the percentage of kids with a college-educated parent who are highly skilled at math is lower than the percentage of such kids among *all* students in Iceland, France, Estonia, and Sweden.

Parents in Palo Alto will always insist that their kids are the exception, of course. And researchers cannot compare small cities and towns around the globe—not yet, anyway. But Hanushek thinks the study significantly undercuts the diversity excuse. "People will find it quite shocking," he says, "that even our most-advantaged students are not all that competitive."

The Success in Massachusetts

Reading the list, one cannot help but thank God for Massachusetts, which offers the United States some shred of national dignity—a result echoed in other international tests. "If all American fourth- and eighth-grade kids did as well in math and science as they do in Massachusetts," writes the veteran education author Karin Chenoweth in her 2009 book, *How It's Being Done,* "we still wouldn't be in Singapore's league but we'd be giving Japan and Chinese Taipei a run for their money."

Is it because Massachusetts is so white? Or so immigrant-free? Or so rich? Not quite. Massachusetts is indeed slightly whiter and slightly better-off than the U.S. average. But in the late 1990s, it nonetheless lagged behind similar states—such as Connecticut and Maine—in nationwide tests of fourth- and eighth-graders. It was only after a decade of educational reforms that Massachusetts began to rank first in the nation.

What did Massachusetts do? Well, nothing that many countries (and industries) didn't do a long time ago. For example, Massachusetts made it harder to become a teacher, requiring newcomers to pass a basic literacy test before entering the classroom. (In the first year, more than a third of the new teachers failed the test.) The state also required students to pass a test before graduating from high school—a notion so heretical that it led to protests in which students burned state superintendent David Driscoll in effigy. To help tutor the kids who failed, the state moved money around to the places where it was needed most. "We had a system of standards and held people to it—adults and students," Driscoll says.

Massachusetts, in other words, began demanding meaningful outcomes from everyone in the school building. Obvious though it may seem, it's an idea that remains sacrilegious in many U.S. schools, despite the clumsy advances of No Child Left Behind.[1] Instead, we still fixate on inputs—such as how much money we are pouring into the system or how small our class sizes are—and wind up with little to show for it. Since the early 1970s, we've doubled the amount of money we spend per pupil nationwide, but our high-schoolers' reading and math scores have barely budged.

Per student, we now spend more than all but three other countries—Luxembourg, Switzerland, and Norway—on elementary and secondary education. And the list of countries that spend the most, notably, has little in common with the outcomes that Hanushek and his colleagues put into rank order. (The same holds true on the state level, where New York, one of the highest-spending states—it topped the list at $17,000 per pupil in 2008—still comes in behind 15 other states and 30 countries on Hanushek's list.)

---

1. The No Child Left Behind Act of 2001 requires individual states to set high educational standards and develop appropriate assessments to improve educational outcomes for students.

The Adoption of Common Standards

However haltingly, more states are finally beginning to follow the lead of Massachusetts. At least 35 states and the District of Columbia agreed this year [2010] to adopt common standards for what kids should know in math and language arts—standards informed in part by what kids in top-performing countries are learning. Still, all of the states, Massachusetts included, have a long way to go. Last year [2009], a study comparing standardized math tests given to third-graders in Massachusetts and Hong Kong found embarrassing disparities. Even at that early age, kids in Hong Kong were being asked more-demanding questions that required more-complex responses.

Meanwhile, a 2010 study of teacher-prep programs in 16 countries found a striking correlation between how well students did on international exams and how their future teachers performed on a math test. In the U.S., researchers tested nearly 3,300 teachers-to-be in 39 states. The results? Our future middle-school math teachers knew about as much math as their peers in Thailand and Oman—and nowhere near what future teachers in Taiwan and Singapore knew. Moreover, the results showed dramatic variation depending on the teacher-training program. Perhaps this should not be surprising: teachers cannot teach what they do not know, and to date, most have not been required to know very much math.

Early last year, President [Barack] Obama reminded Congress, "The countries that out-teach us today will out-compete us tomorrow." This September, Ontario Premier Dalton McGuinty, visiting a local school on the first day of classes, mentioned Obama's warning and smugly took note of the scoreboard: "Well," he said, "we are out-teaching them today."

Arne Duncan, Obama's education secretary, responded to the premier's trash-talking a few days later. "When I played professional basketball in Australia, that's the type of quote the coach would post on the bulletin board in the locker room," he declared during a speech in Toronto. And then his rejoinder came to a crashing halt. "In all seriousness," Duncan confessed, "Premier McGuinty spoke the truth."

"Among the 25 nations participating at 4th grade, the U.S. is sixth with an estimated 37% of its students proficient or better on the 2007 [National Assessment of Educational Progress]."

American Students Perform Favorably Compared to Students in Other Countries

Gerald W. Bracey

In the following viewpoint, Gerald W. Bracey argues that statistics on educational performance show that the United States ranks higher than most nations. Bracey contends that although the United States has a few cities that do not rank very well, he denies that there is a crisis in education. Furthermore, Bracey claims that there is no significant correlation between the performance of students on tests and the level of innovation or economic success of a nation.

Gerald W. Bracey is a fellow at several educational think tanks, a frequently published commentator, and the author of several books on the topic of education, including Setting the

Gerald W. Bracey, "U.S. School Performance, Through a Glass Darkly (Again)," *Phi Delta Kappan*, vol. 90, no. 5, January 2009, pp. 386–387. Reprinted with permission of Phi Delta Kappa International, www.pdkintl.org. All rights reserved.

Record Straight: Responses to Misconceptions About Public Education in the U.S.

As you read, consider the following questions:

1. The author reports that the United States ranked in what place among forty-four countries in math proficiency at eighth grade?

2. What European country does Bracey say Chicago eighth graders fare better than in math proficiency?

3. Which three cities in the United States does the author say score higher "percent proficient" than the average Organisation for Economic Cooperation and Development nation?

I suppose we must expect gloomy predictions about schools from those who have vested interests in depicting them as ruinous, but we shouldn't expect to see such from a place like the American Institutes for Research (AIR). But that's what we get from AIR's Gary Phillips and John Dossey of Illinois State University, authors of *Counting on the Future: International Benchmarks for American School Districts.*

An Inaccurate Assessment

The report, like so many similar reports, begins with false premises and closes with an illogical conclusion. The premises are these:

> Large corporations locate their businesses in U.S. cities; foreign students attend U.S. schools; and U.S. businesses export goods and services to foreign nations. Large urban cities need to know how their students stack up against peers in the nations with which the U.S. does business. This is especially important for students in the fields of science, technology, engineering, and mathematics. The students in these fields will allow our future generation [sic] to remain technologically innovative and economically competitive.

It's hard to imagine a shorter paragraph containing more misinformation. Did BMW build a plant in South Carolina, Mercedes a plant in Alabama, and did Nissan move its U.S. headquarters to Tennessee because of these states' high math scores? Hardly. They built and moved [to these states] because they got enormous tax breaks, no unions, and cheaper labor.

Second, this report compares average scores in the U.S. and selected U.S. cities with average scores in other nations. Such comparisons tell us nothing. Reports such as AIR's concentrate on the supply side of skills and ignore the demand side. Does the market demand more scientists and engineers? Hardly. The U.S. has three new native-born or permanent-resident scientists and engineers for every new scientific and engineering position being created. What the market wants is cheap scientists and engineers, which is no doubt why 65% of new graduates leave science and engineering within two years.

Third, the recent Global Competitiveness Report 2008–2009 from the World Economic Forum (WEF) ranks the U.S. #1—again. Japan's kids were acing tests when *A Nation at Risk*[1] was published 25 years ago and they continued to ace tests even as that nation sank into 15 years of economic recession and stagnation. The link between test scores and a nation's economic health simply isn't there. Does anyone—anyone!—think low test scores created the current crisis? If so, it would have to be the low scores of business school graduates on ethics tests.

A Comparison of Nations

Phillips and Dossey use a linking technique that permits one to estimate how students from other nations would perform if they sat for our NAEP [National Assessment of Educational Progress] tests. The report first summarizes the U.S. generally

1. The 1983 report of President Ronald Reagan's National Commission on Excellence in Education that warned of America's failing schools and called for education reforms to boost student achievement.

Math Proficiency Worldwide

Comparison of the 2007 grade 4 National Assessment of Education Progress (NAEP) in mathematics for the United States and the 2003 grade 4 Trends in International Mathematics and Science Study (TIMSS) results for the percent at and above proficient, based on NAEP achievement levels projected onto the TIMSS scale

Percent at and above proficient

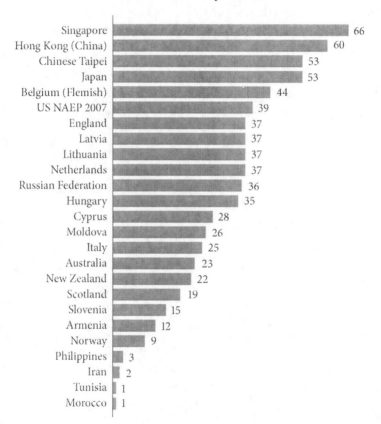

Singapore	66
Hong Kong (China)	60
Chinese Taipei	53
Japan	53
Belgium (Flemish)	44
US NAEP 2007	39
England	37
Latvia	37
Lithuania	37
Netherlands	37
Russian Federation	36
Hungary	35
Cyprus	28
Moldova	26
Italy	25
Australia	23
New Zealand	22
Scotland	19
Slovenia	15
Armenia	12
Norway	9
Philippines	3
Iran	2
Tunisia	1
Morocco	1

TAKEN FROM: Gary W. Phillips and John A. Dossey, "Counting on the Future: International Benchmarks in Mathematics for American School Districts," American Institutes for Research, October 2008.

against other nations participating in the math segment of TIMSS [Trends in International Mathematics and Science Study]. Among the 25 nations participating at 4th grade, the U.S. is sixth with an estimated 37% of its students proficient or better on the 2007 NAEP. At 8th grade, the U.S. is 10th of 44 countries with 31% proficient. These rankings are the seeds of crisis?

Interestingly, only four nations have a majority of students proficient at the 4th-grade level, only five manage it at 8th grade. Singapore is tops in both grades with 66% proficient at 4th grade, 73% proficient at 8th grade. At 8th grade, 14 nations have 5% or fewer proficient. Norway has 9%, Italy 18%, Sweden 21%, Scotland and New Zealand 22%. These countries are generally considered "competitor nations." For four nations, including Saudi Arabia, the percent proficient rounds down to zero.

A Comparison of Cities

The report then considers results from the TIMSS nations held up against "large urban cities" that had participated in the 2007 NAEP. Some cities that are often cited as horrible examples take their lumps here. Chicago has only 16% proficient at 4th grade, 13% proficient at 8th grade—but that's better than Norway's 9%. Yet the WEF ranks Norway higher than high-scoring Taiwan (16th vs. 17th) and almost as high as Japan (9th), Korea (13th), and Hong Kong (11th). Only Singapore at 5th puts what looks like real daylight between itself and Norway. But it ranks behind Sweden in the WEF report, though 73% of its 8th graders are proficient compared to Sweden's 21%. The link between test scores and economies is simply not there.

For Los Angeles, the figures are 19% and 14% and for Atlanta, 20% and 11%. Cleveland and the District of Columbia make double digits only at 4th grade.

But Houston is almost at the median at 4th grade (28%) and above the median at 8th grade (21%). And New York City is at the median in 4th grade (34%) and above it at 8th grade (22%). And Boston scores 27% proficient at both grades. San Diego gets 35% of its 4th graders to the proficient level but falls to 24% at 8th grade.

Two cities that are often perceived as university towns, Austin and Charlotte, do even better. Charlotte finishes higher than the U.S. average with 44% proficient at 4th grade and 34% at 8th grade. This figure ranks it sixth among 25 nations at 4th grade and 10th among 44 at 8th grade. Austin has the same rankings, having 40% of 4th graders proficient and 34% of 8th graders. This means that at 4th grade, Austin and Charlotte are just behind Singapore, Hong Kong, Taiwan, Japan, and Flemish Belgium.

The Significance of Differences

The report examines how the cities stack up against the average of the nations. At 4th grade, Austin, Charlotte, San Diego, and the U.S. as a whole do significantly better than the TIMSS average. Houston and Boston do about the same, while Atlanta, Chicago, Cleveland, Los Angeles, and the District of Columbia do significantly worse.

At 8th grade, Austin, Boston, Charlotte, and the U.S. as a whole do significantly better than the international average. Houston, San Diego, and New York City do about the same. Atlanta, Chicago, Cleveland, Los Angeles, and the District of Columbia do significantly worse.

Keep in mind that these "significant" differences are purely statistical. We have no idea about any practical significance.

Well, you say, when we compare American cities against individual countries or the TIMSS average, we're including some nations whose percent proficient rounds to zero. Thus the report goes on to compare the percent proficient in the cities and the average for the industrialized nations of the Organisation for Economic Co-operation and Development (OECD).

At 4th grade, Charlotte, Austin, San Diego, and the U.S. as a whole score significantly better than the average OECD nation. Boston, Houston, and New York City score about the same, while the other five cities—Atlanta, Boston, Chicago, Cleveland, and the District of Columbia—scored lower. At 8th grade, no city outperforms the OECD average. Charlotte, Austin, and the U.S. as a whole perform as well, but the other cities are all below the OECD average.

An Illogical Conclusion

The report closes with the usual illogical conclusion that because our kids don't match Singapore's in math, "we are already at a competitive disadvantage." I don't think so. I've reported on how employers are emphasizing soft skills and college admissions officers put more weight on extracurricular activities than on SAT [Scholastic Aptitude Test] scores. Equally important, just as these "dark side" reports never consider the demand for skills, they never take into account cultural variables. Most people who do the dirty work in Singapore actually live in Malaysia. Many long-term "guest workers" in Singapore come from the Philippines and can't bring their families with them. Singapore is thus spared the efforts required to educate an economically diverse population.

In [the October 26, 2008, *Boston Globe*], Jay Mathews wrote, "the impression that our schools are losing out to the rest of the world, that we are not producing enough scientists and engineers, is a misunderstanding fueled by misleading statistics." True enough. AIR's statistics are in places misleading, but their worst flaw is that the authors misinterpret them.

> *"It's difficult to overstate how extensive a role the unions play in making America's schools what they are—and in preventing them from being something different."*

Teachers' Unions Have Not Been Good for American Education

Terry M. Moe

In the following viewpoint, Terry M. Moe argues that the immense power of teachers' unions has led to poor public education. Moe claims that because the interests of the unions are different from—and at odds with—the interests of children, bad teachers are protected by a perversely organized system. Moe concludes, however, that the time is particularly ripe for change.

Terry M. Moe is a senior fellow at the Hoover Institution and a member of the institution's Koret Task Force on K–12 Education; he is the William Bennett Munro Professor of Political Science at Stanford University and the author of Special Interest: Teachers Unions and America's Public Schools.

As you read, consider the following questions:

1. According to the author, how much does New York City spend each year on salary and benefits for teachers who have been removed from classrooms?

2. During what two decades, according to Moe, did most teachers in the United States join unions?

3. What three examples does the author give in support of his claim that changes wrought by technology will undermine union power?

Janet Archer painted watercolors. Gordon Russell planned trips to Alaska and Cape Cod. Others did crossword puzzles, read books, played chess, practiced ballet moves, argued with one another, and otherwise tried to fill up the time. The place was New York City. The year was 2009. And these were public school teachers passing a typical day in one of the city's Rubber Rooms—Temporary Reassignment Centers—where teachers were housed when they were considered so unsuited to teaching that they needed to be kept out of the classroom, away from the city's children.

The Union Defended Bad Teachers

There were more than seven hundred teachers in New York City's Rubber Rooms that year. Each school day they went to "work." They arrived in the morning at exactly the same hour as other city teachers, and they left at exactly the same hour in the afternoon. They got paid a full salary. They received full benefits, as well as all the usual vacation days, and they had their summers off. Just like real teachers. Except they didn't teach.

All of this cost the city between $35 million and $65 million a year for salary and benefits alone, depending on who was doing the estimating. And the total costs were even greater, for the district hired substitutes to teach their classes, rented space for the Rubber Rooms, and forked out half a million dollars annually for security guards to keep the teachers safe (mainly from one another, as tensions ran high in these places). At a time when New York City was desperate for money to fund its schools, it was spending a fortune every year for seven-hundred-plus teachers to stare at the walls.

Mayor Michael Bloomberg and Chancellor Joel Klein wanted to move bad teachers out of the system and off the payroll. But they couldn't. While most of their teachers were doing a good job in the classroom, the problem was that all teachers—even the incompetent and the dangerous—were protected by state tenure laws, by restrictive collective bargaining contracts, and by the local teachers' union, the United Federation of Teachers (UFT), which was the power behind the laws and the contracts and the legal defender of each and every teacher whose job was in trouble.

With such a big defensive line, teachers who were merely mediocre could not be touched. So Bloomberg and Klein chose to remove just the more egregious cases and send them to Rubber Rooms. But even these teachers stayed on the payroll—for a long time. They didn't leave; they didn't give up; and because the legal procedures were so thickly woven and offered union lawyers so much to work with, it took from two to five years just to resolve the typical case.

Undermining Education

Sometimes it seems that public education operates in a parallel universe, in which what is obviously perverse and debilitating for the organization of schools has become normal and expected. The purpose of the American public school system is to educate children. And because this is so, everything about the public schools—how they are staffed, how they are funded, and more generally how they are organized to do their work—should be decided with the best interests of children in mind. But this isn't what happens. Not even remotely.

The New York City school district is not organized to provide the best possible education to its children. As things now stand, it can't be. Why? If we could view the district's entire organization, we would doubtless find many reasons. But when it comes to bad teachers alone, the district is wasting millions of dollars because the rules it is required to follow in operating the schools—rules that are embedded in the local collective bargaining contract and state law—prevent it from quickly, easily, and inexpensively removing these teachers from the classroom. Getting bad teachers out of the classroom is essential if kids are to be educated effectively. Yet the formal rules prevent it.

These rules are part of the organization of New York City's schools. The district is literally *organized* to protect bad teachers and to undermine the efforts of leaders to ensure teacher quality. It is also *organized* to require that huge amounts of money be wasted on endless, unnecessary procedures. These undesirable outcomes do not happen by accident. They happen by design.

New York may seem unusual. Its dimensions dwarf those of the typical American school district, and its organizational perversities may be extreme as well. But the kind of problem I discuss here is quite common. Almost everywhere, in districts throughout the nation, America's public schools are typically not organized to provide the nation's children with the highest quality education.

Rules That Protect Bad Teachers

One example: salary schedules that pay teachers based on their seniority and formal credits and have nothing whatever to do with whether their students are learning anything. Another example: rules that give senior teachers their choice of jobs and make it impossible for districts to allocate teachers where they can do the greatest good for kids. Another example: rules that require districts to lay off teachers (in times of reduced revenues or enrollments, say) in reverse order of seniority, thus ensuring that excellent teachers will be automatically fired if they happen to have little seniority and that lousy teachers will be automatically retained if they happen to have lots of seniority.

These sorts of rules are common. But who in their right mind, if they were organizing the schools for the benefit of children, would organize them in this way? No one would. Yet the schools do get organized in this way. The examples I've given are the tip of a very large iceberg. As a result, even the most obvious steps toward better education are difficult, if not impossible, to take.

Researchers have long known, for example, that when a student is fortunate enough to have a teacher near the high end of the quality distribution rather than a teacher near the low end, the impact amounts to an entire year's worth of additional learning. Teacher quality makes an enormous difference. Indeed, even if the quality variation across teachers is less stark, the consequences for kids can still be profound. As researchers Eric Hanushek and Steven Rivkin report, if students had good teachers rather than merely average teachers for four or five years in a row, "the increased learning would be sufficient to close entirely the average gap between a typical low-income student receiving a free or reduced-price lunch and the average student who is not receiving free or reduced-price lunches." In other words, it would eliminate the achievement gap that this nation has struggled to overcome for decades. Good teachers matter, and they matter a lot. Yet our school system is organized to make it virtually impossible to get bad teachers out of the classroom, bases key personnel decisions on seniority rather than expertise, and in countless other ways erects obstacles to providing children with the best possible teachers.

The Influence of Teachers' Unions

Ineffective organization has long been an open secret. *A Nation at Risk* [the Ronald Reagan administration's study of the status of American education] warned in 1983 of a "rising tide of mediocrity" in America's schools—leading to a frenzied era of nonstop reforms that, it was hoped, would bring dramatic improvement. But today the facts show that this dramatic improvement hasn't happened, and that bold reforms are still needed to turn the schools around. The most intensive period of school reform in the nation's history has largely been a failure. So we now have two questions to ponder. To the first, which asks why the public schools are burdened by ineffective organization, we can add a second: why has the reform movement, which for a quarter century has been dedicated to bringing effective organization to the nation's schools, failed to do that? The answer to both questions, I argue, is much the same: these problems are largely due to the power of the teachers' unions.

It might seem that the teachers' unions would play a limited role in public education: fighting for better pay and working conditions for their members, but otherwise having little impact on the structure and performance of the public schools more generally. Yet nothing could be further from the truth. The teachers' unions have more influence on the public schools than any other group in American society.

Their influence takes two forms. They shape the schools from the bottom up, through collective bargaining activities so broad in scope that virtually every aspect of school organization bears the distinctive imprint of union design. They also shape the schools from the top down, through political activities that give them unrivaled influence over the laws and regulations imposed on public education by government, and that allow them to block or weaken governmental reforms they find threatening. In combining bottom-up and top-down in-

The Monopoly of Unions

Since public schools already enjoy a monopoly on nearly $600 billion in annual government education spending, the chief way in which the NEA [National Education Association] and AFT [American Federation of Teachers] minimize competition is by lobbying elected officials to maintain that monopoly—opposing policies such as charter schools, vouchers, and education tax credits that give families easier access to nonunion schooling . . . Union political contributions at the federal level are substantial. In fact, if the NEA and AFT are taken together (not unreasonable, given that they overwhelmingly support the same party and pursue a similar agenda), they constitute the most generous source of federal political donations over the past 20 years. According to a ranking by the Center for Responsive Politics (2009), the NEA and AFT together have spent $56 million on federal political contributions since 1989, roughly as much as [oil giants] Chevron, Exxon Mobil, the NRA [National Rifle Association], and [aeronautics leader] Lockheed Martin combined.

Andrew J. Coulson,
Cato Journal, *Winter 2010.*

fluence, and in combining them as potently as they do, the teachers' unions are unique among all actors in the educational arena.

The Rise of Union Power

It's difficult to overstate how extensive a role the unions play in making America's schools what they are—and in preventing them from being something different.

Before the 1960s, the power holders in America's public school system were the administrative professionals charged with running it, as well as the local school boards who appointed them. Teachers had little power, and they were unorganized aside from their widespread membership in the National Education Association (NEA), which was a professional organization controlled by administrators. In the 1960s, however, states began to adopt laws that for the first time promoted collective bargaining for public employees. When the American Federation of Teachers (AFT) launched a campaign to organize the nation's teachers into unions, the NEA turned itself into a labor union (and eventually kicked out the administrators) to compete, and the battle was on in thousands of school districts. By the time the dust settled in the early 1980s, virtually all districts of any size (outside the South) were successfully organized, collective bargaining was the norm, and the teachers' unions reigned supreme as the most powerful force in American education.

This transformation—the rise of union power—created what was essentially a new system of public education. This new system has now been in equilibrium for roughly thirty years, and throughout this time it has been vigorously protected—and stabilized—by the very union power that created it.

The Political Power of the Unions

The trademark of this new system is not just that the teachers' unions are pre-eminently powerful. It is also that they *use* their power to promote their own special interests—and *to make the organization of schooling a reflection of those interests.* They say, of course, that what is good for teachers is good for kids. But the simple fact is that they are not in the business of representing kids. They are unions. They represent the job-related interests of their *members,* and these interests are *not the same* as the interests of children.

Some things are obvious. It is not good for children that ineffective teachers cannot be removed from the classroom. It is not good for children that teachers cannot be assigned to the classrooms where they are needed most. It is not good for children that excellent young teachers get laid off before mediocre colleagues with more seniority. Yet the unions fight to see that schools are organized in these ways.

And there's more. The organization of schooling goes beyond the personnel rules of collective-bargaining contracts to include all the formal components of the school system: accountability, choice, funding, class size, special education, and virtually anything else policymakers deem relevant. These matters are subject to the authority of state and national governments, where they are fought out in the political process—and decisions are heavily determined by political power.

Here the unions' great strength as political organizations comes into play. The NEA and the AFT, with more than four million members between them, are by far the most powerful groups in the politics of education. They wield astounding sums of money, year after year, for campaign contributions and lobbying. They have armies of well-educated activists in every political district. They can orchestrate well-financed public-relations and media campaigns any time they want, on any topic or candidate. And they have supremely well-developed organizational apparatuses that blanket the country.

They don't always get their way on public policy, of course. The American system of checks and balances makes that impossible. But these same checks and balances also ensure that *blocking* new laws is much easier than getting them passed, and this is how the teachers' unions have used their power to great effect: not by getting the policies they want, but by stopping or weakening the policies they *don't* want—and thus preventing true education reform.

The Chance for Change

From the beginning of the reform era, reformers have focused on the problem of ineffective schools, and thus on fixing the schools themselves. Yet they have failed to resolve this problem because there is another problem—the problem of union power—that is more fundamental, and has prevented them from fixing the schools in ways that make sense and have real promise. If our nation ever hopes to transform the public schools, this problem of union power must be recognized for what it is. And it must be resolved.

But can it be resolved? This is the pivotal question for the future of American education. The answer, I believe, is yes— although major change may take decades.

In normal times, reformers who try to change the system or its underlying power structure will almost always lose. This is the Catch-22 of power: if you try to weaken powerful groups, they will normally be able to use their power to stop you. Yet, fortunately for the nation, *these are not normal times.* American education stands at what political scientists would call a critical juncture. Because of a largely accidental and quite abnormal confluence of events, the stars are lining up in a way that makes major change possible, and in fact will drive it forward. Two separate dynamics are at work.

Two Dynamics Supporting Change

The first is arising "endogenously"—that is, within the education system and its politics. More than at any other time in modern history, the teachers' unions are on the defensive: blamed for obstructing reform, defending bad teachers, imposing seniority rules, and in general, using their power to promote their own interests rather than the interests of kids and effective organization. And open criticism is coming not just from conservatives anymore. It is also coming from liberals, moderates, and Democrats. Key constituencies have become fed up. Fed up with perpetually abysmal schools for disadvantaged kids. Fed up with the party's perpetual impotence with regard to reform. Fed up with what Jonathan Alter of *Newsweek* has called the "stranglehold of the teachers' unions on the Democratic Party." The demand is palpable for the party to free itself to pursue serious education reform in the best interests of children, especially those who need it the most.

But the shifting political tides *will not be enough* to bring about major education reform. Absent some other dynamic, the unions will remain very powerful, with over four million members, tons of money, countless activists, and all their other weapons still intact. Their Democratic allies will allow reform to go only so far before pulling up short. Luckily, another dynamic *is* at work. This one is "exogenous"—arising entirely outside the educational and political systems—and will ultimately dovetail nicely with the political trends that are running against the unions. I'm speaking about the revolution in information technology, one of the most profoundly influential forces ever to hit this planet. It is fast transforming the fundamentals of human society, from how people communicate and interact to how they collect information, gain knowledge, and transact business. There is no doubt that it has the capacity to transform the way children learn, and that it will ultimately revolutionize education systems all around the world, including our own.

The specific kinds of changes wrought by technology—among them the massive substitution of technology for labor, the growing irrelevance of geography for teaching (which means that teachers can be anywhere, and no longer need to be concentrated in districts), and the huge expansion in attractive alternatives to the regular (unionized) public schools—are destined to undermine the very foundations of union power and make it much more difficult for them to block reform and impose their special interests through politics. This will lay the groundwork, over a period of decades, for truly massive reforms—and for the rise of a new system that is much more responsive to children's needs and much better organized to provide the quality education they deserve.

> "There is no strong evidence that unions
> ... [are] at 'the heart' of our education
> problems."

Bipartisan, But Unfounded: The Assault on Teachers' Unions

Richard D. Kahlenberg

In the following viewpoint, Richard D. Kahlenberg argues that the attack on teachers' unions is unwarranted. Kahlenberg claims that collective bargaining is important for democracy and important for education, arguing that educators' interests align more closely with students' interests than other groups. He concludes that teachers' unions can help to bring about educational reform, and he contends that the general public strongly supports the collective bargaining rights of public employees.

Richard D. Kahlenberg is a senior fellow at the Century Foundation and coauthor of Why Labor Organizing Should Be a Civil Right: Rebuilding a Middle-Class Democracy by Enhancing Worker Voice.

Richard D. Kahlenberg, "Bipartisan, But Unfounded: The Assault on Teachers' Unions," *American Educator*, vol. 35, no. 4, Winter 2011–2012, pp. 14–18. Copyright © 2012 by the American Educator. All rights reserved. Reproduced by permission.

As you read, consider the following questions:

1. Kahlenberg argues that collective bargaining not only advances individual interests but also works to balance out the forces of what two entities?

2. Which six states does the author identify as having long forbidden collective bargaining for teachers?

3. What percentage of Americans oppose ending collective bargaining for public sector employees, according to a poll cited by Kahlenberg?

Teachers' unions are under unprecedented bipartisan attack. The drumbeat is relentless, from governors in Wisconsin and Ohio to the film directors of *Waiting for "Superman"* and *The Lottery*; from new lobbying groups like Michelle Rhee's StudentsFirst and Wall Street's Democrats for Education Reform to political columnists such as Jonathan Alter and George Will; from new books like political scientist Terry Moe's *Special Interest* and entrepreneurial writer Steven Brill's *Class Warfare* to even, at times, members of the Obama administration. The consistent message is that teachers' unions are the central impediment to educational progress in the United States.

Part of the assault is unsurprising given its partisan origins. Republicans have long been critical, going back to at least 1996, when presidential candidate Bob Dole scolded teachers' unions: "If education were a war, you would be losing it. If it were a business, you would be driving it into bankruptcy. If it were a patient, it would be dying." If you're a Republican who wants to win elections, going after teachers' unions makes parochial sense. According to Terry Moe, the National Education Association (NEA) and the American Federation of Teachers (AFT) gave 95 percent of their contributions to Democrats in federal elections between 1989 and 2010.[1] The nakedly partisan nature of Wisconsin Governor

Scott Walker's attack on public sector collective bargaining was exposed when he exempted from his legislation two unions that supported him politically: one representing police officers and the other representing firefighters.

What's new and particularly disturbing is that partisan Republicans are now joined by many liberals and Democrats in attacking teachers' unions. Davis Guggenheim, an avowed liberal who directed Al Gore's anti–global warming documentary *An Inconvenient Truth* and Barack Obama's convention biopic, was behind *Waiting for "Superman."* Normally liberal *New York Times* columnist Nicholas Kristof regularly attacks teachers' unions, as does Steven Brill, who contributed to the campaigns of Hillary Clinton and Barack Obama, yet compares teachers' union leaders to Saddam Hussein loyalists and South African apartheid officials. A string of current and former Democratic school superintendents (including New York City's Joel Klein and San Diego's Alan Bersin) have blamed unions for education's woes. Even President Obama strongly supports nonunionized charter schools and famously applauded the firing of every single teacher in Central Falls, Rhode Island.

The litany of complaints about teachers' unions is familiar. They make it "virtually impossible to get bad teachers out of the classroom," says Moe.[2] Critics claim they oppose school choice, oppose merit pay, and oppose efforts to have excellent teachers "assigned" to high-poverty schools where they are needed most.

Growing Democratic support of these criticisms has emboldened conservatives to go even further and call for the complete abolition of collective bargaining for teachers a half-century after it started.[3] Conservative education professor Jay Greene pines for a "return to the pre-collective bargaining era."[4] Teachers' unions "are at the heart" of our education problems, Moe says.[5] "As long as the teachers' unions remain powerful," he writes, the "basic requirements" of educational success "cannot be met."[6] The idea that policymakers can work with "reform" union leaders is, in his view, "completely wrong-headed,"[7] "fanciful and misguided."[8]

Critics suggest that collective bargaining for teachers is stacked, even undemocratic. Unlike the case of the private sector, where management and labor go head-to-head with clearly distinct interests, they say, in the case of teachers, powerful unions are actively involved in electing school board members, essentially helping pick the management team. Moreover, when collective bargaining covers education policy areas—such as class size or discipline codes—the public is shut out from the negotiations, they assert. Along the way, the interests of adults in the system are served, but not the interests of children, these critics suggest.

Criticisms Abound, Evidence Does Not

The critics' contentions, which I'll sum up as collective bargaining and teachers' unions being undemocratic and bad for schoolchildren, have no real empirical support. Democratic societies throughout the world recognize the basic right of employees to band together to pursue their interests and secure a decent standard of living, whether in the private or public sector. Article 23 of the 1948 Universal Declaration of Human Rights provides not only that workers should be shielded from discrimination but also that "everyone has the right to form and to join trade unions for the protection of his interests."[9]

Collective bargaining is important in a democracy, not only to advance individual interests, but to give unions the power to serve as a countervailing force against big business and big government. Citing the struggle of Polish workers against the Communist regime, Ronald Reagan declared in a Labor Day speech in 1980: "Where free unions and collective bargaining are forbidden, freedom is lost."[10]

In the United States, 35 states and the District of Columbia have collective bargaining by statute or by state constitution for public school teachers; the rest explicitly prohibit it, are silent on the matter, or allow the decision to be made at the local level.[11] It is no accident that the states that either prohibit collective bargaining for teachers, or by tradition have never had it, are mostly in the Deep South, the region of the country historically most hostile to extending democratic citizenship to all Americans.

The argument that collective bargaining is undemocratic fails to recognize that in a democracy, school boards are ultimately accountable to all voters—not just teachers, who often live and vote outside the district in which they teach, and who in any event represent a small share of total voters. Union endorsements matter in school board elections, but so do the interests of general taxpayers, parents, and everyone else who makes up the community. If school board members toe a teachers' union line that is unpopular with voters, those officials can be thrown out in the next election.

The title of Moe's most recent book, *Special Interest: Teachers Unions and America's Public Schools*, invokes a term historically applied to wealthy and powerful entities such as oil companies, tobacco interests, and gun manufacturers, whose narrow interests are recognized as often colliding with the more general public interest in such matters as clean water, good health, and public safety. Do rank-and-file teachers, who educate American schoolchildren and earn about $54,000 on average, really fall into the same category?

Former AFT President Albert Shanker long ago demonstrated that it was possible to be a strong union supporter and an education reformer, a tradition carried on today by President Randi Weingarten. Local unions are sometimes resistant to necessary change, but the picture painted by critics of unions is sorely outdated. Unions today support school choice within the public school system, but oppose private school vouchers that might further Balkanize the nation's students. Unions in New York City, Pittsburgh, and elsewhere favor teacher merit pay so long as it includes school-wide gains to reward effort while also encouraging cooperation among teachers. While unions disfavor plans to allow administrators to "allocate" teachers to high-poverty schools against their will (a policy that is reminiscent of forced student assignment for racial balance during the days of busing), both the NEA and the AFT favor paying teachers bonuses to attract them to high-poverty schools.

On the issue that arouses the most controversy, getting rid of bad educators, many teachers' unions today also favor weeding out those who are not up to the job, *not* based strictly on test scores or the subjective judgment of principals, but through multiple measures of performance, including "peer review" plans. In peer review, expert teachers come into a school and work with struggling educators; many of those educators improve, but when the expert teachers do not see sufficient improvement, they recommend termination (and the final decision rests with the superintendent and/or school board). The average fifth-grade teacher has a powerful self-interest in getting rid of an incompetent fourth-grade colleague, which is part of why peer review programs in places like Toledo, Ohio, and Montgomery County, Maryland, have resulted in increases in teacher terminations compared with previous systems in which administrators were in charge. In Montgomery County, for example, administrators dismissed just one teacher due to performance issues between 1994 and 1999, but during the first four years of the district's peer review program, 177 teachers were dismissed, were not renewed, or resigned.[12]

Moreover, there is no strong evidence that unions reduce overall educational outcomes or are, as Moe and other critics suggest, at "the heart" of our education problems. If collective bargaining were really a terrible practice for education, we would see stellar results in the grand experiments without it: the American South and the charter school arena. Why aren't the states that have long forbidden collective bargaining for teachers—Georgia, Mississippi, North Carolina, South Carolina, Texas, and Virginia—at the top of the educational heap? Why did the nation's most comprehensive study of charter schools (88 percent of which are nonunion), conducted by Stanford University researchers and sponsored by pro-charter foundations, conclude that charters outperformed regular public schools only 17 percent of the time, and actually did significantly worse 37 percent of the time?[13] Why, instead, do we see states like Massachusetts, and countries like Finland, both with strong teachers' unions, leading the pack?

Union critics like Moe reply, reasonably enough, that the South suffers from lots of other impediments to high achievement, such as higher levels of poverty, a history of segregation, and lower levels of school spending. Well, yes, but this response begs a question: If factors like poverty and segregation matter a great deal more to student achievement than the existence of collective bargaining, why not focus on those issues instead of claiming that the ability of teachers to band together and pursue their interests is the central problem in American education? Moreover, a 2002 review of 17 studies by researcher Robert Carini finds that when demographic factors *are* carefully controlled for, "unionism leads to modestly higher standardized achievement test scores."[14]

Critics of unions point out that teacher interests "are *not the same* as the interests of children."[15] That's certainly true, but who are the selfless adults who think only about kids? For-profit charter school operators whose allegiance is to shareholders? Principals who send troublemakers back into the classroom because they don't want school suspension numbers to look bad? Superintendents who sometimes junk promising reforms instituted by predecessors because they cannot personally take credit? Mayors who must balance the need to invest in kids against the strong desire of many voters to hold down taxes?

Do the hedge fund billionaires who bankroll charter schools have only the interests of children at heart? Might not it be in the self-interest of very wealthy individuals to suggest that expensive efforts at reducing poverty aren't necessary, and that a nonunion teaching environment will do the trick? When hedge fund managers argue that their income should be taxed at a 15 percent marginal rate, they limit government revenue and squeeze funds for a number of public pursuits, including schools. Is that putting the interests of kids ahead of adults, as the reformers suggest we should always do? Moreover, is the bias of Wall Street—that deregulation is good and unions distort markets—really beneficial for low-income children? Why aren't union critics more skeptical of deregulation in education, given that the deregulation of banking, also supported by Wall Street, wreaked havoc on the economy? And is the antipathy of hedge fund managers toward organized labor generally in the interests of poor and working-class students, whose parents can't make ends meet in part because organized labor has been eviscerated in the United States over the past half-century?

On many of the big educational issues—including levels of investment in education—the interests of educators who are in the classroom day in and day out do align nicely with the interests of the children they teach. Unlike the banks that want government money to cover for their reckless lending, teachers want money for school supplies and to reduce overcrowded classes. Yes, teachers have an interest in being well compensated, but presumably kids benefit too when higher salaries attract more talented educators than might otherwise apply.

Overall, as journalist Jonathan Chait has noted, politicians, who have short-term horizons, are prone to underinvesting in education, and teachers' unions "provide a natural bulwark" against that tendency.[16] Because most voters don't have kids in the public school system, parents with children in public schools need political allies. The fact that teachers have, by joining together, achieved some power in the political process surely helps explain why the United States does a better job of investing in education than preventing poverty. The child poverty rate in the United States is 21.6 percent, the fifth highest among 40 Organisation for Economic Co-operation and Development (OECD) nations. Only Turkey, Romania, Mexico, and Israel have higher child poverty rates. Put differently, we're in the bottom eighth in preventing child poverty.[17] By contrast, when the interests of children are directly connected with the interests of teachers—as they are on the question of public education spending—the United States ranks close to the top third. Among 39 OECD nations, the United States ranks 15th in spending on primary and secondary education as a percentage of gross domestic product.[18]

Moreover, the United States would probably rank even worse on the poverty score were it not for the influence of teachers' unions and the American labor movement generally. Education reformers like Michelle Rhee have adopted the mantra that poverty is just an "excuse" for low performance, blithely dismissing decades of evidence finding that socioeconomic status is by far the biggest predictor of academic achievement. If we could just get the unions to agree to stop protecting bad teachers and allow great teachers to be paid more, Rhee says, we could make all the difference in education. The narrative is attractive because it indeed would be wonderful if student poverty and economic school segregation didn't matter, and if heroic teachers could consistently overcome the odds for students. But educators like Albert Shanker, the head of the AFT from 1974–1997, knew better. He believed strongly that teachers' unions should be affiliated with the AFL-CIO, in part because teachers could do a much better job of educating students if educators were part of a coalition that fought to reduce income inequality and to improve housing and health care for children. Teachers know they will be more effective if children have full stomachs and proper eyeglasses, which is a central reason why the AFT remains an active part of the broader labor movement in trying to help rebuild the middle class.

While many divide the world between teachers' unions and reformers, the truth is that unions have long advocated a number of genuine reforms—inside and outside the classroom—that can have a sustained impact on reducing the achievement gap. They back early childhood education programs that blunt the impact of poverty and have been shown to have long-lasting effects on student outcomes. They back common academic standards of the type used by many of our successful international competitors. And in places like La Crosse, Wisconsin; Louisville, Kentucky; and Raleigh, North Carolina; teachers have backed public school choice policies that reduce concentrations of school poverty, thereby placing more low-income students in middle-class schools and increasing their chances of success.

Moreover, by democratizing education and giving teachers voice, unions can strengthen schools by tapping into the promising ideas teachers have for reform. At the same time, giving teachers greater voice reduces frustration and turnover. It is well documented that while teacher turnover is high in regular public schools, it is even higher in the largely nonunionized charter sector. As researchers David Stuit and Thomas M. Smith have found: "The odds of a charter school teacher leaving the profession versus staying in the same school were 130 percent greater than those of a traditional public school teacher. Similarly, the odds of a charter school teacher moving to another school were 76 percent greater."[19] Some charter advocates have tried to spin the higher turnover rates as a virtue, but according to researcher Gary Miron, "attrition from the removal of ineffective teachers—a potential plus of charters—explains only a small portion of the annual exodus."[20]

Critics of unions also fail to understand that the union leaders benefit immeasurably from the insights of their members. In a much-discussed twist in his book *Class Warfare*, Steven Brill suggests that Randi Weingarten be appointed chancellor of New York City's public schools: once liberated from her obligation to represent teachers, she could use her savvy and smarts to improve education. But this suggestion misses the crucial point that much of a union leader's strength comes from the fact that she or he constantly interacts with teachers and learns from them how education reform theories actually work in practice.

Other union critics also try, unfairly, to drive a wedge between teachers and their elected union leaders. Columnist Jonathan Alter, for example, claims: "It's very, very important to hold two contradictory ideas in your head at the same time. Teachers are great, a national treasure. Teachers' unions are, generally speaking, a menace and an impediment to reform."[21] Interestingly, Moe, citing extensive polling data, concludes that his fellow critics like Alter are wrong on this matter. Moe finds that among teachers, "virtually all union members, whether Democrat or Republican, see their membership in the local as entirely voluntary and are highly satisfied with what they are getting."[22] In a 2009 survey, 80 percent of teachers agreed that "without collective bargaining, the working conditions and salaries of teachers would be much worse," and 82 percent agreed that "without a union, teachers would be vulnerable to school politics or administrators who abuse their power."[23]

Finally, teachers' unions, more than any other organizations, preserve the American system of public schools against privatization proposals. Other groups also oppose private school vouchers—including those advocating on behalf of civil liberties and civil rights, school boards associations, and the like. But only teachers' unions have the political muscle and sophistication to stop widespread privatization. Today, vouchers and similar schemes serve one-third of 1 percent of the American school population. This fact infuriates union critics, including those who see large profit potential in privatization, and delights a majority of the American public.

Most of the public also supports collective bargaining for teachers and other public employees. A *USA Today*/Gallup survey found that by 61 to 33 percent, Americans oppose ending collective bargaining for public sector employees.[24] An NBC News/*Wall Street Journal* poll found that while most Americans want public employees to pay more for retirement benefits and health care, 77 percent said unionized state and municipal employees should have the same rights as union members who work in the private sector.[25] In November, Ohio voters overwhelmingly supported the collective bargaining rights of public employees, voting to repeal an antibargaining law by a margin of 61 to 39 percent.

The public is right on this question. Teachers should not have to go back to the pre-collective bargaining era, when they engaged in what Shanker called "collective begging."[26] Educators were very poorly compensated; in New York City, they were paid less than those washing cars for a living. Teachers were subject to the whims of often autocratic principals and could be fired for joining a union.

Many states are facing dire budget crises, and unions need to be smart about advocating strategies that keep fiscal concerns in mind. That means moving beyond traditional efforts to pour more money into high-poverty schools. Magnet schools, which give low-income students a chance to be educated in a middle-class environment, are an especially promising investment. But this kind of engagement in education policy involves moving in a direction opposite from the one advocated by Michelle Rhee, Governor Scott Walker, and other Democratic and Republican union critics.

As Shanker noted years ago, restricting bargaining to the issue of wages (as many states are now trying to do) is a clever trap in which critics can suggest that teachers care only about money. Collective bargaining should be broadened, not constrained, to give teachers a voice on a range of important educational questions, from merit pay to curriculum. This could help improve the battered image of teachers' unions. But, more important, it could help students.

Notes

1. Terry M. Moe, *Special Interest: Teachers Unions and America's Public Schools* (Washington, DC: Brookings Institution Press, 2011), page 283, table 9–2.
2. Moe, *Special Interest*, 205.
3. Ironically, a half-century ago, Wisconsin became the first state in the nation to pass legislation allowing collective bargaining for public employees, including educators.
4. Jay P. Greene, "Unions and the Public Interest: Is Collective Bargaining for Teachers Good for Students?" *Education Next* 12, no. 1 (Winter 2012), 65.
5. Moe, *Special Interest*, 6.
6. Moe, *Special Interest*, 342.
7. Moe, *Special Interest*, 242.
8. Moe, *Special Interest*, 244.
9. United Nations General Assembly, "Universal Declaration of Human Rights," December 10, 1948, www.un.org/en/documents/udhr.
10. Ronald Reagan, Labor Day speech at Liberty State Park (Jersey City, NJ, September 1, 1980), www.reagan.utexas.edu/archives/refrence/9.1.80.html.
11. American Federation of Teachers, "States with Statutory Collective Bargaining for K–12 Teachers" (Washington, DC: American Federation of Teachers' Center for Collective Bargaining, 2011).

12. Stacey M. Childress, Denis P. Doyle, and David A. Thomas, Leading for Equity: The Pursuit of Excellence in Montgomery County Public Schools (Cambridge, MA: Harvard Education Press, 2009), 84.

13. Center for Research on Education Outcomes, *Multiple Choice: Charter School Performance in 16 States* (Stanford, CA: CREDO, 2009), http://credo.stanford.edu/reports/multiple_choice_credo.pdf.

14. Robert M. Carini, "Teacher Unions and Student Achievement," in *School Reform Proposals: The Research Evidence*, ed. Alex Molnar (Tempe, AZ: Education Policy Research Unit, 2002), http://nepc.colorado.edu/files/Chapter10-Carini-Final.pdf, page 10.17.

15. Terry M. Moe, "The Staggering Power of the Teachers' Unions," *Hoover Digest* (2011, no. 3), www.hoover.org/publications/hoover-digest/article/84076.

16. Jonathan Chait, "Learning Curve," *New Republic*, April 7, 2011.

17. Organisation for Economic Co-operation and Development, OECD Family Database, "Child Poverty," chart CO2.2.A, last updated February 28, 2011, www.oecd.org/dataoecd/52/43/41929552.pdf.

18. Organisation for Economic Co-operation and Development, OECD Family Database, "Public Spending on Education," chart PF1.2.A, last updated December 20, 2010, www.oecd.org/dataoecd/45/48/37864432.pdf.

19. David Stuit and Thomas M. Smith, "Teacher Turnover in Charter Schools" (research brief, National Center on School Choice, Peabody College of Education and Human development, Vanderbilt University, Nashville, TN, June 2010), www.vanderbilt.edu/schoolchoice/documents/briefs/brief_suit_smith_ncspe.pdf.

20. Gary Miron, testimony prepared for hearing of the House Committee on Education and the Workforce, Washington, DC, June 1, 2011, http://edworkforce.house.gov/UploadedFiles/06.01.11_miron.pdf.

21. Quote by Jonathan Alter in *Waiting for "Superman,"* directed by Davis Guggenheim, 2010.

22. Moe, *Special Interest*, 109.

23. Public Agenda, "Supporting Teacher Talent: The View from Generation Y Full Survey Results," question 40, parts c and d (data collected April 16, 2009–June 22, 2009), www .publicagenda.org/pages/supporting-teacher-talent-view -from-Generation-Y-topline.

24. Ruy Teixeira, "Public Opinion Snapshot: Public Backs Collective Bargaining Rights for State Workers," Center for American Progress, February 28, 2011, www.american progress.org/issues/2011/02/snapshot022811.html.

25. Hart/McInturff, NBC News/*Wall Street Journal* Survey, Study #11091, February 24–28, 2011, question 16, http://msnbcmedia.msn.com/i/MSNBC/Sections/NEWS /A_Politics/___Politics_Today_Stories_Teases/2-24-28-11 .pdf.

26. Albert Shanker, "The Flagrant One-Sidedness of the Taylor Law," Where We Stand, *New York Times*, September 9, 1972, http://source.nysut.org/weblink7/DocView.aspx?id =1267.

Periodical and Internet Sources Bibliography

The following articles have been selected to supplement the diverse views presented in this chapter.

| Andrew J. Coulson | "A Less Perfect Union," *American Spectator*, June 2011. |

Tom DeWeese "American Education Fails Because It Isn't Education," American Policy Center, April 11, 2011. http://americanpolicy.org/2011/04/11/american-education-fails-because-it-isnt-education-2.

Eric Hanushek "The 'War on Teachers' Is a Myth," *Hoover Digest*, vol. 1, 2011.

Eric Hanushek and Paul E. Peterson "Your Child Left Behind," *Hoover Digest*, vol. 2, 2011.

Susan Headden "A Test Worth Teaching To: The Race to Fix America's Broken System of Standardized Exams," *Washington Monthly*, May–June 2012.

Jack Jennings "Long-Term Gains in Minority Education: An Overlooked Success?," *Huffington Post*, May 8, 2011. www.huffingtonpost.com/jack-jennings/an-overlooked-success_b_857247.html.

Cheryl Miller "The End of History in America's Classrooms," *Weekly Standard*, October 12, 2010.

Adam B. Schaeffer "Education Cost Top Problem for Local Government," *Investor's Business Daily*, February 2, 2011.

Andrew Smarick "The Turnaround Fallacy," *Education Next*, Winter 2010.

OPPOSING
VIEWPOINTS®
SERIES

CHAPTER 2

Are School-Choice Alternatives a Good Idea?

Chapter Preface

Proposals for allowing a choice in public education have been around as long as public schools have existed. Prior to the nationwide establishment of public schools, educational choice—including whether or not to educate at all—was simply up to parents. With the advent of public schools, however, public education is supported by all taxpayers, and all children must receive a certain level of schooling. Parents have the choice of whether or not to send their children to public school, and they have the ability to influence education policy through elected officials and being active in their local school district. Nonetheless, with federal policies such as No Child Left Behind and various state mandates on curricula, many of the facets of public school education are not open to choice by parents or students. The argument for more choice in public schooling takes a variety of forms, but what they all have in common is a desire to give more choice to parents than currently exists.

The use of school vouchers as a vehicle for choice involves giving parents a voucher equivalent to the amount of money spent per child in public school for use at a private school of their choosing. The idea of using vouchers as a way to opt out of public schools is not a new one; in the nineteenth century, Catholics asked state legislatures for state money to set up Catholic schools as an alternative to public schools. Their request was denied and most states passed constitutional provisions forbidding the use of public funds for religious schools. In 2002, however, the US Supreme Court held that public funds could be used to pay for education in religious and other private schools without violating the US Constitution's directive on separation of church and state, as long as aid went directly to parents in the form of vouchers. According to the National Conference of State Legislatures, as of October

2011, Louisiana, Indiana, Ohio, Wisconsin (Milwaukee), and the District of Columbia offer vouchers to low-income students. The use of school vouchers will likely expand around the country as a result of the Court's decision.

Similar to the option of school vouchers, but avoiding the use of direct monetary transfer, are tuition tax credits. According to the National Conference of State Legislatures, tuition tax credit programs were being used in eleven states as of September 2012. These programs allow individuals and corporations to allocate a certain portion of their owed state taxes to private, nonprofit school tuition organizations that in turn offer scholarships to students to attend one of their approved private schools, which include religious schools. Although the tuition tax credit programs do not give parents a voucher to use to attend private schools, by offering a reduction in taxes owed for participating in the program, the program essentially amounts to a monetary transfer of government funds.

In addition to these two school-choice options that allow parents some monetary support for sending children to private schools, there are also school-choice options within the public school system. Charter schools are one such option. Publicly funded and tuition free, they differ from traditional public schools by being free of some state regulations, although not from requirements on student performance. According to the National Alliance for Public Charter Schools, there were 5,275 charter schools in the 2010–2011 school year, making up more than 5 percent of all public schools.

Whether through vouchers, tax credits, or charter schools, alternatives to public schooling aimed to increase choice are not without controversy. Critics charge that diverting money and resources from the existing public school system will worsen the quality of public education, primarily benefitting families who already have the resources to send their children to private school. Additionally, there is widespread concern about the use of government funds for religious schooling, with many arguing that such a practice violates the First Amendment. Supporters of school choice claim that their right to choose how to educate their children is paramount and contend that competition is good for traditional public schools because they will be forced to improve. Nonetheless, due to widespread dissatisfaction with the quality of public school education, alternatives to public school are popular and are likely to continue to be developed and debated, as evidenced by the viewpoints in this chapter.

| "The practical solution to America's education problems is to privatize the government school system."

The Educational Bonanza in Privatizing Government Schools

Andrew Bernstein

In the following viewpoint, Andrew Bernstein argues that the solution to poor educational quality and the coercive nature of the current education system is to turn government schools into private schools. Bernstein claims that the free market is better equipped to offer a variety of high-quality education choices. Furthermore, he contends that a decrease in current taxes, the competitiveness of the free market, and the existence of charity will ensure the ability of all parents to send their children to school.

Andrew Bernstein is a lecturer in philosophy at the State University of New York–Purchase, and author of Capitalist Solutions: A Philosophy of American Moral Dilemmas.

As you read, consider the following questions:

1. What two policies does Bernstein claim coercively force parents to send their children to government schools?

Andrew Bernstein, "The Educational Bonanza in Privatizing Government Schools," *The Objective Standard*, vol. 5, no. 4, Winter 2010–2011, pp. 22–30. Copyright © 2011 by The Objective Standard. All rights reserved. Reproduced with permission.

2. The author claims that less than what percent of students in America attend private schools?

3. Bernstein cites the increase in parents who choose to homeschool their children in order to refute what objection to school privatization?

American education is in shambles. One in three fourth graders scores below the "basic level"—the lowest ranking deemed proficient—on the reading portion of the National Assessment of Education (NAEP) exams. Among low-income students, half score below that level. In some of America's larger cities, fewer than half the students earn a high school diploma; in Detroit, only one quarter do.[1] Roughly one million children drop out of school each year. Forty-five million Americans are marginally illiterate. Twenty-one million cannot read at all.[2]

Such statistics indicate not merely the current state of American education, but a decades-long trend in educational deterioration. Since 1983, 10 million Americans have reached twelfth grade without learning to read at the basic level. In 1986, the national test score average for eleventh graders taking the NAEP literature and history test was 54.5 percent correct on the history portion, and 51.8 percent correct on the literature portion.[3] In 1995, a nationally administered history test found that only one student in ten was grade-level proficient in the subject; the majority failed to reach a basic level.[4] In 1996, U.S. high school seniors scored near the bottom on an internationally administered math exam.[5] According to a study published in 1999, a "nationwide assessment of math skills found that 'only 14 percent of eighth graders scored at the seventh-grade level or above'"[6] and "fewer than half of twelfth-graders can do seventh-grade work in mathematics."[7] In 2000, math students in America ranked below those in Malaysia, Bulgaria, and Latvia.[8]

Why is education in America—the world's wealthiest, most-advanced nation—so abysmally bad? A central reason is the existence of America's government-run schools.

The many problems with government schools include the way they are funded, their lack of competition and economic incentive, the fact that children are forced to attend them, the schools' resultant unaccountability regardless of performance, and various other conflicts inherent in a school system based on force. Consider these in turn.

Local, state, and federal governments finance the government schools by seizing wealth from productive men, largely via property taxes, but also by means of sales and income taxes, both personal and corporate.[9] Thus the schools are funded not voluntarily, based on merit, but coercively, regardless of merit.

Indeed, on the premise that poor academic performance can be remediated primarily by increased spending, the schools receive progressively *more* money, not less, as they educationally regress. New York City in 2003, for example, in an attempt to improve the dismal academic performance of its government schools, increased spending by $7 billion, only to be dismayed by results of the 2007 NAEP exams, showing meager improvement in some areas and deterioration in others.[10]

The gradual worsening of the government schools imposes gradually heavier financial liabilities on the taxpayers who are forced to support them. The government says, in effect, "The schools are underperforming because we do not violate individual rights sufficiently; we must do so on an even wider scale."

For many families, the taxes they pay to support the government schools make it impossible for them to send their children to a private school, for they are financially unable to pay twice for education. Making matters worse, truancy laws mandate that children attend school until age sixteen. This combination of coercive policies means that many students are *forced* to attend government schools.

The current arrangement makes the government school system akin to a monopoly, in that it is impervious to competition.

By analogy, suppose the government established a state-run automobile company; legally required all adults to own a car, which they received "free" of charge; and, by means of property, sales, and income taxes, financed the government-car producer, thus making it monetarily impossible for millions of Americans to purchase a privately-manufactured automobile. Such a "business" would gain its income and "customers" by means of a rights-violating system, and it would receive the same income and "customers" regardless of whether its "customers" deemed its product satisfactory. The government-car producer would lack any and all economic incentive to excel; no matter how woeful its product, it would be kept in "business" by wealth taken coercively from taxpayers. This is what the government school system does in the realm of education.

Further, government schools create irresolvable conflicts regarding curricula, textbooks, and teacher training. In order for the government to ensure that its schools are providing government-quality education, the state must establish an agency—call it the Bureau of Education—to oversee the schools, curriculums, textbooks, and teacher training. Who controls the Bureau? In a dictatorship, the government controls it and employs the state schools to ram propaganda down the throats of its subjects. In a mixed economy, such as America's, competing interest groups vie to gain control of the Bureau, seeking to impose their preferred educational standards on the nation's youth.

Consider just a few of the conflicts arising from the current American system. Some groups want schools to teach creationism; others want them to teach evolution. Some want schools to teach the "virtues" of socialism and the "crimes" of America; others want them to teach the virtues of freedom and the unprecedented accomplishments of America. Some want schools to teach that America is a Christian country; others want them to teach that America is a secular republic. Some want schools to teach the "look-say" or "whole language" method of reading; others want schools to employ phonics.

Such conflicts follow logically from the coercive methods by which government schools are funded, populated, and operated.

By contrast, private schools entail none of these problems.

It is common knowledge that private schools are generally academically superior to government schools, and this superiority is borne out on various tests. For instance, in the area of reading, private-school fourth graders in 1994 scored nineteen points higher than their government school counterparts on the NAEP exam.[11] Likewise, in the field of math, also during the 1990s, the disparity between private school and government school achievement, on average, over the course of high school, was equivalent to 3.2 years of learning.[12] More recently, in 2008, educational researcher Andrew Coulson reported on a comprehensive study—analyzing twenty-five years of educational research from eighteen nations—that compared government schools to private schools. The analysis demonstrated not merely the academic superiority of private education, but, more revealingly, that "the private sector's margin of superiority is greatest when looking at the least regulated, most market-like private schools."[13]

One school that demonstrated both the superiority of the private model and the problems for private schools posed by government schools was Westside Preparatory School in Chicago, founded in 1975 by Marva Collins. Collins was a school-teacher in Chicago who, frustrated by the bureaucratic restrictions of the government schools, resigned and opened

Westside Prep. She took in many low-income and minority children deemed incorrigibly uneducable by the same government schools she had fled and transformed them into consummate students. She jettisoned the look-say and whole-language methods of teaching reading used in the government schools, taught phonics instead, and made reading a vital part of every aspect of her curriculum, including mathematics. She did not organize classes based exclusively on age, but let students progress as rapidly as they were able, and used advanced students to assist in the teaching of novices. Both she and her school became justly famous for the academic excellence achieved by their students.[14] Unfortunately, due to insufficient enrollment and funding, Westside Prep closed in 2008—while government schools in Chicago continued to receive both students and funding by means of coercion.

Countless comparisons of private schools to government schools reveal that the former generally outperform the latter. The question is: Why?

The main reason for private school superiority is that such schools are *immune* to the problems that inescapably plague government schools.

A private school cannot force customers to purchase its product, nor can it compel anyone to finance its existence, nor can it regulate or curtail the activities of its competitors. Because private schools are legally forbidden to use force, their existence and programs entail no violation of rights. Having to earn their customers and money, private schools possess strong economic incentive to provide excellent educational services. If they want to stay in business and flourish, they must make money by satisfying the educational requirements of students and their families; if they fail to do so, they face bankruptcy. (Even nonprofit private schools must compete for students and funding. If they fail to deliver a satisfactory educational product, families send their children to a competitor that does. And if they fail to succeed in their stated mission, their philanthropic financiers will find other venues for their philanthropy.)

Further, private schools pose no irresolvable problems of curriculum, textbooks, or teaching methods. The *owners* of private schools decide what subjects will be taught, the methods by which they will be taught, and the price at which they will offer their services. Parents voluntarily purchase the service for their children (or not) and continue to purchase it only if satisfied with the service and its price.

If a private school chooses to teach the theory of evolution in its biology curriculum, it is free to do so, and potential customers are free to decide whether they want that for their children. If another private school chooses to teach creationism, it is free to do so, and potential customers are free to decide whether they want *that* for their children. If a private school chooses to focus on the three Rs to the exclusion of painting, music, or drama, it is free to do so, and potential customers are free to patronize the school or not. If another private school chooses to focus on the arts, or to focus on trade skills, or to offer any variety of subjects, it is free to do so, and potential customers are free to do business there or not.

The philosophy of education is a complex and controversial issue, and people's needs and values can differ in countless ways. In a system of private schools, everyone is free to decide what he will do with his money and where he will educate his child; no one is forced to finance schools he deems unworthy or to patronize ideas he deems false or immoral.

In short, private schools do not violate rights; thus, they are free of the myriad problems that accompany rights violations. In other words, private schools are not only moral but also—and consequently—*practical.*

History demonstrates this as fully as do current educational practices.

Prior to the mid-19th century, government schools did not exist in America. All schools were private, and education was widespread and outstanding. For example, in the Middle Atlantic colonies during the pre-Revolutionary period, professional educators established numerous schools to satisfy the demand for education.[15] Philadelphia, for instance, boasted schools for every subject and interest. Between 1740 and 1776, 125 private schoolmasters advertised their services in Philadelphia newspapers—this in a city whose population was miniscule relative to today. Professional educators provided mentoring services in English, contemporary foreign languages, science, and a wide variety of other topics.[16] Children who grew to be such brilliant scientists, writers, and statesmen as Benjamin Franklin, Thomas Jefferson, and George Washington received their education at home or in private schools.

(As to higher education, by the late-18th century six private colleges operated in the colonies: Yale, the College of New Jersey [Princeton], the College of Philadelphia [Penn], Dartmouth, Queen's [Rutgers], and Rhode Island College [Brown].)[17]

Predictably, the educational results of such a free educational market were superb. The literacy levels of Revolutionary America were remarkably high. For example, Thomas Paine's book, *Common Sense*, written in plain style but enunciating sophisticated political principles, sold 120,000 copies during the colonial period to a free population of 2.4 million (akin to selling 10 million copies today).[18] The essays of *The Federalist*, written by Hamilton, Madison, and Jay in support of a Constitution for the nascent republic, were largely newspaper editorials written for and read by the common man.

Sales of American books and educational materials in the early- and mid-19th century likewise indicate a high national literacy rate. Between 1818 and 1823, while the U.S. population was under 20 million, Walter Scott's novels sold 5 million copies (the equivalent of selling 60 million copies today).

Early in the 19th century, *The Last of the Mohicans* by James Fenimore Cooper likewise sold millions of copies.[19] The *McGuffey's Readers*, first published in 1836, routinely used such terms as "heath" and "benighted" in third-grade texts. They asked such questions as "What is this species of composition called?" and gave such assignments as "Relate the facts of this dialogue." The fourth-grade reader included selections from Hawthorne, and the fifth-grade text, readings from Shakespeare. "These were not the textbooks of the elite but of the masses," explains Thomas Sowell. "[F]rom 1836 to 1920, *McGuffey's Readers* were so widely used that they sold more than 122 million copies."[20]

Given the high quality of education in early America, it is no surprise that two renowned French visitors observed and reported on the phenomenon. In an 1800 book Vice President Thomas Jefferson commissioned, titled *National Education in the United States of America*, Pierre Du Pont de Nemours reported that Americans received an education far superior to that of other peoples. "Most young Americans," he wrote, "can read, write, and cipher. Not more than four in a thousand are unable to write legibly."[21] Several decades later, Alexis de Tocqueville wrote in *Democracy in America* that Americans were the most educated people of history.[22]

Private schools in America have provided and continue to provide high-quality education.

Unfortunately, private schools today constitute less than 11 percent of America's educational system. According to the National Center for Educational Statistics, in school year 2009–2010, nearly 49.8 million students attended government schools, while 5.8 million were enrolled in private schools.[23] Because of the numerous coercive laws earlier discussed, almost 90 percent of American children are *compelled* to attend educationally crippling government schools. This is not merely a tragedy. It is a man-made tragedy; indeed, an atrocity.

What is the solution?

One key political solution to the abysmal state of education in America is to privatize the government schools. For an indication of what would happen to education in America if the government schools were privatized, consider the industries that are either fully or essentially private. Examine the quality, availability, and prices of automobiles, cell phones, CDs, MP3 players, jeans, breakfast cereals, and pain relievers. Consider the quality, availability, and prices of services such as hair styling, car repair, plumbing, and dentistry. If we focus on any one of these, we can see that the private nature of the businesses involved is what drives quality up, prices down, and makes such a diverse array of goods and services available to millions.

For instance, when was the last time anyone complained about a shortage of high-quality, low-priced cell phones? Observe that there are countless varieties of cell phones, optional features, and calling plans. Cellular service producers competing for business provide customers with sparkling new, high-tech phones *free of charge* upon contracting to purchase their service. Just over a century ago, people had no telephone service. Now they receive a personal, portable phone—a technological marvel—for free. Why are cell phones and calling plans so inexpensive, technologically advanced, and abundant? The answer is that the industry is relatively free of government interference. Producers of goods and services in a free market know that if they provide quality products for reasonable prices they will make money and that if they do not they will go out of business.

The economic bottom line is that if a producible good or service is in demand in a free market, profit-seeking businessmen will endeavor to supply it at affordable prices. Education is no exception.

In a fully privatized, free market of education, profit-seeking businessmen would provide quality educational services at prices affordable to millions. And because they would have to meet consumer demand in order to thrive, businessmen would provide a sweeping diversity of services matching actual student needs. For example, observing that many people value the full academic curriculum and want their children to learn the classic three Rs of reading, writing, and arithmetic, entrepreneurial educators would provide such a service effectively and affordably. Likewise, observing that many of these same people want their children later to advance to science, mathematics, literature, and history, educators would provide these services as well, because they could make money doing so.

The same is true of vocational training. Some families demand only the basics of academics, and then want their children to branch out into one of many vocational fields—whether business, farming, baking, construction work, or countless other productive fields. In a free market, profit-seeking educators would supply such services as efficiently and inexpensively as possible—lest competitors provide a better value and put them out of business.

This truth applies also to the field of special education. Some individuals need specialized instruction. For example, some are gifted in specific ways—intellectually, musically, athletically—and require highly focused, advanced training. Others suffer from debilitating psychological or physiological ailments. Some are sadly afflicted with varying degrees of mental retardation. In a free market, where there is a demand for various forms of special education, profit-seeking businessmen will compete to supply them.

All the evidence culled from the current state of education, from history, and from the logic of economics points without exception to a single conclusion: Private schools competing for students and profits in free (or freer) markets produce quality, affordable educational services to satisfy customer demand.

Politically speaking, the practical solution to America's education problems is to privatize the government school system—to convert the government schools into private schools. And the reason this is the practical solution is that it is the *moral* solution. A fully private school system would recognize and respect the rights of everyone involved. It would leave educators and customers fully free to produce and purchase educational products and services in accordance with their own needs and preferences. . . .

Before we turn to *how* the government school system should be privatized, let us address a couple of common objections to the goal of privatization.

One objection is that some parents do not value their children's education enough to pay for it. To the extent that there are such parents, this is hardly a reason to violate the rights of all Americans and destroy the possibility of a good education for millions of other children. People who have children and do not care enough to educate them should be socially ostracized and, when appropriate, prosecuted for parental neglect. But they should not be held up as a reason to violate Americans' rights and keep American education in the sewer.

The fact is that the overwhelming preponderance of parents value their children's education *enormously* and, when free to choose how they would spend their money, would procure that value just as they do food, clothing, shelter, and medical care. Observe in this regard the current trend toward home schooling in America. An increasing number of parents, now more than a million, value their children's education so much and are so dissatisfied with government schools that they have chosen to home school their children—despite the fact that they are still forced to finance the government schools they do not use. (Not surprisingly, the educational results achieved by home schoolers are generally outstanding. For example, by eighth grade most home-schooled children test four grade levels above the national average.)[24]

If parents choose not to provide their children with a proper education, that is their right—and the children will, for a time, suffer the consequences of their parents' irrationality. But children are not mindless replicates of their parents; as they grow into adulthood they can and often do make fundamentally different choices. For example, the children of religious parents sometimes choose secularism; the offspring of bigoted parents often choose individualism; and the children of alcoholic or drug-addicted parents often choose clean living. Human beings possess free will, and, as numerous parents ruefully learn, their children frequently do not passively accept their families' values.

Even in today's government-thwarted education market, many centers of adult education prosper. A fully free market in education would enable educational entrepreneurs to expand this market immensely. Competition among private schools and tutors providing both academic and vocational training for the adult market would increase; prices would drop; options would abound. In such a marketplace, the few children whose backward parents had neglected to educate them could seek education on their own in their early years of adulthood, then move on and live lives of greater wisdom and superior career opportunities.

Finally, it is important to emphasize that there is no right to an education—just as there is no right to food, shelter, or medical care. A right involves the freedom to act on one's best judgment and to pursue the values of one's choice. It does not involve access to a good or service at someone else's expense. If a person (or a citizenry) is forced to provide others with education (or anything else), then his rights are violated and he becomes, to that extent, a slave of those he involuntarily serves. A free market in education would both obviate such manifest immorality and provide immensely better options in all educational fields.

Another objection to a fully privatized educational system is that if taxpayers were not coerced to finance government schools, some families would be unable to afford quality education. The first thing to note in answer to this objection is that the coercively funded and operated government schools are precisely what make it impossible for customers to receive quality education. Another important point is that with the government monolith slain, the property, income, and sales taxes that had been levied to sustain it could and should be repealed. With their tax burden substantially diminished, families would retain more of their income and be fully free to spend it on their children's education. Yet another point is that in a full private market for education, competition among private schools, teachers, and tutors would increase dramatically. This inevitably would drive prices down, making education increasingly affordable.

As for those families that somehow in a free market for education still could not afford to pay for any education for their children, observe that even today many private schools offer scholarships to worthy students who cannot meet the tuition.[25] In a fully free market for education, such scholarships would increase and abound. Private schools are highly competitive with one another, and they all seek to showcase the value and superiority of their product. Consequently, it is in their rational self-interest to attract students who will make them shine. Scholarships are a crucial means of doing so.

It is also worth noting that voluntary charity flourishes in America even when we are taxed at today's obscene rates. According to Giving USA Foundation's annual report on philanthropy, "Charitable giving in the United States exceeded $300 billion for the second year in a row in 2008," and "Education organizations received an estimated $40.94 billion, or 13 percent of the total."[26] So long as the government does not prohibit educational charities, Americans will contribute to such charities.

In short, in a fully private market for education, the few families unable to afford quality education would find no shortage of scholarships and/or charities available to assist them. Objections to privatizing the government schools simply do not hold water.

Now let us turn to the question of how government schools could be privatized.

There are, no doubt, several viable means by which this could be done, but one straightforward way is simply by auctioning off schools and their corresponding properties to the highest bidders. Sold schools would either continue under private ownership, or the properties would be used for noneducational purposes. If the schools became private schools, competition in a free market would ensure a drive toward improved education and decreased prices. If some of the properties were deployed for noneducational purposes, the resultant increase in demand for education in that area would motivate profit-seeking educational entrepreneurs to meet the demand with other venues. Either way, the market would soon teem with private schools, teachers, and tutors competing to supply the educational service demanded by millions of families whose only earlier alternative was the abysmally bad government school system.

Such a transition would necessarily take some time, and the government would have to provide fair notice and appropriate grace periods to enable government-dependent families to adjust to the free market. For instance, the government could enact a law declaring that, effective immediately, the government would begin auctioning off school properties, with transference of ownership to occur at the end of a five-year grace period. This would enable all teachers, tutors, and educational entrepreneurs to ramp up their businesses. And it would give all parents substantial time to assume full responsibility for the education of their children.

The enactment of such a policy would be followed by an explosion of private schools and tutoring services, some large-scale, others small; some in private homes (as Marva Collins began), some in multistory buildings; some religious, some secular; some profit-driven, some not. The teeming diversity of schools and the high level of educational results would soon rival those of America in the centuries before the imposition of government schooling.

We who recognize the vital nature of education to the lives of individuals and to the health of a society must demand the privatization of government-run schools and work toward the establishment of a fully private market in education. The time to advocate this change is now.

Endnotes

1. Dan Lips, "Still a Nation at Risk," www.heritage.org/Research/Commentary2008/05/Still A Nation at Risk.
2. "Reading, Literacy & Education Statistics," www.readfaster.com/education.asp.
3. Diane Ravitch and Chester Finn, *What Do Our 17 Year Olds Know?: A Report of the First National Assessment of History and Literature* (New York: Harper & Row, 1987), pp. 1, 43, 120; Andrew Coulson, *Market Education: The Unknown History* (New Brunswick, NJ: Transaction Publishers, 1999), pp. 188–89.
4. Coulson, *Market Education*, pp. 8–10.
5. C. Bradley Thompson, "Cognitive Math Abuse in Our Classrooms," www.aynrand.org/site/News2?page=NewsArticle&id=5410.
6. Coulson, *Market Education*, p. 9.
7. Coulson, *Market Education*, p. 15.
8. Thompson, "Cognitive Math Abuse."
9. "Trends in Educational Funding—Public Schools: Where Does The Money Come From?," http://social.jrank.org/pages/965/Trends-in-Educational-Funding-Public-Schools-Where-Does-Money-Come-From.html.

10. Sol Stern, "In School Reform, Billions of Dollars But Not Much Bang," www.manhattaninstitute.org/html/miarticle.htm?id=4167.

11. Coulson, *Market Education*, pp. 279–86.

12. Coulson, *Market Education*, p. 280.

13. "Markets of Competing Private Schools Outperform Public School, Study Based on 25 Years of Educational Data Effectively Settles the Debate," Cato Institute news release, September 10, 2008, www.cato.org/pressroom.php?display=news&id=157. Coulson's full report, "Markets vs. Monopolies in Education: A Global Review of the Evidence," is available here: http://www.cato.org/pubs/pas/pa620.pdf.

14. Marva Collins and Civia Tamarkin, *Marva Collins' Way* (New York: Putnam, 1990), pp. 126–37.

15. Hans Sennholz, ed., *Public Education and Indoctrination* (Irvington-on-Hudson, NY: Foundation for Economic Education, 1993), p. 38.

16. Sennholz, *Public Education*, pp. 22–23, 26, 38–39, 44.

17. Sennholz, *Public Education*, p. 23. Harvard was founded by the Great and General Court of the Massachusetts Bay Colony and named for its first donor, John Harvard. The College of William & Mary and King's College (Columbia University) were founded by royal charter.

18. Sheldon Richman, *Separating School and State* (Fairfax, VA: The Future of Freedom Foundation, 1995), p. 38.

19. Richman, *Separating School and State*, p. 38.

20. Thomas Sowell, *Inside American Education: The Decline, the Deception, the Dogmas* (New York: The Free Press, 1993), p. 7.

21. Pierre Du Pont de Nemours, *National Education in the United States of America*, translated from the second French edition of 1812 and with an introduction by B. G. Du Pont (Newark, DE: University of Delaware Press, 1923), pp. 3–4; quoted in Sennholz, *Public Education*, pp. 23–24.

22. Sennholz, *Public Education*, p. 44; John Taylor Gatto, "Our Prussian School System," *Cato Policy Report*, March/April 1993, p. 1.
23. National Center for Educational Statistics, U.S. Department of Education, Fast Facts, http://nces.ed.gov/fastfacts/display.asp?id=372.
24. Isabel Lyman, *The Homeschooling Revolution* (Amherst, MA: Bench Press International, 2000), pp. 59–69.
25. Melissa Kelly, "Teaching at Private vs. Public Schools," http://712educators.about.com/od/jobopenings/a/private-public.htm.
26. "U.S. Charitable Giving Estimated to Be $307.65 Billion in 2008," Giving USA Foundation, http://www.philanthropy.iupui.edu/News/2009/docs/GivingReaches300billion_06102009.pdf.

> "The value of a strong public school sys-
> tem could not be more obvious than it
> is now, as we face the prospect of losing
> it altogether."

The Republican War on Education

Ruth Conniff

In the following viewpoint, Ruth Conniff argues that the battle over Wisconsin's Senate Bill 22 (since defeated) is evidence of a frightening war on public education that threatens to privatize schools. Conniff contends that the proposal to replace public schools with charter schools—both physical and virtual (online)—is opposed by large numbers of the public and is un-democratic. Conniff claims the support for privatization comes from big business and politicians who are beholden to lobbyists, not from teachers and others who care about education.

Ruth Conniff is the political editor of the Progressive, *a monthly magazine with a liberal perspective.*

As you read, consider the following questions:

1. What is the single largest budget item for each of the fifty states, according to Conniff?

Ruth Conniff, "The Republican War on Education," *Progressive*, vol. 75, no. 5, May 2011.

2. The author cites a study by Stanford University showing that what percentage of charter schools performed better and what percentage performed worse than public schools?

3. Conniff cites what examples of interaction between teacher and students, recounted by a Wisconsin teacher, that are not available through a virtual education?

The public outpouring was incredible. People flooded into the capitol building in Madison, Wisconsin, from the urban neighborhoods of Milwaukee and from tiny towns in the northern and western corners of the state. They came to oppose Republican plans that would wipe out rural school districts, drain resources from city schools, and dismantle an entire statewide system of public education.

They packed a hearing room and two overflow rooms, and waited all day to speak. Hour after hour, teachers, parents, and citizens gave impassioned, often tearful testimony. Jon Sheller, a former member of the Montello school board, and his daughter, social studies teacher Yedda Ligocki, talked about their little town, with 750 schoolchildren. "As in most small school districts," Sheller said, the school "is the heart of the community."

"The athletics, the musicals, other school activities are the life of Montello," added Ligocki.

Governor Scott Walker's unprecedented $900 million cut to school funding, coupled with a scheme [Senate Bill (S.B.) 22] to create a state-run system of charter schools, will kill off both the school and the town, they said. Under S.B. 22, the bill they came to oppose, students and funds that used to go to schools like Montello's will be siphoned off to virtual charter schools run by a state board of political appointees.

"There will be no turning back," Sheller said. "Small schools and their communities will wither and die—and for what? A political maneuver to allow privatization of public education at the expense of Wisconsin's history as a leader in student achievement. This is giving away our future."

Wisconsin is on the leading edge of a national assault on public education. Walker made a big name for himself with his explosive move to bust public employee unions and take away teachers' bargaining rights. Now comes the next phase.

"We've been hearing about this for years now," says Democratic state representative Sondy Pope-Roberts. "I see Wisconsin as the first domino in a line. As this falls, I see other states hoping to achieve our quote-unquote success ... by crushing unions and taking public schools private."

Wisconsin has long had a strong public school system. But the conservative Bradley Foundation in Milwaukee has also been a national incubator for vouchers and other school privatization efforts.

"We started by being the first state to have a voucher school, in Milwaukee," Pope-Roberts says. "Now we will be the first state to ... basically create charter school districts."

Instead of being approved by local school boards, under S.B. 22 these charters would be overseen by a nine-member board appointed by the governor and leaders of the legislature.

The bill would encourage the rapid expansion of virtual charters, which would receive the same per-pupil tax dollars as bricks-and-mortar schools, and could enroll students all over the state.

Walker's other proposals include lifting the income cap for vouchers, so wealthy families could receive public funds to send their kids to private schools.

The war on public schools is part of the conservative dream to "get government down to the size where you can drown it in the bathtub," as conservative guru Grover Norquist so memorably put it.

K–12 education is the single largest budget item for each of the 50 states. So it stands to reason that privatizing education is the largest front in the conservative war on government.

Hence the jarring attacks on teachers by Walker and his political allies in Ohio, Michigan, Indiana, and Pennsylvania.

But it turns out that drowning students and teachers in the bathtub isn't all that popular with the public.

"I'm seeing this kernel of negativity and meanness in this bill," said Milwaukee resident Lorraine Jacobs in her testimony before the senate education committee in Madison.

As Lisa Scofield, a parent in Spring Green who teaches in the River Valley School District, put it, "This is not about education. It's about money and control, and you are taking it away. How can you even pretend to strengthen education as you dismantle our state's largest democratic institution?"

On the statewide expansion of charter schools, 120 people testified. Of these, only fifteen were in favor, and twelve of those fifteen were people with a direct interest in charter schools.

Republican senator Alberta Darling, the supposed author of the bill, introduced it flanked by its real authors—state and national charter school organizations. "These gentlemen represent a massive network," she declared.

Todd Ziebarth of the National Alliance for Public Charter Schools testified that Wisconsin "fails to provide autonomy" to charters. David Hansen of the National Association of Charter School Authorizers said S.B. 22 would make Wisconsin a better "policy environment," allowing more charters to open. If they failed, his organization could simply close them down.

This idea that it's no big deal to close down schools is perhaps the biggest disconnect between business-minded school "reformers" and the parents and teachers who came out to plead with their legislators not to destroy the public school system.

"I don't want my children's school in someone's portfolio," said Scofield, objecting to the business lingo used by the bill's proponents. "I want it in my community, with local control."

"I just wonder who is benefitting from this," she added. "Because it's not my kids."

"Charter schools are public schools," the charter advocates repeatedly intoned. John Gee, executive director of the Wisconsin Charter Schools Association, went even further, saying kids who can't afford private education need a way out of failing schools: "Ultimately, this is a social justice issue," he said, to a chorus of groans.

Gee was referring to historic racial divisions over school choice. When the Bradley Foundation made private-school vouchers into a national crusade, it pushed African American parents in Milwaukee out front on the issue. After all, who wants to argue with low-income, minority parents that their kids should be trapped in lousy schools?

The Madison Urban League's Kaleem Caire testified that S.B. 22 would make it easier for him to open a charter school for African American boys who are not well served by the public schools.

But overall, Walker's education proposals face opposition from both public school advocates and black leaders like Milwaukee's state senator Lena Taylor, who acknowledges that school choice is a tough issue.

"What we've done with this budget is to set up a secondary system of education with its own rules," says Democratic state representative Fred Clark.

If Wisconsin Republicans succeed in setting up their new statewide system of charter schools, Madison school board member Marjorie Passman testified, "those not chosen by lottery will return to the dying embers of our public school system."

"Add vouchers to the picture," Passman said, "and you'll actually have the poor paying for the rich to attend school."

The Rush to Privatize Education

From Idaho to Indiana to Florida, recently passed laws will radically reshape the face of education in America, shifting the responsibility of teaching generations of Americans to online education businesses, many of which have poor or nonexistent track records. The rush to privatize education will also turn tens of thousands of students into guinea pigs in a national experiment in virtual learning—a relatively new idea that allows for-profit companies to administer public schools completely online, with no brick-and-mortar classrooms or traditional teachers.

Lee Fang, Nation, *December 5, 2011.*

That, in a nutshell, is the vision of Walker and the coalition of interest groups that helped draft his education policies.

There is nothing remotely democratic about it. In fact, it is the brainchild of a network of national privatization think tanks and lobby groups. Just listen to the buzzwords that pop up over and over as Republican governors and legislators across the country attack teachers' unions, cut education budgets, and privatize schools.

Governor Walker used the word "tools" with Tourette's-like frequency during a press conference on his education program.

"We're giving our schools and local governments the tools they need" to make needed reform, he said, which amounts to "a net benefit to school districts."

If districts seize the "tools" and drive a hard bargain with teachers, they can save a lot of money, the governor asserted.

There is something funny about that word "tools."

It popped up again in Ohio, when Governor John Kasich announced a massive 16.4 percent cut to the state's education system. A press release from a think tank called Ohio Education Matters, which helped draft Kasich's plan, praised the governor's education effort, saying it "provides the right tools to help schools meet lower spending levels."

Those "tools" include cutting teacher benefits and "expanding opportunities for digital education." Digital education turns out to be the business of the group's parent organization, KnowledgeWorks, which markets a "portfolio of innovative approaches" to schools in seventeen states.

On the cover of the January 2011 issue of the pro-business American Legislative Exchange Council's magazine, *Inside ALEC*, there is a large photo of a toolbox and the headline "State Budget Reform Toolkit." ALEC drafts boilerplate legislation and pushes a pro-privatization agenda to state legislators around the country.

While there are good charter schools that work with local districts, independent charters are part of the "toolkit" of privatization and budget cutting around the nation. Robert Bobb, emergency manager of the Detroit Public Schools, has proposed a massive conversion of the city's schools to charters to deal with budget cuts. The rationale: Replacing all of Detroit's teachers with non-union personnel would save the district money.

Nor are charters better. In Philadelphia, a 2010 federal investigation turned up evidence of rampant fraud and mismanagement in the city's charters. The only comprehensive, national study of charters, by Stanford University, found that only 17 percent outperformed public schools, 37 percent did significantly worse, and the remaining 46 percent were no better. Likewise, Milwaukee voucher students perform worse in state tests than their public school peers. But liquidating state education funds, especially if you don't have to pay union wages or benefits, especially if you don't even have to maintain a physical building, means big money.

On education, money is lined up against students, teachers, and local communities—from the inner city to little farm towns.

It is telling that in Wisconsin, just as the Republicans won both houses of the legislature and moved into leadership positions, top staffers left state government altogether to take new jobs—as school privatization lobbyists. "The voucher groups are the heavies now," says Democratic state representative Mark Pocan. "Bankers and realtors have become the B team."

James Bender, former chief of staff for now-majority leader Jeff Fitzgerald, is currently a lobbyist for School Choice Wisconsin.

Brian Pleva, who ran the powerful Republican Assembly Campaign Committee, joined indicted former assembly speaker Scott Jensen at the Washington, D.C.–based American Federation for Children, a spinoff of the Michigan-based group All Children Matter, which has poured millions into phony issue ads in state legislative races. All Children Matter was founded by Michigan billionaires Dick and Betsy DeVos.

American Federation for Children spent $820,000 in the last election cycle in Wisconsin—almost as much as the $1 million spent by the state's most powerful coalition of business groups, Wisconsin Manufacturers and Commerce.

School choice groups form, dissolve, and then spring up again with new, patriotic-sounding names in each election cycle, says Mike McCabe, executive director of the watchdog group Wisconsin Democracy Campaign. That way they can remain nonprofits, instead of 527s [election campaign groups organized under Section 527 of the Internal Revenue Code], and they don't have to disclose their donors.

So there you have it: money and political power bearing down on public school teachers and kids with all the force of a mighty, well-financed, nationally organized lobby.

Patricia Schmidt, a white-haired elementary school music teacher from Republican education committee chair Senator Luther Olsen's district, told the committee "Wautoma schools are bracing for the worst."

Because of budget cuts, Schmidt said, she is driving to nearby Redgranite and teaching 100 extra students. "Our music program is very strong, and many of our students would drop out if they couldn't sing in the choir or play in the band, because they're not doing so well in their other classes," she said. Virtual schools would never fill the gap if her school closed, she added. She pleaded with the senators on the committee to come see the students and teachers for themselves.

Weirdly, bill sponsor Darling, who seemed distracted for much of the hearing, woke up from her reverie and thanked the music teacher for doing such a good job with the kids.

Few politicians want to appear in public being mean to white-haired music teachers.

But at the hearing, Republican state legislators had to sit and listen to their constituents tell them that they are going down in history as the people who killed their hometowns.

It's a pretty damn dramatic problem for Darling, Olsen, and others who are facing energized recall campaigns, thanks to Walker's scorched-earth program.

Drowning government in the bathtub is all well and good until you're the one who has to do the wet work.

So we got the bizarre scene in the hearing room: platitudes from politicians about "reforming" education in order to "help children," and citizens reacting with shock to the reality of brutal budget cuts and a vicious, predatory privatization scheme.

While Darling fiddled with her cell phone and whispered to her staff, Montello's Ligocki tried to describe what is important about local schools and their real, flesh-and-blood teachers.

She talked about her relationship with her high school English teacher and mentor, Miss Maasz.

When Maasz was about to lose her battle with cancer, Ligocki went to see her. "I asked her to tell me everything I needed to know about being a teacher in the few minutes we had to talk," Ligocki said. "She summarized decades of teaching experience with this sentence: 'When you walk into that classroom, your number one job is to love your students, and the ones who are the hardest to love are the ones who need it the most.' That sentence did more to prepare me for teaching than I could have imagined."

Ligocki went on to describe working in a school where half the kids qualify for free or reduced lunch, in an area plagued by poverty and alcoholism. "Many of our students' parents can't or don't give them the care they need," Ligocki said. "I don't just teach my kids, I love them. I raise them."

She talked about keeping extra food on hand for kids who are hungry. She told how she intervened when she saw that they were being abused. She explained how she earns their trust so they are willing to make themselves vulnerable and to try their hardest to learn.

Recently, during a training in online teaching, Ligocki said she asked her instructor, a virtual school teacher, about his relationships with students. "He said it was mostly limited to e-mails and comments on discussion boards."

The same day, she said, she went to a funeral for a beloved local math teacher, Andy Polk, a young husband and father who was killed in a tractor accident.

Students and teachers stood in the rain for two hours waiting to get inside the school for the visitation. "Students made huge displays with poems, pictures, and their favorite Mr. Polk sayings," she said.

"The shortcomings of a virtual education could not have been more obvious that day."

And the value of a strong public school system could not be more obvious than it is now, as we face the prospect of losing it altogether.

| "The choice of increasing student outcomes by moving to vouchers is becoming more and more of a no-brainer."

School Vouchers Are a Good Alternative to Public Schools

Gary Jason

In the following viewpoint, Gary Jason argues that allowing parents to use vouchers to pay for their children to attend the school of their choice is the solution to the problems present in the American public education system. Jason claims that recent research shows that voucher schools have better outcomes than public schools with respect to student performance, improving competition, improving graduation rates, and decreasing school violence.

Gary Jason is an adjunct philosophy professor at California State University–Fullerton and a senior editor of Liberty, *a libertarian journal.*

As you read, consider the following questions:

1. According to the author, per capita education spending has increased by what factor over the last quarter of a century?

2. Jason cites a study showing that voucher competition led to gains in reading performance in what two groups of public school students?

3. The author contends that a study of the Milwaukee voucher program shows that among voucher students, the graduation rate was how much higher?

The failure of the American K–12 public school system has been obvious for decades. Some of us fossils can recall the public uproar that accompanied the release of the report "A Nation at Risk" back in 1987, documenting the mediocre at best, disastrously bad at worst performance of the nation's public schools.[1]

A Solution to the Education Problem

The public school special interest groups (the PSSIGs)—that is, public school administrators, education department professors, "labor studies" professors, textbook publishers, and most notoriously teachers unions and their members—managed to turn the outrage into support for jacking up spending.

Over the last quarter-century, we have nearly doubled our national per capita spending—we now outspend per capita for K–12 education every other nation on Earth but one. But our national student scores have remained flat, while internationally, we have dropped in ranking among developed nations from 14th during the 1970s down to 24th place [in 2011].

Fabulous news, however: our students still outscore the other kids of the world on—self-esteem!

Milton Friedman, the Nobel Prize–winning economist and public intellectual, devised an elegantly simple but profound solution to the problem: vouchers. Under the voucher concept, the money we the taxpayers give—yes, it is our money,

1. *A Nation at Risk* was the 1983 report of President Ronald Reagan's National Commission on Excellence in Education that claimed America's schools were failing and called for education reforms to boost student achievement.

not the PSSIGSs'—to support public education is divided equally and goes directly to the children (through their parents), as opposed to being funneled through a giant rent-seeking machine. A brilliant, cut-to-the-chase concept: empower the users of a government-promoted service to pick the venue that best suits them, as opposed to what suits the providers of the service.

This fits well with Kantian [after eighteenth-century German philosopher Immanuel Kant] ethics: it respects the dignity of autonomous individuals by letting them choose the path that leads to their greatest self-fulfillment.

Voucher Students' Performance

Recent studies confirm consequentially what reasoning suggests logically. For example, a meta-study [a study of many studies] by the superb social scientist, Greg Forster, reviews the literature on voucher programs, and it is quite positive.

He notes that of the ten "gold standard" studies of vouchers—that is, studies that look at the performance of kids who won the lottery to go to voucher schools versus those who entered the lottery but lost (so had to attend public schools instead—nine show statistically significant gains in academic performance, and the one exception did show gains, just not at the level of statistical significance. By comparing students who got the vouchers with those who tried but didn't get them, these studies effectively rule out other possible explanations for the academic gains, such as parental or student ambition.

Forster also reports that of the 19 empirical studies of the impact voucher schools have on the surrounding public schools, 18 confirm what one would expect *a priori* [without having to see evidence], viz. [namely], that competition from the voucher schools would force the public ones to improve their services. The remaining study shows no impact—but no harm, either.

Reasons for School Vouchers

Even if vouchers did not improve test scores for participants and public schools, there would still be other reasons to implement them. Vouchers put students into schools that graduate more students, earn significantly greater satisfaction from parents, provide better services for disabled students, improve racial integration and students' civic values, save the public money, and so forth.

There are also other reasons one might support vouchers independent of their impact on test scores. Perhaps the most important argument is that they return control of education to parents, where it had rested for much of our nation's history. The seizure of power over education by a government monopoly and attendant interest groups (especially unions) has had far-reaching implications for our nation. The American founders would have viewed it as incompatible with a free and democratic society, as well as a realistic understanding of the natural formation of the human person in the family.

However, when all these issues have been considered, the empirical question of how vouchers impact student test scores remains—and it remains important. Vouchers do, in fact, improve test scores for both participants and public schools. The benefits of competition in education are clearly established by the evidence. The only remaining question is whether the evidence will be permitted to shape public debate on the question of vouchers.

Greg Forster, Foundation for Education Choice, March 2011.

The Impact of Public Schools

Another study by Matthew Carr provides yet more evidence of the validity of the voucher concept.

Carr researched the Ohio voucher program, called the Educational Choice Scholarship Program ("EdChoice") and passed by the legislature there in 2005. EdChoice provides vouchers to a small number of public school students. EdChoice was fiercely opposed by Ohio's PSSIGs then, and current Republican Governor [John] Kasich is facing even fiercer PSSIG resistance now as he struggles to quadruple the number of vouchers available to students in failing public schools.

Carr's study focuses on the crucial claim that voucher schools make public schools improve their quality of service through the force of competition (what he terms "the voucher threat"). Carr found that the public schools facing the voucher threat showed statistically significant gains in reading compared with those who didn't.

Interestingly, the gains are most concentrated in the "tails of the Bell-shaped curve"—that is, the most advanced and least advanced students. As he puts it, this suggests that the public schools facing voucher competition put their focus on improving their services to the two groups they view as most likely to flee to private schools.

Neither Forster nor Carr reviews the studies done in other countries—such as Denmark; New Zealand; Sweden; and Quebec, Canada—that have national voucher programs. But those studies show that vouchers work to improve student outcomes, and that teachers like the results just as the parents do.

Other Benefits of School Vouchers

Even more exciting is the recent work by researchers investigating the effects of voucher programs on such non-academic but still vitally important phenomena as graduation rates and rates of campus violence. Here the results are even more dramatic.

The 2010 study of the D.C. voucher program done by the U.S. Department of Education—a study that President [Barack] Obama shamefully suppressed while he killed the

D.C. voucher system (even as he was finding the best private school for his own privileged children)—shows that the students who went to voucher schools had a 21% higher graduation rate than students who applied for vouchers but lost the lottery (91% versus 70%).

A similar study of the Milwaukee voucher program showed an 8% higher rate of graduation among voucher students than among the voucher applicants who went to public school (77% versus 69%).

And studies have shown that the voucher schools have lower rates of violence.

As states continue to struggle with their budgets, in the face of ever-higher expenses for public services, the choice of increasing student outcomes by moving to vouchers is becoming more and more of a no-brainer—which is why during the last year, several states adopted or expanded voucher programs.

"*Most students with vouchers can only afford to attend private or parochial schools that, in many cases, are only marginally less bad than their public schools.*"

False Choice: How Private School Vouchers Might Harm Minority Students

Matthew McKnight

In the following viewpoint, Matthew McKnight argues that although school vouchers have been proposed as the solution to the problem of the education achievement gap along racial lines, the evidence does not support vouchers as the answer. McKnight claims that there are numerous problems with voucher programs, such as funding, which prevent vouchers being used for high-performing private schools without additional money. Furthermore, McKnight contends that voucher programs do not address the problems minority students face with respect to diversity and inclusion.

Matthew McKnight is a reporter for the New Yorker, *a weekly magazine of culture, criticism, and commentary.*

As you read, consider the following questions:

1. According to the author, in what year did the District of Columbia first implement the use of school vouchers?

2. McKnight claims that the maximum funding under the newly reinstated voucher program in Washington, DC, is what amount per year?

3. Instead of enacting school voucher programs, McKnight proposes spending public money on what?

For decades, policy wonks, lawmakers, and educators have wrestled with the phenomenon of the achievement gap in U.S. schools. The answer to the essential question—why does such a racialized gap exist?—has proven elusive. Race itself, poverty, location, lack of stability at home, and bad teachers has each been the culprit du jour at one time or another. Recently, however, many conservatives have decided that the problem might be the whole of public education—so they have sought to direct more funds toward private schools.

On March 31, the U.S. House of Representatives passed a bill to reinstate the school voucher program in the District of Columbia. The program delivers funding for low-income parents to send their children to private and independent schools. It was launched in 2003 as a five-year pilot but was discontinued by the Obama administration in 2009. (Students with vouchers were allowed to keep them until they graduated, but no new students could be enrolled in the program.) Although Obama continues to oppose the program, it was attached as a rider onto last week's House budget deal, which passed the Senate on Thursday [April 14, 2011]. The conventional wisdom among those—namely Republicans—backing the program's revival says that students with vouchers are all receiving top-notch educations, free of the problems that students at public schools face.

But there is growing evidence that suggests otherwise. There are problems with education in America that are so deeply rooted that not even private and independent schools escape them, which renders the notion of school vouchers out of touch with the nuanced problem of the achievement gap that it attempts to solve. It is worth giving a closer look to the real nature of the private-school environments where low-income children with vouchers often end up.

At face value, vouchers' main function—delivering choice to low-income parents with children in failing schools—seems like a laudable goal. Except, that is, when it doesn't work. In its most recent study of the D.C. Opportunity Scholarship Program (OSP), as the District's vouchers regime is called, the federal Department of Education's Institute of Education Sciences (IES) reported that there have been "no statistically significant impacts on overall student achievement in reading and math after at least four years." Patrick Wolf, the lead investigator on the study, ultimately supported OSP in his February testimony to the Senate Committee on Homeland Security and Governmental Operations. In the same testimony, however, he admitted that interpreting the program's effectiveness "is bound to be somewhat subjective."

Inadequate funding is part of the problem. In D.C., students who accepted vouchers before the program was discontinued generally attended one of two types of schools: parochial schools, and private or independent schools. But tuition at the city's most elite, highest-achieving private schools are far too expensive for both the previous voucher allotments ($7,500 per year) and the increase proposed in the new bill ($2,000 per year). A smaller number of students were able to make up the difference from other funding sources in order to attend the more costly private schools. But, this means that most students with vouchers can only afford to attend private or parochial schools that, in many cases, are only marginally less bad than their public schools.

The Voters' Choice: State Referenda on Vouchers

State	Year	Results
Maryland	1972	Rejected 55% to 45%
Michigan	1978	Rejected 75% to 26%
Colorado	1992	Rejected 67% to 33%
California	1993	Rejected 70% to 30%
Washington	1996	Rejected 64% to 36%
Michigan	2000	Rejected 69% to 31%
California	2000	Rejected 71% to 20%
Utah*	2007	Rejected 68% to 32%

* Voters in Utah repealed a program already created by the state legislature, as opposed to voting on a proposed program.

TAKEN FROM: Coalition for Public Schools, "Fact Sheet: The Case Against Private Schools Vouchers," www.coalition4publicschools.org, 2009.

Problems with voucher programs persist outside the District, too. In late March, Wisconsin's Department of Public Instruction released findings from the study of a similar program in Milwaukee that, when it began 21 years ago, was thought to be the standard-bearer for school choice programs. The *Journal Sentinel* reported, "Students in Milwaukee's school choice program performed worse than or about the same as students in Milwaukee Public Schools in math and reading on the latest statewide test, according to results released Tuesday that provided the first apples-to-apples achievement comparison between public and individual voucher schools."

But the flaws in voucher programs run deeper than what mere test scores can show. For many students who accept vouchers, there is a broader issue—the fact that private school education comes with its own sets of problems for minority students that proponents of vouchers either aren't aware of or choose not to acknowledge. Within the walls of many private schools, there are realities that create gaps between white students and low-income minority students.

These gaps have to do with a sense of inclusion. Psychologists Greg Walton and Geoffrey Cohen have dedicated years of study to the impact that the quality of a person's social connection has on his or her achievement. Their 2007 research paper concluded, "[I]t seems that Black students globalized the implications of social hardship into a conclusion about their potential to fit and succeed in an academic setting." More to the point, the authors wrote:

> We suggest that, in academic and professional settings, members of socially stigmatized groups are more uncertain of the quality of their social bonds and thus more sensitive to issues of social belonging. We call this state *belonging uncertainty*, and suggest that it contributes to racial disparities in achievement.

The study found no such results among Caucasian students. Rather, as shown by a more recent study that builds on Walton and Cohen's research, stereotypes, and feeling the risk that one might confirm stereotypes, also negatively influence performance among minorities. Barnard [College] Professor Steven Stroessner calls this "stereotype threat." He writes that, in performance-based situations in which a person actually is or expects to be "the single representative of a stereotyped group . . . or a numerical minority," lowered performance results most often occur. Stroessner adds that "minority status is sufficient but not necessary for stereotype threat"; indeed, "a reminder of a stereotype . . . or even just a reminder of a person's group membership (typically race or gender) that is tied to the stereotype" can be other factors.

Curious about real-life examples of this phenomenon, I talked to students, parents, and administrators at various private schools in D.C. Dominic Vedder, 17, an African American senior at the elite, private Sidwell Friends School in D.C., notices the impact of "belonging uncertainty" and "stereotype threat." He came to Sidwell in ninth grade from KIPP DC KEY, a public charter school and part of a nationwide network that has recently come under scrutiny; although Sidwell accepts vouchers, he is not the recipient of one. "Sometimes, especially if you haven't been at Sidwell for a long time, you can definitely get the feeling of [being] an outsider, because there are a lot of people who have been with each other since kindergarten," Vedder said. He also pointed to the sharp racial imbalances, among students and teachers, as obstacles to a successful transition to Sidwell. When asked how he overcame them—he admits the change of schools incited a drop in his grades—Vedder said, "I stay involved in school, hang out with my friends [after] school," and participate in extra-curricular activities. In other words, it was through great effort that he found success.

But it's not so easy for other minority students transferring from public into private schools, often with the help of vouchers, to find success. (And not all private schools, as previously mentioned, are nearly as excellent, academically and otherwise, as Sidwell.) Recently, the researchers intervened against "belonging uncertainty" by engaging black college freshmen in an hour-long exercise aimed at conveying that every student—regardless of race—faces uncertainty about belonging in a new community. They found that such interventions could reverse the impact that uncertainty has on a minority student's academic performance. Unfortunately, however, voucher programs don't always come equipped with interventions to help minority students transition into their new school environments.

To be sure, some private schools across the country work to improve diversity and inclusion, and should continue to do so. And, even when achievement gains aren't clear for students with vouchers, there may be other factors—such as parent satisfaction—that come into play when determining the best place to send children to learn.

But the fact remains that vouchers, including D.C.'s reviv-ing program, generally ignore the factors that work directly against their success. The ultimate fallacy of vouchers is that they are designed to deliver choices, not outcomes. In that process, minority students stand a serious chance of losing out. It would be wise, instead, to devote public money and energy to creating thriving public schools, open to all students and focused on their achievement, regardless of background.

"In a tax-credit program . . . the amount
is . . . defined entirely by the individual
choice of the donating citizens."

In Defense of School-Choice
Tax Credits

David French

*In the following viewpoint, David French argues against the idea
that school-choice tax credits cost the government money. French
claims that unlike school vouchers, which use government funds,
tax credits use private funds thereby avoiding any charge of
harm to other taxpayers. French contends that tax credits would
ultimately save the government money on the savings from expanding private schools. French is a senior counsel at the American Center for Law and Justice.*

As you read, consider the following questions:

1. Why does French think it is misleading to say the "government ends up with less money" because of the tax-
   credit school-choice plan?

2. According to the author, who determines a citizen's total
   tax liability?

3. How does the government end up with more money under the Arizona tax-credit plan, according to the author?

Robert, I'm beginning to get the sense we're going to have to agree to disagree on the merits of Arizona's tax-credit school-choice plan. But before I let our little dispute pass into history, I've got to take issue with this statement:

> There is no difference between (A) having the government spend money on a program, and (B) having the government give dollar-for-dollar credits so that individuals can "donate" (i.e., divert their tax dollars) to that program. Either way, the government ends up with less money, the individual has not foregone a single dollar, and the program has more money.

I'm not quite sure how you can say there's "no difference." The differences are, in fact, vast—economically, fiscally, and conceptually. In every voucher program ever created, the vouchers represent an actual expenditure from the government treasury according to budgeted dollar amounts as limited by the specific appropriation. In a tax-credit program, by contrast, the direct money transfer is not from government to private citizen but from private citizen to private entity (the tuition organizations), and the amount is not a finite, budgeted amount but instead—like normal charitable contributions—defined entirely by the individual choice of the donating citizens. Thus, private choice defines the scope of the program. Whether the tuition organizations spend $50,000 or $50 million is up to the decisions of individuals, not the legislature.

Next, I think it's misleading to say the "government ends up with less money." There was considerable record evidence that the tax-credit program actually saved the government considerable money. If Arizona's private schools were to close tomorrow, vast state expenditures would be required to house

Public Opinion on School Tax Credits

A proposal has been made to offer a tax credit for educational expenses (fees, supplies, computers, and tuition) to low- and moderate-income parents who send their children to public and private schools. Would you favor or oppose such a proposal?

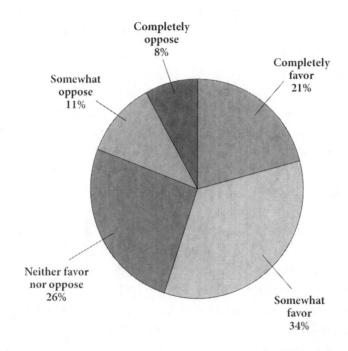

Completely oppose
8%

Completely favor
21%

Somewhat oppose
11%

Somewhat favor
34%

Neither favor nor oppose
26%

TAKEN FROM: *Education Next* and the Program on Education Policy and Governance at Harvard University, "*Education Next*–PEPG Survey 2011," April–May 2011. educationnext.org.

and educate tens of thousands of new students. The cost of the tax credit is far, far smaller than the cost of educating a child in an Arizona public school.

Finally, I love your phrase "divert their tax dollars." I prefer to describe it as being forced to pay less of their own money to the Arizona government. As Justice Kennedy himself said, "Private bank accounts cannot be equated with the Arizona State Treasury." The starting position for any citizen is that all the money they earn is theirs, not the state's, and then the individual determines their total tax liability (the portion of their money they pay to the government) according to applicable law. That law creates a marginal income-tax rate but also a myriad of deductions, credits, and other mechanisms that work together to define the actual tax dollars owed. Thus, the effective tax rate has long been quite different from the defined marginal rates, and I don't think it's accurate to define the difference as "diverted tax dollars." I don't think anyone would describe a lowered marginal tax rate or other tax cuts in that manner, so why define other—less sweeping—mechanisms that lower your tax liability as "diverted tax dollars?"

If I go to my neighborhood Super Walmart, and I carry with me a bundle of coupons, pick up an extra pack of Viva paper towels because of a two-for-one deal, and then bite the bullet and buy off-brand Four Loko instead of the real thing, I don't think of the savings as my "diverted grocery dollars." Instead, I just pay my grocery bill and am happy to have more money in my pocket.

Under the Arizona tax-credit plan, the government ends up with more money because of the vast cost savings inherent in expanded private education, individuals still pay actual money into the program in amounts they determine, and the program ends up with the amount of money the citizens want it to have. That's a plan conservatives can support.

> "A ... tuition tax credit program would harm public schools and local taxpayers."

Tax Credits for School Choice Do Not Benefit Taxpayers and Students

National Education Association

In the following viewpoint, the National Education Association (NEA) argues that the use of tax credits to fund parents' decisions to send children to private school is poor public policy. The NEA contends that the use of tax credits does not improve student performance and has a negative economic impact on public schools. The NEA also claims that the use of tax credits is an inequitable policy that benefits the wealthy, and it denies that individual taxpayers should be allowed choice in this area. The NEA is the nation's largest professional employee organization, with members working at every level of education, committed to advancing the cause of public education.

As you read, consider the following questions:

1. What two methods of using tax credits to offset the cost of private education does the author identify?

2. What reason does the NEA give in support of its view that students who switch from public to private school because of tax credits will not save school districts money?

3. Identify one of the two analogies the NEA uses in support of its view that taxpayers should not get tax refunds for choosing to send their children to private school.

Efforts to subsidize private education take a variety of forms, with the most familiar being the private school voucher provided directly to parents. But there are other less direct ways governments subsidize private schools. One such method is to provide a tax credit to parents to offset their personal education expenses (education tax credit). Another is to allow individuals and corporations to reduce their tax bills by sending what they would otherwise owe in taxes to a foundation that turns the money into private school vouchers (tax credit voucher). Like directly funded vouchers, these tax loopholes do nothing to improve public schools, while actually reducing the amount of money available for proven school improvement strategies.

A Lack of Benefits from Tax Credits

Tax credit vouchers have *not* been proven effective in improving student academic performance. Research indicates that when student demographics are taken into account, public school students perform as well if not better than private school students. Students attending traditional public high schools are also just as likely to attend college as those attending private high schools.

Those who promote private school tax subsidies claim that the risk of losing students to private school forces public schools to improve. There is no credible research supporting this alleged positive competitive impact.

A common argument advanced in favor of private school tax credits is that they would save states money by encouraging families to switch from public schools to private ones. A study of individual tax credits in Arizona, however, showed that they were used primarily by families whose children already attended private school. In such cases, these programs represent net revenue losses for states.

Even in situations where students do switch from public school to private school, school districts may not experience savings, because districts cannot reduce their fixed costs— maintenance, utilities, debt service, transportation, etc.—in proportion to the number of students who leave. Rather than save money, school districts must make do with less.

The Problem of Inequity

A nationally recognized economic consulting firm determined that a proposed tuition tax credit program would harm public schools and local taxpayers, who would have to make up any funding shortfall resulting from reduced state expenditures and federal aid. Public school students would experience the most direct impact, as they would attend less well-funded schools or have to travel to distant public schools after neighborhood schools closed due to declining enrollment and funding.

As with most tax cuts, the financial benefits of education tax subsidies accrue primarily to the wealthy. In the case of an individual education tax credit, the financial benefits are enjoyed only by families that itemize their taxes, and can afford to pay tuition and then later reduce their tax bill by all or some of their costs. The fiscal benefits of tax credit vouchers are also enjoyed primarily by those who can afford to make donations to foundations that will use the money to grant vouchers. The foundations that convert charitable donations into vouchers are also treated differently than other charitable foundations. Because taxpayers receive credits against their tax bills for contributions to voucher foundations, rather than mere reductions of their taxable income, taxpayers seeking to maximize their charitable giving may favor voucher-granting foundations over other worthy causes.

To make private school tax subsidies politically palatable and less vulnerable to legal challenge, proponents often include in their proposals credits for public school expenses or contributions to public school extracurricular funds. Because families in less affluent communities cannot afford to make donations to their children's schools, the benefits of public school tax credits accrue primarily to wealthy school districts, increasing the disparities between rich and poor neighborhoods. The inclusion of provisions aimed at public school parents is more about making the proposals *appear* equitable than about actually providing public schools with equitable funding.

The Role of Taxes

Government provides public services for the benefit of *all* members of society. Taxpayers do not get to pick and choose which of these services their tax dollars will support, and which they would prefer not to fund. Taxpayers who buy books, for example, should not receive a tax rebate for not patronizing the public library. Nor should taxpayers who prefer country clubs to public golf courses receive rebates to compensate them for the additional cost of that private choice. Likewise, taxpayers who choose to send their children to private school should not receive tax refunds to pay tuition.

These private school tax subsidies increase the complexity of an already complex tax system. To claim an education tax credit, taxpayers must retain and submit receipts for all claimed education expenses. To minimize the risk of fraud in a tax credit voucher program, the state Department of Revenue would have to compare the contributions that taxpayers claim they made to voucher foundations with the receipts reported by those groups, and also confirm that the donations were used to fund vouchers that were actually used in eligible schools. In Arizona, the chief economist for the state Department of Revenue warned that the program contained "lots of possibilities for abuse."

Tax credit vouchers and education tax credits are just the latest in a long list of schemes that have diverted attention from what our children and our schools really need—programs and funding to recruit, train, and retain the best teachers; smaller classes so they can devote enough attention to each child; high-quality early childhood education programs so children come to school ready to learn; tutoring to ensure that those who fall behind aren't left behind, and the active involvement of parents and the community. All students deserve the right to a great public school, and it is with these kinds of investments—not education tax subsidies—that we will achieve this goal.

Periodical and Internet Sources Bibliography

The following articles have been selected to supplement the diverse views presented in this chapter.

Americans United for Separation of Church and State	"10 Reasons Why Private School Vouchers Should Be Rejected," February 2011. www.au.org/church-state/february-2011-church -state/featured/10-reasons-why-private-school -vouchers-should-be.
Robert J. Birdsell and Mary Claire Ryan	"Where Credit Is Due," *America*, November 28, 2011.
Lindsey Burke	"Why Market Forces Are Good for Education," *Atlantic*, February 3, 2012.
Michael Chingos and Paul Peterson	"The Effects of School Vouchers on College Enrollment," Brookings Institution, August 2012. www.brookings.edu/events/2012/08/23 -school-vouchers.
Lee Fang	"How Online Learning Companies Bought America's Schools," *Nation*, December 5, 2011.
Jack Jennings	"School Vouchers: No Clear Advantage in Academic Achievement," *Huffington Post*, July 27, 2011. www.huffingtonpost.com/jack-jennings/ school-vouchers-no-academic-advantage_b _909735.html.
Michael A. LaFerrara	"Toward a Free Market in Education: School Vouchers or Tax Credits?," *Objective Standard*, Spring 2011.
Paul E. Peterson	"Let the Charters Bloom," *Hoover Digest*, vol. 3, 2010.
Richard W. Rahn	"Put Department of Education in Timeout," *Washington Times*, November 3, 2010.
Katrina Trinko	"Why School Vouchers Are Worth a Shot," *USA Today*, April 19, 2011.

OPPOSING
VIEWPOINTS®
SERIES

CHAPTER 3

Should Religion and Religious Ideas Be Part of Public Education?

Chapter Preface

The US Constitution protects religious freedom in the United States. The First Amendment to the Constitution states, "Congress shall make no law respecting an establishment of religion, or prohibiting the exercise thereof." The first portion, known as the establishment clause, prohibits the government from establishing any official religion. The second portion, known as the free exercise clause, prohibits the government from barring the exercise of religion. These clauses form the foundation of religious freedom in the United States, forbidding government from promoting any particular religion while also allowing people to practice any religion that they choose. Balancing these two principles in the public sphere can be challenging, and this tension is particularly evident in the public schools, where social battles over the role of religion have been ongoing for decades.

The First Amendment's guarantee of freedom from government establishment of religion and guarantee of free exercise of religion applies to the public schools. The US Supreme Court has held that the public school context is one in which government must be particularly careful about establishing or endorsing religion: "What to most believers may seem nothing more than a reasonable request that the nonbeliever respect their religious practices, in a school context may appear to the nonbeliever or dissenter to be an attempt to employ the machinery of the State to enforce a religious orthodoxy." (*Lee v. Weisman*, 505 US 577 [1992]). Over the last few decades the Court has concluded that public school officials may not engage in activities that endorse a particular religion—such as starting the day with a prayer, posting religious material, such as the Ten Commandments, in the classroom, or teaching creationism instead of evolution in science classes—to avoid violation of the establishment clause.

Although the Court has held that public school officials may not endorse religion, the Court has recognized that the free exercise clause of the First Amendment protects the rights of students to exercise their religion: "There is a crucial difference between government speech endorsing religion, which the Establishment Clause forbids, and private speech endorsing religion, which the Free Speech and Free Exercise Clauses protect." (*Board of Education of Westside Community Schools v. Mergens*, 496 US 226 [1990]). Thus, as long as student religious activity at school is private, it is protected. The US Department of Education clarifies that "students may read their Bibles or other scriptures, say grace before meals, and pray or study religious materials with fellow students during recess, the lunch hour, or other noninstructional time to the same extent that they may engage in nonreligious activities." However, the Department of Education also notes that student religious expression, as with other privately initiated student expression, may be limited when students are engaged in school activities and instruction, cautioning that "the Constitution mandates neutrality rather than hostility toward privately initiated religious expression."

History shows that even when the Supreme Court decides the issue, not everyone agrees with the outcome. This chapter demonstrates that debates about school prayer, Bible classes, and the teaching of intelligent design and creationism continue despite the fact that the Court has reached conclusions on these issues, as people disagree about the extent to which religion and religious ideas should be a part of public education.

| "History textbooks have been scrubbed
  clean of religious references."

Public Schools Have Been Overly Sanitized of Religion

John W. Whitehead

In the following viewpoint, John W. Whitehead argues that attempts to keep religion out of school have gone too far. Whitehead claims that recent incidents show that an irrational understanding of the separation of church and state has led to a misguided belief that religion must be entirely expelled from public schools. Whitehead claims that America's history and founding support the view that public life ought to include many viewpoints, including religious ones.

John W. Whitehead is an attorney, author of The Rights of Religious Persons in Public Education, *and founder and president of the Rutherford Institute, which promotes civil rights, especially religious rights.*

As you read, consider the following questions:

1. According to the author, what two messages were conveyed to the public school student who was prevented from giving his presentation on Jesus to the entire class?

2. Whitehead says that secularists often cite what principle to justify the censorship of religious expression?

3. According to the author, what role did religion play in early public school curriculum in the United States?

Our young people are growing up in a world in which *God* is the new four-letter word. Look around and you will find that while it is permissible for children in many public school systems and homes to read novels with graphic language and watch sexually explicit commercials on TV, talking about God or religion is taboo.

Attacks on Religion in School

Few objections are raised over the kind of music kids are listening to on their MP3-players at school during non-instructional time. However, lawsuits are constantly being filed over whether students should observe a moment of silence at the start of the school day. Two incidents that perfectly illustrate my point recently came across my desk.

The first incident involves Wade, a fourth grader from Colorado. Wade's class was given a "Hero" assignment, which required each student to pick a hero, research the person and write an essay. The student would then dress up and portray the chosen hero as part of a "live wax museum" and give an oral report in front of the class.

However, when the 9-year-old chose Jesus as his hero, school officials immediately insisted that he pick another hero. (You have to wonder whether school officials would have objected had Wade chosen the Dalai Lama—or even the Rev. Martin Luther King Jr.—as his hero.) After Wade's parents objected, the school proposed a compromise: Wade could write the essay on Jesus. He could even dress up like Jesus for the "wax museum." However, he would have to present his oral report to his teacher in private, with no one else present, rather than in front of the classroom like the other students.

A Zero-Tolerance Attitude

In an attempt to avoid offending anyone, America's public schools have increasingly adopted a zero-tolerance attitude toward religious expression. . . . Such politically correct thinking has resulted in a host of inane actions, from the Easter Bunny being renamed "Peter Rabbit" to Christmas concerts being dubbed "Winter" concerts, and some schools even outlaw the colors red and green, saying they're Christmas colors. And . . . simply because someone is offended by the title, students cannot play music that has no words and is performed with no religious intent.

John W. Whitehead, Liberty,
January–February 2010.

The message to young Wade, of course, was two-fold: first, Jesus is not a worthy hero, and second, Jesus is someone to be ashamed of and kept hidden from public view. Yet do we really want our young people to grow up believing that freedom of speech means that you're free to talk about anything as long as you don't mention God or Jesus?

Wade is not the only school-aged child being singled out for censorship because of a particular religious viewpoint. For instance, a third grader at an elementary school in Las Vegas, Nevada, was asked to write in her journal about what she liked most about the month of December. When the child wrote that she liked the month of December because it's Jesus's birthday and people get to celebrate it, her teacher tapped her on the shoulder and informed her that she was not allowed to write about religion in school.

The Separation of Church and State

Much of the credit for this state of affairs can be chalked up to secularist organizations that have worked relentlessly to drive religion from public life. John Leo, a former contributing editor at *U.S. News and World Report*, painted a grim picture of those who operate under the so-called guise of safeguarding the separation of church and state so that all faiths might flourish. Leo's article, written seven years ago, was an eerie foreshadowing of our current state of affairs:

> History textbooks have been scrubbed clean of religious references and holidays scrubbed of all religious references and symbols. Some intellectuals now contend that arguments by religious people should be out of bounds in public debate, unless, of course, they agree with the elites.
>
> In schools the anti-religion campaign is often hysterical. When schoolchildren are invited to write about any historical figure, this usually means they can pick Stalin or Jeffrey Dahmer, but not Jesus or Luther, because religion is reflexively considered dangerous in schools and loathsome historical villains aren't. Similarly a moment of silence in the schools is wildly controversial because some children might use it to pray silently on public property. Oh, the horror. The overall message is that religion is backward, dangerous and toxic.

Unfortunately, as the many cases that I deal with demonstrate, things have only gotten worse since John Leo wrote those words. How do we explain why these instances of discrimination have become the rule, rather than the exception?

Plain and simple, an elite segment of society that views God as irrelevant has come to predominate. As Christopher Lasch details in his book *The Revolt of the Elites and the Betrayal of Democracy* (1995):

> Public life is thoroughly secularized. The separation of church and state, nowadays interpreted as prohibiting any public recognition of religion at all, is more deeply en-

129

trenched in America than anywhere else. Religion has been relegated to the sidelines of public debate. Among elites it is held in low esteem—something useful for weddings and funerals but otherwise dispensable. A skeptical, iconoclastic state of mind is one of the distinguishing characteristics of the knowledge classes. Their commitment to the culture of criticism is understood to rule out religious commitments. The elites' attitude to religion ranges from indifference to active hostility.

The Threat of Extreme Secularism

Those who have adopted this secular outlook frequently cite the "wall of separation between church and state" as justification for censoring, silencing and discriminating against religious individuals, especially in the public schools. The threat posed by this extreme secularism is that religion and religious people are not merely kept separate from the school system but are instead forced into a position of utter subservience.

Moreover, contrary to history and tradition, most Americans have now come to accept the assumption that religious faith has no real bearing on civic responsibility or morality. This is because the extreme concept of the separation of church and state has literally been drilled into their heads through the schools, the media and the courts.

This is not to say that the concept of a wall of separation between church and state is not an important part of our cultural and legal landscape. However, the wall of separation is not the issue in the myriad of cases that arise in schools today. The issue in such instances is the religious believer versus the secular state. It is also a denial of everything this country stands for in terms of the freedoms of speech, religion and a respect for moral traditions.

The History of Religion in America

Contrary to the propaganda peddled by various separatist organizations, those who founded this country were not antireligionists. Take Thomas Jefferson, for example, who coined the *wall of separation* phrase. While Jefferson was correct in arguing that churches should not interfere in the workings of government, he did not intend to seal religion off hermetically from public life. In fact, Jefferson was a religious person who on two separate occasions—once while President—reduced the New Testament to include what he believed were the true teachings of Jesus (absent the virgin birth and the miracles). Jefferson's conclusion was that Jesus' teachings were "the most sublime and benevolent code of morals which has ever been offered to man."

American public education was established on the precept that it would accommodate religion. For example, the Northwest Ordinance, enacted by the Continental Congress in 1787, recognized the importance of religion in its provision setting aside federal property for schools. This section of the Ordinance provided: "Religion, morality, and knowledge being essential to good government and the happiness of mankind, schools and the means of education shall forever be encouraged." Thus, according to the Northwest Ordinance, religion was part of the foundation of American public schools.

In fact, the historical record reveals that religion was integrated into the early public school curriculum. Textbooks referred to God without embarrassment, and public schools considered one of their major tasks to be the development of moral character through the teaching of religion.

While the cultural landscape has changed greatly since the founding of the country, one thing has not: America still stands for freedom and pluralism. What this demands is an equal voice for all viewpoints. This includes religion. If we do not maintain this ideal, then the only alternative is a form of secular society and government that respects no one's freedom or opinions at all.

| "Neutrality is the appropriate stance for the government to take toward religion."

Public Schools Are Rightfully Neutral on Religion

Americans United for Separation of Church and State

In the following viewpoint, the organization Americans United for Separation of Church and State argues that disallowing religious promotion in public school while protecting individual student religious expression is the correct approach in a religiously diverse country. The author contends that despite much misunderstanding, religion has not been purged from the school realm but only government sponsorship of it.

Americans United for Separation of Church and State is a nonpartisan educational organization dedicated to preserving the constitutional principle of church-state separation.

As you read, consider the following questions:

1. According to the author, did the US Supreme Court decision in *Engel v. Vitale* (1962) forbid students from praying at school at any time?

2. Are teachers allowed to use the Bible in class, according to Americans United for Separation of Church and State?

3. What two historical incidents does the author cite in support of the view that neutrality was the logical outcome of the history of religion in American schools?

Few issues in American public life engender more controversy than religion and public education. Unfortunately, this topic is all too often shrouded in confusion and misinformation. When discussing this matter, it's important to keep in mind some basic facts.

Ninety percent of America's youngsters attend public schools. These students come from homes that espouse a variety of religious and philosophical beliefs. Given the incredible diversity of American society, it's important that our public schools respect the beliefs of everyone and protect parental rights.

The schools can best do this by not sponsoring religious worship. This principle ensures that America's public schools are welcoming to all children and leaves decisions about religion where they belong: with the family.

Prayer in Public School

The U.S. Supreme Court has been vigilant in forbidding public schools and other agencies of the government to interfere with Americans' constitutional right to follow their own consciences when it comes to religion. In 1962, the justices ruled that official prayer had no place in public education.

This decision is widely misunderstood today. The court *did not* rule that students are forbidden to pray on their own; the justices merely said that government officials had no business composing a prayer for students to recite. The *Engel v. Vitale* case came about because parents in New York challenged a prayer written by a New York education board. These

Christian, Jewish and Unitarian parents did not want their children subjected to state-sponsored devotions. The high court agreed that the scheme amounted to government promotion of religion.

In the following year, 1963, the Supreme Court handed down another important ruling dealing with prayer in public schools. In *Abington Township School District v. Schempp*, the court declared school-sponsored Bible reading and recitation of the Lord's Prayer unconstitutional.

Since those rulings, a myth has sprung up asserting that Madalyn Murray O'Hair, a prominent atheist, "removed prayer from public schools." In fact, the 1962 case was brought by a group of New York parents who had no connection to O'Hair, and the 1963 case was filed by a Unitarian family from the Philadelphia area. O'Hair, at that time a resident of Baltimore, had filed a similar lawsuit, which the high court consolidated with the Pennsylvania case.

It is important to remember that in these decisions the Supreme Court did not "remove prayer from public schools." The court removed only *government-sponsored* worship. Public school students have always had the right to pray on their own as class schedules permit.

Bible Reading in Public School

Also, the Supreme Court did not rule against official prayer and Bible reading in public schools out of hostility to religion. Rather, the justices held that these practices were examples of unconstitutional government interference with religion. Thus, the exercises violated the First Amendment.

Nothing in the 1962 or 1963 rulings makes it unlawful for public school students to pray or read the Bible (or any other religious book) on a voluntary basis during their free time. Later decisions have made this even clearer. In 1990, the high court ruled specifically that high school students may form clubs that meet during "non-instructional" time to pray, read religious texts or discuss religious topics if other student groups are allowed to meet.

The high court has also made it clear, time and again, that objective study *about* religion in public schools is legal and appropriate. Many public schools offer courses in comparative religion, the Bible as literature or the role of religion in world and U.S. history. As long as the approach is objective, balanced and non-devotional, these classes present no constitutional problem.

In short, a public school's approach to religion must have a legitimate educational purpose, not a devotional one. Public schools should not be in the business of preaching to students or trying to persuade them to adopt certain religious beliefs. Parents, not school officials, are responsible for overseeing a young person's religious upbringing. This is not a controversial principle. In fact, most parents would demand these basic rights.

Religion in Public Education

A passage from the high court's ruling in the 1963 Pennsylvania case sums up well the proper role of religion in public education.

Justice Tom Clark, writing for the court, observed, "Nothing that we have said here indicates that such study of the Bible or of religion, when presented objectively as part of a secular program of education, may not be effected consistent with the First Amendment." Clark added that government could not force the exclusion of religion in schools "in the sense of affirmatively opposing or showing hostility to religion."

The court's ruling suggested simply that a student's family, not government, is responsible for decisions about religious instruction and guidance. There was respect, not hostility, toward religion in the court's ruling.

Knowledge of Religion's Role in Public Schools

Percent of respondents who know that, according to rulings by the US Supreme Court, a public school teacher . . .

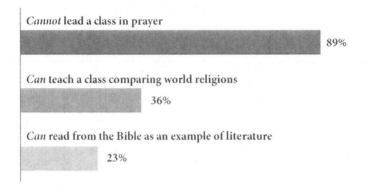

Cannot lead a class in prayer

89%

Can teach a class comparing world religions

36%

Can read from the Bible as an example of literature

23%

TAKEN FROM: The Pew Forum on Religion and Public Life, "US Religious Knowledge Survey," Pew Research Center, September 28, 2010. www.pewforum.org.

Justice Clark concluded, "The place of religion in our society is an exalted one, achieved through a long tradition of reliance on the home, the church, and the inviolable citadel of the individual heart and mind. We have come to recognize through bitter experience that it is not within the power of government to invade that citadel, whether its purpose or effect be to aid or oppose, to advance or retard. In the relationship between man and religion, the State is firmly committed to a position of neutrality."

A Logical Outcome of Neutrality

Some critics of the high court's rulings have suggested that these church-state rulings have no precedence in American history. On the contrary, the decisions are the logical outcome of a debate that has been under way in our country for many decades.

Public education for the masses, as conceived by Horace Mann and others in the mid 19th century, was intended to be "non-sectarian." In reality, however, schools often reflected the majority religious view, a kind of nondenominational Protestantism. Classes began with devotional readings from the King James Version of the Bible and recitation of the Protestant version of the Lord's Prayer. Students were expected to take part whether they shared those religious sentiments or not.

Catholic families were among the first to challenge these school-sponsored religious practices. In some parts of the country, tension over religion in public schools erupted into actual violence. In Philadelphia, for example, full-scale riots and bloodshed resulted in 1844 over which version of the Bible should be used in classroom devotions. Several Catholic churches and a convent were burned; many people died. In Cincinnati, a "Bible War" divided the city in 1868 after the school board discontinued mandatory Bible instruction.

Tensions like this led to the first round of legal challenges to school-sponsored religious activity in the late 19th century. Several states ruled against the practices. Compelling children to recite prayers or read devotionals from certain versions of the Bible, these courts said, was not the job of public schools. They declared government-imposed religion a violation of state constitutions and the fundamental rights of conscience. Eventually, the U.S. Supreme Court adopted this view as well, applying the church-state separation provisions of the First Amendment of the U.S. Constitution.

Guidelines for Religion in Schools

The high court's decisions have worked well in practice. In 1995, a joint statement of current law regarding religion in public schools was published by a variety of religious and civil liberties organizations. This statement served as the basis for U.S. Department of Education guidelines intended to alleviate concerns about constitutional religious activities in schools.

These guidelines, which were sent to every public school in the nation, stressed that students have the right to pray or to discuss their religious views with their peers so long as they are not disruptive. But the guidelines went on to state that public schools are prohibited from sponsoring worship or pressuring students to pray, meditate, read religious texts or take part in other religious activities.

These are common-sense guidelines, but they are not enough for some people. Misguided individuals and powerful sectarian lobbies in Washington continue to press for religious majority rule in the nation's public schools. They advocate for school prayer amendments and other measures that would permit government-sponsored worship in the schools. They want their beliefs taught in the public schools and hope to use the public schools as instruments of evangelism.

The Need for Religious Neutrality

Americans must resist these efforts. They must protect the religious neutrality of public education. Being neutral on religion is not the same as being hostile toward it. In a multi-faith, religiously diverse society such as ours, neutrality is the appropriate stance for the government to take toward religion. Under this principle, public schools can allow for individual student religious expression without endorsing or promoting any specific faith.

The United States has changed since its founding in 1787. A nation that was once relatively religiously homogeneous has become one of the most pluralistic and diverse on the face of the globe. Scholars count over 2,000 different denominations and traditions in our country.

The answer to disputes over religion in public schools is simple: Keep the government out of the private religious lives of students. Leave decisions about when and how to pray (or whether to pray at all) to the home. This is the course the Supreme Court has adopted, and we are a stronger nation for it.

As Supreme Court Justice Anthony Kennedy said in a June 1992 opinion, "No holding of this Court suggests that a school can persuade or compel a student to participate in a religious exercise. . . . The First Amendment's Religion Clauses mean that religious beliefs and religious expressions are too precious to be either proscribed or prescribed by the State."

> "*Secular humanism . . . [is predomi-*
> *nant] in kids' school-day devotions.*"

The Ruling Religion in Schools

Kurt Williamsen

In the following viewpoint, Kurt Williamsen argues that al-
though displays of Christianity have been removed from the
public schools and other public places, other religions have not
suffered the same fate. Williamsen claims that the most domi-
nant religion taught in public schools is secular humanism,
which denies the existence of God but endorses a particular ethi-
cal system. Williamsen contends that the promulgation of secular
humanism is having dire consequences for society.

Kurt Williamsen is associate editor of the New American, *a*
publication of the conservative John Birch Society.

As you read, consider the following questions:

1. Williamsen claims that bans on public Christianity are meant to have what effect?

2. According to the author, what is the core moral teaching of secular humanism?

Kurt Williamsen, "The Ruling Religion in Schools," *New American*, vol. 28, no. 1, January 9, 2012, p. 44. Copyright © 2012 by the New American. All rights reserved. Reproduced by permission.

3. What premise are the statistics about children from fatherless homes, cited by the author, intended to support?

Christmas came again—along with the numerous lawsuits and public prohibitions against public displays of Christianity. Many agree with making Christianity invisible because the phrase "separation of church and state" is repeated so often that even school kids can recite it with little prompting.

But even aside from the fact that there is no such phraseology in the Constitution or Bill of Rights, that Congress has opened with a prayer since its inception, that several states had state religions, and that every state's constitution opens with praise to God, it's a ludicrous notion: As Christianity is heaved out of the public sphere, other religions take its place.

In fact, bans on public Christianity are strictly meant to eliminate Christian morals, not to adhere to the law. This should be obvious to anyone: While prayers are yanked from commencement ceremonies, and our Christian roots are removed from social studies/history classes, the Islamic religion is welcomed.

As Janet Levy at *American Thinker* noted, students at Excelsior Middle School in Discovery Bay, California, had to take Muslim names, recite Islamic prayers, and celebrate Ramadan. Carver Elementary in San Diego provided prayer time for Muslims, removed pork from menus, and segregated classes by gender. "The University of Michigan, a taxpayer-funded school, has provided separate prayer rooms and ritual foot baths, requiring bathroom modifications costing over $100,000, for Muslim observances." Also, the federal government is forcing the Berkeley, Illinois, school district to adjust its time-off policy so that a teacher may take a pilgrimage to Mecca during the school year. The list goes on.

And Islam is not even the dominant religion taught in public schools; "secular humanism"—which posits that humans are the central beings of the universe and that science,

logic, and reason should be the basis for morality and decision making—takes those honors in kids' school-day devotions.

Yes, secular humanism is a religion!

What is religion? It is any system of beliefs, practices, and
ethical values underlying a code of behavior and a philosophy.
(No, religion is not the "worship" of a supreme God; otherwise, Shintoism and Buddhism would not qualify as religions.)
As part of "humanist" religious education, public schools
teach that no family situation is inherently better than another
and that morals are relative and should be reevaluated for
each situation—essentially saying there is no absolute right or
wrong (teaching ethics, of a sort). Schools eradicate God from
any part in creation, inculcating kids with the idea that evolution is how all species came about (teaching a belief system),
and schools preach a creed of "social justice" that espouses a
reverence for Mother Earth, fairness through government re-
distribution, and a victim group mentality (teaching and insti-
tuting personal practices).

In fact, U.S. courts have ruled that secular humanism is
indeed a religion; they just somehow couldn't find it in the
schools.

It should come as no surprise that a belief system initiated
in schools through a reliance on illogic, falsehoods, ignorance,
and political correctness propagates more of the same.

Here are several of hundreds of examples: Someone who
states in schools that homosexuality is aberrant, high-risk behavior would be punished severely as a bully and a bigot for
demeaning homosexuals' beliefs—for making homosexuals
feel bad about themselves—but disparaging Christian beliefs
to Christian kids is somehow not a problem.

Secularists insist that youth have the freedom and encouragement to experiment with sex—running a gauntlet of disease and possible death—but also say that government should

have the power to regulate equally personal decisions, such as what people eat and drink and what medical treatments they may receive.

And they teach that every type of family unit is equally desirable despite the fact that 63 percent of youth suicides are from fatherless homes, as are 90 percent of all homeless and runaway children, 85 percent of all children that exhibit behavioral disorders, and 80 percent of rapists motivated with displaced anger.

The children of cohabitating parents fare poorly as well, experiencing high rates of drug abuse, depression, physical and sexual abuse, and poverty, as well as dropping out of high school.

Ironically, as with all studies, undoubtedly, at least one scientific study somewhere will completely contradict these facts, which were gleaned from scientific studies. So much for the superiority and sanctity of science.

According to secularists, "reason" can provide societal guidance. Unfortunately without the prospect of divine retribution, too many find it logical and reasonable to lie and falsify to promote their beliefs.

When it comes to "a separation of church and state," it might be nice if people practiced what they preach.

> *"It's time that we scientists stopped acting like ... the theory of evolution ... was somehow inferior to creationism and intelligent design, and we could not win the competition for best ideas fairly and openly."*

Mr. Dawkins, Tear Down This Wall!

Satoshi Kanazawa

In the following viewpoint, Satoshi Kanazawa argues that creationism and intelligent design should be taught alongside evolution in schools in order to allow the ideas to compete fairly and openly. Kanazawa claims that he is not endorsing the teaching of creationism because he believes it is true but because he thinks it should be subjected to examination since so many people believe it. Kanazawa contends that to deny the open assessment of these theories in schools is akin to the failure of communist societies to properly teach the theory of capitalism. Satoshi Kanazawa teaches management at the London School of Economics in the United Kingdom.

Satoshi Kanazawa, "Mr. Dawkins, Tear Down This Wall! Why Creationism and Intelligent Design Should Be Taught in Schools," *Psychology Today*, March 22, 2009. Copyright © 2009 by Psychology Today. All rights reserved. Reproduced by permission.

As you read, consider the following questions:

1. According to Kanazawa, why did Communist political leaders not allow their citizens to be accurately exposed to the theory of capitalism?

2. What does Kanazawa believe will happen when an intelligent child is exposed to the theory of evolution and the theory of creationism?

3. The author infers that by failing to support the teaching of creationism and intelligent design, scientists are sending what message about evolution?

I am somewhat unusual as a scientist and evolutionary psychologist, in that I strongly support the teaching of creationism and intelligent design in schools. I personally don't understand why my fellow scientists in general and evolutionary psychologists in particular oppose it so vehemently. Perhaps it's because I'm old enough to remember (and to have been educated during) the Cold War.

It's sobering to recall that it is the 20th anniversary of the fall of the Berlin Wall this year, and that all of my undergraduate students were born into the world where there were no East and West Germany. To them, East and West Germanies are as historically quaint as East and West Roman Empires are to me. During the Cold War, we taught our children what capitalism was and what communism was, whereas children going to school in the Soviet Union and the rest of the Eastern Bloc countries never learned what capitalism was. They learned falsely negative views of capitalism and equally falsely positive views of communism. My wife was one of these children.

The communist political leaders did not allow their citizens to be exposed to accurate portrayals of capitalism because they knew, deep down, that anyone who learned what capitalism truly was would naturally opt for it instead of communism. They therefore could not allow their citizens to learn what it was. We, on the other hand, had no such worry, because we knew that anyone who carefully compared capitalism and communism would naturally opt for capitalism. We did not build a wall to keep our people in; anybody who wanted to emigrate to the Soviet Union was free to go. We had entry visas; they had exit visas. Communists had to build a wall to keep their people in, because they knew what would happen if they didn't. We all learned that they were right in October 1989. We won the Cold War, not because we didn't allow our citizens to learn about communism, but because capitalism was a genuinely superior economic and social system than communism.

No one who has a better idea or product is ever afraid of an open competition; politicians who can win a majority of the votes fairly and openly never rig the election. So why are scientists, who are supposed to be all for academic freedom of expression and thought, actively trying to suppress creationism and intelligent design in schools? Why are they afraid of an open competition? Why are they acting like Stalin or Mugabe?

Teach our children both evolution and creationism in schools. Any intelligent child who is confronted with comprehensive and accurate views of evolution and creationism will naturally opt for evolution. Those who don't and instead believe in creationism deserve to live in the dark. Not everybody deserves the truth.

Of course, there is the argument that we shouldn't teach creationism in schools because it is not true. It is true that it is not true. But then virtually everything they teach in the sociology and women's studies departments on every college campus throughout the world is false. Yet nobody is calling for sociology and feminism to be censored and banned from schools, and I for one would certainly not support such censorship. I believe anyone who wants to study sociology and women's studies should be entirely free to do so. Any intelligent student who is confronted with comprehensive and accurate views of evolutionary psychology and sociology will naturally opt for evolutionary psychology. Those who don't and instead believe in sociology deserve to live in the dark. Not everybody deserves the truth.

Another possible objection is the separation of church and state mandated by the Constitution. Maybe the Constitution needs to be amended slightly to allow the teaching of creationism in schools (although I personally don't think the teaching of creationism in public schools is a major breach of the separation of church and state). The Constitution is not a perfect, prescient document (after all, it's not the Bible!); that is why there have been so many amendments to it. Whether we like it or not, creationism—the fact that so many people believe in it, especially in the US—is a fact of life that we can neither change nor ignore. It is better to confront it head on and expose its flaws than to ignore it, hiding behind the Constitution. If we continue to ignore creationism in school, the children can never eliminate the possibility in their mind that it just might be true.

I think it's time that we scientists stopped acting like our product—the theory of evolution by natural and sexual selection—was somehow inferior to creationism and intelligent design, and we could not win the competition for best ideas fairly and openly. We should stop acting like the communists during the Cold War.

"Students . . . are not taught the critical thinking skills they need to evaluate questions about evolution and become good scientists."

Debate About Evolution Should Be Taught in Science Class

Casey Luskin

In the following viewpoint, Casey Luskin argues that it is necessary for science students to learn about some of the scientific doubts about the theory of evolution. Luskin claims that the push to teach evolution as settled fact amounts to a kind of censorship. He denies that debate about evolution needs to involve any endorsement of religion or religious theory and claims that attempts by proponents of evolution to paint it as such is disingenuous.

Casey Luskin is an attorney with the pro–intelligent design Discovery Institute and coauthor of Traipsing into Evolution: Intelligent Design and the *Kitzmiller v. Dover Decision.*

As you read, consider the following questions:

1. According to Luskin, what was the original reason for the controversy over the proposed biology textbooks in Louisiana?

2. Luskin claims that proponents of Darwinian evolution refer to scientific views that they dislike in what way?

3. The author claims that what fraction of Americans believe that students need to know about criticisms of evolutionary theory?

Critical inquiry and freedom for credible dissent are vital to good science. Sadly, when it comes to biology textbooks, American high school students are learning that stubborn groupthink can suppress responsible debate.

The Biology Textbook Controversy

In recent weeks [in December 2010], the media have been buzzing over a decision by the Louisiana State Board of Elementary and Secondary Education to adopt biology textbooks. A Fox News summary read "Louisiana committee rejects calls to include debate over creationism in state-approved biology textbooks. . . ." There was one problem with the story. Leading critics of evolution in Louisiana were not asking that public schools debate creationism, or even that they teach intelligent design. Rather, they wanted schools to simply teach the scientific debate over Darwinian evolution.

The controversy began because the biology textbooks up for adoption in Louisiana teach the neo-Darwinian model as settled fact, giving students no opportunity to weigh the pros and cons and consider evidence on both sides.

One textbook under review (*Biology: Concepts and Connections*) offers this faux critical thinking exercise: "Write a paragraph briefly describing the kinds of evidence for evolution." No questions ask students to identify evidence that

The Controversy About Evolution

While it is routinely asserted that the theory of evolution is no more controversial than the theory of gravity, this is mere bluster. The central claims of Darwinian evolution—that random mutation and natural selection (or some similarly unguided process) are sufficient to produce increasingly complex life forms—cannot be confirmed through experimentation in the way that the theory of gravity can be confirmed. Even if it were shown through experimentation that a Darwinian mechanism could produce a more complex life form from a simpler ancestor, it does not prove that this mechanism did *in fact* produce such an effect in the past. Explanations on the origins of complex life forms through Darwinian mechanisms will never approach the degree of certainty that one can have in other scientific concepts such as gravity, the heliocentric arrangement of the solar system, or Boyle's Law.

To assert that there is controversy over Darwinism is simply to state the obvious. Darwin's theory is controverted scientifically, and because of its implications, it remains controversial for purposes of public education.

David K. DeWolf,
"The 'Teach the Controversy' Controversy,"
University of St. Thomas Journal of Law & Public Policy,
Fall 2009.

counters evolutionary biology, because no such evidence is presented in the text. If the modern version of Charles Darwin's theory is as solid as most scientists say, textbooks shouldn't be afraid to teach countervailing evidence as part of a comprehensive approach. Yet students hear only the prevailing view.

A Subtle Form of Censorship

Is this the best way to teach science? Earlier this year a paper in the journal *Science* tried to answer that question, and found that students learn science best when they are asked "to discriminate between evidence that supports . . . or does not support" a given scientific concept. Unfortunately, the Darwin camp ignores these pedagogical findings and singles out evolution as the only topic where dissenting scientific viewpoints are not allowed.

Courts have uniformly found that creationism is a religious viewpoint and thus illegal to teach in public school science classes. By branding scientific views they dislike as "religion" or "creationism," the Darwin lobby scares educators from presenting contrary evidence or posing critical questions—a subtle but effective form of censorship.

The media fall prey to this tactic, resulting in articles that confuse those asking for scientific debate with those asking for the teaching of religion. And Darwin's defenders come off looking like heroes, not censors.

Those who love the First Amendment should be outraged. In essence, the Darwin lobby is taking the separation of church and state—a good thing—and abusing it to promote censorship. But one can be a critic of neo-Darwinism without advocating creationism.

Valid Doubts About Evolution

Eugene Koonin is a senior research scientist at the National Institutes of Health and no friend of creationism or intelligent design. Last year [in 2009], he stated in the journal *Trends in Genetics* that breakdowns in core neo-Darwinian tenets such as the "traditional concept of the tree of life" or "natural selection is the main driving force of evolution" indicate that the modern synthesis of evolution "has crumbled, apparently, beyond repair."

Likewise, the late Phil Skell, a member of the US National Academy of Sciences, considered himself a skeptic of both intelligent design and neo-Darwinian evolution. He took issue with those who claim that "nothing in biology makes sense except in the light of evolution" because, according to Dr. Skell, in most biology research, "Darwin's theory had provided no discernible guidance, but was brought in, after the breakthroughs, as an interesting narrative gloss."

In a 2005 letter to an education committee in South Carolina, Skell wrote: "Evolution is an important theory and students need to know about it. But scientific journals now document many scientific problems and criticisms of evolutionary theory and students need to know about these as well."

The Need for Debate

Skell was right, and polls show that more than 75 percent of Americans agree with him. The Louisiana textbook debate reflects the public's gross dissatisfaction with the quality of evolution instruction in biology textbooks.

The Louisiana Board should be applauded for rejecting censorship and adopting the disputed textbooks despite their biased coverage of evolution. Students need to learn about the evidence supporting the evolutionary viewpoint, and the textbooks present that side of this debate. But the books themselves should not be praised because they censor from students valid scientific questions about neo-Darwinian concepts—concepts that are instead taught as unquestioned scientific fact.

Students are the real losers here, because they are not taught the critical thinking skills they need to evaluate questions about evolution and become good scientists. When we start using the First Amendment as it was intended—as a tool to increase freedom of inquiry and promote access to scientific information—then perhaps these divisive controversies will finally go away.

"The fallout from this decades-long campaign to dismantle evolution education and re-insert religious ideology into public school science classes is substantial and disturbing."

Neither Creationism nor Debate About Evolution Should Be Taught in Schools

Heather Weaver

In the following viewpoint, Heather Weaver argues that attempts by creationists to influence science curricula should be resisted. Weaver contends that there is a long history of attempts to teach creationism in public schools, including recent attempts to teach intelligent design and to manufacture controversy about evolution where none exists. Weaver claims that the campaign is silencing teachers and harming science education.

Heather Weaver is a staff attorney for the American Civil Liberties Union Program on Freedom of Religion and Belief.

As you read, consider the following questions:

1. In what year and in what state was a law passed, later found unconstitutional, that prohibited the teaching of evolution, according to the author?

Heather Weaver, "Saving Souls," *Index on Censorship*, vol. 40, no. 4, November 2011, pp. 87–92, 94–95, 97–98. Index on Censorship is the world's leading free speech magazine. Subscribe here: www.indexoncensorship.org/subscribe.

2. In what year did the US Supreme Court strike down a law that required the teaching of creationism alongside evolution, according to Weaver?

3. The author cites a poll finding that what percentage of Americans believe that most scientists do not endorse evolution as a valid scientific principle?

In 1925, the Tennessee Legislature passed the Butler Act, a law that prohibited public school employees from teaching 'any theory that denies the Story of the Divine Creation of man as taught in the Bible', including any theory 'that man has descended from a lower order of animals'. The statute led to the prosecution and conviction later that year of John T. Scopes, a high school biology teacher who dared to discuss evolution with his students. Scopes was represented by the American Civil Liberties Union (ACLU), a then relatively new organisation dedicated to preserving individual rights and liberties guaranteed by law. The proceedings—dubbed the 'Scopes Monkey Trial' by the media—attracted international attention, and the conviction was ultimately overturned. The Tennessee law was never enforced again and similar evolution bans across the country were, over a number of decades, defeated.

The Teaching of Evolution

Eighty-six years later, the teaching of evolution is no longer a criminal act in any state. Indeed, though an organised movement of creationists has doggedly pursued various strategies to gain judicial approval for anti-evolution laws and other policies that seek to inject creationist beliefs into public school science curricula, American courts have repeatedly ruled that it is unlawful to censor the teaching of evolution in public schools or to use those schools to promote religious doctrine such as creationism. Despite its spectacular losses in the courts of law, however, the creationist movement marches on, and there is troubling evidence that it is growing increasingly successful in the court of public opinion, the political arena and public school classrooms.

Earlier this year [2011], for example, the ACLU received a complaint from the parent of a fifth-grade student at an Alabama public school. His daughter's teacher had abruptly halted a science lesson after the topic of evolution had come up in the class textbook. The teacher announced that she would not read or discuss the issue further because 'some of us believe in God' and 'some of us believe that the world was made in seven days and that God created man and the trees'. When the ACLU pressed the school district regarding the incident, officials dismissed the teacher's actions as a 'stray comment' and claimed that they follow all state educational guidelines, which include teaching biological evolution. The ACLU continues to investigate the incident and is seeking documents that might help show whether, in fact, the school district's teachers are censoring evolution lessons in science classes. If so, however, they would scarcely be alone.

A study published in *Science* last January [2011] showed that only 28 per cent of US public high school biology teachers provide adequate instruction in evolution. According to the study, which was based on a national survey of public high school biology teachers, 13 per cent of teachers 'explicitly advocate creationism or intelligent design by spending at least one hour of class time presenting it in a positive light'. The remaining 60 per cent 'fail to explain the nature of scientific inquiry, undermine the authority of established experts, and legitimise creationist arguments'. As appears to be the case with the Alabama school teacher who refused to continue with her science lesson, many teachers within this failing 60 per cent no doubt intentionally undermine the teaching of evolution because they perceive it as conflicting with their personal religious views.

The Creationists' Tactics

Many other teachers, however, merely want to avoid controversy and a backlash from students and parents, according to the study's authors, Penn State University political scientists Michael Berkman and Erik Plutzer. As Plutzer explained to Ars Technica, a science and technology news website: 'The challenge is for these teachers to stay out of trouble. They have to teach in a cautious way to avoid complaints from either side. They want to avoid what everyone wants to avoid, which is being called to the principal's office.' With polls showing that more than two-thirds of Americans support teaching creationism in public schools—either as a replacement for or alongside evolution—it is not surprising that this caution has led to instruction that not only understates the scientific case for evolution but also gives credence to and endorses creationist religious beliefs.

Creationist leaders are well aware of their success on this front and will not ease the pressure on teachers any time soon. They blame the discoveries of modern science, especially evolution, for destroying traditional notions of both God and man, giving rise to moral relativism, and thereby causing a host of societal ills. For them, then, the fight against evolution is a central battle in the so-called culture wars; it is a fight to reclaim our humanity and save our souls by restoring America and Americans to God. With the stakes so high, creationists will thus continue to do whatever they must to suppress the teaching of evolution in public schools, no matter the cost; and in light of the courts' refusal to sustain outright attacks on evolution or permit teaching creationism alongside it, that means targeting teachers directly and indirectly.

Among other tactics employed in recent years, creationists have sponsored a barrage of proposed laws that would authorise teachers to introduce fabricated 'weaknesses' of evolution into individual science classes. They have also launched a

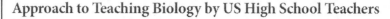

Approach to Teaching Biology by US High School Teachers

Advocate of

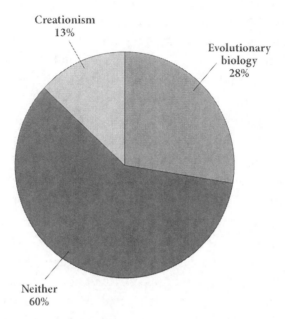

Creationism
13%

Evolutionary
biology
28%

Neither
60%

Based on responses to the National Survey of High School Biology of 926 US public high school biology teachers. Total does not add up to 100 because of rounding.

TAKEN FROM: Michael B. Berkman and Eric Plutzer, "Defeating Creationism in the Courtroom, But Not in the Classroom," *Science,* January 28, 2011.

high-profile anti-evolution propaganda campaign. These tactics aim to popularise creationist doctrine and anti-evolution beliefs. They ultimately seek to fashion a cultural environment that further emboldens willing teachers to flout the law by teaching creationism outright, while the remaining teachers are bullied into presenting students with incomplete and inaccurate information about evolution. Unfortunately, if the *Science* study is any indication, these tactics appear to be working.

The History of the Creationist Movement

To grasp just how insidious the creationist movement has become, it is helpful to understand its history. As Eugenie Scott and Nicholas Matzke of the National Center for Science Education chronicle in their 2007 paper, 'Biological Design in Science Classrooms', significant opposition to evolution education began in the 1920s 'as a by-product of the acrimonious split of American Protestantism into "fundamentalist" and "modernist" camps'. While modernists treated the Bible as 'allegorical and a product of human history', fundamentalists adopted 'a strict doctrine of biblical inerrancy, wherein the entire text of the Bible was considered to be divinely inspired truth and without error (and usually, but not always, to be interpreted literally)'.

Fundamentalists' original focus on evolution education in the public schools makes even more sense for the contemporary creationist movement. Thanks to mandatory attendance laws, the public schools offer access to a wide audience of students and families, including those of other faiths and non-believers. By targeting students in elementary and secondary school, creationists reach children when they are most impressionable and likely to internalise religious beliefs. By delivering religious doctrine through trusted teachers, they increase the likelihood that students will be less resistant to or questioning of religious doctrine, especially where, as is often the case today, the religious doctrine is cloaked in pseudo-science terms.

But the advantages of this approach are the very factors that have doomed it under the law. The First Amendment of the US Constitution contains the 'Establishment Clause', which prohibits the government from promoting or advancing religion. The US Supreme Court, the highest court in the country, has been particularly vigilant about enforcing this principle in public schools because of compulsory attendance laws, the vulnerability of children, and the special trust that families place in the government to educate their children with exploiting that opportunity to religiously indoctrinate them. As a result, the Supreme Court and lower courts have repeatedly rejected both efforts to incorporate instruction in creationism, creation-science, and intelligent design into public school curricula and efforts to undermine the teaching of evolution because of its perceived conflict with the Bible. After each judicial defeat, however, creationists have adapted their tactics and unrepentantly pressed forward, prompting many to comment on the irony of an evolving anti-evolution movement.

Defense of Evolution in the Courts

Though the Scopes Trial shone a light on the exploitation of the public schools to promote creationism and censor teaching about evolution, due to the fundamentalist movement and laws such as the Butler Act, evolution education in secondary public schools largely ground to a halt for several decades. It was not, as Scott and Matzke note, until the 50s and 60s—when fears arose that the country was falling behind the Soviet Union in technology and science—that evolution was reintroduced into many public school curricula via federally funded and commissioned textbooks written by scientists.

That effort was helped along by a 1968 Supreme Court decision [*Epperson v. Arkansas*] overturning a state ban on teaching evolution in public schools. Susan Epperson, a tenth grade biology teacher at Little Rock Central High School, challenged the Arkansas law, which prohibited public school teachers from teaching, or using textbooks that teach, human evolution. Much to the dismay of fundamentalists, the Supreme Court agreed that the law was an unconstitutional 'attempt to blot out a particular theory because of its supposed conflict with the biblical account, literally read'.

The events of the 50s and 60s, as well as the *Epperson* ruling, prompted supporters of creationism to alter their approach. They next tried to dress up their religious belief as 'creation-science' and mandate that it be given 'equal time' alongside evolution in science classes. The Supreme Court once again rebuffed the attempt to suppress evolution teaching and promote creationism. In 1987, [in *Edwards v. Aguillad*] the Court struck down Louisiana's Balanced Treatment for Creation-Science and Evolution-Science in Public School Instruction Act. The law forbade the teaching of evolution in public schools unless accompanied by instruction in creation-science. The Court ruled that the 'state may not constitutionally prohibit the teaching of evolution in the public schools, for there can be no non-religious reason for such a prohibition'. Nor, the court added, could the state require 'the presentation of a religious viewpoint that rejects evolution in its entirety'.

The Intelligent Design Movement

Unable to banish evolution from public school classrooms and barred from using public schools to promote creationism, the creationist movement shifted course again, claiming to have developed a new scientific theory to rival evolution: so-called 'intelligent design', which posits that nature is so irreducibly complex that it must have been created by an 'intelligent designer'. In 1998, the Discovery Institute, a leading purveyor of intelligent-design creationism, produced a document detailing its plan to use intelligent design theory to drive a 'wedge' into the scientific community, combat the growing acceptance of evolution in America, and 'replace it with a science consonant with Christian and theistic convictions'. Key prongs of the wedge strategy included: (1) producing 'solid' scholarship, research and argument (2) formally integrating teaching about intelligent design into public school science standards and curricula and (3) popularising design theory among influential leaders, the media, and in the 'broader culture'.

The movement never came close to reaching the first goal: intelligent design proponents were unable to produce any credible scientific research to buttress their belief. In addition, the campaign to formally incorporate intelligent design into public school curricula as a legitimate alternative to evolution also failed after a federal judge ruled in [2005] that intelligent design is just another extension of creationism, there is no scientific evidence to support it, and it cannot be taught in public schools. . . .

After the court's ruling in [*Kitzmiller v.*] *Dover*, creationism advocates were again forced to adapt their legal strategies. Their hopes of formally incorporating creationism, via intelligent design theory, into public school curricula dashed, they turned to subtler, more indirect ways to undermine evolution education. Drawing on intelligent design theory's argument that evolution contains 'gaps' in information, they have increasingly focused on the claim that there is controversy in the scientific community regarding the purported 'strengths and weaknesses' of evolutionary theory. They attack those who oppose incorporating this alleged controversy into science curricula as trampling free speech and seeking to brainwash students against critical analysis of scientific matters.

A Campaign of Misinformation

Specifically, under the pretexts of protecting the academic freedom of those who question evolution and fostering students' critical thinking skills, creationism advocates have been instrumental in proposing a number of state laws that would encourage and authorise public school teachers to present the so-called 'weaknesses' of evolution and other purportedly controversial scientific theories, such as global warming. More than 40 bills of this type have been proposed in 13 states over the past seven years. Creationists have also sought to inject the 'weaknesses' argument into state science educational standards, which govern public school science curricula and textbook approval processes.

The invocation of 'academic freedom' and 'critical analysis' to defend and advance a campaign singularly aimed at censoring proven scientific principles and promoting, in their stead, untested and unverifiable religious ideology would be laughable if it weren't for the serious risk that these tactics pose to sound science education. As Judge [John] Jones so artfully laid out in the *Dover* case, there is, of course, no controversy in the scientific community about the soundness of evolution as a scientific principle any more than there is a dispute over the validity of the theory of gravity. The purported 'weaknesses' that sponsors of these measures hope will be presented to students are recycled claims—universally rejected by scientists— that have been made for years by creationism and intelligent design advocates. There is no academic freedom in the right to provide demonstrably false information to students, and ensuring that information presented in science classes meets basic, well-established scientific standards enhances students' ability to engage in critical analysis.

Fortunately, due to strenuous opposition by the ACLU and other groups, nearly all of these legislative efforts have, thus far, been defeated. (Louisiana remains the only state to have passed an 'academic freedom' bill—the Louisiana Science Education Act.) But the campaign of misinformation has nevertheless been remarkably effective in confusing the public about the scientific support for evolution. While 57 per cent of Americans believe that humans and other living things have evolved over time, according to a poll conducted this September [2011] by the Public Religion Research Institute, only half (51 per cent) of those polled knew that there is also a broad scientific consensus supporting evolution. Over a quarter of respondents erroneously believed that scientists are divided on the question, and a mind-boggling 15 per cent of those polled thought that most scientists do not endorse evolution as a valid scientific principle. Seizing on this confusion, creationists have, in recent years, ramped up their propaganda efforts to gain and solidify public support for their cause. . . .

The Creation of a Controversy

After trying for decades, with little success, to enact formal legal change that would censor the teaching of evolution and instead permit creationist beliefs to be advanced in public schools, creationists appear to be embracing another approach that targets teachers more indirectly. By spreading misinformation and propaganda about evolution and inflaming the public debate over it, they have managed to create a cultural environment in which some teachers feel inspired to violate the law on their own by teaching creation, and many others—cognisant of the potential backlash from parents and students who might otherwise, however wrongly, perceive the teachers as challenging or denigrating their religious beliefs by endorsing evolution as a proven scientific concept—feel pressured to self-censor their science lessons.

Even the current legal strategies (relating to evolution's so-called 'strengths and weaknesses') avoid any direct attacks on evolution or direct advocacy of creationism or intelligent design. Instead, creationists now seek to exploit teachers' instincts to avoid controversy by giving them legal cover to present information that will placate those who dispute evolution on religious grounds.

The fallout from this decades-long campaign to dismantle evolution education and re-insert religious ideology into public school science classes is substantial and disturbing. Nearly three-quarters of students are receiving an inadequate foundation in science education. As creationists ratchet up and hone their current strategies targeted at teachers, these figures may grow worse. Consequently, millions of students are and will continue to be ill-prepared for the rigours of higher education and less likely to pursue careers in scientific fields. Much like the mid-20th century, when we discovered that the country was falling behind the world in technology and science, the US continues to lag far behind other nations in science education: a 2009 study by the Organisation for Economic Co-operation and Development rated US science students in the bottom ten of the top 30 industrialised nations.

The Threat to Science Education

Creationists' treatment of evolution as opinion, rather than scientific fact, is also likely to encourage devaluing scientific discovery in other contexts as well. Indeed, global warming deniers have already hitched their wagons to the evolution 'debate' by casting global warming as another 'scientific controversy' about which science curricula should remain circumspect.

In addition to the serious harm caused to science education, the use of public schools to advance religious ideology infringes the constitutional rights of every student to be free from government-imposed religious indoctrination. It also usurps the rights of parents, not the government, to control the religious upbringing of their children. And it creates religious dissension that undermines a core function of the public school system, which, as one Supreme Court justice [Felix Frankfurter, in *McCollum v. Board of Education*] has observed, was '[d]esigned to serve as perhaps the most powerful agency for promoting cohesion among a heterogeneous democratic people' and must, therefore, be kept 'scrupulously free from entanglement in the strife of [religious] sects'.

Though the courts and legislatures have traditionally marked the frontline for combatting the creationist movement, the battlelines are shifting. Make no mistake, it remains important to defend those judicial victories and to ensure that no ground is yielded in the legal sphere. But to truly protect science education in US public schools, we also must look beyond the courts and devise strategies to ease the pressure on science teachers to self-censor or otherwise compromise their instruction in evolution—starting with a plan to open the public's eyes to the overwhelming evidence and support for evolution in the scientific community, the primacy of evolution as a fundamental principle of biology and science, and the importance of sound science to our individual and common welfare.

Periodical and Internet Sources Bibliography

The following articles have been selected to supplement the diverse views presented in this chapter.

Americans United for Separation of Church and State	"Praying for Legal Behavior: Why Teachers Should Not Be Preachers," *Church & State*, October 2010.
Jay Bookman	"Religion Better Off When Separate," *Atlanta Journal-Constitution*, October 6, 2009.
Kristin Friedrich	"Evolution's Non-Debate," *Natural History*, June 6, 2009.
David Harsanyi	"The More You Know: Should School Boards Silence the Debate over Evolution?," *Reason.com*, April 1, 2009. http://reason.com/archives/2009/04/01/the-more-you-know.
Wendy Kaminer	"The Devilish Details of School Prayer," *Atlantic*, January 30, 2012.
Lauri Lebo	"The *Scopes* Strategy: Creationists Try New Tactics to Promote Anti-evolutionary Teaching in Public Schools," *Scientific American*, February 28, 2011.
William R. Mattox Jr.	"Teach the Bible? Of Course," *USA Today*, August 17, 2009.
Martha McCarthy	"Beyond the Wall of Separation: Church-State Concerns in Public Schools," *Phi Delta Kappan*, June 2009.
Jeff Passe and Lara Willox	"Teaching Religion in America's Public Schools: A Necessary Disruption," *Social Studies*, May–June 2009.

OPPOSING
VIEWPOINTS®
SERIES

CHAPTER 4

How Should the Education System Be Improved?

Chapter Preface

There is widespread agreement in America that there is room for improvement in the education system. A 2012 Gallup poll showed that only 5 percent of Americans believe public schools provide children with an excellent education, and only 8 percent of Americans report complete satisfaction with the quality of education that students receive from kindergarten through grade twelve. However, when attempting to decide exactly what improvements should be implemented, very little consensus exists.

Suggestions for improving the public schools abound: In an open-ended question posed by a 2009 Gallup poll, 17 percent of respondents suggested better-quality teachers; 10 percent urged a return to the basic curriculum of reading, writing, and arithmetic; 6 percent urged better school funding; 6 percent suggested a reduction in class size; 6 percent wanted better pay for teachers; 5 percent demanded more parental involvement; 4 percent wanted improved testing standards; 4 percent suggested better discipline; and 4 percent thought there should be more teachers. Other suggestions included school vouchers, more religion, better security, year-round school, and the abolition of teachers' unions.

While there is no limit to the number of improvements that may be implemented, given adequate public support and funding, the ability to reach some kind of consensus on what improvements are necessary may prove to be the biggest hurdle. Even in situations where there is broad consensus about the existence of a problem, there is not always widespread support to address that problem. In the forty-fourth annual *PDK/Gallup Poll of the Public's Attitudes Toward the Public Schools* in 2012, Phi Delta Kappa and Gallup reported that a whopping 97 percent of Americans agreed that improving the nation's urban schools was either very important or fairly important. Nonetheless, when the same Americans were asked whether they would be willing to pay more taxes to provide funds to improve the quality of the nation's urban public schools, only 62 percent said they would be willing. Even with a majority willing to spend more money, it is unclear whether any agreement could be reached about how the money should be spent.

Agreement on the existence of a problem may be the strongest area of consensus, as the viewpoints in this chapter demonstrate. Looking at the different proposals for education reform, it becomes clear that not only are there competing views about what reforms would result in improvement, suggestions for improvement are oftentimes completely contradictory. Such a lack of consensus threatens to thwart any efforts to improve the current US education system.

> *"While Washington spends huge sums on things that are education-related, the riches produce almost nothing of educational value."*

Federal Spending on Education Should Be Cut

Neal McCluskey

In the following viewpoint, Neal McCluskey argues that federal government spending on education should be drastically reduced. McCluskey contends that since the 1970s, spending on education has risen, with no positive educational outcomes to show for it. McCluskey claims that continued education spending by the federal government is driven by politics, not by results.

Neal McCluskey is the associate director of the Cato Institute's Center for Educational Freedom and author of Feds in the Classroom: How Big Government Corrupts, Cripples, and Compromises American Education.

As you read, consider the following questions:

1. According to McCluskey, by what percentage did federal spending on education per student increase from 1970 to 2006?

Neal McCluskey, "For the Nation's Sake, Cut Education Spending," *The Daily Caller*, January 25, 2011. Copyright © 2011 by Neal McCluskey. All rights reserved. Reproduced by permission.

2. According to the author, by how much did reading scores on the National Assessment of Educational Progress increase from 1971 to 2008?

3. Total federal spending on education in the 2008–2009 academic year amounted to how much, according to McCluskey?

If President [Barack] Obama cares about restoring sanity to federal finances, he will demand deep cuts to education spending. That's right: In tonight's [January 25, 2011,] State of the Union address, he will call to axe most of Washington's educationally worthless outlays.

Unfortunately, Mr. Obama is likely to prove that he doesn't care all that much about attacking the nation's crushing debt. According to several sources, he'll not only place education spending off limits, he might make increasing it a focal point of tonight's address.

Federal Spending on Education

But wait: Debt or no debt, isn't having an educated citizenry crucial to the nation's future? Isn't he right to protect education funding?

Education is, indeed, very important. But while Washington spends huge sums on things that are education-related, the riches produce almost nothing of educational value. If anything, the feds keep stuffing donuts into an already obese system.

Federal elementary and secondary education spending has risen mightily since the early 1970s, when Washington first started immersing itself in education. In 1970, according to the federal *Digest of Education Statistics*, Uncle Sam spent an inflation-adjusted $31.5 billion on public K–12 education. By 2009 that had ballooned to $82.9 billion.

On a per-pupil basis, in 1970 the feds spent $435 per student. By 2006—the latest year with available data—it was

Federal On-budget Funding for Education by Category

Selected fiscal years, in billions of constant fiscal year 2010 dollars

Year	Total	Elementary/ Secondary	Post-secondary	Other education	Research at educational institutions
1965	$36.9	$13.5	$8.3	$2.6	$12.6
1975	$90.5	$41.2	$29.7	$6.2	$13.3
1980	$89.7	$41.7	$28.9	$4.0	$15.1
1985	$74.6	$32.3	$21.4	$4.0	$16.9
1990	$84.7	$36.1	$22.4	$5.6	$20.7
1995	$100.6	$47.2	$24.7	$6.6	$22.0
2000	$110.0	$56.1	$19.2	$7.0	$27.7
2009	$165.8	$89.6	$37.0	$8.3	$30.8

Note: Detail may not sum to totals because of rounding

TAKEN FROM: Thomas D. Snyder and Sally A. Dillow, "Digest of Education Statistics 2010," National Center for Education Statistics, US Department of Education, April 2011.

$1,015, a 133 percent increase. And it's not like state and local spending was dropping: Real, overall, per-pupil spending rose from $5,593 in 1970 to $12,463 in 2006, and today we beat almost every other industrialized nation in education funding.

Higher Costs Without Results

What do we have to show for this?

Certainly more public school employees: Between 1969 and 2007, pupil-to-staff ratios were close to halved. Not coincidentally, these same people politick powerfully for ever more spending and against reforms that will challenge their bloated monopoly. They also routinely defeat efforts to hold them accountable for results.

This constant feeding of special interests is why we've gotten zilch in the outcome that really matters—learning. Since the early 1970s, scores on the National Assessment of Educational Progress—the "Nation's Report Card"—have been utterly stagnant for 17-year-olds, our schools' "final products." In 1973 the average math score was 304 (out of 500). In 2008 it was just 306. In reading, the 1971 average was 285. In 2008 it was up a single point, hitting 286.

The higher education tale is much the same, especially for student aid, the primary college dumping ground for federal dollars. According to the College Board, in 1971 Washington provided $3,814 in inflation-adjusted aid per full-time equivalent student. By 2009–10 that figure had more than tripled, hitting $12,894.

By most available indicators this has been money down the drain. For instance, only about 58 percent of bachelor's seekers finish their programs within six years, if at all. Literacy levels among people with degrees are low and falling. And colleges have raised their prices at astronomical rates to capture ever-growing aid.

Political Reasons for Continued Spending

What's the total damage?

It's impossible to know exactly because so many federal programs touch on education, but the *Digest* provides a decent estimate. In the 2008–09 academic year, Washington spent roughly $83 billion on K–12 education and $37 billion on higher education. (The latter, notably, excludes student-loan funds that fuel the tuition skyrocket but generally get repaid, as well as federally funded research conducted at universities.) Add those together and you get $120 billion, a sum that's doing no educational good and, therefore, leaves no excuse for not applying it to our $14 trillion debt.

And yet, it seems President Obama will not only protect education spending, he might fight to increase it. Why?

He could certainly believe that huge spending on education is a good thing. That, though, might mean he hasn't
looked at all at what we've gotten for our money.

Unfortunately, it might also be that education is the easiest
of all issues through which to buy political capital, whether
from special interests like teachers' unions, or busy parents
who don't have time to research what education funds actually produce. It's also ideal for demonizing opponents who
might demand discomfiting fiscal discipline.

Of course, misguided intentions and political exploitation
have been at work for decades in education, so this isn't new.
We are now well past the point where we can ignore results.
Today, we simply cannot afford to keep throwing money away.

| "*The kids who have the greatest need for public education are suffering the deepest cuts.*"

Federal Spending on Education Should Not Be Cut

Robert L. Borosage

In the following viewpoint, Robert L. Borosage argues that in the wake of the economic recession, cuts in education are unfair and dangerous. Borosage claims that research shows the importance of funding early childhood education and a wide variety of educational programs. He contends that the calls by politicians for increased educational quality while states are slashing budgets constitute empty rhetoric.

Robert L. Borosage is the founder and president of the Institute for America's Future and codirector of its sister organization, the Campaign for America's Future.

As you read, consider the following questions:

1. According to the author, how many states have eliminated funding for pre-kindergarten programs?

2. Borosage cites a study finding that school budgets have been cut in how many states?

3. The author claims that since 1929, significant spending on education has only happened during what two events?

Wall Street's excesses blew up the economy. Now the question is who pays to clean up the mess. Across the country, our children are already paying part of the bill—as their schools are hit with deep budget cuts. A new report—*Starving America's Public Schools: How Budget Cuts and Policy Mandates Are Hurting Our Nation's Students*—released today [October 13, 2011,] by the Campaign for America's Future and the National Education Association, looks at five states to detail what this means to kids in our public elementary and secondary schools. (Full disclosure: I co-direct the Campaign.) The findings are sobering.

The Importance of Education

Every study shows the importance of early childhood education. Analysts at the Federal Reserve discovered that investments in childhood development have, in the words of Fed Chair Ben Bernanke, such "high public as well as private returns" that the Fed has championed such investments to noting they save states money by reducing costs of drop outs, special education, and crime prevention. Yet across the country, states are slashing funding for pre-kindergarten and even rolling back all-day kindergarten. Now pre-K programs serve only about one-fourth of 4-year-olds. Ten states have eliminated funding for pre-K altogether, including Arizona. Ohio eliminated funding for all-day kindergarten.

Every parent and teacher knows the importance of smaller classes, particularly in the early years when individual attention is vital. Yet across the country, schools have cut some 270,000 jobs since 2007 and are facing layoffs of nearly 250,000

Reaction to Cutting Government Spending in Education

Do you favor or oppose cutting government spending in education?

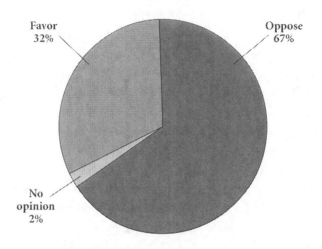

Note: Total does not add up to 100 because of rounding.

TAKEN FROM: Frank Newport and Lydia Saad, "Americans Oppose Cuts in Education, Social Security, Defense," Gallup, January 26, 2011. www.gallup.com.

public school workers next year, many of them teachers. In Chester Upland, Pa., 40% of the teachers were eliminated, with class sizes rising from 21 to 30 in elementary schools and to 35 in high schools, causing students to walk out.

Intelligence comes in many forms. Successful schools offer a well-rounded curriculum—not just the basics, but art and music, social studies, extra-curricular activities, physical education. But now schools across the country are forced to terminate or charge extra for anything beyond the core curriculum. In York, Pa., art, music and physical education was eliminated in elementary schools. In Medina, Ohio, students returned to find courses in French, German, art, music, and Advanced Placement Science and Math were eliminated.

The Slashing of State Budgets

And children, needless to say, are extremely diverse. They learn in different ways, at different rates, and face different challenges. Public schools educate the poor and the affluent, those with developmental challenges and those who are gifted. Yet across the country, schools are slashing funds for special learning instruction, for advanced placement courses. Increasingly parents face extra fees for programs. In Medina, Ohio, for example, it costs $660 to play a high school sport, $200 to join the school choir, $50 to act in a student play.

Even as budgets are slashed for public schools, more and more state education money is getting siphoned off to private contractors to pay for elaborate tests, and to vouchers and corporate tax credits to subsidize private and charter schools. We're cutting billions out of educating kids while increasing spending on testing how they are doing.

The Center for Budget and Policy Priorities reports that school budgets have been cut in some 34 states and the District of Columbia. In Arizona, the cuts average about $530 per pupil. In Florida, $1 billion was cut in next year's budget, or about $542 per student. Not surprisingly, these cuts fall hardest on the poorest districts that can't afford to make up for them the way more affluent districts can. The kids who have the greatest need for public education are suffering the deepest cuts.

Americans sensibly value education. Every political candidate promises our children will have the best education in the world. Yet Washington seems largely oblivious to the carnage taking place in our schools. Part of the president's American Jobs Act was special funding to avoid more teacher layoffs. A filibuster by Republican Senators kept that from even coming up for debate, much less a vote.

The Grim Reality of Spending Cuts

Meanwhile a furious argument continues about what standard teachers and schools should be held accountable to. The administration, still touting its Race to the Top program, wants the reauthorization of No Child Left Behind to set the standard that all children should be "college ready" by the year 2020. Senator [Tom] Harkin introduced a more sensible standard of requiring "continuous improvement" from all schools.

But schools are eliminating kindergarten, laying off teachers, cramming 35 kids in a class, cutting advanced placement classes, and levying steep fees for kids to be in the band or play on an athletic team. Continuous improvement? Race to the Top? The grim reality facing our kids mocks the rhetoric.

Jeff Bryant, author of the *Starving America's Public Schools* report, notes that there have been only two previous times since 1929 when this nation cut spending significantly on its children's education—once in the midst of the Great Depression and once in the midst of World War II. With schools facing budget cutbacks while the largest generation of kids since the boomers flood the classrooms, this is likely to be the third. The bankers who caused the mess got bailed out. The military budget exceeds Cold War levels. The richest 1% of Americans, who make as much as the bottom 60% of Americans, pay the lowest tax rates since the Great Depression. But our kids and their schools are getting the bill for an economic mess they didn't create. No wonder Occupy Wall Street [a protest movement] is spreading across the country.

| "Merit-pay systems are . . . an essential tool for designing schools and systems that can excel in tight times."

Merit Pay for Teachers Should Be Used to Improve Education

Frederick M. Hess

In the following viewpoint, Frederick M. Hess argues that paying teachers with a one-size-fits-all system is not the best method of compensation. Merit pay, he claims, can reward productivity and encourage the development of teaching talent in needed areas. He cautions against utilizing merit pay based on test scores alone and encourages a more dynamic system.

Frederick M. Hess is resident scholar and director of education policy studies at the American Enterprise Institute and author of The Same Thing Over and Over: How School Reformers Get Stuck in Yesterday's Ideas.

As you read, consider the following questions:

1. According to the author, what have step-and-lane pay scales in the teaching profession rewarded?

Frederick M. Hess, "Spend Money Like It Matters," *Educational Leadership*, vol. 68, no. 4, Dec–Jan 2010–2011, pp. 51–54. Permission conveyed through Copyright Clearance Center, Inc. Republished with permission of Educational Leadership.

2. Hess suggests that schools might pay an excellent reading teacher extra for what reason?

3. According to the author, what is the problem with merit pay based on past performance?

Do you think that employees who are good at their work ought to be rewarded, recognized, and have the chance to step up into new opportunities and responsibilities? I do. If you're with me on this, you embrace the principle of merit pay—whether you know it or not.

A Reasonable Assumption

Because, although we all have that childhood friend or distant cousin who lives on a commune somewhere and inveighs against the evils of bourgeois materialism, most of us think it makes sense for a talented, hardworking engineer, dentist, accountant, or babysitter to be rewarded for his or her efforts.

There are two crucial provisos here. First, endorsing this principle doesn't mean signing on to the raft of slack-jawed merit-pay proposals that would-be reformers have championed in recent years. Merit pay is only useful if it's done smart, which entails using it to help attract, retain, and make full use of talented educators.

Second, understand that there's no proof that rewarding talented, hardworking folks "works." You can comb through decades of economics journals and issues of the *Harvard Business Review* without finding any proof that paying and promoting good employees yields good results. The premise just seems like a reasonable assumption; you either buy it, or you don't.

That's how I come at merit pay. I don't imagine that paying bonuses for bumps in test scores, as though we were compensating traveling encyclopedia salesmen in the 1950s, is going to improve teaching or learning. And I don't think that value-added calculations are themselves a comprehensive or reliable measure of teacher quality, even in grades where we can calculate such numbers with a reasonable degree of statistical accuracy. But money and metrics are invaluable tools in shaping a 21st century teaching profession.

The Point of Merit Pay

The point of rethinking pay is not to bribe teachers into working harder. Rather, merit pay is a tool for redefining the contours of the profession. Today's step-and-lane pay scales, built around seniority and credits completed, suggest that the primary way to determine how much teachers are worth is how long they've been on the job and how many courses they've sat through. I don't believe that's a good or useful way to gauge a teacher's value.

There's nothing innately wrong with step-and-lane compensation. Indeed, when introduced in the first decades of the 20th century, it was a sensible response to the massive gender inequities that characterized schooling. At that time, women were routinely paid half as much as their male counterparts. Because male teachers were far more prevalent in the high schools, many districts employed de facto pay scales in which high school teachers dramatically outearned their K–8 counterparts for no discernible reason. In that era, standardizing pay made sense.

By the 1970s, however, schools could no longer depend on a captive influx of talent regardless of the terms of employment. Whereas limited alternatives had meant that more than half of women graduating from college became teachers in mid-20th-century America, the figure today is closer to 15 percent. Meanwhile, new college graduates are much less likely to stick to a job for long stretches, the competition for college-educated talent has intensified, and we can now more or less distinguish teachers who excel at helping students master important content and skills.

All this adds up to a new workforce environment in which the step-and-lane, industrial-era model that flourished as a best practice in post–World War II auto and steel plants is unduly confining. Step-and-lane pay is ill-suited to attracting and retaining talent in the new world of career changers, scarce talent, and heightened expectations.

Merit pay is not a substitute for high-quality instructional materials, pedagogy, or curriculum. Rather, rethinking pay can help make employees feel valued, make the teaching profession more attractive to potential entrants, and signal that professional norms are displacing those of the industrial model. None of this "fixes" schools, but it does establish a firmer, more quality-conscious basis for dramatic improvement.

The Issue of Productivity

As cash-strapped states and school systems look ahead to lean years, it's vital to recognize that one-size-fits-all pay is insensitive to questions of productivity. Although the term *productivity* is regarded as an irritant in most education conversations, it refers to nothing more than how much good a given employee can do. If one teacher is regarded by colleagues as a far more valued mentor than another, or if one reading instructor helps students master skills much more rapidly than another, it's axiomatic that some teachers do more good than others do (that is, that some are more productive than others).

One-size-fits-all compensation means that we're either paying the most effective employees too little, paying their less effective colleagues too much, or, most times, a little of each. In a world of scarce talent and limited resources, this is a problem. Savvy leaders recognize the benefits of steering resources to employees who do the most good, as these are the employees whom schools most need to keep and from whom they need to most effectively wring every ounce of skill.

Thus, a crucial element of a well-designed merit-pay system is rewarding employees who not only do a terrific job but also do so in a way that extends their effect on students and schools. Rewarding prized mentors who choose to mentor more colleagues (while continuing to get high marks from them) or boosting pay for terrific classroom teachers who choose to take on larger student loads (while continuing to excel) are ways to use limited resources to amplify the contributions of skilled professionals.

Using Pay to Solve Problems

One-size-fits-all pay also inhibits efforts to leverage the opportunities for differentiation and specialization that new technologies and staffing models offer, such as the use of part-time professionals by the Boston-based Citizen Schools. Today, school systems casually operate on the implicit assumption that most teachers will be similarly adept at everything. In a routine day, a 4th grade teacher who is a terrific English language arts instructor might teach reading for just 90 minutes. For schools blessed with such a teacher, this is an extravagant waste of talent, especially when one can stroll down the hallway and see a less adept colleague offering 90 minutes of pedestrian reading instruction. If we're sincere about the centrality of early reading proficiency, using these educators in this fashion is simply irresponsible.

One approach to using talent more wisely might entail overhauling teacher schedules and student assignment so that the single exceptional English language arts instructor would teach reading to every student in that 4th grade. Colleagues, in turn, would shoulder that teacher's other instructional responsibilities. However, this is not an even swap. Excellent reading instructors are rare; we should refashion compensation to recognize their importance. If that encourages other teachers to develop their skills and pursue this role, so much the better. Districts with a plethora of talent can then revise staffing accordingly. The point is that salary should be a tool for solving problems by finding smarter ways to attract, nurture, and use talent; it should not be an obstacle to doing so.

After all, we pay thoracic surgeons much more than we do pediatric nurses—not because we think they're better people or because they have lower patient mortality rates, but because their positions require more sophisticated skills and more intensive training and because surgeons are harder to replace. By allowing pay to reflect perceived value, law and medicine have made it possible for accomplished attorneys or doctors to earn outsized compensation without ever moving into administration or management. That kind of a model in education would permit truly revolutionary rethinking in how we recruit, retain, and deploy effective educators. That's a far cry from today's ill-conceived proposals to slather some test-based bonuses atop existing pay scales.

A Viable Path Forward

Unfortunately, too many would-be reformers hear the call for rethinking pay as a charge to impatiently rush forth and "fix" compensation in a furious burst of legislation. As a result, promising efforts to uproot outdated, stifling arrangements get enveloped in crudely drawn and potentially destructive policies.

Education reformers have trouble accepting that unwinding long-standing arrangements and replacing them with sensible alternatives will take time, humility, and a lot of learning. The fix-it-now approach to pay, with its overreliance on value-added measurements, turns a blind eye to the technical challenges involved and to the fact that reading and math scores are a profoundly limited proxy for instructional effectiveness. This approach also runs the risk of stifling the kind of smart use of personnel that reformers are trying to encourage. Principals who rotate their faculty by strength during the year or who augment classroom teachers with guest instructors or online lessons are going to clash with evaluation and pay systems predicated on linking each student's annual test scores to a single teacher. Even in the states that have spent the most time on these assessment and data systems, value-added scores are available for only a sliver of instruction and for only a minority of teachers. Devising new one-size-fits-all merit-pay systems around this limited population is both premature and nonsensical.

Right now, the smart move is to explore ways to base an increasing share of teacher pay on various measures of performance, drawing on potential metrics that seem useful and reliable in a given district. Labor market conditions should be a consideration; if it's more difficult to find effective math teachers than effective social studies teachers, pay should reflect that. In a world of accountability, there is an increased role for simple principal evaluation. Given the collaborative nature of much good teaching, it makes sense to import a key element of 360-degree evaluation and factor in systematic evaluations of teachers by their colleagues regarding which teachers make the largest contributions to the school and their peers. Measures of productivity; value-added calculations, where appropriate; and systematic classroom observation also have roles to play.

Just as many educators comfortable with step-and-lane pay recoil from such changes, many would-be reformers reject my counsel of patience and seek to "fix" teacher pay immediately. But K–12 is a sprawling, complex exercise. Spasmodic solutions born of frustration can lead to flawed policy—as with No Child Left Behind, which overreached in ways that undermined the law's more sensible provisions.

Designing the Right Merit-Pay Systems

Merit pay should reward performance, value, and productivity. We can measure these in many ways—by scarcity of individuals in the labor market, annual evaluation by peers, professional observations, supervisor judgment, and so forth. The contemporary obsession with student test scores as the only metric of interest has been an unfortunate distraction.

Student achievement must be an important factor, but we should employ it deliberately, with an eye to a teacher's actual instructional duties and responsibilities. Too often, we rely on test scores simply because we don't have anything else. That's not a problem specific to merit pay; that's our peculiar failure to import widely employed practices and tools from other professions.

Second, it's a mistake to imagine there's one universal way to design pay systems. Why debate about whether Google, the Red Cross, or Microsoft has the "right" compensation model? There are a slew of reasonable approaches, depending on organizational context and needs. Rather than searching for proven pay models, education leaders would be better off identifying the problems they're trying to address and asking how reconfiguring pay might help them solve those problems.

Third, the aim must be to craft systems that can evolve. The whole point of pay is to help attract and leverage talent. We need an approach that succeeds in tapping specialists, online instructors, part-time educators, and others who can best serve students. Rather than cement in place new merit-pay systems predicated on improving test scores for a teacher who spends 45 minutes a day for 180 days with the same 24 students, let's design systems that can reward unconventional forms of excellence.

For instance, an online tutor who lives thousands of miles away but who can help struggling students make remarkable leaps in mastery of algebra is an invaluable asset. The same is true of a retired army sergeant who may be ill-equipped to teach a middle school class but who may be able to inspire and mentor 15 middle school students or of a teacher who builds a dynamic arts or science program. Today, there is little room in teacher pay scales to recognize or reward—or, sometimes, even make possible—these kinds of contributions. The attempt to superimpose rigid hierarchies atop an otherwise unchanged profession was one of the big stumbling blocks for career ladders and merit-pay proposals in the 1980s. Let's take care not to repeat those mistakes.

Finally, today's test-based merit-pay systems have nothing to say when it comes to productivity. They funnel more dollars to teachers who yield higher test scores. The reward is a bonus for past performance; it does nothing to amplify a teacher's effect on students and schools. Well-designed merit-pay systems should reward teachers who choose to take up opportunities to do more good—such as instructing additional students, leveraging particular skills, or assisting colleagues—making their increased pay a pound-wise investment for their districts or schools.

This means that merit-pay systems are not, as some would argue, a frilly luxury that is unaffordable in today's bleak fiscal climate. Rather, they are an essential tool for designing schools and systems that can excel in tight times. Merit pay should shift dollars from employees and roles that do less good for students toward those that matter most. This will entail discomfort and disruption and require an array of compromises and adjustments. But if merit pay is to be more than a gimmick, it must be part and parcel of a push to rethink the shape of teaching and schooling.

| "Merit pay [based on test scores] will
  not make education better."

What's Wrong with Merit Pay?

Diane Ravitch

In the following viewpoint, Diane Ravitch argues that merit pay based on test scores is misguided and will make education worse. Ravitch contends that merit pay used in this way rewards results in a very narrow portion of the curriculum. Regardless, she claims that research shows merit pay has no impact on test scores.

Diane Ravitch is a research professor of education at New York University, a senior fellow at the Brookings Institution, and former assistant secretary of education responsible for the Office of Educational Research and Improvement in the US Department of Education.

As you read, consider the following questions:

1. According to the author, merit pay for increased test scores encourages teachers to teach only what?

2. A merit-pay experiment in New York City cost taxpayers how much annually, according to Ravitch?

3. Which subjects does Ravitch claim will get too little attention in school if merit pay based on test scores is utilized?

The subject today is merit pay, an important topic because President Obama has decided to hang his hat on this idea. It has not yet been explained, however, just what he means by merit pay. Does he mean that teachers should be paid more for teaching in what are euphemistically called "hard to staff" schools? Paid more for teaching in areas where there are shortages, such as certain kinds of special education or subjects such as math and science? Or paid more for mentoring other teachers or teaching longer days?

I would call such compensation "performance pay," rather than merit pay, because teachers would be paid more for doing more. But I have a feeling that what the Obama administration has in mind is paying teachers more based on their students' "value-added" test scores, meaning that when their students' scores increase, the teachers will get "merit pay" to reward their supposedly superior teaching.

I believe that this is the direction in which the administration is heading, which explains why millions of dollars will be spent on data warehouses in every state and why Education Secretary Arne Duncan has told the governors that they will get their stimulus money only if they collect and report data to the federal government. This was an odd request in that some of the information he asked for is already available, such as the gap between state and National Assessment of Educational Progress scores (data previously published and no secret).

There are several reasons why it is a bad idea to pay teachers extra for raising student test scores. Doing so would

- Create incentives for teachers to teach only what is on the tests of reading and math, thus narrowing the curriculum to only the subjects tested;

- Encourage not only teaching to the test but gaming the system by such mechanisms as excluding low-performing students and outright cheating;

- Ignore a wealth of studies showing that student test scores are subject to statistical errors, measurement errors, and random errors and that the "noise" in these scores is multiplied when used to make high-stakes personnel decisions;

- Overlook the fact that most teachers in a school are not eligible for such "merit" bonuses—only those who teach reading and math and only those for whom scores can be obtained in a previous year;

- Fail to acknowledge that many factors play a role in student test scores, including student ability, student motivation, family support (or lack thereof), the weather, distractions on testing day, and so on;

- Not reckon with the fact that tests must be given at the beginning and the end of the year, not midyear as is now the practice in many states. (Which teacher would get credit and a bonus for score gains: the one who taught the student in the spring of the previous year or the one who taught her in the fall?)

I believe that merit pay of the stupidest kind is coming and that it will do nothing to improve our schools. The Manhattan Institute recently released a study showing that merit pay had no impact on test scores in 200 New York City schools that had tried it. In fact, scores went down in larger schools that offered bonuses. (It is possible that scores may go up in later years; this is only the first year, after all.) But this little experiment in schoolwide bonuses is costing taxpayers $20 million a year.

The way in which this study was released is highly interesting. Usually when the Manhattan Institute releases a study,

A Study of Merit Pay

In this paper we present evidence on the impact of NYCDOE's SPBP [New York City Department of Education's School-Wide Performance Bonus Program] during the program's first year of implementation. Because the number of schools meeting eligibility criteria under the SPBP guidelines required more than the amount of money budgeted for the program, NYCDOE's Research and Policy Support Group assigned schools to the SPBP intervention by random lottery. Our evaluation design takes advantage of the fact that schools were randomly lotteried into the SPBP intervention.

Our findings suggest that the SPBP has had negligible short-run effects on student achievement in mathematics. The same holds true for intermediate outcomes such as student, parent, and teacher perceptions of the school learning environment. We also find no evidence that the treatment effect differed on the basis of student or school characteristic. An exception is the differential effect of SPBP eligibility by school size, which suggests student performance in larger schools decreases when SPBP was implemented. . . .

Although a well-implemented experimental evaluation design would suggest that our estimates have strong internal validity, readers should interpret these initial findings with caution when considering the possible impact of this or any other program.

Matthew G. Springer and Marcus A. Winters, Center for Civic Innovation at the Manhattan Institute, April 2009.

it holds a press conference to announce the results. This study, however, arrived with no fanfare; its results were quietly posted on the web with no press conference, no press release. I suspect that had the scores flown upward, the study would have been released with all the bells and whistles.

My prediction is that merit pay of the kind I have described will not make education better, even if scores go up next year or the year after. Instead, it will make education worse, not only because some of the purported gains will be based on cheating and gaming the system but because they will have been obtained by paying scant attention to history, geography, civics, the arts, science, literature, foreign languages, and all the other subjects needed to develop smarter individuals, better citizens, and people who are prepared for the knowledge-based economy of the twenty-first century. Nor will it identify better teachers. Instead, it will reward those who use their time for low-level test preparation.

Is it possible to have an educational system that miseducates students while raising their test scores? I think so—and we may soon prove it.

Periodical and Internet Sources Bibliography

The following articles have been selected to supplement the diverse views presented in this chapter.

Andrew Biggs and Jason Richwine	"Public School Teachers Aren't Underpaid," *USA Today*, November 16, 2011.
Bruce Buchanan	"Beyond the Basics," *American School Board Journal*, May 2008.
Dana Goldstein	"Is Merit Pay a Distraction in the Fight for Meaningful Education Reform?," *American Prospect*, March 30, 2009.
Susan Harman	"Pay-per-Score: Arne Duncan and Merit Pay," *Dissent*, July 9, 2009.
Frederick M. Hess and Linda Darling-Hammond	"How to Rescue Education Reform," *New York Times*, December 5, 2011.
Jim Hull	"Cutting to the Bone: At a Glance," Center for Public Education, October 2010. www.centerforpubliceducation.org/Main-Menu/Public-education/Cutting-to-the-bone-At-a-glance.
Neal McCluskey	"Behind the Curtain: Assessing the Case for National Curriculum Standards," *Cato Policy Analysis*, February 17, 2010.
John Merrow	"The Influence of Teachers," *Independent School*, Winter 2008.
Kenneth A. Strike	"Small Schools: Size or Community?," *American Journal of Education*, May 2008.
Joel Westheimer	"No Child Left Thinking," *Independent School*, Spring 2008.

For Further Discussion

Chapter 1

1. Amanda Ripley and Gerald W. Bracey disagree about what the comparative performance of American students says about the US education system. Do the two disagree about the facts of the research, the interpretation of the research, or both? Explain your answer, citing from the viewpoints.

2. Terry M. Moe and Richard D. Kahlenberg have competing views about the impact of the teachers' unions on education. How do you think Kahlenberg would respond to Moe's concern about the difficulties schools face in getting rid of bad teachers?

Chapter 2

1. Andrew Bernstein believes that the privatization of government-run public schools will lead to more freedom for parents in educational choices, whereas Ruth Conniff raises concerns that privatization will remove educational control from communities. Based on what each of them argues, do you think privatization would lead to more educational freedom or less? Explain your answer, citing from the viewpoints.

2. Both Matthew McKnight and the National Education Association argue against alternatives to public school— through vouchers and tax credits, respectively—due to how the programs will affect the most disadvantaged students in the current system. What solution might a proponent of school-choice alternatives, such as Gary Jason or David French, offer in an attempt to alleviate this concern?

Chapter 3

1. Among the viewpoints of John W. Whitehead, Americans United for Separation of Church and State, and Kurt Williamsen, which two viewpoints are the most compatible? Explain your answer.

2. Satoshi Kanazawa uses an analogy between the refusal to teach creationism and intelligent design in schools and the refusal to teach about capitalism in former communist countries. List the ways in which the two are not analogous and then assess whether this is a strong analogy for Kanazawa's purpose.

3. What is the core disagreement between Casey Luskin and Heather Weaver on the issue of teaching debate about evolution in public schools? Why?

Chapter 4

1. Frederick M. Hess argues in favor of developing effective merit-pay systems. Based on the content of his viewpoint calling for cuts in education spending, do you think Neal McCluskey could endorse Hess's proposal? Why or why not?

2. Diane Ravitch argues against a particular kind of merit pay. Do you think she would endorse the kind of merit-pay systems proposed by Frederick M. Hess? Explain your answer.

Organizations to Contact

The editors have compiled the following list of organizations concerned with the issues debated in this book. The descriptions are derived from materials provided by the organizations. All have publications or information available for interested readers. The list was compiled on the date of publication of the present volume; the information provided here may change. Be aware that many organizations take several weeks or longer to respond to inquiries, so allow as much time as possible.

American Civil Liberties Union (ACLU)
125 Broad Street, 18th Floor, New York, NY 10004
(212) 549-2500
e-mail: infoaclu@aclu.org
website: www.aclu.org

The American Civil Liberties Union is a national organization that works to defend Americans' civil rights as guaranteed in the US Constitution. The ACLU works in courts, legislatures, and communities to defend First Amendment rights to freedom of speech, freedom of the press, and freedom of religion; the right to equal protection; the right to due process; and the right to privacy. The ACLU publishes the semiannual newsletter *Civil Liberties Alert*, as well as other publications, including "ACLU History: Maintaining the Wall: Freedom of—and from—Religion."

American Policy Center (APC)
PO Box 129, Remington, VA 22734
(540) 341-8911
e-mail: admin@americanpolicy.org
website: www.americanpolicy.org

The American Policy Center is a privately funded, nonprofit, grassroots action and educational foundation dedicated to the promotion of free enterprise and limited government regulations of commerce and individuals. The APC focuses on the issues of environmental policy and its effect on private property rights; national federal computer data banks and their effect on individual privacy rights; the United Nations and its effect on American national sovereignty; and federal education policy and its effect on local schools and parental rights. APC publishes *The DeWeese Report* and special reports on the above issues.

Americans United for Separation of Church and State (AU)
1301 K Street NW, Suite 850E, Washington, DC   20005
(202) 466-3234 • fax: (202) 466-2587
e-mail: americansunited@au.org
website: www.au.org

Americans United for Separation of Church and State is a nonprofit educational organization dedicated to preserving the constitutional principle of church-state separation. AU works to defend religious liberty in Congress and state legislatures, aiming to ensure that new legislation and policies protect church-state separation. AU publishes several books and pamphlets, including *Religion in the Public Schools: A Road Map for Avoiding Lawsuits and Respecting Parents' Legal Rights.*

Becket Fund for Religious Liberty
3000 K Street NW, Suite 220, Washington, DC   20007
(202) 955-0095 • fax: (202) 955-0090
website: www.becketfund.org

The Becket Fund for Religious Liberty is a public-interest law firm protecting the free expression of all religious traditions. Among other practice areas, the Becket Fund defends private religious expression by public school students and works to ensure that private religious schools can educate students without government interference or discrimination. At its website, the Becket Fund has information about its legal cases, including its US Supreme Court case briefs.

Cato Institute
1000 Massachusetts Ave. NW, Washington, DC   20001-5403
(202) 842-0200 • fax: (202) 842-3490
website: www.cato.org

The Cato Institute is a public-policy research organization dedicated to the principles of individual liberty, limited government, free markets, and peace. The institute is dedicated to increasing and enhancing the understanding of key public policies and to analyzing their impact on the principles identified above in many research areas, including education and child policy. The Cato Institute issues many publications, including the quarterly *Regulation* magazine, the bimonthly *Cato Policy Report*, and the periodic *Cato Journal*.

Center for Education Reform (CER)
910 Seventeenth Street NW, 11th Floor
Washington, DC   20006
(800) 521-2118
website: www.edreform.org

The Center for Education Reform aims to improve the accuracy and quality of discourse and decisions about education reform, leading to fundamental policy changes. The CER campaigns for policies that create more educational choice, including the establishment of charter schools. The CER website offers numerous articles on issues such as charter schools, online learning, teacher quality, and standards and testing.

Center for Public Education
1680 Duke Street, Alexandria, VA   22314
(703) 838-6722 • fax: (703) 548-5613
e-mail: centerforpubliced@nsba.org
website: www.centerforpubliceducation.org

The Center for Public Education is a resource center set up by the National School Boards Association. The center works to provide information about public education, leading to more understanding about US schools, more community-wide involvement, and better decision making by school leaders on behalf of all students in their classrooms. Among the many publications available at the center's website is "The Changing Demographics of America's Schools."

Center for Science & Culture (CSC)

Discovery Institute, Seattle, WA   98104

(206) 292-0401 • fax: (206) 682-5320

e-mail: cscinfo@discovery.org

website: www.discovery.org/csc

The Center for Science & Culture is a Discovery Institute program that supports research by scientists and other scholars challenging various aspects of neo-Darwinian evolution theory and developing the theory of intelligent design. The CSC also encourages schools to focus more on weaknesses of the theory of evolution in science education. The CSC has numerous papers, policy positions and videos available on its website, including *Teaching About Evolution in the Public Schools: A Short Summary of the Law.*

Center on Education Policy (CEP)

2140 Pennsylvania Ave. NW, Room 103, Washington, DC 20037

(202) 994-9050 • fax: (202) 994-8859

e-mail: cep-dc@cep-dc.org

website: www.cep-dc.org

The Center on Education Policy is a national, independent advocate for public education and for more effective public schools. The organization works on national, state, and local levels to inform the government and the public, via publications, meetings, and presentations, about the importance of the public education system. Reports on issues regarding all aspects of the education system, such as federal education programs, testing, vouchers, and ways to improve public schools, can be found on the CEP website.

Character Education Partnership
1025 Connecticut Ave. NW, Suite 1011
Washington, DC 20036
(202) 296-7743
website: www.character.org

The Character Education Partnership is a nonprofit, nonpartisan, nonsectarian coalition of organizations and individuals committed to fostering effective character education in schools. It provides tools, methods, and strategies to empower teachers, parents, and community members to help schools achieve the goals of character development. The partnership publishes annual reports assessing the status of character education in the United States, and also provides online resources such as "11 Principles of Effective Character Education."

Education Commission of the States (ECS)
700 Broadway, #810, Denver, CO 80203-3442
(303) 299-3600 • fax: (303) 296-8332
e-mail: ecs@ecs.org
website: www.ecs.org

The Education Commission of the States is an interstate compact created in 1965 to improve public education by facilitating the exchange of information, ideas, and experiences among state policy makers and education leaders. As a nonprofit, nonpartisan organization involving key leaders from all levels of the education system, ECS creates unique opportunities to build partnerships, share information, and promote the development of policy based on available research and strategies. ECS provides policy research and analysis on current educational issues; sponsors state, regional, and national policy conferences; and publishes the bimonthly journal the *Progress of Education Reform.*

First Amendment Center
1207 Eighteenth Ave. South, Nashville, TN 37212
(615) 727-1600 • fax: (615) 727-1319
website: www.firstamendmentcenter.org

The First Amendment Center works to preserve and protect First Amendment freedoms by providing information and education. The center serves as a forum for the study and exploration of free-expression issues, including freedom of speech, of the press, and of religion, and the rights to assemble and to petition the government. The First Amendment Center publishes a number of articles, including "Evolution and Creation."

Friedman Foundation for Educational Choice
One American Square, Suite 2420, Indianapolis, IN   46282
(317) 681-0745 • fax: (317) 681-0945
website: www.edchoice.org

The Friedman Foundation aims to promote universal school choice as the most effective and equitable way to improve the quality of K–12 education in America. The foundation was founded upon the ideals and theories of Nobel laureate economist Milton Friedman and economist Rose D. Friedman, who believed that when schools are forced to compete to keep the children they educate, all parties win. The Friedman Foundation publishes studies and reports such as "Moms and Schools Survey," available at its website.

National Center for Fair & Open Testing (FairTest)
PO Box 300204, Jamaica Plain, MA   02130
(617) 477-9792
website: www.fairtest.org

The National Center for Fair & Open Testing advances quality education and equal opportunity by promoting fair, open, valid, and educationally beneficial evaluations of students, teachers, and schools. FairTest's Assessment Reform Network aims to facilitate the exchange of information and ideas among teachers, parents, and organizations seeking to improve student assessment practices in their communities. FairTest publishes numerous fact sheets available at its website, including "A Better Way to Evaluate Schools."

National Education Association (NEA)
1201 Sixteenth Street NW, Washington, DC   20036-3290
(202) 833-4000 • fax: (202) 822-7974
website: www.nea.org

The National Education Association is an educator member-ship organization that works to advance the cause of public education and the rights of educators and children. The NEA focuses its efforts on improving the quality of teaching, in-creasing student achievement, and making schools safe places to learn. Among the magazines that the NEA publishes are *NEA Today* and *Thought & Action.*

Progressive Policy Institute (PPI)
1101 Fourteenth Street NW, Suite 1250
Washington, DC   20005
(202) 525-3926 • fax: (202) 525-3941
website: www.progressivepolicy.org

The Progressive Policy Institute works to advance progressive, market-friendly ideas that promote American innovation, eco-nomic growth, and wider opportunity. Numerous articles can be found on the PPI website, including such titles as "Improv-ing Charter School Accountability: The Challenge of Closing Failing Schools."

US Department of Education
400 Maryland Ave. SW, Washington, DC   20202
(800) 872-5327
website: www.ed.gov

The US Department of Education's mission is to promote stu-dent achievement and preparation for global competitiveness by fostering educational excellence and ensuring equal access. It engages in the following four major types of activity: 1) es-tablishing policies related to federal education funding, ad-ministering distribution of funds and monitoring their use; 2) collecting data and overseeing research on America's schools; 3) identifying major issues in education and focusing national attention on them; 4) enforcing federal laws prohibiting discrimination in programs that receive federal funds. The Department of Education publishes a variety of newsletters on specific topics relating to education, and its National Center for Education Statistics compiles annual information through its National Assessment of Educational Progress (NAEP).

Bibliography of Books

Phil Boyle and
Del Burns

Preserving the Public *in Public Schools: Visions, Values, Conflicts, and Choices.* Lanham, MD: Rowman and Littlefield Education, 2012.

Dave F. Brown

Why America's Public Schools Are the Best Place for Kids: Reality vs. Negative Perceptions. Lanham, MD: Rowman and Littlefield Education, 2011.

Evans Clinchy

Rescuing the Public Schools: What It Will Take to Leave No Child Behind. New York: Teachers College Press, 2007.

Lisa D. Delpit

Multiplication Is for White People: Raising Expectations for Other People's Children. New York: New Press, 2012.

Sara Dimerman

Character Is the Key: How to Unlock the Best in Our Children and Ourselves. Hoboken, NJ: Wiley, 2009.

Julie Duckworth

The Little Book of Values: Educating Children to Become Thinking, Responsible, and Caring Citizens. Bethel, CT: Crown House, 2009.

Greg Forster and
C. Bradley
Thompson, eds.

Freedom and School Choice in American Education. New York: Palgrave Macmillan, 2011.

Charles L. Glenn   *Contrasting Models of State and School: A Comparative Historical Study of Parental Choice and State Control.* New York: Continuum, 2011.

Steven K. Green   *The Bible, the School, and the Constitution: The Clash That Shaped Modern Church-State Doctrine.* New York: Oxford University Press, 2012.

Jay P. Greene   *Why America Needs School Choice.* New York: Continuum, 2011.

H. Wayne House, ed.   *Intelligent Design 101: Leading Experts Explain the Key Issues.* Grand Rapids, MI: Kregel, 2008.

William H. Jeynes   *A Call for Character Education and Prayer in the Schools.* Santa Barbara, CA: Praeger, 2010.

Emile Lester   *Teaching About Religions: A Democratic Approach for Public Schools.* Ann Arbor: University of Michigan Press, 2011.

Judd Kruger Levingston   *Sowing the Seeds of Character: The Moral Education of Adolescents in Public and Private Schools.* Westport, CT: Praeger, 2009.

Charles Murray   *Real Education: Four Simple Truths for Bringing America's Schools Back to Reality.* New York: Random House, 2009.

Warren A. Nord — *Does God Make a Difference? Taking Religion Seriously in Our Schools and Universities.* New York: Oxford University Press, 2010.

Diane Ravitch — *The Death and Life of the Great American School System: How Testing and Choice Are Undermining Education.* New York: Basic Books, 2010.

Mike Rose — *Why School? Reclaiming Education for All of Us.* New York: New Press, 2009.

H. Svi Shapiro, ed. — *Education and Hope in Troubled Times: Visions of Change for Our Children's World.* New York: Routledge, 2009.

Stephen D. Solomon — *Ellery's Protest: How One Young Man Defied Tradition and Sparked the Battle over School Prayer.* Ann Arbor: University of Michigan Press, 2009.

Joel Spring — *American Education*, 15th ed. New York: McGraw-Hill, 2012.

Keith Stewart Thomson — *Before Darwin: Reconciling God and Nature.* New Haven, CT: Yale University Press, 2008.

Paul Tough — *How Children Succeed: Grit, Curiosity, and the Hidden Power of Character.* Boston: Houghton Mifflin Harcourt, 2012.

Herbert J. Walberg — *Tests, Testing, and Genuine School Reform.* Stanford, CA: Education Next Books, 2011.

Bob Wise

Raising the Grade: How High School Reform Can Save Our Youth and Our Nation. San Francisco: Jossey-Bass, 2008.

Index

CPSIA information can be obtained
at www.ICGtesting.com
Printed in the USA
FFOW01n0357070214
3478FF

TABLE OF CONTENTS

ACKNOWLEDGEMENTS

We wish to express appreciation to the following publishers for permission to print articles:

Desclée de Brouwer, Paris for the use of four articles from the series "Etudes Carmélitaines," vol. *Direction spirituelle et psychologie* (1951), pp. 173-263.

Institut Catholique, Paris for the use of one article from its bulletin *Nouvelles de l'Institut Catholique de Paris*, special issue "Thérèse de Lisieux: Conférences du Centenaire, 1873-1973" (1973), pp. 107-23.

Editorial de Espiritualidad, Madrid for use of the first three sections of an article appearing in the volume *Introducción a la lectura de Santa Teresa* (1978), pp. 43-88. (The fourth section will be translated and published in *Carmelite Studies* sometime in the near future.)

We also wish to express our thanks and recognition to several persons who have collaborated in the preparation of this volume by the translations they have prepared, viz., to Sr Kathleen Kirk, OCD, Fr Christopher Latimer, OCD, Fr Michael Dodd, OCD, Fr John Clarke, OCD and Br Steven Payne, OCD. Thanks go to Miss Jeannette Mallon, OCDS for typing parts of the manuscript and to Mr Robert Mastro, publications consultant, for graphics work.

ABBREVIATIONS

To facilitate reading of the notes we will adopt the following abbreviations of the major works of Sts John of the Cross, Teresa of Avila and Thérèse of Lisieux. Given the multiplicity of English-language translations of their writings, an entirely satisfactory system of citation is not possible. In a general way, however, choice of the contemporary I.C.S. versions will be preferred unless the authors of articles decide either to make their own translation or to supply the text of some other published translation. (When needed, introductory editorial or translators' notes will explain special usages adopted for particular articles.)

ST JOHN OF THE CROSS

A = The Ascent of Mount Carmel
N = The Dark Night
C = The Spiritual Canticle
F = The Living Flame of Love

In A and N the first number
indicates the book

ST TERESA OF AVILA

L = The Book of Her Life
W = The Way of Perfection
C = The Interior Castle
F = Book of the Foundations

In C the first number indicates the Dwelling

ST THERESE OF LISIEUX

S = Story of a Soul, From the Original Manuscripts
LC = Last Conversations

INTRODUCTION

Few people were surprised ten years ago with the Church's declaration of Teresa of Avila as the first woman Doctor of the Church. Bringing the mystical "Daughter of the Church" to this honor and status seemed like an evidently well-founded course of action to both Carmelites and non-Carmelites alike. But Pope Paul VI's proclamation was greeted by the Order of Carmel with particular satisfaction and enthusiasm.

This "doctorate," conferred on a woman who laid the foundations of her own religious order even as she worked for the reform of a more ancient order, can justly be regarded as an honor that redounds to the good of both groups of Carmelites throughout the world. She stood for and fought for deep prayer life in the Church; they are members of a family which now continues to pursue living prayer in its life. Her desire to drink in deeply the refreshing experience of God's personal loving-kindness in prayer is the fundamental desire of all Carmelites.

On the tenth anniversary of Teresa's arrival among the revered *doctores ecclesiae* the arrival on the scene of a new Carmelite series is a symbolic, though real, affirmation that the ideal embraced, sought after and attained by Teresa of Jesus through her Carmelite vocation is still valid. We feel that all she learned from Carmelites before her and all she passed on to those who now enjoy reading her lively writings still is significant for the present as it is for the future. Because of this we are happy to contribute to English-language spiritual literature studies about the witness of Carmel to humankind's encounter with the mystery of God.

Carmelite Studies would wish to imitate, after a fashion, what Teresa of Avila did in her times. Just as she described in her writings her own experience of the "intimate sharing between friends . . . alone with him who we know loves us," this series will devote its volumes to describing the varied ways, the many instances, the rich personal histories which exemplify Carmel's manner of experiencing that "intimate sharing" which is prayer. Our main purpose is to make available to an English-language

vii

reading audience exegesis of the written and lived witness of Carmel to the life of prayer—to supply keys of understanding to Carmel's heritage, history and spirituality. How we will attempt to accomplish this goal through a "binary" approach will become evident from the closing paragraph of these editorial comments. Just briefly, though, we would point to one particular preoccupation *Carmelite Studies* will borrow from St Teresa in order to answer the perhaps inevitable question as to why there should even be a new publication of this type.

Teresa's renewal efforts in Carmel took place in a period of conciliar renewal unleashed in the Church by the Council of Trent. Several hundred years previously the Order of Carmel itself began its existence in an era of great struggles over renewal in the medieval Church: St Albert of Jerusalem, Latin-rite bishop of the local church, delivered the *Rule* to the hermits of Mount Carmel in or around 1209, a year which stood a bit more than mid-way between the third and fourth Lateran (reform) Councils. Currently, our generation is living out a renewal council's call to revision and reform. *Carmelite Studies* hopes to further the progress of renewal for contemporary Carmelites and for as many others as are attracted to study the spirituality of our order. This new series of the Institute of Carmelite Studies would want to contribute to the ideal of renewal dear to our order and take to heart, as it does so, the following advice of St Teresa:

> Let it never be said of them, as it is said of some other Orders, that they do nothing but praise their beginnings. It is we who are the beginners now; but let them continually strive to be beginners too, in the sense of growing better and better all the time (*Foundations*, 29).

Over the past decade the Institute of Carmelite Studies has been striving to produce reliable and handsome translations of the masterpieces of our Carmelite writers. Now with *Carmelite Studies* we will have a forum for no less important commentaries on those classics of Carmelite literature. To carry out its role *Carmelite Studies* will aim to achieve a balance that assures a "binary" effect between diverse qualities. For instance, along with *original pieces* on the one hand there will also be *transla-tions* of articles. In this way we plan to make available in English a *corpus* of significant writings on Carmelite topics by European and other authors which have remained inaccessible to all who do not read foreign-language publications. Our Institute has frequently received requests from interested readers for translations of this kind. Then, woven into a fabric of competent *study* will be definite *pastoral lessons*, however the author chooses to express them. Furthermore, the structure of each issue will contain two parts: a first cluster of articles will articulate a particular *timely theme* selected by the editor and the other members of the I.C.S.; then, the second part will contain a *miscellany* of other articles which need have nothing else in common except that they treat topics concerning Carmelite matters.We trust that the former section's thematic approach will satisfy desires to see questions of contemporary concern compared to varied facets of Carmel's own view of life; while the latter will ensure pleasant variety to our readers and greater scope to prospective authors in their choice of subjects of interest. (For this first volume the number of translated studies tends to predominate, especially in the first, thematic section on spiritual direction. We feel certain that those four articles—which are appearing together in English translation for the first time—form a distinct contribution to the evolution of spiritual direction as a pastoral art and service to the People of God.)

It is our hope that all the articles of this and of subsequent volumes do prove "pleasant" to the reader, even as we invite comments on the journal and promise to listen carefully to reactions submitted, in order to assure ongoing evaluation of *Carmelite Studies*.

John Sullivan, OCD
Editor

SPIRITUAL DIRECTION IN THE TERESIAN CARMEL

SPIRITUAL DIRECTION ACCORDING TO ST JOHN OF THE CROSS

Lucien-Marie Florent, O.C.D.

Father Lucien-Marie has written many books and articles about Carmelite spirituality, and the most noteworthy is perhaps his article on St John of the Cross in the highly respected and much consulted Dictionnaire de Spiritualité.

I t is an easily verifiable fact that the angle from which spiritual direction is examined in the works of St John of the Cross is that of deviations, even perversions, of direction. We need not probe very deeply to become aware of the saint's severity toward bad directors. Certain sentences constitute such a striking warning that, once read (even if only casually), they can never be forgotten: "Many spiritual directors cause great harm to a number of souls."[1] The paradoxical vehemence of this assertion, which is not unique, does not fail to surprise us. We perceive rather quickly that the criticisms leveled at bad directors fall into three principal categories:

(1) The most obvious, which for this reason will claim less of our attention, involve an excessive and downright defect. Here there is question of moral perversions: the vehement passage in which the saint reproaches certain directors for an almost husband-like jealousy of their directees is too famous to bear repeating here.[2] His next reproach is hardly more indulgent and

3

is aimed at directors whose faith and whose sense of consecration to God are so weak that they lead away from the religious life those whom God has called to it. Here we are obviously in the area of faults that are rather strictly those of the moral order.

(2) In a second series of complaints, it is not the morality of the director that is under fire, but rather his ignorance. In its various forms this is characterized by a more or less sectarian dogmatism and by the priority granted by the director to his own security, even to the detriment of the spiritual development of the person he is supposed to be helping approach God. Instead of transmitting the flame, he seems to be too much of a spiritual extinguisher. Behind this ignorance we readily suspect an affective factor: a wrong love of self and of one's personal security. And this poisonous narcissism does not fail to render such ignorance culpable. "He who recklessly errs will not escape a punishment corresponding to the harm he caused, for he was obliged, as is everyone, to perform the duties of his office well and not be mistaken."[3]

(3) Finally, there are certain deviations regarding direction which differ clearly from the first two categories. They take on an even greater importance now that recent studies in psychology enable us to better measure their consequences. A careful explanation is still required here. The principle appears banal: "The disciple will become like the master, and as is the father so will be the son."[4] But it is no longer a question of voluntary influence nor of culpable ignorance. Here the influence is not calculated but is nevertheless inevitable. Unconsciously or involuntarily, the director influences his directee with his own faults, his preferences, even his imbalance. Hence, at least when it is a matter of a director leading a soul called to a deeply interior life, we realize how strictly indispensable is the factor of personal experience. Strictly speaking, it is the word *experience* which applies in spiritual direction, not *holiness*, even though these two words often overlap: when involved with the interior life, experience can hardly be anything other than holiness, at least "in fieri" or on the way to fulfillment, if not yet consummated. But the opposite is not always true. For it is not beyond imagining that one could

be a saint, while still showing a certain psychological imbalance. The latter may very well not impede holiness, but it renders the one so afflicted more or less unsuited for the role of spiritual counselor. The grace of spiritual direction does not flow directly from sanctifying grace. Not just everyone is qualified to be a spiritual director. To fill this role effectively, certain psychological conditions are required which do not flow primarily from personal sanctity. One may think that Father de Foucauld made great progress in the ways of sanctity and yet at the same time doubt whether he could without any reservations be recommended as a perfectly qualified spiritual counselor. St John of the Cross says that it is rare for a director to be universally suited for spiritual direction. We see one explanation of this overall truth in the fact that, if the director shows certain psychological defects which do not pertain to the order of personal holiness, he will not be capable of guiding souls who are afflicted with the same defects. Thus for lack of this factor of personal realization of necessary corrections, the director who is most competent with regard to speculative knowledge will remain, in certain cases, incapable of leading the soul effectively to God. There are stages that must have been lived through in order to be thoroughly understood. Moreover, there are certain stages of development that one must have completed in order to be capable of helping others to pass through them (for one accomplishes more than is realized by one's own effort). There are purifications that one must first have experienced if one is not to impede the progress of a soul who is taking the same road.

Thus the director's lack of experience first makes itself felt in a negative manner: "Although the foundation for guiding a soul to spirit is knowledge and discretion, the director will not succeed in leading the soul onward in it, when God bestows it, nor will he even understand it, if he has no experience of what true and pure spirit is."[5] Lack of personal experience on the part of the director, however intelligent and prudent he may be, is liable to impede the directee instead of causing him to advance, and may even make him deviate from the path which God has called him to follow.

In various ways, several texts of St John of the Cross repeat this same assertion: for lack of this factor of preliminary personal experience, many directors theorize, more or less successfully, when they ought to be entering into the depth of another's personal experience, the paths of which they cannot even guess if they have not first traveled them.

But this negative harm is accompanied by another positive one. If the directee does not have a strong personality, or if he has not been led by God far beyond the point where his director is, the director, intentionally or not, will mark him with his own defects and will make him practise, out of season, and maybe even desire more profoundly what is no longer suitable for him in the stage of the interior life he has arrived at. A sort of spiritual osmosis takes place. "Assuredly, I wish I knew how to speak of this, because I think it is difficult to explain how the spirit of the disciple is secretly fashioned after that of his spiritual father."[6] And again: "He [the spiritual director] cannot avoid—even though unaware—affecting his disciple with this attitude and pleasure, if the disciple is not more advanced than he."[7]

There need not be a calculated intention to reach such a serious lack of objectivity. Without prejudging the possible factor of culpability, but remaining on the level of psychological analysis (the psychological factor conditions, to be sure, moral behavior), we can speak of the perversion of spiritual direction. Whereas normally spiritual direction ought to be the means of facilitating the journey of the directee to God, and whereas, by right, spiritual direction should place at the disposal of the directee all the resources the director has, and the latter should be totally self-sacrificing in fulfilling this task, it can actually become for the director the occasion of his turning the directee toward himself and attaching him to himself. This occurs, not in the excessive mode of an affective disorder, but as a form of assimilation to the director's manner of being, while the soul is really asking that his own manner of being be respected. It is easy to understand how, even without deliberate calculation, this attitude is not without a certain narcissism, a cult of self and of one's own manner, from which it is not easy to remove all culpability.

The severity of St John of the Cross with regard to sham spiritual direction is such that we might often prefer not to draw the inevitable conclusions: "It is not given to all persons to guide souls, since it is extremely important whether the director does badly or well in such a serious matter."[8] We could compile a whole litany of bad directors: "Builders of the tower of Babel,"[9] "Job's comforters,"[10] "blacksmiths, who know no more than how to hammer,"[11] "little foxes that destroy the flourishing vineyard,"[12] "destroyers of the Lord's vineyard,"[13] "the blind leading the blind,"[14] and "barriers or obstacles at the gate of heaven."[15]

This severity, in a concrete manner, presents us with the problems of spiritual direction: it should stimulate our effort and point out paths of research.

For if spiritual direction is a difficult art, it is nevertheless very necessary. How can we forget the many illusions that souls have with regard to themselves? The Prologue of the *Ascent* clearly indicates them,[16] both positively and negatively, as does the Prologue to the *Maxims*.[17] Thus it is doubly important to be aware of them, for directors "are obliged to be careful and understand what they are doing."[18]

"THEOLOGICAL" SPIRITUAL DIRECTION

It would be too simplistic and dangerously inexact to set asceticism in opposition to the mystical life, or to extol the cultivation of the theological virtues to the exclusion of the moral virtues: no question here of placing in opposition to each other the members of a living organism, all of which have a role to play, nor of choosing between them. The security of the theological virtues rests upon the foundation of the moral virtues, and the latter reach their full development only in a theological climate. Rather it is a matter of specifying in which focal point the synthesis takes place of the different elements involved in spiritual direction, or, again, what the effort of the director is actually aiming at.

Without expressly mentioning it, the lengthily developed title

of the *Ascent of Mount Carmel* traces the plan of spiritual
direction as St John of the Cross understands it. The text formally
presupposes the primacy of divine action. For a predominantly
voluntaristic spirituality, this theme hardly makes any sense, but
appears as inexpressive as a photographic negative. The latter
must always be viewed as a function of the luminous impression
which will make of it a positive picture. Thus this text:

> "The Ascent of Mount Carmel
>
> explains how to reach divine union quickly. It presents instruction
> and doctrine valuable for beginners and proficients alike that they
> may learn how to unburden themselves of all earthly things, avoid
> spiritual obstacles, and live in that complete nakedness and
> freedom of spirit necessary for divine union."

If the divine initiative in the highest stages of the spiritual life
assumes such importance that the soul can do no more than
maintain itself in a state of passivity, it must also be affirmed that
this divine action is essential from the humble beginnings on,
even though it may manifest itself in more disguised form. All the
soul can do is practice totally absolute poverty, on both the
temporal and the spiritual levels. God takes care of all the positive
work. If the person strives to be poor, it is impossible that God
will not communicate himself to him. "It is more impossible
than it would be for the sun not to shine on clear and uncluttered
ground. As the sun rises in the morning and shines upon your
house so that its light may enter if you open the shutters, so
God . . . will enter the soul that is empty, and fill it with divine
goods."[19] This is one of the assertions that flows perhaps most
often from the saint's pen and surely one of those that must
always be presupposed in his reasoning. The fact that this
initiative from God takes on different forms according to the
different stages of the spiritual life does not prevent its always
prevailing over a disorderly agitation on the part of the soul in a
domain that is utterly beyond it.[20] What is true of certain
characteristic stages must be generalized, while respecting the
required nuances. God is the "chief agent,"[21] it is he "who
actuates this love and pours it forth in the soul."[22] Let us not

forget that the most lofty directions given by St John of the Cross in the *Living Flame* are useful not only for souls who are already well advanced, "but also for all others who are seeking their Beloved."[23] Through all the stages of the spiritual life, God's desire does not change, and it inspires his manner of acting from the beginning.[24] In the soul's journey toward God, despite initial deficiencies, despite stages of aridity when it seems that God is absent, all the activity of the soul, however intense it may be, can only be a response and never an initiative. The sense of the transcendence of God and of his action, for God acts "in no other manner than as God,"[25] dominates the views of St John of the Cross with regard to the spiritual life. "It is God's task"[26] to lead the soul to the life that transcends all natural life, however refined the latter may be. It is he who is "the supernatural artisan"[27] of the soul's sanctification.

Rather than multiply texts, we do better to consider one of those vehement affirmations that we are sometimes startled to hear fall from the lips of one who is ordinarily so restrained in his language: "These directors should reflect that they themselves are not the chief agent, guide, and mover of souls in this matter, but that the principal guide is the Holy Spirit, who is never neglectful of souls, and that they are instruments for directing them to perfection through faith and the law of God, according to the spirit God gives each one."[28]

Almost all the essential points of doctrine of St John of the Cross regarding spiritual direction are contained in this text. First there is the unconditioned primacy of the divine action: "the chief agent, guide, and mover of souls in this matter is not they themselves, but the Holy Spirit." Then there is the purely instrumental role that must be rightly attributed to directors, after the affirmation of the primacy of God: "they are only instruments." Next he emphasizes the primordial importance of faith and God's law, which in the ordinary usage of St John of the Cross includes all the underlying asceticism necessary for one who wishes to respond to God's overtures. Finally there is the obligation of directors not to issue rules in the abstract, but to adapt their advice to the subjective needs of souls, taking into account the historical factors of their development: "according to the spirit God gives to each one."

The logical consequence of the primacy of the divine initiative is that the director can have only a *disposing* role. This is the adjective that best describes the role of the director. This is not to be understood in an essentially chronological sense, as if the director should always precede historically God's action and prepare for it, but in a metaphysical sense: "Let directors be content with disposing them for this according to evangelical perfection, which lies in nakedness and emptiness of sense and spirit; and let them not desire to go any further than this in building, since that function belongs only to the Father of lights . . ."[29] The title of the *Ascent* clearly expresses its purpose of helping the soul to overcome whatever is an obstacle to its progress and especially to reject whatever is only a remote means of approaching God. The job of the director is to place the soul in this "disposition,"[30] to teach the soul to remove the obstacles which counter God's action and to lead it to total interior detachment. God takes care of the rest, that is to say, of all the work of positive construction. The director helps the soul to prepare to receive a gift that only God can provide, and then to accept it in a manner adapted to the gift itself, and finally to develop it.

It is possible that in the beginning of the spiritual life and at certain more difficult times the role of the director may include a certain amount of initiative, but, if the words are not mutually contradictory, this is always a secondary initiative.

Inversely, when the soul is in full passivity, when all initiative, even what is secondary, is impossible to the director, he will always remain, in every sense of the term, God's witness, the one who verifies from outside the interior action of the Holy Spirit. As a paradoxical but incontestable consequence, St John of the Cross, who seems to minimize the role of the director (whom he reminds that he is never the soul's principal guide), upholds the indispensable character of his role even in the highest stages, since even then the director will always remain the one who visibly approves the soul and, in God's name, authenticates the

quality of this life which it is not his to give. A bit like St John the
Baptizer, the friend of the Bridegroom and witness to the nuptials
of the Bridegroom, the director can be only the respectful witness
to a work over which he does not have paternity.

This conception of the director's role allows us to delve deeper
into its essence according to the views of St John of the Cross. If
he judged that the role of the spiritual director remains substantially the same at the beginning and at the end of the spiritual life,
as the soul takes its first steps on the road as well as when God
leads it into the regions where there is no road anymore, this is
because his notion of this role was quite different from what one
ordinarily comes across. Certainly he does not forget, and he even
reminds the soul, that prudence and humility oblige him not to
trust in himself.[31] A soul without a guide is like a garden without
a wall,[32] like an isolated piece of coal that will never be kindled,[33]
like a blind man who has much trouble finding his way when all
goes well, not to mention when he falls.[34] No, St John of the
Cross is not unaware of the rules of prudence and he knows how
beneficial this virtue is when one places the care of one's soul in
the hands of an experienced master.

Yet, to reduce his doctrine to a sort of code entirely dominated
by prudence would be to distort and cut it off from what is
essential to it. An indirect consideration will permit us to proceed
further in this research. If certain people assert that the final goal
of spiritual direction is, by means of adequate formation of the
directee, to render direction useless, this is because they consider
direction solely from the point of view of the moral virtues and of
asceticism. One thinks of the sports coach who ceases to be of use
as soon as his pupil knows as much as he does. It seems that we
would then remain on the level of human initiative, of ascetical
training, of technique. When a pupil arrives at the point where he
possesses the technique of his master as well as or maybe even
better than the master himself, there would seem to be no reason
for him to continue to take lessons.

This kind of consideration is foreign to the thinking of St John
of the Cross. For him, the spiritual director is someone quite
different from a teacher of technique. Even when the directee is

fully passive, even when he is at a degree of union which his particular director is far from achieving, St John of the Cross advises him, even though it be in vain, to seek the aid he needs to respond to God's overtures.

What defines the relationship of the directee to the director is not primarily nor directly the virtue of prudence; nor is it the humility of a person who knows himself to be a disciple with still much to learn. Although this assertion requires precise qualification, it is faith which defines the relationship of the directee to the director. In the religious life, the whole external organization is based on the obedience of the subject to the superior, who represents God. Likewise, taking due account of the considerable differences which separate the external organization of the religious life from the secret domain of the relationship of the soul with God, it can be said that in spiritual direction, as in the obedience of a subject, the director is "substituted in place of God."[35] It is regretable that St John of the Cross dealt little with this problem and did not treat of it expressly. To complain of him in this regard would be to forget that his role as practitioner of the spiritual life dispensed him from theoretical explanations, to which he rarely applied himself! But the principles that he set forth and the concrete applications that he suggested manifest his profound thought on the subject. It is no more nor less than the conception of the Church, both visible and invisible, which is involved in spiritual direction as he envisions it. The mystery of the Church is the prolongation of the mystery of the Incarnation. Faith rests, as on its unique foundation, upon Christ and upon the Church that is one with him. And this faith indicates to us not only what we must believe, but also what we must do: "We must be guided humanly and visibly in all by the law of Christ the man and that of his Church and of his ministers. This is the method of remedying our spiritual ignorances and weaknesses; here we shall find abundant medicine for them all. Any departure from this road is not only curiosity, but extraordinary boldness. One should disbelieve anything coming in a supernatural way, and believe only the teaching of Christ, the man, as I say, and of his ministers who are men."[36] Doubtless this passage extends far beyond spiritual direction and embraces the whole problem of the

Church's magisterium. But what interests us here is precisely his relating the problem of spiritual direction to that of the ordinary magisterium of the Church. To remedy our "spiritual ignorances and weaknesses," there are not only the official definitions of the Church, but also the private instructions of the one who incarnates the Church for the soul. Certainly one need not adhere as absolutely to the instructions of a spiritual director as one does to the definitions of the Church, but the same order of motivation is operative. Commenting on the text of St Matthew: "Where two or three are gathered together, I am in the midst of them" (18:30), St John of the Cross adds: "It is noteworthy that he did not say: where there is one alone, there I am; rather he said: where there are at least two. Thus God announces that he does not want the soul to believe only by itself the communications it thinks are of divine origin, nor that anyone be assured or confirmed in them without the Church or her ministers."[37] It seems that, in the individual domain as well as in the quite special realm of the soul's guidance, this is a sort of delegation of the ordinary power of the Church: "The effect, light, strength, and security of many divine communications are not completely confirmed in a soul, as we stated, until it discusses them with one whom God has destined to be spiritual judge over it, who has power to bind, loose, approve, and reprove."[38] This last assertion, one of the saint's strongest, is interesting in that it clearly attaches the particular case of the director of conscience to the ordinary power of the Church. We can in this sense invoke the text of Father Labourdette: "The Church has received the objective deposit of divine revelation; it pertains to the Church to set it forth to all generations, to every human intelligence."[39]

No doubt, in all these texts, we can sense in the background the presence of the "illuminists"[39a] who were so damaging to the true spiritual current of sixteenth-century Spain. It is because of them that St John of the Cross insists so much upon the imperative of not leaving the soul alone in its relations with God, but of subjecting all things to the judgment of someone who is God's visible witness. The same preoccupation impels St John of the Cross to highlight the necessity of not allowing oneself to be guided blindly according to the illuminations of an unverified spirituality, but to have recourse first to the certitudes of natural reason. It is perhaps paradoxical to note that in certain cases recourse to natural reason is opposed not to adherence to faith, but rather to the spontaneous impulse of personal illuminations. It can also be said that to affirm the obligation of recourse to natural reason is to affirm the benefit of spiritual direction that is based on a relationship of faith: "God is so content that the rule and direction of man be through other men, and that a person be governed by natural reason, that he definitely does not want us to bestow entire credence upon his supernatural communications, nor be confirmed in their strength and security until they pass through this human channel of the mouth of man."[40]

Certain people may be astonished by this, but such a clear statement on the part of St John of the Cross establishes against the "illuminists" the necessity not only of never dispensing oneself from the considerations of natural reason, but especially from that of living our whole spiritual life within the perspectives of the Incarnation, i.e., of God made man, and also of his Church, both visible and invisible, both interior and related to God through the ministry of men. St Paul himself did not find assurance regarding "his Gospel," the one that Our Lord himself had revealed to him, until he had been to confer with St Peter and the Apostles.[41] Analogically it is the same step that is taken by a person going to ask of a qualified witness to God no longer simply the truth of what he should believe but also the appropriateness of his projects and, still more, the authentication of his personal manner of dealing with God. Leo XIII, in a well-known and very clear text, does not hesitate to refer spiritual direction to the magisterium of the Church and thus to make the directee's attitude of faith the basis of the relationship that binds him to his director:

> . . . experience itself teaches us that these warnings and impulses from the Holy Spirit are very often perceived only with the aid and, as it were, the preparation of the external magisterium. St Augustine says on this subject: "He cooperates in the birth of the fruit who, from outside, waters the good tree and cultivates it by whatever means and he who, from within, gives it growth by his

personal action." (*De Grat. Christ.*, c. xix) This observation flows
from the common law of Providence which has established that
men generally be saved by other men and that likewise those called
to a higher degree of sanctity should be led there by men "so that,
following the saying of St John Chrysostom, God's instruction
comes to us through men." (*Hom. I*, in *Inscr. altar*) We find at the
very origins of the Church a famous manifestation of this law:
although Saul breathing threats and carnage (Acts 9:1) had heard
the voice of Christ himself and asked: "Lord, what do you want me
to do?" it was to Damascus that he was sent, to Ananias: "Enter
into the city, and there you will be told what you must do."[42]

In practice we see how intimate is the act of faith brought
about by recourse to the spiritual director: it involves the inner-
most life of the soul. Speaking of interior graces by means of
which the soul receives certain truths concerning human events
with a certitude so strong that it must be adhered to, St John of
the Cross demands that this soul have recourse to the spiritual
director anyway, not to learn anything more, but by so doing to
make an act of faith which consists in not being guided by oneself
but by the instructions of God's representatives: "Although a man
may consider his knowledge certain and true, as we pointed out,
and be unable to cast off that passive interior assent, he must not,
on account of this conviction, fail to believe and give the assent of
reason to the instructions and commands of his spiritual director,
even if they are extremely contrary to what he feels. In this way
one will be led by faith to the divine union, for a soul must
journey to it more by believing than by understanding."[43] It
seems impossible to doubt that, for St John of the Cross, recourse
to a visible minister of God, in order to be guided by him in the
ways of divine union, constitutes an act of faith that is very
interior and thus realizes within the depths of the soul the mystery
of the visible and invisible Church, the mystery of the Christ-
Man.

Moreover, the faith that constitutes the basis of the relationship of the directee to the director is the essential nourishment
which the director should give to his directee. The practical
cultivation of faith is something so evident in St John of the Cross

that it would be tedious to gather all the texts from his works that express this, as well as the testimonies of those who benefited from his direction. . . : "He used to teach that manner of living in faith which consists solely in dependence upon God and attentiveness to him . . . He wanted souls to progress by relying on the light of faith." In conversation he had a special grace, that of radiating faith: "When he spoke, his words penetrated souls, restoring their serenity, removing all temptation or doubt and permeating them with light and with faith."[45]

One might say without exaggeration that his only direction is always to develop faith in souls, whatever the circumstances. He deplores the fact that souls are not "grounded in faith,"[46] nor detached "so as to soar to the heights of dark faith."[47] One must "guide the soul through faith to the divine union."[48] All distinct knowledge, no matter how lofty, is not worth one act of faith. Faith alone is the adequate means of union, the only means proportionate to the goal to be attained. This is the unique theme of the night of the understanding in the *Ascent* and in numerous passages in his other works. Since faith, in spite of its obscurity, gives us God himself, it is understandable that the principal concern of the director should be to help his directee in every way to live by faith.

We need not repeat that St John of the Cross's faith is not opposed to love, but to hodgepodges of sensitivity. The concrete and lived faith that he demands of his disciples is a faith enriched with all the love possible, a faith "through which we love God without understanding him."[49]

This unconditional primacy of the theological virtues, and especially of faith, governs what we might call the interiority of spiritual direction as St John of the Cross conceives it. We may be surprised by the little importance he seems to attach to all that pertains to the exterior attitude. The witnesses of his life certainly noted this trait: "He spoke more of the interior than of what was demanded in practice." This surely does not mean that he underestimated exterior behavior, for it is well known how faithful he was to the practices of his religious life, but he was greatly concerned that behavior be rooted in the theological life.

The true source of behavior can only be the theological life, and the theological life normally develops into correct moral behavior. For St John of the Cross there is never such a thing as pure asceticism. It always tends toward union with God as toward its normal goal.

Thus from two different points of view the doctrine of St John of the Cross regarding spiritual direction must be related to faith: (1) as it defines the relationship of the directee to the director, and (2) as it expresses the essential content of the instructions which the director should give. Certainly, let us repeat, this cultivation of faith excludes neither prudence nor the moral virtues; in fact, it includes and presupposes them, but it is faith which always draws up the essential axis of the road to be traveled.

"SUBJECTIVE" SPIRITUAL DIRECTION

Although that aspect of the doctrine of St John of the Cross which concerns spiritual direction and which we have qualified as theological evokes some discussion, the general outline of this doctrine seems certain. Even if we sometimes experience difficulty in expressing certain points of the Mystical Doctor's teaching on this subject, the cultivation of faith is so frequently extolled that we cannot essentially challenge this theological aspect of spiritual direction as he conceives it.

Much less emphasis seems to have been given to another aspect of his teaching which, for lack of a better term, we shall call the subjectivism of St John of the Cross. The importance of the strictly doctrinal line of the *Ascent* or of the *Living Flame* has held the attention of authors who have studied the works of the Mystical Doctor, to the detriment of all that deals with the art of direction in these works. It is, however, this second aspect that gives value to the first, that matches it to reality and provides its efficacy. As almost always happens, it is criticism, sometimes harsh despite their respectful manner, from modern authors against what we might call "traditional" spiritual direction which has led us to study more extensively this side of sanjuanist doctrine. We can describe as follows the series of facts which have led us to go deeper into this study. Indisputably, a number of directors (whom we must always suppose to be well intentioned) commit practical errors of which the souls entrusted to their care suffer the consequences. Psychologists called in to deal with these errors declare that real mental disorders can sometimes derive from them. One thing must be noted: these errors almost always result from ignorance of the subjective data. Too many spiritual directors, preoccupied with principles, forget that souls are not abstract products, that they are not all identical, and supposedly not all capable of putting into practice the theoretical principles of the spiritual life. There is no question of doubting for an instant the value of these principles. It is simply a matter of asking ourselves whether, confronted with these principles, all souls have the same capacity for implementation. Do they all have among their aptitudes that sort of coefficient which theoretical principles are likely to presuppose?

Now is a good time to quote the courageous lines written by Dr Odier about this:

Theoretical moralities or certain spiritualistic doctrines seem to address themselves to a type of person taken in an abstract and general sense, independently of all personal and particular psychological structure. Their postulates would seem to be in accordance with the following premises:

In principle the receptivity and the capacity to respond to moral, spiritual and religious appeals is equal and constant in all civilized beings—or those born in a civilized community—and are free from mental illness. In all persons one would seem to grant *a priori* to the ego and to the moral conscience a virtual aptitude to conform to the prescriptions of such and such a normative and legislative morality. This would amount to saying that ego and moral conscience are assumed to be able at any time and in any place to constitute a "functional unity" in order to be able to harmonize their functions. This premise would in turn postulate the admission of a homogeneous moral conscience, always identical with itself, presenting a proper and indefinitely perfectible framework and pursuing its specific ends in an autonomous fashion. Correlatively, its deficiencies would be attributed to its own imperfection.

However, a precise analytical investigation demonstrates that these postulates are *false*.

Consequently, in the area of spiritual direction one is not justified in proposing or imposing the same demands upon everyone of whatever age. To do so would be to base oneself upon an abstract and "metamoral" concept. Is it not the mission of the psychologist to point out the real dangers of metamoral and even metaspiritual concepts?

It is the "flock" who face these dangers, not their directors. It is, in fact, an abuse into which certain guides of souls easily fall. It consists in declaring that if a given subject, under ordinary conditions, does not manage to accept such and such a norm as an obligation, or refuses to conform his conduct to it, it is always "his fault"; it is always his "bad spirit" that leads him astray. It is never the law imposed upon him that is at fault, nor the one who imposes it upon him. His responsibility is presumed to be complete, as all social morality and spiritual doctrine are supposed to correspond to the human nature for which they have been rightly conceived. And the postulate of this correspondence is implicitly maintained in the mind of the guide applying such doctrine, by the very fact that he applies it. Confronted with the uncertain and troublesome results of his work, he never gets around to asking himself whether the author of the same doctrine, in conceiving it, might not have been oblivious to the psychological conditions required for its application to human souls . . ."[50]

As far as St John of the Cross is concerned, the many depositions of witnesses in the Processes of Beatification and Canonization show in him a constant concern not to make abstract oracular pronouncements but to respond to the spiritual needs of souls. The witnesses reveal a real admiration for the flexibility with which the saint applied a doctrine whose broad, simple lines might have caused one to fear rigidity. To a person disturbed about this point, the saint replied that the more holy directors are, "the better they penetrate the human condition."[51] Mary of the Mother of God asserts that he knew very well how to apply to each individual soul the beneficial remedy.[52] One of his disciples, in trying to describe the saint's attitude with regard to souls, points out two traits which highlight his understanding of the subjective data of souls: "He readily gained insight into two things without which no spiritual master can safely lead those whom he is directing: to know the tastes and the maturity of each of the souls, and to recognize what God wanted of them in order to lead them in a reasonable and secure manner."[53] Martin of St Joseph confirms this flexibility in the saint; he knew how to adapt himself to the needs of religious as well as laity, of great and small, of learned and ignorant. He had a gift of penetration of spirits and a very small indication would suffice to enlighten him about the real needs of his directees, even when the latter were incapable of expressing what they were experiencing.[54] Far from being some kind of an unfeeling theoretician, he impressed people with his patience in guiding souls, "putting up with their imperfections, repeating tirelessly his instructions and leading souls without violence, according to their imperfect steps, to perfection; and by weak means, to strength; accommodating the means to the end."[55] This deposition is particulary valuable and shows to what extent the saint was attentive to adapting the law to the capacities of souls, not to limit the law, but to draw forth progressively the capacities of souls to the demands of the law. (And this deposition is all the more precious in that it comes from Blessed Ann of St Bartholomew, who had heard this from the lips of St Teresa herself.)

Diego de la Concepción explains how the saint used to proceed: He had such concern for each soul in particular that he listened every day to the confidences of his religious, and helped them to gain insight into themselves. An even more important and very noteworthy point is that he explained his manner of acting and did not conceal his displeasure with "pure theoreticians." He "opposed those spiritual masters for whom everything consisted in preaching sermons to their novices and who did not make an effort to get to know their spirit and to guide them."[56] There is no need to multiply these quotations, which seem to have been made expressly to protest in advance against any deformation of the true image of St John of the Cross. No one was less doctrinaire than he: the flexibility of his practical instructions impressed all who benefited from his spiritual direction. In his contacts with souls, he carefully avoided ready-made formulas. He was never a man of one technique. He believed in the transcendence of a doctrine of faith which, because it is transcendent, is never incarnated identically in individual persons. He knew that his role was not to bend souls to the postulates of abstract principles, but to respond to their essentially individual and often variable needs.

How could any attentive reader be led into error on this point? Even his written works bear witness to the constant concern the Mystical Doctor had to avoid the rigidity inherent in one impersonal approach, valid for all. How often he points out the considerable individual differences that distinguish souls from one another and prevent their being treated in a uniform manner. Whether he is treating of the trials of the night or of the joys of the espousals, at every point along the spiritual journey he spreads out the broad range of multiple individual expressions.

Jean Baruzi has rightly noted this in a way that deserves to be quoted. He is commenting on a text from the *Spiritual Canticle* that is very rich in meaning: "devout souls . . . run here and there, that is, they run from different directions and in different ways . . . each according to the spirit and the state which God has given to them: run, I say, with so many differences of works and spiritual exercises on the road to eternal life." [57] Baruzi adds: "As for the multiplicity of ways that he reproaches spiritual directors for not being able to discern, one might say that he never ceases to keep the image before him, despite an apparent rigidity.

> Following your footsteps,
> the young girls run along the roads.

"He sees young creatures running: joyful dances, supple leaps along the roads that they discover. He is pleased with this rich originality that he discovers through adventures that are never identically reproduced." [58]

Study of the works of the Mystical Doctor reveals the apparently paradoxical combination of clear universal principles with an ever keen sense of individual expressions. The latter cannot be reduced to one abstract type that will be valid for all souls and they are even variable for the seasons of a given person's life. Not only does the saint always presuppose differing individual expressions, but he often is at pains to make the synthesis which will comprise the whole truth. He has good reason to fear from certain spiritual fathers a rigid interpretation of principles which, on the contrary, demand so much flexibility. Even when his declaration is categorical, we must never forget his insistence that, in order to realize the ideal in all its purity, one must sometimes make use of detours. Does not God himself bend with condescension to the weakness of souls and adapt himself to their manner of being? Why should we presume to be less understanding than he? St John of the Cross is well aware that certain means, mingled as they are with the human element and laden with less than perfect factors, but proportionate to the actual needs of souls, are worth more than an absolutely pure instruction to which the individual could not adapt. Some might accuse the saint of contradicting himself: it matters little. He does not hesitate to warn his disciple against a facile simplification of his principles. In their living expression, they demand such flexibility that sometimes one might suspect that they are being denied. However, it is only a question of transposing them smoothly to the level of real life. Have we not noticed that even the essential articulations of his doctrine are not formulated in absolute terms but are accompanied by the adverb *"ordinarily,"* so weighty in actual practice? When we think that the most elementary theme of the sanjuanist itinerary, that which concerns the night of sense and the night of spirit, is itself subjected to the possibility of foreseen exceptions! The Canticle of the absolute,[59] which orders total mortification of our inordinate instinctive tendencies, appeals as if by intrinsic necessity to the two adverbs which govern its application: "operating with order and discretion."

For the same reason, the description of the different forms in which the night of sense can be concretely realized in souls takes different subjective capacities so much into account that some people have managed to be totally mistaken about the principle that clarifies these individual variations.[60] There is no question of reserving the road to contemplative union for certain souls, by virtue of some unqualified divine decree. But God is well aware that many souls respond only halfheartedly or not at all to his overtures. For his part, "He would want all to be perfect."[61] But there are too few souls who are capable of bearing the trials that he sends to lead them to perfection. For after all, he explains, there is a whole gamut with an indefinite number of nuances running from those generous souls (and clearly they are so by the grace of God) with whom the trial of the night constantly increases, to those souls who are so weak that God can at most keep them, by intermittent trials, from faults of the grossest gluttony. The same gamut is mentioned a few pages further on, based essentially on the greater or lesser generosity of souls. There are some very courageous souls. There are some very weak ones. Between the two extremes, all sorts of nuances are encountered.

But there are other factors whose influence is added to these. Many causes of variability are revealed as one observes souls. St John of the Cross is aware of the basis of individual differences, what we can simply call material causality. There is no question of denying the unchangeable character of principles (which in this case play the role of formal causality), but the principles are incarnated in living subjects and spiritual direction is concerned with particular beings. Among these factors, some belong to the supernatural history of the soul, while others arise from what we'd call purely human psychology, namely differences of character or of temperament; but it is evident that all without exception fall under predestination: "that has no measure other than the will of God," says St John of the Cross.[62] No one, to our knowledge, has ever thought of denying the primacy of divine activity, and it is simply to avoid a useless objection that we make note of this point. But on the level of human psychological analysis, natural and supernatural, we find ourselves confronted with factors that we are able to describe, thanks to information furnished by St John of the Cross. First we must take into account the point of departure of the spiritual itinerary: the night of sense certainly did not descend upon a St Thérèse of the Child Jesus in exactly the same way that it did upon a Father de Foucauld. St John of the Cross notes briefly: ". . . according to the greater or lesser amount of imperfection that must be purged from each one."[63] The divine action, and consequently the advice of the director charged with facilitating this action, are also in propor-

tion to the degree of sanctity to which God predestines each soul.
Union with God is not an absolute that can be measured quanti-
tatively like the realities described in the mathematical physics of
our contemporaries. One soul may have arrived at the fullness of
its growth before God and yet be less "large" than another. More
than once St John of the Cross refers to this relative characteristic
of the perfection of individual souls: "in the measure of the degree
of love to which God wishes to raise a soul."[64] And even if we
should presuppose a same point of departure and a same point of
arrival, the routes could be very different, in length and in
quality, according to the greater or lesser generosity of souls. "In
my Father's house are many mansions" (Jn 14:2).

After having enumerated these factors of variability that flow
from the moral order, we must take note also of those that flow
from the psychological order. Individual nuances are such that
"hardly one spirit will be found like another in even half its
method of procedure."[65]

Why should we shrink from the conclusions that flow from
this? One of these conclusions which becomes most immediately
evident is that particular applications of the immutable law must
be as nuanced as are the souls themselves. St John of the Cross
never hesitated before conclusions of this kind. We cannot
overemphasize the force of a passage too often neglected in
practice, that on which the saint—ordinarily a fierce critic of the
sensible, in that it cannot lead directly to God and also in that it
can serve to nourish a greedy sensitivity—serenely affirms that
"there are souls who are greatly moved toward God by sensible
objects."[66] In this way one not only can but should use sensible
objects: none is excluded *a priori*. This is also what happens in
souls who are totally purified, who have rediscovered the plan of
God as it was realized in the original innocence of creation before
the fall. But what the saint maintains is that certain souls, by
virtue of their natural balance and of the supernatural gifts
received from God, go to God effectively by means of the sensible.
Thus he does not hesitate to condemn directors too preoccupied
with personal security, who prefer to take refuge in an intransigent attitude, to the detriment of souls. It is clear that these souls
are the exception, but the flexibility of the saint's doctrine

deserves to be emphasized, for there is a sort of vehemence in his declarations, and history tells us to what extent he himself enjoyed the beauties of God's creation.

The sanjuanist doctrine has until now been too little studied from this angle. Is it not evident that it is in the order of material causality that the study of purely theoretical doctrine will make the most progress? Modern psychological discoveries offer immense possibilities for explanation and application of the teachings about the night. It would be quite presumptuous to neglect to develop these possibilities.

At the exhibits of the armorers of Toledo one can see swords whose blades are literally rolled into a circle. Nothing better illustrates the quality of the temper and the flexibility of the steel. One must never separate the abstract study of the principles of sanjuanist doctrine from that of individual factors of variability. For flexibility is not something added *post factum* to the tempered blade. Principles are never found in isolation or in a pure state in the real world. They are always incarnated. This same synthetic method should always prevail in the study of the practical doctrine of the ways that lead to God.

With St John of the Cross, it is precisely the combination of principles enriched with all possible understanding and perceptive consideration of their concrete conditions of realization which explains the astonishing flexibility of his doctrine.

We state the problem badly if we give the director a choice between application of principles and the welfare of souls, as if it were a matter of two opposed realities. It cannot be denied, sad to say, that many unskillful directors conceive things in this way: and this inevitably causes much harm that we would be wrong not to recognize. St John of the Cross recognized this with a sort of vehemence. One could hardly be more severe than he, and it was to remedy this situation that he wrote. The role of the spiritual master is not to impose artifically upon the soul the yoke of ready-made instructions immediately valid for all, but to lead the soul to that interior freedom of which the *Living Flame* speaks in lyric terms: "O spiritual master, guide it to the land of promise flowing with milk and honey. Behold that for this holy liberty and idleness of the sons of God, God calls the soul to the desert, in which if journeys festively clothed and adorned with gold and silver jewels, since it has now left Egypt and been despoiled of its riches, which is the sensory part. Not only this, but the Egyptians are drowned in the sea of contemplation, where the Egyptian of sense, not finding a foothold or some support, drowns and thereby frees the son of God, which is the spirit that has emerged from the narrow limits and slavery of the operation of the senses . . ."[67]

Far from keeping the man in some kind of constraint, as we do with children upon whom we are trying to impose from without the principles of hygiene and also of morality—we ought always to try to see to it that they are assimilated interiorly as rapidly as possible—the saint wants the director to keep the soul "in leisure and in repose, with peace and serenity."[68] He multiplies paraphrases, which give the thought a singular insistence. Every author betrays himself by the dominant words of his vocabulary. The vocabulary of St John of the Cross, in this regard, reveals in an astonishing fashion the supple interior workings of his direction. In what has rightly been called "a treatise of spiritual direction," there is nothing that smacks of spartan training or heroism. There is only flexibility, freedom, peaceful tranquility and interiorization.[69] With an insistence that could be judged incorrect from a strictly literary point of view, all the sternness is directed against people who are rigid in practical instructions, in *a priori* judgments considered valid for all souls. On the contrary, St John of the Cross's positive instructions tend in the direction of an overall gentleness, of putting at ease the soul who is called to live from within a doctrine of freedom and peace. The Spirit of God "is loving, tranquil, solitary, peaceful, mild, and an inebriator of the spirit, by which the soul feels tenderly and gently wounded and carried away, without knowing by whom, nor from where, nor how."[70]

We can thus better understand his lack of sympathy with blacksmiths who know only how "to hammer and pound,"[71] or with the "mass production" director spoken of by witnesses in the process of beatification, and we realize why Quiroga points out that the saint's special grace was "to pacify and quiet souls."

Direction and St John of the Cross 27

Only a person who is sure of the quality of the principles he is putting into operation and well aware of the particular needs of souls can have the boldness and flexibility of which the work and the life of St John of the Cross bear such eloquent testimony.

CONCLUSION

Step by step, following a method that is dear to those who are sincerely searching (*via intentionis,* as the scholastics of yesterday used to say), we have discovered the principal characteristics of the doctrine of St John of the Cross with regard to spiritual direction. Above all, there is the cultivation of faith which, from the beginning, imposes itself as an absolute, whether it be to define the relationship of the directee to the director or to sum up the essential content of the instructions given by the saint. It soon became evident to us, however, that we might be in danger of falling into an intransigence totally foreign to the saint's particular manner, if we were to hold too rigidly to this doctrinal line. For his life and his works show insistently the important role he attributed to material causality. St John of the Cross wants a director to be truly aware of the concrete situation, attentive to the subjective needs of souls, to their past, and to their future vocation. In everyday life the unchanging principles of doctrine always appear immersed in particular human surroundings. It is the synthesis of these two elements which makes for the solidity and the flexibility of the saint's teaching.

Reinforced by these conclusions, we would like to review rapidly what has been said in order of discovery, but this time transcribing it into a logical sequence. A partial synthesis seems possible between the findings of modern psychology and the traditional instructions furnished by a St John of the Cross, and it is this synthesis that we would like to attempt.

(a) Dr Odier has highlighted the role of a sort of pre-morality, which he also calls psychological morality.[72] It is in conformity with the data of thomistic psychology to affirm that the practice of morality normally presupposes a psychologically healthy organism. The essential function of this pre-morality is to throw light upon the true motives of our action, by an insistence upon interior honesty. Present-day psychologists show us how to arrive at what by instinct, or thanks to the clarity of their observations, the moralists of all ages have demanded, often not without bitterness. Before acting for a virtuous goal (this antecedence is logical, not chronological), one must be freed from unconscious motivations which, in fact, sometimes weigh more heavily than conscious motivations in the decisions we make. It is not by virtue of calculation but with a spontaneity of which the lives of the saints often furnish us with some precocious examples that each of us seeks to deceive himself by attributing, in a conscious manner, honorable reasons for acting; whereas in fact our decision is already made for other reasons much less honorable, or which we judge, rightly or wrongly, to be less honorable. To speak figuratively, we must remove the screens whose colored silks agreeably hide the misery of dusty corners.

St Thérèse of the Child Jesus was perhaps two years old, hardly more, when someone presented her with a tiny straw basket in which had been placed two cherries, one for her and the other for her sister Céline. Returning home, she discovered that one of the cherries had fallen out on the way. She burst into tears, "because Céline's cherry was lost." No one would accuse a two-year-old of perverse calculation. Her spontaneously proprietary nature had immediately found the solution for the disaster under the "generous" guise of sadness that she manifested over the loss endured by her sister.

(b) On the level of conscious deliberation, which is properly its own domain, classical asceticism takes on an analogous task. It is basically the same psychological rhythm which is transposed. In the (supposedly) clear area of our deliberate desires, we must jealously watch over the purity of our intentions, over our own self-denial, over the sincerity of our private or public attitude. Thus we must eliminate the inordinate affective factors which distort our judgment. All our activity, instead of being governed by egoism, must be inspired by a true altruism, whether in our love for God or in our love for others. On more or less refined levels, there is always the same work of clarification in order to achieve the same purity in the motives of our actions.

(c) And it is the same interior rhythm which is discovered in the course of the passive purifications. Here it is no longer a case of unconscious psychological dispositions, nor of work executed voluntarily with the grace of God, but of the remaking of the whole spiritual organism, simultaneously weak and impure, in order to arrive at a practice of the theological virtues that will have as little human stain as possible. To eliminate from this essentially supernatural organization whatever human (psychological) infirmity and (moral) impurity there may be;[73] to bring it about that we believe, that we hope, that we love, no longer as children of men but as children of God; to remove the obstacles which stand in the way of the development of the essential spiritual life; all this is the work that God effects directly in the soul by means of the passive purifications, as St John of the Cross describes in the night of sense and in the night of spirit. Analogically, it is the same work, no longer accomplished by the soul, but by God himself on the level of the soul's supernatural life (moreover, as St John of the Cross tells us, this work of God within us clarifies even the unconscious motivations of which we spoke initially).[74] It seems, in fact, that there are not three different mechanisms here, although the realities to which they apply are very diverse.

So the history and the doctrine of St John of the Cross allow us to affirm that his attitude as director of souls was inspired instinctively by principles which scientific research now allows us to discover through great effort. Here is an example of the first case envisioned.

A religious named John of St Ann was in anguish about predestination. The saint showed him "how all his trouble was self-love because he was not seeking in God his greatest glory and how to love him more, but his own self-interest. His thoughts showed this clearly, since he was anxious to know whether God would give him glory or would deprive him of it. He showed him that this self-love was what was weakening his faith, hope and love and was precipitating his going astray. He taught him to love God and to seek to please him in all that he did, without regard to his preoccupation on the subject of heaven or hell. By doing that, he would find heaven, because that would lead him there, and he would avoid hell, where one goes by self-love. And thus he cured him."[75]

Whereas the religious consulting him was convinced of the supernatural character of the difficulties he was experiencing, the saint placed the problem on the natural level of basic sincerity, the sincerity one must have with regard to himself. It was sufficient to point out where the true problem lay for the person to find the solution immediately. Actually, the question, when properly formulated, caused the badly formulated one to vanish.

Can we not interpret in this sense many passages in the *Ascent* where the saint refuses to resolve problems which are only errors of judgment rooted in a badly purified affectivity? Love of too humanly decorated oratories hardly concealed from his eyes a love of what glitters. The oratory was a pious pretext. Likewise for those who call *prayer* what should really be called *recreation*, i.e., time spent in some place agreeable to the senses. How many errors of judgment and of behavior flow simply from a lack of affective rectitude! Bringing to light the real terms of a problem often succeeds in dissipating pseudo-difficulties. For the basic sincerity that the saint demands is that which one must have with regard to oneself.

Classical asceticism—rethought by the saint in function of the goal that he set for himself and which greatly exceeds it— furnishes many applications of what has appeared to us as being a mechanism for clarifying our conscious desires. We should quote here the very beginning of the *Ascent of Mount Carmel* and many other texts of his doctrine as well as the life of the saint. Let us cite this exclamation, the lyricism of which is so moving:

"Ah, my Lord and my God! How many go to you looking for their own consolation and gratification and desiring that you grant them favors and gifts, but those wanting to give you pleasure and something at a cost to themselves, setting aside their own interests, are few."[76] Maxim 20, which must have been given so many times as instruction, renders exactly the same tone: "He who acts out of pure love for God, not only is unconcerned whether men see him, but does not act even so that God may know it; for even if God should not know it, he would not cease to render him the same services, with like joy and equal purity of love."[77] One of his spiritual daughters, Mary of the Blessed Sacrament, understood so well the lesson of her father that she repeated it almost verbatim in the Process of Beatification: "He taught that the one who suffers pain for God ought not to seek consolations; that if the servants of God could render great services to the divine majesty of the Lord, this would be, if possible, without God's knowing it, without expecting any response, but they would render them solely for love of him, so much would they desire that God be served only for himself."[78] Why multiply testimonies which show the intense desire of the saint for purity in our motives and in our behavior?

But the most original part of his work is that which shows the action of God in the soul taking supremacy over personal activities. For this work of moral clarification is impossible for the soul, however generous it may be, to carry out successfully by its own conscious efforts, even aided by the grace of the supernatural virtues. The passive nights have no purpose other than to eliminate from our relations with God the impurities that we would be incapable of discovering there, and *a fortiori* of purifying by ourselves. The source of the initiative changes, the rule that measures the action is no longer the same, and yet it is always a demand for deep purity which governs the steps to God himself and his action in the soul. At the end of the purifications, the soul is capable of having, in its relationships with God as well as in its relationships with its neighbor, an innocence which recalls that of the terrestrial paradise. This is total purity of a soul in which all impurity has vanished.

It seems that St John of the Cross found—thanks to this supernatural instinct from the gifts of the Holy Spirit—the right words to describe what a spiritual director should be. Modern findings of psychology explain what he simply affirmed. They show it to be well founded. Is it not a true joy for the mind to contemplate the synthesis which governs the successive attitudes of the director with regard to the soul, a synthesis as firm in its doctrinal line as it is flexible and bold, if necessary, in its applications? The disciple of St John of the Cross in spiritual direction must maintain an attitude which is found analogically identical in the first fundamental indications of psychological morality, in so-called classical asceticism, and in the course of the passive purifications. And it is important that with humble prudence those who are heirs of the Mystical Doctor seek tirelessly to preserve his authentic teaching. (Trans. C. Latimer)

NOTES

1. F, 3, 31.
2. F, 3, 59.
3. F, 3, 56.
4. F, 3, 30.
5. *Ibid.*
6. A, 2, 18, 5.
7. A, 2, 18, 6.
8. A, 2, 30.
9. A, Prologue, 4.
10. *Ibid.*
11. F, 3, 43.
12. F, 3, 55.
13. *Ibid.*
14. F, 3, 29.
15. F, 3, 62.
16. A, Prologue.
17. Maxims, Prologue, 4.
18. F, 3, 62.
19. F, 3, 46.
20. F, 3, 3.
21. F, 3, 46.
22. F, 3, 3.
23. F, 3, 1.
24. F, 3, 6.
25. F, 3, 40.
26. F, 3, 47.
27. *Ibid.*
28. F, 3, 46.
29. F, 3, 47.
30. *Ibid.*
31. Maxim 14.
32. Maxim 11.
33. Maxim 13.
34. Maxim 17.

35. Precuation "Against the Devil," 2, 12.

36. A, 2, 22, 7.

37. A, 2, 22, 11.

38. A, 2, 22, 16.

39. Marie-Michel Labourdette, "La théologie, intelligence de la foi, *Revue Thomiste*, 46 (1946), 16.

39a. EDITOR'S NOTE: See article by Teófanes Egido, *infra*, p. 130.

40. A, 2, 22, 9.

41. A, 2, 22, 12.

42. Leo XIII, *Testem Benevolentiae*, January 22, 1899.

43. A, 2, 26, 11.

44. Fr Alphonse of the Mother of God, Apostolic Process of Segovia, in *Procesos de Beatificación y Canonización*, vol. 5 of *Obras de San Juan de la Cruz* ed. Silverio de Santa Teresa (Burgos: Ed. de "El Monte Carmelo," 1931), p. 370. Hereinafter called "Procesos."

45. Fr Martin of St Joseph, Informative Process of Baeza, *Procesos*, p. 13.

46. A, 2, 18, 2.

47. *Ibid.*

48. A, 2, 18, 26.

49. C, Prologue, 2.

50. Charles Odier, *Les deux sources de la vie morale, consciente et inconsciente* (Neuchâtel: Eds. de la Baconnière, 1947), pp. 243–45.

51. Henri Chandebois, *Portrait de S. Jean de la Croix, la flûte de roseau* (Paris: Grasset, 1947), p. 126.

52. Mary of the Mother of God, Information Process of Baeza, *Procesos*, p. 36.

53. Joseph of Jesus-Mary Quiroga, *Historia de la vida y virtudes del Venerable P Fr Juan de la Cruz* (Brussels: J. Meerbeeck, 1628), Ch. 7.

54. Martin of St Joseph, Informative Process of Baeza, *Procesos*, p. 117.

55. Alonso of the Mother of God, "Vida, virtudes y milagros del santo Padre Fray Juan de la Cruz," MS 13460, Biblioteca Nacional, Madrid, Bk. 1, ch. 22.

56. Crisogono of Jesus, *Vida y obras de San Juan de la Cruz* (Madrid: B.A.C., n.d.), p. 306. EDITOR'S NOTE: the author does not indicate the edition of this classic work and so it has not been possible to provide the reference to the quote given in the English translation *Life of St John of the Cross*.

57. C, 17, 2.

58. Jean Baruzi, *S. Jean de la Croix et le problème de l'expérience mystique* (Paris: Lib. Felix Alcan, 1924), p. 272.

59. A, 1, 13.

60. N, 1, 10; also N, 1, 14.

61. F, 2, 27.

62. N, 1, 14.

63. N, 1, 14, 5.

64. *Ibid.*

65. F, 3, 59.

66. A, 3, 24, 4.

67. F, 3, 38.

68. F, 3, 34.
69. F, 3, 38.
70. *Ibid.*
71. F, 3, 43.
72. Odier, *Les deux sources*, p. 158.
73. See Lucien-Marie Florent, "A la recherche d'une structure essentielle de la nuit de l'esprit, *Etudes Carmélitaines*, 23 (1938, Oct.), 262–81.
74. N, 1, 4.
75. Cited by Baruzi, S. *Jean de la Croix et le problème* (1924 ed.), p. 298, note 2.
76. N, 2, 19, 4.
77. Maxim 27 in French Edition = Maxim 20 of *I.C.S.* ed., p. 668.
78. Mary of the Blessed Sacrament, Informative Process of Caravaca, *Procesos*, p. 205.

SPIRITUAL DIRECTION IN THE MAJOR WORKS OF ST TERESA

Pierluigi Pertusi, O.C.D.

Father Pierluigi is now a missionary in Japan and has held various teaching posts in the Discalced Carmelite Order.

S t Teresa gives us valuable teaching for the study of spiritual direction. Thanks to her remarkable gift of psychological intuition, the result of natural sharpness, her constant attention to observing the phenomena of the spiritual life, and also and especially her interior purity, she was able to penetrate to the soul's depths. I have tried to study Our Holy Mother under this aspect of teacher of psychology by looking for that knowledge she had of the psychological depths of human beings, and the derived teaching she has left us for spiritual direction. From this perspective, we shall also see her preoccupation with uncovering the subtle illusions which might or do infiltrate the whole evolution of the spiritual life: illusions which, as we know, often have their origin in the influence of the subconscious. Certain acts, certain forms of behavior which take on the appearance of virtue, or even seem to be sublime moments in the supernatural life, cannot hide their inferior origin from the sharp eye of St Teresa. She knows that the depth of our being cherishes evil tendencies; she also knows that very often a person does not succeed in discerning these tendencies, which never show their real face. "... I am

35

convinced that the devil does us less harm than our own imagination and our evil caprices, especially if there is melancholy involved. Women are naturally frail, and the self-love which influences them is very subtle. Many people have come to me, men and especially women, and I have also talked with the nuns of this monastery: how clearly I have seen that very often these people deceive themselves without wishing to!"[1]

Anyone who desires manifest proof of the intuition and the experience of St Teresa with this capacity for self-deception should read the magnificent little treatise on the "Manner of Visiting the Monasteries of the Nuns of the Order of Our Lady of Mount Carmel". What insistence that the visitor not trust what the nuns say! Certainly they do not wish to deceive; on the contrary, they are sure of themselves and want to tell the truth, but in these conversations with the visitor they are mistaken.[2] "I am amazed," notes the experienced prioress, "when I see how cleverly the devil makes each sister believe that she is telling the greatest truth in the world."[3] Nature,[4] passion, self-love[5] each has its own word to say: ". . . considering our self-love, it is very rare that we blame ourselves for our fault and recognize ourselves."[5]

Based on such a keen intuition of frequent illusions in the spiritual life, the teaching of St Teresa on spiritual direction will be welcome to modern directors, justly anxious to find a reliable road in line with the increasingly more precise conclusions of psychologists about the mistakes incited by the subconscious.

Before developing the implications of St Teresa's teaching on spiritual direction, it seems indispensable to explain what she says about illusions, taking care to note the physiological and psychological elements described; it will then pertain to psychologists to determine the influence of the subconscious on each illusion and the mechanism of each illusion through studies whose conclusions cannot but help directors. I have gathered what seemed to be the most relevant material for the following five points: manifestations of fervor, practice of virtue, melancholy, prolonged suspension of psychic activity, interior words. I do not speak of visions because that subject would require too long an explanation, and the matter has already been covered by excellent research. On each of the five points which form the first part of this study I will give a description, the psychological elements, the criterion used by the saint to distinguish illusions from reality, and the effects of these illusions—all very briefly. I shall leave for the second part and its treatment, *ex professo*, of spiritual direction, the advice St Teresa gives concerning each of these five points.

ILLUSIONS IN THE SPIRITUAL LIFE

Pseudo-Fervor

On the witness of St Teresa, manifestations of religious fervor and spiritual consolations sometimes contain elements foreign to the life of the spirit, most of the time unconscious tendencies in which the spiritual person is basically seeking, without perceiving it, his own sensible satisfaction more than the love of God.

St Teresa speaks of sensible devotion, movements of the heart that are very common, which seem to stifle the spirit; there are impetuous transports into which "natural weakness" sometimes creeps, or which "can pertain in great part to the sensory portion of the soul."[7] There are sweet sentiments which a person can attain for himself in prayer or meditation.[8] The saint has noted to what extent the spiritual person is prone to obtain for himself these sensible satisfactions. Our nature is so eager for delights that it tries everything to procure them.[9] These satisfactions closely resemble the very sentiments which earthly things excite in us. They do not open the heart, rather they tighten it. Tears burst forth, which passion seems somehow to have provoked. Temperament and sense are somewhat at the origin of it all.[10]

These sentiments may be so violent as to manifest themselves exteriorly: "Consolations in the spiritual life are sometimes mixed with our own passions (and) are the occasion of loud sobbing; and I have heard some persons say they experience a tightening in the chest and even external bodily movements that they cannot restrain. The force of these passions can cause nosebleeds and other things just as painful."[11]

Even on the subject of vehement desire for the beatific vision, which God himself enkindles in very advanced persons and which causes them a delicious torment, St Teresa notes that "a weak constitution is wont to cause these kinds of suffering, especially in the case of tender persons who will weep over every little thing. A thousand times they will be led to think they weep for God, but they will not be doing so. And it can even happen, when tears flow in abundance (I mean, that for a time every little word the soul hears or thinks concerning God becomes the cause of tears), that some humor has reached the heart thereby contributing more to the tears than does love for God . . ."[12]

According to St Teresa, many of the phenomena of the spiritual life: transports, tears, ardent desires . . . accompanied by sensible satisfaction of varying intensity, arise from causes of a non-spiritual nature. These bear the names of nature, passion, sensitivity, and sometimes exercise a causality outweighing that of the love of God, the connatural spiritual cause of the above mentioned phenomena. Since they present themselves to the person under a facade, he is easily deceived and often attributes everything to divine action or to a desire for God.

More than subtle analysis, it was observation of the effects following manifestations of fervor which allowed St Teresa to decide when these manifestations proceed from mixed causes. These impetuous transports and sweet feelings leave the head exhausted and the spirit overcome.[13] They do not open the heart but rather tighten it.[14] Soon after they have arisen in the heart the soul "is quickly left cold because however much it may desire to light the fire and obtain this delight, it doesn't seem to be doing anything else than throwing water on it and killing it."[15]

Again in the case of these psychological phenomena, St Teresa is careful to point out something very important: "You will indeed know when this fire is the source of the tears, for they are then more comforting and bring peace not turbulence, and seldom cause harm. The good that lies in the false tears—when there is any good—is that the damage is done to the body (I mean when there is humility) and not to the soul."[16] The great Spanish mystic remarks, however, that the studied intensification of these vehement desires for God may greatly injure one's health.[17]

It may also interest psychologists to know the attitude of the saint towards these phenomena. We could ask: should we absolutely refuse these manifestations of feeling which clearly show they lack a spiritual origin and are perhaps satisfying deep unconscious tendencies? Is it not that which is demanded of a pure spirit, conscious and free of subjection to any hidden tendency of the psyche?

These lines seem to offer a good resume of St Teresa's thought: "It is for these reasons sometimes that these tears flow and desires come, and they are furthered by human nature and one's temperament; but finally, as I have said, they end in God regardless of their nature. They are to be esteemed if there is the humility to understand that one is no better because of experiencing them."[18] The saint adds on the same subject further on: "The whole experience ends in the desire to please God and enjoy His Majesty's company."[19]

Consistent with herself, St Teresa does not believe we ought to reject totally sensible consolations, or free ourselves of them at all cost; it is better to treat them with a prudent moderation which precludes the injury they cause and permits their good effects. She gives the soul the following advice: to go gently about moderating the causes of the increase of this fire;[20] to accustom oneself to work interiorly by earnestly striving to avoid exterior feelings;[21] to curb gently such transports, without suffocating them, by means of some appropriate reflection;[22] to shorten one's prayer in spite of all the sweetness one finds in it, when bodily strength begins to feel it or the head to ache from it[23]—in a word, mortification. To mortify oneself even in these intense desires is good, "for mortification helps in everything,"[24] so we do not fall into illusion and always act with caution in these matters.[25]

I should like to underscore the wisdom of this advice, even from a simple psychological point of view. Mortification and a prudent fear that everything may not come from God, always accompanied by humility,[26] are the most suitable means for lessening the intensity of desire for sensible consolations, a desire which predisposes a person to illusions. This mortification and this hesitation are conducive to the reflection and vigilance over oneself, which the saint recommended so much,[27] and to having recourse to a spiritual guide. On the other hand, this mode of acting does not suppress the benefits which, according to St Teresa, may come to a person from sensible fervor, that is, a greater love and desire for God. The manifestations of sensible fervor are not really rejected, but only restrained and purified in the proper degree. Thus, as the saint says, even if their origin is some other source than the love of God, they end up in a love and desire for God, now not disguised, but authentic.

False Virtues

Another error coming from the subconscious and which, much more than pseudo-fervor, may entail serious harm to the spiritual life, consists in believing oneself virtuous when one is not; in being convinced without reason that one possesses a particular virtue. An especially dangerous error, this conviction makes one neglect the practice of virtue; even humility finally suffers from it.[28] Such a lover of solid virtue as St Teresa had her eyes open to this possibility. Here are some examples of illusions pointed out by the saint.

When certain people who are aware of their humility practice prayer, they imagine they desire to be publicly humiliated and to receive insults for love of God. Actually, it is "all imagination"; the facts reveal quite other sentiments: these persons would hide a tiny fault they have committed! And let someone charge one to them without cause, well then, God help us.[29]

But even proof to the contrary does not destroy the conviction some have that they are humble. In their eyes everything is transformed so as to leave their certainty intact: ". . . they have engaged so long in the practice of virtue they think they can teach others and that they are more than justified in feeling disturbed. . . . For everything in their minds leads them to think they are suffering these things for God . . . they canonize these feelings in their minds and would like others to do so . . . and please God they will not think their grief is for the faults of others and in their minds turn it into something meritorious."[30] They are not even capable of refusing the least mark of esteem one might give them; if necessary they will go in search of it; and yet their conviction remains intact.[31] Religious persons also know how to disguise this seeking for honor. St Teresa is thinking of scholars who, in maintaining points of honor, are deluded to the extent of believing they have a right to them, even according to God's law.[32] She is thinking of certain religious who are terribly sensitive to questions of seniority because they are provided for by law. St Teresa uncovers the real tenor of these feelings: "The fact is that since we are inclined to ascend—even though we will not ascend to heaven by such an inclination—there must be no descending."[33]

So this is how pride assumes so many different guises before people: it does not wish at any cost to call one's humility into question.

And on the subject of humility, St Teresa mentions illusions of another kind. These are different tendencies which mask themselves under the guise of humility, to which they have a certain resemblance—in order not to appear what they really are.

True humility doubtless has as its directing norm the knowledge of one's faults, since, as St Thomas says (following St Augustine), humility holds fast to truth, not to falsity.[34] St Teresa thinks—and rightly so—that we have nothing good of ourselves, that misery and nothingness are our natural lot;[35] we are even unskillful in the little we do.[36] But the saint's good sense is on the alert to recognize certain convictions in regard to one's own misery and nothingness which are not true humility; they do not spring from grace: impure in origin, they are very harmful. This kind of humility engenders faintheartedness. St Teresa is speaking specifically of persons who shelter their cowardice under the cover of humility.[37] She also points out the excessive timidity met with in certain people, and which they take for humility;[38] others baptize their fear, their cowardice and lack of courage to undertake great things with the name of humility.[39]

To distinguish true humility from counterfeits St Teresa resorts almost exclusively to examination of the effects, rather than to introspection or analysis. Humility which hinders us from desiring and undertaking great things for the Lord is false; it is cowardice.[40] True humility does not trouble the soul but floods it with peace and serenity; expands it and makes it more ready for the service of God. Far from producing these effects, false humility causes the contrary: it agitates, troubles, narrows the soul and turns everything upside down; in short, it is very painful.[41]

It is not difficult to explain the mechanism by which cowardice, excessive fear and other similar sentiments take on the appearances of humility with spiritual persons. Because these persons do not possess true humility, which is sincerity in face of one's own deficiencies—because they wish to keep a good opinion of themselves—they fear really seeing themselves. For that reason, they transform their natural cowardice, without perceiving it, into what resembles it in the spiritual life: humility.

St Teresa speaks also of false poverty: "We think we are very poor in spirit and have the habit of saying so . . . So often do we say we have this virtue that we end up believing we have it."[42] In reality, this is nothing but an illusion which, as the saint says, may last twenty years and even a lifetime. With the real virtue lacking, one easily seeks to satisfy his desire to have something at his disposal. Under the influence of the fixed conviction that one is poor, that one wishes for nothing, this desire is transformed. The object of desire becomes necessary, indispensable for one's support. "I must live to serve God; it is his Will that we support our bodies." "And," adds the saint, "join to this a thousand other reasons, which the devil, disguised as an angel of light, puts into the mind—for all this is excellent in itself. Thus he persuades a person that he is poor, that on this point there is nothing else remaining to be done."[43] But if a religious receives a gift, "it is a wonder if he judges that he does not need it."[44] St Teresa uncovers similar illusions in regard to poverty in persons of the world who claim to be virtuous.[45]

Bodily penance also furnishes matter for illusions. Some neglect it because . . . they wish to preserve their health to serve the Lord. These are the spiritual persons, orderly about everything, of whom the third mansions speak: "The penance these souls do is well balanced, like their lives. They desire penance a great deal so as to serve our Lord by it. Nothing of this is wrong . . ."[46]

On the other hand, some give themselves to excessive penance: "The devil tempts us in regard to excessive penances so that we might think we are more penitential than others and are doing something."[47] Subtle transformation of self-love of this kind is so shrewd that it wins out even when it is a matter of imposing physical pain on oneself. St Teresa told of her own case: "Once while thinking of the distress it caused me to eat meat and not do penance, I understood that sometimes my distress was more a matter of self-love than a desire for penance."[48]

St Teresa also speaks of illusory great desires for the apostolate which arise in prayer. She puts her daughters on guard against these desires and gives a shrewd psychological reason for her advice: ". . . sometimes the devil gives us great desires so that we will avoid setting ourselves to the task at hand, serving our Lord in possible things, and instead be content with having desired the impossible."[49] A clever disguise for laziness in people who want to excel in their own eyes.

In regard to solitude St Teresa points out another disguise for laziness and sensuality. She asks herself "whence comes . . . the vexation we usually feel when one or the other of these duties [obedience or charity] prevent our spending a great part of the day in deep recollection and immersed in God. . . . The first, and chief, of them is a very subtle self-love, which creeps into us in such a way that, without our perceiving it, we are seeking our satisfaction rather than that of God. So it is really evident," she notes perceptively, "that when we have begun to taste how sweet the Lord is, there is more pleasure in keeping the body at rest and the soul in spiritual joy, than in giving ourselves up to action."[50]

Another illusion, whose origin St Teresa imputes to the devil, but which may easily come from hidden tendencies, consists in being worried about the faults and sins of others. This attitude entails loss of peace and hinders the exercise of prayer; it can induce a person to interfere inopportunely, even with superiors, for the correction of the offenders.[51] Obviously all this does not proceed from a healthy source. And yet, in some way we persuade ourselves that it is virtue, perfection, zeal for the glory of God; we think in all sincerity that this worry caused by the failures of our neighbor comes solely from the desire that God be not offended, from regret at seeing him insulted.[52]

That was a whole series of illusions about virtue, capable of paralyzing the spiritual life if they are not dispelled in time. Happily, it is not impossible to recognize them.

When dealing with beautiful sentiments concerning virtue, the first rule of prudence consists in not believing, on the witness of interior dispositions, that we really possess virtues. Real virtues demand works. St Teresa often comes back to this indispensable proof of authenticity. A superficial look at our conduct is not enough; our works have to be scrutinized. A superficial look may deceive us, an attentive examination cannot.[53] And to avoid all illusion, especially in the highest degrees of the spiritual life, St Teresa wishes us to examine ourselves in even the smallest things.[54] She is convinced that, by acting in this way, we shall see the revelation of the true contours of our works. Even if we see in ourselves the works of virtue, it is better that we always maintain a certain mistrust: "The truly humble person," says St Teresa, "always walks in doubt about his own virtues."[55]

The saint gives another counsel which is always useful: to avoid all illusion, we must choose a capable guide, who is not in illusion himself. We shall throw more light on this point in the second part of this study.

Melancholy

One of the best known and most frequent cases of illusion, in which the subconscious plays a great role, is melancholy. St Teresa examines this case thoroughly; she often met and advised men and women attacked by this evil.[56]

Here are the observations of the Holy Reformer on the nature of this evil: in general it strikes people whose imagination is weak.[57] Melancholy, St Teresa says, forms and builds chimeras in the imagination;[58] its chief effect is the weakening of the reason: "Sometimes the evil is so violent that it entirely takes away the use of reason. . . . But there are those in whom this faculty is weakened, but not extinguished . . . intermittently they are even sound in mind."[59]

The obscuring of reason and preponderance of imagination bring on a mania for doing their own will in everything. ". . . these people," says St Teresa, "are especially inclined to doing what they please, to saying whatever comes into their head, to exposing others' faults which will cover up their own, to having their own way everywhere. In a word, they are people who have no self-control."[60] Sometimes they really do not have the strength to control themselves; but then it is not lack of strength that hinders them, but some fault. In this illness one risks getting used to acting without control, even in the healthy intervals.

Characteristic of the malady is great cunning; when necessary it can play dead. Great is its ingenuity to carry out its caprices. As we have already seen, St Teresa admits there are many degrees of it. Not everyone infected with it is equally difficult and dangerous; if they are humble and gentle, they do not harm anyone.[61]

The coexistence of virtue with melancholy shows well the limits of the latter. St Teresa knew many persons "who have almost entirely lost their reason, but are humble and who dread offending God so much that, in spite of the torrents of tears which they shed in secret, they never swerve from what they are told to do. They bear their sickness as others put up with bodily illnesses. Their martyrdom is harder, and so their glory will be greater in heaven." Humility and obedience, fear and love of God alone,[62] suffice to curb these sick people.

A correct diagnosis of melancholy should also take account of the great harm it causes. First of all, the patient's torment is a real purgatory, as the saint says: ". . . these persons suffer interiorly a very painful and very meritorious death in consequence of their desolations, their fantasies, their scruples. . . ." If the illness is not taken care of in time, they will lose their minds entirely.[63]

The most serious harm is spiritual, both to the sick person and to his community. Melancholy destroys the whole edifice of perfection; the devil uses it to seize power over souls and make them follow their passions without control. The very eternal salvation of these sick people may be at stake. If such people live in community, it takes only one of them to disturb a whole monastery, says St Teresa, speaking of women's monasteries. Besides, the illness is contagious: "Nuns who are well may imagine—so miserable is our nature—that they too are infected with melancholy, and so people should put up with everything from them."[64]

Such are the descriptive details which St Teresa gives on the nature and effects of melancholy. She deals at greater length with the treatment to apply to this sickness—something we shall speak about in the second part.

Prolonged "Suspension"

Another psychological phenomenon which St Teresa noticed and in which the subconscious can have a considerable part, consists in certain deep suspensions, common with many good people when they receive the favor of some sweetness in prayer.

These persons feel themselves captivated by the least exercise of piety and they give in at once to the feeling that is overcoming them. So they remain absorbed for seven or eight hours, in the most serious cases.[65] The body is seized, but the will, the memory and the understanding are not at all so. Still, their activity lacks all control. Some people, without being subject to this kind of fainting, allow their imagination to concentrate too much, even upon aspects of highest prayer. If they have had some vision or received some extraordinary grace, they believe they are constantly seeing an object which they have seen only once, or continually feeling the presence of a grace that is completely past.[66]

In St Teresa's judgment, these phenomena have their roots in a great desire to enjoy in every possible way the pleasure which accompanies spiritual graces. When they concern people of weak constitution and of a tenacious temperament or imagination which foster this desire, they cling with all their might to the object, even a spiritual one, which causes sensible pleasure, and remain totally absorbed in it.[67]

Here are some quotations from the saint: ". . . this sweetness surpasses all the pleasures of the world. Now suppose there is question of a person of weak constitution and whose mind, or rather imagination, is not versatile, but who, once he has begun to study a subject, continues his study and never seeks distraction. It will be with her as with many people who, when they think of something, even something unrelated to God, stay completely absorbed, or, thinking of a thing, pay no attention to what is under their very eyes: these are indolent natures, who get distracted and don't seem to know what they were going to say. This is a little of what happens in the state I am speaking of, according to the different characters, temperaments and degrees of weakness. If melancholy comes in along with this, oh: then it will fill the imagination with a thousand pleasant illusions."[68] Excessive penance, lack of food and sleep predispose a person to these suspensions. Those exhausted by penance "have no sooner begun to taste the sensible sweetness of love than they surrender themselves up to it entirely," we read in the *Foundations*.[69] In a more general way, St Teresa adds: "If there is a weak constitution involved, that is enough for the transport of spirit to overcome and captivate it."[70] Nature remains overcome by the spiritual consolations.[71]

The following text is especially complete: "Since they feel some consolation interiorly and a languishing and weakness exteriorly, they think they are experiencing a spiritual sleep . . . and they let themselves become absorbed."[72]

The bad effects of this absorption are considerable. In the first place, no spiritual profit, wasted time: in this state, works cannot be meritorious. Then, if the person does not try to prevent the repetition of these suspensions, he risks losing his health and slowly causing his death or at least losing his mind.[73]

The opinion of psychologists on these phenomena should be of extreme interest to spiritual directors. Without a doubt, St Teresa's explanations admit of further clarification from both the physiological and psychological point of view.

Interior Words

What does St Teresa say of interior words attributed to God under an illusion that prevents a person from recognizing in them the fruit of his own psychic activity?

People subject to this phenomenon assert that they see, hear, understand.[74] Actually, it is failings of the imagination that are deceiving them. According to St Teresa, interior words may also come simply from the mind as it stirs up its activity in an intense desire for extraordinary graces.[75] There may be other causes hidden from us.[76] "A person could be recommending something to God with great feeling and intensity and think he understands something about whether it will be done or not. . . ."[77] Such a person is like one who composes little by little what he wants to hear said.[78]

In the *Life*, St Teresa manifests the conviction that the spiritual person always knows when he is the author of pseudo interior words: "If they are something the intellect [imagination?] fabricates, no matter how subtly it works, a person will know that it is the intellect that is composing something and speaking. The difference is that in the one case the words are composed and in the other they are listened to. The intellect will see that it is not then listening because it is working."[79] In the *Interior Castle*, on the other hand, St Teresa seems to admit the possibility of a sincere conviction on the part of the person who says he really hears and sees something.[80]

Psychologists could greatly clarify this problem of interior words; their studies would be very appropriate in these times when entire books of interior words are published—words whose supernatural origin seems to be entirely reliable.

I shall not stop to add the signs which distinguish true words from false. These signs are found together in chapter 25 of the *Life*.

DIRECTION

The preceding treatment sought to bring to light St Teresa's profound knowledge of illusions in the spiritual life. An analysis of all her works would multiply instances of this knowledge. There is no psychic phenomenon along the way of perfection about whose origins St Teresa did not wonder: whether it comes from God, from virtue, or, on the contrary, whether it is a deception of the devil, or, simply a product of the lower psychic forces. The great mystic of Avila never loses sight of the influence of these forces in describing the whole spiritual life, and, consequently, in her advice for spiritual direction.

I intend to examine spiritual direction according to St Teresa precisely under this aspect. For brevity's sake, the study embraces only the essential points; besides, as has been said, we have the good fortune of possessing a complete study of spiritual direction according to St Teresa in the fine book *I Want To See God* by Fr Marie-Eugène (II, ch. 8).

I shall speak of the need for direction, of the behavior of the penitent in direction, of the qualities of the director and of the way he should deal with the penitent: all envisaged in relation to illusions and the influence of the subconscious.

Need for Direction

To prove the need for spiritual direction, St Teresa stresses especially the two following reasons: the need of knowing oneself perfectly, as one is before God, and the need to proceed in everything as God's will requires by leaving aside one's own will. The depths of the subconscious are hidden from us and their influence makes matters of conscience appear to us under a false light. As a result, it is impossible for us to direct ourselves according to objective reality or conformably to the real will of God.

Naturally, this need of spiritual direction admits of degrees according to individuals and the phases of the spiritual life. Women are more easily deceived than men and for that reason have more need than they for direction. Direction becomes strictly necessary when the spiritual life presents extraordinary phenomena. But a certain spiritual direction is necessary at every stage of the spiritual life and for every individual, if he really wishes to advance toward perfection. The primary need to escape from the detrimental influence of the subconscious is the basis of this general necessity for direction.

We can see how St Teresa proved the great benefit of spiritual direction in the marvelous 5th chapter of the *Foundations*. The saint wishes to explain to us that obedience is the shortest way and the most effective means for arriving at perfect conformity to the will of God, a conformity equivalent to perfection: "We are not masters of our own will so as to be able to employ it entirely for God, until we have subjected it to reason." Now, St Teresa sees the insurmountable difficulty which the subconscious opposes to this subjection: by ourselves we shall not reach it; obedience alone can lead us to such control of our will. "It is not by the help of nice reasoning that we reach it," we read in the *Foundations*: "our nature and our self-love are so inventive in this area that we shall never attain it. In fact very often the most reasonable thing looks like folly to us because we have no desire to do it. I should never finish if I had to describe here the struggles that go on within us and all that the devil, the world and our sensuality raise up against us, to make us turn from right reason." Another person can see clearly more easily than we can in this struggle between the requirements of the will of God and the reasons formulated by a mind clouded by unknown influences. In the case of spiritual direction, taking his superior or confessor as arbitrator, a person may also trust in these words of our Lord: "He who hears you hears me." Surrendered into the hands of his director, he no longer has to fear that the deceits of "nature" and "self-love will influence his decisions." [81]

We find the same reasoning in the *Third Mansions* teaching prompt obedience in spiritual matters. Certain people who are extremely structured in all their activities and to whom the Lord had granted and is granting his consolations, seem particularly prone to believe themselves in possession of true virtues. To know themselves well and really give themselves to the practice of virtue, they must obey a director. "And even if they are not members of a religious order, it would be a great thing for them to have—as do many persons—someone whom they could consult so as not to do their own will in anything. Doing our own will is usually what harms us. And they shouldn't seek another of their own making, as they say—one who is so circumspect about everything; but seek out someone who is very free from illusion about the things of the world. For in order to know ourselves, it helps a great deal to speak with someone who already knows the world for what it is."[82]

In St Teresa's thought, then, obedience to a director is an effective means of gradual liberation from illusions and from the influence of the subconscious: a person thereby comes to know himself as he really is and to act with full freedom of spirit.

The Role of the Directee

For direction to bear its fruits of light and liberation, a person has to know how to practice it. I shall limit myself to showing how St Teresa taught others, and practiced herself, extreme openness in direction. "Reveal to your superior and to your confessor all your temptations, your imperfections and your repugnances."[83] This openness should be absolute, and should be practiced with candor and simplicity.[84] "I have never heard anyone say that there can be anything better than obeying the confessor in everything and not hiding anything from him." "What is necessary, Sisters, is that you proceed very openly and truthfully with your confessor. I don't mean in regard to telling your sins, for that is obvious, but in giving an account of your prayer. If you do not give such an account, I am not sure you are proceeding well, nor that it is God who is teaching you. He is very fond of our speaking as truthfully and clearly to the one who stands in his place as we would to him and of our desiring that the confessor understand all our thoughts and even more our deeds however small they be."[85] St Teresa is here speaking of people who are very advanced; in order to judge the extraordinary graces which they receive, their director has to be able to rely on an openness that is perfectly exact. But the advice is proportionately applicable to all states. St Teresa herself always acted in this way, at least from the time when she had directors: "I always tried to speak with complete clarity and truthfulness to those with whom I conversed about my soul. I desired that they know even about any first stirrings, and I accused myself of matter that was doubtful and questionable with arguments against myself."[86]

It is not necessary to emphasize to what extent the practice of this advice is apt to unveil the influence of the subconscious in the spiritual life. When a person manifests all his thoughts, and, as far as possible, even his first stirrings; when he gives an account of his works, "even the smallest", in the long run everything hidden deep in the soul comes to full view. And the director, on the strength of this knowledge, is in a position to interpret the person's behavior and to show him the way to go.

The directee, in turn, must make up his mind to follow the advisements of obedience at any cost. The subconscious does not cease to exert its influence upon the speculative judgment just because we commit ourselves to obedience. St Teresa foresees the interior struggle that must be waged not to depart from the direction received: ". . . now entirely annihilating our own desires, now the direction received: winning only after a thousand battles, and thinking the judgment given in our case to be folly, we shall come, by means of this painful exercise, to resign ourselves to doing what we are commanded. We shall do it in the end, whether it costs us pain or not . . ." And St Teresa gives such submission its proper name: not abdication of personality, nor slavery, but liberation and self-mastery. The person gains control of himself, becomes fully master of his mind and will, and in future is beyond the influence (unconscious but real and tyrannical) of hidden tendencies.[87]

To escape the snares of these lower forces, women religious have, besides, a very effective means at their disposal: openness with the superior or novice mistress. I speak of sisters as more easily exposed to illusions; but the same is proportionately true for religious men. With reason, St Teresa has insisted very much on this point (see *Const.*, chap. 14: How the nuns should behave in fulfilling their duties), and it is with much wisdom that new constitutions of the Discalced Carmelites have repeated and emphasized it. It is only too evident that community life promotes extremely well our knowledge of people. Openness in direction alone obviously cannot give the director complete knowledge of the person, as modern schools of characterology, biotypology and psychoanalysis intend to; such knowledge, without being absolutely indispensable, is nonetheless very useful for understanding people's behavior. St Teresa had the intuition that this was so, and, besides advising the sisters to be open with the prioress, she wished the latter to make a study of each one's temperament and life, so as to know each one thoroughly. "We may conclude from these examples and from many others, how useful it is for each nun to make her prayer entirely known to the prioress. For her part, the prioress should examine very carefully the temperament and the virtue of the sister, and inform the confessor of it, so that he may be able to judge with greater certainty."[88] Certainly the intervention of the prioress with the confessor is a very delicate matter and repugnant to our mentality. But it remains true that candid openness with the superior, the daily witness of the conduct of the subjects whose temperament he studies, obtains abundant light for getting to know ourselves, light which will then show up in our manner of dealing with the confessor: we shall be more sincere, more objective in speaking of personal matters.

Qualities Required of the Director

According to St Teresa, the director must have the following qualities to obtain deep knowledge of a soul: good judgment, some experience, adequate training.[89] A good acquaintance with psychology, which takes into account nature's possibilities, as well as some solid theology, which knows how to appreciate the efficacy of grace in the psychological life, are also valuable in a director.

Following St Teresa we must emphasize fully another quality demanded of a director for perfect knowledge of the penitent: sanctity, along with an indispensable detachment from created things. St Teresa counsels this very thing to persons who wish to know themselves well and not allow themselves to be caught by the mirage of their own reasonings, to choose a director "free from illusions about the things of this world."[90] Interior purity, the fruit of detachment, seems to be the best disposition for understanding what is confided to him, without allowing himself to be imposed upon by the directee's words. As we said at the beginning, there is no doubt we owe St Teresa's inspired psychological intuitions not only to her natural perceptiveness and her penetrating mind, but to her great interior purity.

A close connection exists, it seems to me, between this purity and that gift of discernment of spirits which St Teresa often mentions. This gift perhaps does not always signify a true grace *gratis data*; sometimes it seems to indicate a natural gift of psychological intuition which experience and, above all, great interior purity have sharpened.

Behavior of the Director in Regard to the Directee

The need for the director's vigilance in the matter of illusions is clearly shown by the preceding remarks. St Teresa's teaching illustrates splendidly this principle of spiritual direction. The greater a person's progress in prayer, the stronger is St Teresa's concern that he avoid illusions. The Mother of Spirituality ("Mater Spiritualium") has a passion for walking and enabling others to walk in the truth. Truth here is to mean not only the exclusion of all duplicity and hypocrisy—which is obvious; but also in the sense of excluding even unconscious illusions, as for example taking for humility what is basically nothing but cowardice, etc. An act which proceeds unconsciously from the depths of the psyche does not constitute a sin, it may even be meritorious in the eyes of God; but the continuance of mistaken conduct, the persistence of an error of judgment affecting the spiritual life is bound at least to hinder the soul's progress.

Hence the need that the director, if he does not wish to fall into illusion, be alert and know how to discern the effects of grace from manifestations of deep natural tendencies, tendencies perhaps too much repressed, which have had to be modified, transformed, disguised, even under the most specious spiritual forms in order to come to the surface. In this discernment, the director, as we saw above, can base himself upon the openness of the penitent and an attentive examination of his actions.

Once the influence of forces alien to the spiritual life has been discovered, the advice St Teresa gives for different cases will guide the director in the practical judgment he ought to make. It is not a matter of always eliminating at any cost the influence which has been uncovered, but of using it, if possible, to lead a life that is more virtuous and more united to God.

Thus, for example, faced with transports of sensible fervor, the saint advises simply modifying them, as we have seen in the first part—allowing them to go on, since they may do good. Purification will come in its own time.

As for illusions that concern virtue, the case is different: these are dangerous. It belongs to the director to disillusion the penitent, by inducing him (according to St Teresa's advice) not to set so much value on his own thoughts and desires, and to test himself by his works.

With melancholy, the case is still more complex. It is worth the effort of following the saint's advice in detail. The best remedy for people afflicted with melancholy is to keep them busy with duties so that their imagination has no leisure to work itself up. Also one should shorten their prayer-time, forbid them to fast, have them eat fish only rarely. Medicine is an option, but St Teresa does not seem to have had great confidence in the rudimentary medicine of her day: "From time to time medicine may be used to relieve this humor and make it more bearable."[91]

The saint is categorical about how to deal with the sick person: the sister afflicted with melancholy must *give up her whims*. To obtain this result, gentleness is to be used, and, if that does not suffice, severe commands: ". . . they must understand well that they are not going to follow their whims, and that in no way will they be allowed to follow them when the time comes to obey." If she wishes to attain her end, the prioress should behave with great love, like a true mother, but without allowing the sick sisters to perceive it. "Tenderness and skill" will "easily" obtain submission.[92]

Sometimes, the saint knows by experience, good manners are not enough. Then recourse must be had to all possible means to reduce the sick ones to submission; going on even to applying the severest punishments, including confinement. This particular remedy, among many others adopted, is, according to St Teresa, the most effective way to save these people who remain untouched by any loving remedy.[93]

I should like to stress the saint's observations concerning the influence of the will in crises of melancholy. In many cases the will is free to some extent and the person is responsible for the evil done; on the other hand, for an honest and virtuous person melancholy can be a source of great merit. This gives an indication of what directors have to instil in these sick people. A serious effort of the will is demanded so as not to offend God and to progress in doing good. St Teresa insistently exhorts the melancholic individuals to be humble and obedient, to fear and love God.[94] It comes spontaneously to mind to ask psychologists whether this effort of the will also has a therapeutic effect on melancholy.

We would ask them the same question in regard to the attitude to take toward melancholic people, as St Teresa indicates. I mean especially the vigor the saint calls for to prevent, by necessary threats and punishments, the faults the sickness brings on. Is this manner of treating the sick solely a means of preventing very great evils, especially in community life, or can it be also part of a specific remedy for the disease?[95]

The advice of psychologists may also help directors on the other two points examined in the first part: suspensions and interior words. St Teresa's advice can be summed up in a few words. It is possible to resist prolonged absorptions, and a person must do all that he can to distract himself and not allow himself to be deceived. People subject to these suspensions should be occupied with duties which distract them. In case of weakness, penance and fasting must be forbidden and more food and sleep ordered.[96]

As to interior words, St Teresa thinks that they can be eliminated easily; all that is needed is not to make much of them and not sustain a desire for them.[97] With melancholic individuals, the best remedy is always to keep them "as busy as possible" so that they pay no attention to what they believe they hear.[98]

The task of directors is to point out to souls the safe path to follow; to fulfill this duty they will find firm support in St Teresa's advice.

She places great trust in directors. She never ceased urging strict obedience to the spiritual father as the most fitting means to avoid illusions and comply with the will of God. When this

obedience and real concern not to offend God is present the saint
wishes us to act with all confidence and peace.[99] To people who
believe they are in some mystical state, but do not show the signs
characteristic of it, she says: "If one proceeds with humility,
strives to know the truth, is subject to a confessor, and communicates with him openly and truthfully, it will come about . . . that
the things by which the devil intends to cause death will cause
life, however many the haunting illusions he wants to scare you
with."[100] In the saint's thought, the effectiveness of this spiritual
attitude is not limited to illusions of diabolical origin, but
extends to all illusions.

This openness of conscience with the director and with superiors is really at the heart of the teaching St Teresa has left us on
how to thwart the subtle illusions of our subconscious. It seems to
me that it is above all by fidelity to this Teresian doctrine of
spiritual direction that Carmel has produced and continues to
produce a whole line of souls who are spiritually complete and
completely balanced.

It is for directors to make themselves worthy of the confidence
St Teresa places in them and to acquire the qualities she wishes to
see in a good director, especially purity of life and genuine
knowledge of the depths of God and the depths of the soul. St
Teresa, who so loved learning, would have watched with satisfaction the present-day progress of psychology. She, who already
called on the rudimentary medicine of her time in pathological
cases, would certainly have taken advantage of the scientific
conclusions that have been really established and proved useful
for the spiritual life.

It is with the same breadth of view and the same desire for truth
that we ask of the humane sciences the light to penetrate more
deeply into the psyche. (Trans. K. Kirk)

NOTES

1. F, 4, 2.
2. *Method for the Visitation of Monasteries of Discalced Carmelite Nuns*, par.
54, *Peers*, pp. 240; and passim.
3. *Method*, par. 53, Peers, p. 254.

4. *Method*, par. 5, *Peers*, p. 240.
5. *Method*, par. 51, p. 254.
6. *Ibid*.
7. L, 29, 9.
8. C, 4, 1, 4.
9. L, 15, 4.
10. C, 4, 1, 6.
11. C, 4, 2, 1.
12. C, 6, 6, 7.
13. L, 29, 9.
14. C, 4, 1, 5.
15. L, 15, 4.
16. C, 6, 6, 8.
17. *Ibid*.
18. C, 4, 1, 6.
19. C, 4, 2, 1.
20. L, 29, 9.
21. L, 29, 12.
22. W, 19, 10.
23. W, 19, 13.
24. W, 19, 10.
25. C, 6, 6, 6.
26. C, 4, 1, 6.
27. W, 19, 11.
28. W, 38, 8 and C, 5, 3, 9.
29. C, 5, 3, 10.
30. C, 3, 2, 1, 3 and 5.
31. W, 38, 1 (note of Escorial MS).
32. W, 36, 4.
33. W, 36, 5.
34. *Summa Theologica*, IIa-IIae, q. 161, a.3 ad 2um.
35. C, 6, 10, 7.
36. W, 18, 1.
37. L, 13, 2.
38. W, 28, 3.
39. C, 1, 2, 11.
40. *Ibid*.
41. W, 39, 2.
42. W, 38, 9.
43. W, 38, 9 (note of Escorial MS).
44. *Ibid*.
45. C, 3, 2, 1-7.
46. C, 3, 2, 7.
47. W, 39, 3. See C, 1, 2, 11.
48. Relation 57 = Spiritual Testimony No. 62 (Toledo, early 1577), I.C.S. ed., p. 362.

49. C, 7, 4, 14.
50. F, 5, 4.
51. C, 1, 2, 16.
52. W, 38, 6.
53. *Ibid.*
54. C, 6, 9, 12.
55. W, 38, 9.
56. F, 7, 4; 4, 2.
57. F, 7, 9.
58. C, 6, 2.
59. F, 7, 2.
60. F, 7, 3.
61. F, 7, 4.
62. F, 7, 2.
63. F, 7, 5.
64. F, 7, 10.
65. F, 7, 6.
66. F, 6, 2.
67. F, 6, 6. See C, 4, 3, 11 ff.
68. F, 6, 2.
69. *Ibid.* See C, 4, 3, 11.
70. F, 6, 3.
71. C, 4, 3, 11.
72. *Ibid.*
73. F, 6, 12.
74. C, 6, 3, 2.
75. C, 6, 7; 9, 9. Also L, 25, 1.
76. C, 6, 3, 6.
77. L, 25, 3.
78. C, 6, 3, 10.
79. L, 25, 3.
80. C, 6, 3, 3.
81. F, 5, 11.
82. C, 3, 2, 12.
83. Maxim 18.
84. W, 39, 3; 40, 4.
85. C, 6, 9, 12.
86. L, 30, 3.
87. F, 5, 7.
88. F, 8, 9.
89. L, 5, 3; 13, 14; C, 5, 1, 8; C, 6, 8, 8 and 9, 11.
90. C, 3, 2, 12.
91. F, 7, 8.
92. F, 7, 9.
93. F, 7, 4.
94. F, 7, 5.

95. For persons led by deep faith and still capable of human acts the obsolete remedy of monastic emprisonment (a sometimes effective treatment by isolation before application of biological methods) would have been the equivalent of a healthy "affective shock" spoken of by Prof. Lhermite. The sharp observations of St Teresa, whose fermness as Reformer was joined to her goodness as *Madre*, should prove interesting to chaplains of psychiatric and penal institutions and should be read in their entirety by them.

96. F, 6, 5.

97. C, 6, 3, 4.

98. C, 6, 3, 2.

99. C, 6, 6, 2.

100. W, 40, 4.

SPIRITUAL DIRECTION IN THE LETTERS OF ST TERESA

Marcel Lépée

Marcel Lépée draws upon his qualified knowledge of St Teresa to write this article. He published another article on "St Teresa and the Devil" in the famous volume Satan *of the series "Etudes Carmélitaines."*

S t Teresa's ideas and advice on spiritual direction,[1] such as they are found in her main works, were suggested to her by her own observations, by her personal life story and by the discussions of her time.

The confidences of her friends[2] and her daughters made clear for her what everyone knows and what she more than anyone else had occasion to learn: while there are excellent directors, there are also very mediocre ones. She could cite names and recount more than one anecdote, as she does, about imperious directors who "pen up" souls like cattle, directors who are too compassionate and always ready to justify weakness, careless directors who allow a person made to soar to go on at "a snail's pace," fearful directors whom the least mystical state baffles and who see the devil everywhere.

Furthermore, she judges what happens to others by what has happened to herself. A woman of uncompromising sincerity, she had made her own the honesty she so admired in her father; she detests any form of falsehood. And she is courageous. God had called her while she was still very young and drawn her by his grace, so that she should have radiantly risen straight toward him as a result. Instead, what delays, what fruitless efforts, hesitation, anguish! She now sees well that she had to struggle not only against the world and the devil, but against herself, against everything in her that feared being sacrificed if it appeared in full daylight and which, to avoid death, tried to keep her soul in a "fatal shadow": how she needed a good judge and a good guide! And she remembered the time when she didn't even have a director; she remembered those confessors who, far from pointing out to her what God expected from her love, calmed her remorse over serving him poorly by soft words and easy solutions. She remembered second-rate directors who did not see into her state very well and pronounced precipitously on mystical disturbances and especially the visions which her good judgment feared: some said "this is all from God and you have nothing to be afraid of"; others cried that "this is all from the devil and you must repel the image of the Lord with a scornful gesture." She also remembered the energetic Vincent Barrón, who had caused her to make such rapid progress; the Jesuits Cetina and Pradanos, whose advice had been so prudent; Francis Borgia and Peter of Alcantara, who really understood and reassured her; Balthasar Alvarez who, though he had scruples and doubts, defended her against hostile murmuring and did not mortify her except to make her will more flexible; and finally the very learned Ibañez and Dominic Bañez, so skilled in distinguishing the essential from the accessory, who placed her with such a firm hand in the presence of the "Truth."

St Teresa applied these examples and these memories to the lively discussion then going on between the "spirituals" and the learned. Who should direct people of prayer whom God called to the mystical life? Men "of experience," claimed one side, the mystics, for only they who have had to beware of the same dangers, to practice the virtues in the same degree, to undergo the same states, are prepared to understand them. Theologians, according to the other side, teachers, for God destines them to give his Church light and grants them the graces necessary to do so; men "of experience" are only the blind leading the blind. Just observe what goes on; think of those little groups of over-excited women who gather about some visionary "beata," or of those religious simpletons, more directed than directors, who unconsciously lead people to the Inquisition with the cool assurance of blissful ignorance. After some hesitation which is visible in the *Life* (written in two or three drafts), St Teresa, as can be seen in the *Castle*, took the side of the learned, that is, the authorized interpreters of God's word. "In spite of all this, she was not without fears at times," she writes to Rodrigo Alvarez, "and it seemed to her that spiritual people could be deceived as well as she. She wanted to speak with very learned men, even though they might not be given to prayer, for she only wanted to know whether all her experiences were in conformity with Sacred Scripture."[3] The best director is the great theologian, provided he is virtuous. If he does not practice prayer, he will perhaps come to it, drawn by his directee; and if he practices it, that is all that is necessary.

St Teresa bore in mind this past with its stock of observations and reflections in the last years of her life,[4] when she wrote to inexperienced young prioresses, to Gratian as visitator or provincial, and to her friends, to bring up the subject of spiritual direction. But she also had the cares of foundress and had to answer concrete questions. Hence the double value of her correspondence on this point.

TERESA ON DIRECTION AND DIRECTORS

It goes without saying that the Holy Mother wanted good confessors for her convents. "May it please God to preserve (the then current confessor) for us for many years," she writes from Malagón to Louise de la Cerda. "With him here, I can leave without any worry."[5] A little later, she experienced the fruitful influence of St John of the Cross at the Incarnation. And she declares to Gratian in regard to the monasteries where the Discalced nuns were being asked to bring the Reform: "What would help most in this case is good confessors . . . You must work hard on this point . . . If you show yourself strict about exterior matters and the sisters have no one to support them interiorly, they will have much to suffer. That is what I noticed myself till the day when they gave us Discalced Fathers for confessors at the Incarnation."[6] In 1571, she was received at the Incarnation in an uproar; in 1577, her daughters there defied excommunication by the Mitigated for reelecting her prioress, and when a little later there was mention of imposing that office upon her, she exclaimed: "I will do everything possible to avoid it; without the (former) confessors it would be foolish to accept."[7]

Each convent should have several confessors available: "The Father Provincial[8] does not want the sisters to go always to the same confessor, and that does not seem good to me either."[9] In this instance the father provincial was merely the foundress' mouthpiece; and the proof is that in 1581 she reminded him: "I know what terrible torments they endure in other monasteries where their freedom for the spiritual life is too constrained; a person so bound up could hardly serve God well; that is a temptation of the devil for her."[10] The Constitutions of Alcalá conform to her thinking, perhaps rather timidly, when they prescribe that the prioress may have recourse for her convent to extraordinary confessors, "Discalced Carmelites or religious of another Order," even outside the three occasions a year "permitted by the Council of Trent."[11]

It is the saint herself who appoints the confessors when she founds a house. Thereafter the choice belongs to the prioress, even if it means rendering an account. St Teresa considers it "an extravagance" for the confessor to name his own successor;[12] really a dangerous abuse, this would make the confessor the owner of his office. Should preference be given to the Carmelite Friars of the Reform? At first the saint thought not. A decision of Gratian's, which she rated excellent, after prescribing that each house have "four or five" confessors named by him, adds that the fathers, "avoiding all conversation with women, are not to be confessors for the Discalced Nuns."[13] And such seems to have been St. Teresa's wish: "The sisters are all young and, believe me, my Father, the safest thing is for them not to have contacts with the fathers. There is nothing I am so much afraid of in our monasteries."[14] And again: "Take precautions that wherever there is a monastery of the fathers none of them goes to disturb the sisters."[15]

Perhaps the rule was not absolute.[16] In 1579 we see Madre Teresa appealing to the Carmelite Fathers of the Reform for spiritual direction for two troubled monasteries. She entrusts Malagón to Fr Philip, who accepted only with reluctance. And she wrote to Mary of St Joseph, prioress of Seville: "The Father Vicar General[17] has ordered the Discalced Carmelite Fathers to hear your community's confessions."[18] "I limit myself to asking one thing: that you and your sisters have as little as possible to do with anyone else than the Discalced Carmelite Fathers for the spiritual direction of your souls . . . Assuming that from time to time the community or some sister may wish to speak to others than our Fathers, do not oppose it."[19] "Do not allow her to confess to anyone but the Fathers of the Order."[20] These instructions are confirmed by a letter to Nicholas Doria, who was then at Seville: "In case some sister wishes to confess to some other priest than the ordinary confessor, she should be allowed to do so. But take care to appoint him; one from the convent of Our Lady of Los Remedios, whomever you wish."[21] It is not surprising, then, that the Constitutions of Alcalá authorize choosing confessors from among the Carmelites of the Reform,[22] nor that in 1582 St Teresa called Fr Philip to Burgos.

Besides, Madre Teresa had had painful experiences. In several of her monasteries confessors full of good will, but busying themselves in what did not concern them, had caused serious unrest. For example at Seville, Garciálvarez had naively supported two Carmelites in their mania for denouncing others; at Malagón, Gaspar de Villanueva had seconded a cabal against the interim superior; at Avila, the good—even too good—Julian had tried to make the rule easier. The authority of confessors had to be limited to prevent their abusing their office.

"Please determine once and for all that the vicars[23] for the nuns should not be their confessors; I insist on this point; it is a very important thing for our monasteries. Profitable as it may be for the sisters to go to confession to our Father, as Your Paternity says and as I myself am aware it is, I would prefer that they be unable to do so and that things remain as they are, to seeing each confessor become the vicar of the monastery." The "superior" should not be at the same time the nuns' confessor: "There are serious disadvantages in the places where this is the case, as I have found; and just one of these which I have seen very clearly has been enough [to convince me of this]."[24]

The holy Mother did not like a confessor to remain in office too long. "God deliver me from these confessors to whom they go for many years!"[25] She did not even like too frequent or too lengthy interviews. Anne of Jesus, an energetic prioress whose strong personality was governed only by St John of the Cross, had reduced things to a minimum in her convent. Teresa tells Mary of St Joseph about it: "The prioress of Beas writes me that the sisters of her monastery have only one confessor to whom they tell nothing but their sins, and that they all make their confessions in a half-hour; she adds that that is the way it ought to be everywhere."[26] Doubtless that was going too far; but the saint had not a word of blame (it is true that at Seville, with Mary of St Joseph, they had fallen into the opposite extreme) and she writes to Gratian four years later: "The most outstanding blessing the sisters can be given is not to allow the confessor to have anything to do with them except to hear their sins; in regard to looking out for recollection [in the monastery], the confessors' whole role is to warn the provincials."[27] "Frequent conversations," she assures Gratian, "do no good."[28] It does not seem good to her that "the sisters always go to the same confessor"; the too-frequent "conversations" they are having at Malagón "worry" her.[29]

However, everything has to depend on circumstances to a certain extent. It is not a general principle that the confessors do nothing but hear and remit sins. "Since you are there," she writes to Gaspar de Villaneueva, confessor at Malagón, "why do they go to the mother prioress about their interior life, when it seems they do not find any consolation from her?"[30] And to Mary of St Joseph: "For your prayer, there is nothing against your speaking to Garciálvarez;[31] it is not of a kind that will bring on censure;[32] I give the same advice to the other sisters who follow that way. It would seem strange to do otherwise, especially when our Father Visitator has prescribed it."[33]

But prudence is always necessary. St Teresa recommends it to Gratian, who is too guileless himself to suspect malice: "I can feel and show you great love, for many reasons, but all the sisters would not understand how to do the same ... I know whom I am dealing with and—besides—my age allows it; still, the sisters think they can say and do what they hear me say or see me do."[34] She recommends it to Mary of St Joseph, and particularly in regard to Gratian: "If you show the prudence I have advised you, I will be very pleased."[35] "For charity's sake, let the sisters act with great prudence; in that monastery there is a nun to whom a nothing seems enormous."[36] We have seen what fears she had of the young sisters' having too regular relationships with the Carmelite Fathers: "Our whole future is at stake," she writes to Gratian, "in taking care to deny devout fanatics the least opportunity of ruining [the interior life] of the spouses of Christ. We always have to foresee the worst that can happen in such a case in order to prevent it; the devil makes use of such occasions to creep in without being noticed; it is from this point and from the reception of a great many nuns into the monasteries that I have always feared the most disastrous effects."[37] She did not want the Carmelites to raise their veils to speak to the confessors, and "I say as much," she specifies, "if it is a case of men religious, of whatever Order they may be, and especially of our Discalced Carmelite Fathers."[38]

In this advice and these precautions we see her thinking. Though she knew by name and by character the greater part of her daughters, her point of view is collective; she is thinking less of *one* Carmelite to be guided to God than of maintaining the fervor of a whole Carmel. A Carmel holds women more complicated and difficult to get to know than one would think: "You amuse me," she says to Mariano, "when you tell me you will know what this girl is just by seeing her. We are not so easy to get to know, we women. After you have heard their confessions for years, you are amazed at how little you have really known them; this is because they are not exactly aware of themselves to expose their faults, and you judge them solely by what they tell you."[39] A Carmel in sixteenth century Spain was made up of young women from a world of agitated religious sentiment. Care was taken to require that they have common sense; they were pious, they were "saints", as their Mother said. But, living within the cloister and within themselves, though they often reached the highest mystical states, it could also happen that they did not master nature enough to escape its deceits. Hence certain mistakes and aberrations were justified as devotion; certain faults were disguised as duty; certain morbid symptoms could reach the point of scandal.[40] St Teresa, who was so fearful of illusions and of becoming the sport of the devil, was fearful of the same in her houses. For the evil spirit prowls around the cells; he makes use of the "natural" and occasionally of "a lack of intelligence";[41] by every means he troubles these "little hidden recesses of the Good God." And the harm is all the greater in that public opinion, kept on the look-out by the Carmelites of the Observance, maliciously gossips about unpleasant incidents and decries illuminism: the least imprudence can bring on fatal consequences.

For holiness to flourish in the Carmels, there must first be peace. For peace imperceptibly kills off the secret contradictions in the inmost soul; it allows one to see deviations better and then to set them right more easily, even hypocritical ones; it is the friend of the light that makes spells vanish; it is the condition for joy which, even during severe trials, draws people to God. How many nuns "remain peacefully" in their monastery as a result![42] May nothing trouble them! "The affliction you now[43] have has greatly distressed me, for it is of a kind to upset you all . . . These are painful trials; but I tell you they are nothing in comparison with the pain I would feel if I saw imperfections among you, or people who are disturbed; as long as that is not the case, these stories of sicknesses do not torment me very much."[44] "Believe me, I dread one discontented nun more than a whole crowd of devils."[45] "I fear everything else less than the loss of this deep joy which Our Lord keeps up in them. I know well what a nun without joy is."[46]

Peace, order, tranquillity in order: such is the goal, for the most part, of the recommendations of the foundress in regard to spiritual direction.

Certainly, confessors are needed, first to hear and absolve sins, and then to watch over the interior life of each one. There should even be several, for God does not lead everyone "by the same path"[47] and it is a great loss to a person not to be understood.[48]

But the first rule is that the confessor must not act except by his learning and his virtue.[49] If he allows relationships that are too human to become established between himself and his penitents, if confidences take too familiar a turn, or if both persons are too young and too naive, not only will the reputation and consequently the peace of the monastery soon begin to suffer, but souls will be troubled by influences whose nature, unknown to them, can easily be guessed.

In the second place, the confessor must be prudent. He is not the only one who is responsible for opening, under God, these well-closed retreats; others also are charged with this duty and with uniting these fervent people closely to the Church. He has no business with questions of authority and administration. The monasteries have their constitutions; they have their superiors, visitators and provincials; any intrusion on his part will produce disorder and cause factions. And even in the direction of souls, the superiors have their word to say; they have to keep the spirit of the reformed Carmel very pure in their area of responsibility. This regards the prioress especially, who is a mother. True, it is not her place to demand of the sisters "in regard to their interior way, prayer, or temptations, a manifestation of conscience which they do not wish to make."[50] But it is not enough for her to impose exterior regularity, endeavoring "to make herself loved so as to be obeyed."[51] Either by herself or by the mistress of novices she ought, as many allusions and many words of advice in the *Letters* point out, to train her daughters in prayer; moreso, she must not only keep up an atmosphere of fervor, but also watch over the spiritual "path" each sister is taking, and examine very closely extraordinary kinds of prayer, if any occur. In this matter it is not easy to establish precise limits between her role and that of the spiritual director; there may be conflicts, which is another reason why the director should be careful not to compromise peace, whose first condition is harmony of influences. In any case, every precaution is taken lest the convents degenerate into those conventicles of visionaries where, to the devil's great satisfaction, an imprudent priest is the dupe and accomplice of dubious enthusiasm.

TERESA AS DIRECTOR

One has the impression that St Teresa often bases her advice on specific cases. Some of these concern spiritual direction only remotely; she is then acting rather as superior, but not without indicating how she thinks souls should be dealt with.

"Don't be so foolish, my daughter; Beatrice has her all worked up," she wrote bluntly to Mary of St Joseph [52] about two Carmelites, Beatrice of the Mother of God and Marguerite of the Conception. The one, a visionary, had more imagination than judgment, and the other much more naïveté than intelligence. Constantly in the confessional or the parlor with the confessor, Garciálvarez, an excellent man but of limited acumen, they brought about some great problems for the community, and thanks to the machinations of the Carmelites of the Observance, ended by calumniating the prioress and Fr Gratian in a sordid fashion. There were serious results, with the deposition of the prioress among them; but once the Discalced were removed from the authority of the Mitigated Carmelites, they had no trouble establishing the truth.

How should the guilty ones be treated? Madre Teresa returns to this subject frequently, and her instructions are a marvelous combination of kind gentleness and unflinching firmness, especially in regard to Beatrice. She asks urgently how the "poor little thing" is doing. "Don't show the least resentment to that sister." "I don't think of her as a bad nun but as a deluded person with a weak imagination and ready to fall into the devil's traps." [53] "Tell me about those two poor little sisters; I am very worried about them. Be good to them and take every suitable means to bring them, if possible, to see their fault." [54] "I am asking Sister Beatrice of the Mother of God and Sister Marguerite, as I have already implored the other sisters, not to speak any more of the past, except with Our Lord or with the confessor."[55] Yes; but they will be careful now to act with honesty and openness. And they will see to making satisfaction to those concerned; without that "they will not enjoy peace and the devil will not stop tempting them."[56] "I assure you, my Mother, it is not reasonable to allow such things to go by without punishment. The perpetual imprisonment they have decided to on her,[57] as you tell me, would be the suitable thing for her and it would be good that she never come out of it." "She must be made to retract all her lies."[58] The exercise of motherly love, we see, does not dispense her from satisfying justice—quite the contrary, order is always necessary to assure peace. And it does not seem that great measures had to be employed. The repentance of the two Carmelites was so sincere that one of them, Marguerite of the Conception, accompanied Mary of St Joseph to the foundation at Lisbon, and Beatrice of the Mother of God died in the odor of sanctity.

The case of the visionaries is of interest precisely in regard to spiritual direction. St Teresa, whom her visions had disturbed so much, had little liking for such phenomena among her daughters. This is well seen in the example of Beatrice of the Mother of God (the denouncer—though at that point she had not yet denounced anyone) and Isabel of St Jerome at Seville. "You must know," Teresa writes to Mary of St Joseph, "there are girls with unhealthy imaginations—though not in our monasteries;" (she allows motherly affection to sway her judgment) "everything that comes into their heads they think they see; and the devil must help them to this."[59] Now Isabel and Beatrice, whose prayer seemed "very high," claimed they received revelations. The saint was sceptical: "The great number, alone, of these visions is grounds for suspicion." If I had been there "there would not have been so many stories." "I am fearful for these sisters." What is to be done? First, avoid attaching much importance to these things,[60] not even to speak of them, in conversation or otherwise, to forbid them to write about them,[61] to watch their prayer closely.[62] And finally to resort to an appropriate medication: "Please advise Sister St Francis to have Isabel of St Jerome eat meat as soon as Lent is over and not to let her fast."[63] "I was very glad to hear that our Father ordered the two sisters whose prayer is so high, to eat meat."[64] "As for Sister St Jerome, you must order her to eat meat for some days and to stay away from prayer. She has a weak imagination and thinks she sees or hears everything she meditates on."[65]

To sum up, on the strength of her experience St Teresa was always ready to respond lovingly to the questions put to her and give advice, so that she herself sometimes acted as director. And not only for her daughters, as might be expected, like Mary-Baptist,[66] but more surprising, for many others, in particular Gratian, Don Teutonius de Braganza, the future archbishop of Evora, even for the learned Bañez, and finally for her brother Lawrence.

She sometimes gave her opinion on a degree or kind of prayer: "The vision Paul (=Gratian) "says he had had of Joseph's grandeur" (that is Jesus Christ's) "is very high."[67] "I am very much pleased with your kind of prayer."[68] "That restful prayer of which you speak is the prayer of quiet; it is described in the little book you have."[69] One notices also that she readily connects interior difficulties with "humors" and scruples with that psychasthenia which she calls "melancholy": "As to these interior trials you tell me of, the greater they are the more you must disregard them; they are obviously a weakness of the imagination and a bad humor."[70] "I answer about Paul's scruples,[71] which you are describing: is he able or not to use his faculties? It seems to me that at the time he wrote he must have been under the influence of some melancholy; I say the same thing when he has these scruples. It is obvious from the very arguments he uses."[72] But the devil tries to increase this distress: "The devil sees it well, and doubtless must contribute" to your trials.[73] Sometimes he shows himself more directly: "This fear of which you tell me certainly comes from your spirit's feeling the presence of the bad spirit. You do not see him, it is true, with your bodily eyes, but your soul must see or feel him."[74]

The most remarkable thing in these counsels, however, is how intent they are upon calming people, getting them back on their feet, if one may so speak, bringing them peace. "That you are not satisfied with yourself is not surprising; but do not worry yourself when the fatigue of the journey and the impossibility of arranging your time as usual have occasioned some negligence. As soon as your body gets some rest, your soul too will find peace again."[75] "When you feel distressed, don't fail to go somewhere from time to time where you can look at the sky; take a little walk; you will not be leaving aside prayer when you do this; we really have to support our weakness skillfully so as not to force nature too much. And all that is seeking God, since it is for love of him that we resort to such means. It is necessary to lead the soul gently."[76] "Your imperfections do not surprise me at all; I am full of them myself; and yet I see I've found much more leisure to keep solitude here."[77] "The drynesses you tell me about make me believe that Our Lord is treating you already like a strong soul. What he wants to do is to test you to see whether the love you have for him in joy will keep up in aridity. In my opinion it is a special favor; so don't be at all troubled by it."[78] "I should like very much to speak to you some day about these fears you have. You are losing time by them, and you are a little lacking in humility in not wanting to believe me."[79] "Don't be at all surprised at not keeping all your recollection in the midst of so many concerns; that is not in our power. Provided that once your work is finished you go back to your excellent way of life, I will be satisfied."[80] "Blessed be God that Paul[81] is enjoying interior peace!"[82] "It seems to you that you are giving in to these temptations—nothing of the sort; you are even deriving merit from all of it. For the love of God, do manage to get well; force yourself to eat well; do not keep solitude and don't tire yourself out with thinking; keep yourself busy as you are able and with whatever you are able."[83] There would be no end of quotations. So that God may act and his action, if he wills, produce supernatural restlessness and anxiety as well as sublime sufferings and joys in the higher regions of the soul, it is well that calm and peace reign in the humbler regions.

Interesting above all are the saint's letters to her brother Lawrence: these are real letters of spiritual direction. Lawrence had entrusted his soul to her; he had even promised to obey her, a promise which his sister had accepted only with reluctance, insisting that he not bind himself to it by vow. She started out by writing to him about all kinds of things: herself, her health, her interior trials, her work and her ecstasies. She gave him a lecture on the management of his large fortune; and it was not to dissuade him from taking good care of it—quite the contrary. Doubtless it was not right for him to become totally absorbed in business or anything of that kind "for, in the eyes of the world, one is less esteemed for it."[84] But it would be better for him to have real estate than revenues, and he ought to busy himself with it. Even while congratulating him on leaving his children something preferable to any property, that is, honor, she advises him to put his accounts in order: "Time well spent, like that given to looking after the welfare of one's children, does not detract from prayer." "The time you will spend for the Serna[85] will be well employed, and when summer comes you will be glad to go and spend some time there. Jacob did not cease to be a saint because he was busy with his flocks; nor Abraham, nor St Joachim; but since we want to avoid work everything makes us tired." And what an idea to want to get rid of his silver plate and tapestries in a spirit of poverty! Such things are indifferent: "Just be detached from them," and "since some day you must marry off your children, it is right that you should have a home furnished in keeping with your position."

Her advice about asceticism is very prudent. There has to be bodily mortification, certainly; Teresa even sends her brother two hair-shirts and gives him permission to take the discipline. But she condemns all excess:[86] "I don't know what these *Paternosters* mean that you tell me you recite while taking the discipline; I have never ordered you anything like that. Read my letter again and you will see; keep strictly to what I wrote there; you are to take the discipline twice a week; and then, during Lent, wear the hairshirt once a week. But if it does you harm, you will stop it. As you are very sanguine, I am quite doubtful about it; on the other hand I forbid you to take the discipline any more than that, for any excess would tire your eyes; besides, in the beginning it is a greater penance to be moderate; by doing so you really break your will. You will tell me if you feel any harm from the hair-shirt after you have worn it." No exaggeration in vigils either: "When sleep comes, don't drive it away." "As to sleep, I advise you—and if necessary, I order you—not to take less than six hours. We are already old; and so, believe me, we have to take care of our bodies; otherwise they will crush our spirits, which is a terrible trial." "God prefers your health and your obedience to your penances." In conclusion she states: mortify yourself first by bearing with your unbearable brother Peter.[87]

Lawrence had complained of the sensual troubles to which the mystics are sometimes exposed. She reassures him delicately, but without false modesty: "These evil feelings you give me an account of and which happen to you after prayer, should not worry you. I have never experienced anything like that, I admit; the Lord, in his goodness, has always preserved me from these passions. I imagine that because the soul's joy is excessive, nature must be affected by it. With His Majesty's help this will pass, provided you attach no importance to it." "That will not be able to hurt your prayer; the best thing is to pay no attention to it."

And finally she becomes the judge of her directee's prayer and pronounces on its quality and degrees. "I don't know why you want these fears and terrors, since His Majesty leads you by the way of love . . . The prayer which God gives you is incomparably better than that which consists of thinking of hell." He is not to trust too much in a certain sensible fervor: "that ardor you tell me you feel is very unimportant for devotion; it would likely harm your health, if it were excessive." A curious physiological explanation follows: "As you are sanguine, the great movement of the spirit along with the natural heat which flows from the superior part and reached the heart, may be the cause of it; however, I repeat, it is not a sign that the prayer is higher."

When he does not receive "supernatural" graces Lawrence practices meditation. "The kind of meditation you make when you are not in the prayer of quiet is very good, thank God." But the prayer of quiet is very ordinary with him. True, it is less sublime than he believes: "How foolish you are to think that that prayer you speak to me about is like that which kept me from sleeping! It has nothing to do with it; I was making much greater efforts to get to sleep than to stay awake." However, it is truly high, and Teresa is drawn to give him a full lesson on the wound of the soul: "It is a touch of love made upon the soul; if it grows greater you will understand what you told me you couldn't make out in my couplets. You then feel very keen pain, great grief, without knowing from what, and it is extremely delight- ful . . . When the soul is truly wounded with that love of God, it puts aside that of creatures without any trouble—I mean it has no more attachment here below . . . The feeling of the presence of the Lord and the sweetness which the person then enjoys, pass, it is true, as if he had never experienced it; that is just what you are complaining of; but this must be understood only of the impres- sions of the senses which God has summoned to share the joy which is filling the soul, and not of the soul itself, which always possesses that favor and remains no less rich in graces, as the effects of its love immediately begin to show."

"Peace, my sisters, peace: that is the Lord's word, the word he so often addressed to his apostles," St Teresa writes in the *Interior Castle*.[88] Peace, that is her great care when she is directing her brother, lavishing her advice upon her friends, or organizing spiritual direction in her convents.

We do not reach perfection without going through some difficult periods. The body has its sicknesses; nature its meander- ings; the soul, which "shares" the weaknesses of the former and which tends to be misled by the latter, is subject to illusions and risks being caught in many a trap. The danger grows worse in disorder; and is all the greater then because the devil is always around, and crouching in the shadows, lies in wait for the least trouble as specially favorable occasions.

In monasteries, then, the confessor will be discreet and pru- dent, provision will be made so that his functions will not oppose the exercise of authority nor favor, even without his knowledge, the deceits of the heart. Analagously, whoever directs one person will take care to react against any excess, to keep away human fears, to discipline gently and not turn everything upside down,[89] to organize various plans for life according to "truth," in short, to bring about peace. When the interior life is intense and above all when mystical states arise, order and peace are always beneficial, at least at a certain level of activity. And at all levels the condition for security, worthwhile action and success is the acceptance of the duties of one's state of life, obedience to superiors, continual integration of the individual's life with his social milieu and with the Church. St Teresa had established that order for herself and gained, not without effort, that peace: she wishes them for everyone. She had attained that integration in the highest degree: she makes it a duty for everyone. The love of God may attain the highest folly, which is nothing but highest reasonableness; but if the folly is to be reasonable it is fitting that reason be respected in its humble demands.

The lesson which this incomparable ecstatic gives spiritual directors, then, is a lesson of common sense and realism. She seems to have seen extremely well that the call of God, spiritual strain and divine action are likely to produce, at the point of departure and all along the route, imbalance and sickness in the body, in the conscience and especially perhaps in those regions of the soul which conscience cannot reach. The disproportion is too great between the Reality the person hopes to grasp or whose influence he feels, and the realities of this world to which he had more or less happily adapted himself. And then, in order to live again, we have to die as well; but there are so many things in us that do not want to die, and at the bottom of them all that proud depth of being, that "I-know-not-what" of which St John of the Cross speaks! Condemned to death, these things defend themselves by falsehoods. Unless a person is solidly established in God "beyond neurosis" there is danger that his instincts will establish illusory symbols, "idols," in place of such a demanding God, and the evil spirit will make himself into an angel of light. If we remain in peace, take care to maintain interior harmony and harmony with the world, humbly accept our situation and all the providential arrangements of our existence, then sufferings, joys, sorrows, revelations, ecstasies—far from being suspect—will be the various periods of a drama far superior to all natural conflicts and troubles: the drama played out between ourselves and God, the drama of the experience of God. And this drama, as violent as it may be at times, will end in peace; life made divine will find in everything both its nourishment and its expression; moral effort will become an effort of fullness. Granting that this is what the interior life should be, perhaps we would be able to define with precision, at least theoretically, the respective role of doctors, spiritual directors and religious authorities in its evolution. (Trans. K. Kirk)

NOTES

1. There is no difference between *confession* and *direction*; when St Teresa speaks of the *confessor* she always means one who not only hears and absolves sins, but who also advises, encourages and directs.

2. People spoke of their confessors as readily as they do today of their doctor. For example, Guiomar de Ulloa advised her friend Teresa to turn to John de Pradanos.

3. Spiritual Testimony No. 58 (Seville, 1576 to Rodrigo Alvarez), I.C.S. ed., p. 350. This last phrase was not written without ulterior motives: St Teresa is skillfully answering those who threatened her with the Inquisition. But her testimony is too determined to be challenged, as her life story confirms: on January 17, 1570 she writes to her brother Lawrence de Cepeda: "I always seek out learned men for what concerns my soul."

4. Nearly all her letters which have been preserved date from this period.

5. May 18, 1568. She probably means Fr Carleval, a Calced Carmelite. EDITOR'S NOTE: The passages of St Teresa's letters appearing here are all translated by our translator.

6. January 9, 1577.

7. That is, St John of the Cross, then in prison in Toledo, and his companion. May 14, 1578 to Jerome Gratian.

8. =Gratian.

9. July 1577 to Gaspar de Villanueva.

10. February 21, 1581 to Gratian.

11. Constitutions of Alcalá (1581), No. 44 in *The Teresian Ideal* (Grand Rapids: Carmel of O. L. of Guadalupe—private publication, 1968), p. 516.

12. November 26, 1576 to Mary of St Joseph.

13. (Andrew of the Incarnation) "Memorias Historiales," A-C, 71. Unpublished MS, Biblioteca Nacional, Madrid.

14. June 15, 1576 to Gratian.

15. January 9, 1577 to Gratian.

16. This is evident, given the attentive direction of their sisters by John of the Cross and Gratian, and given the words of Chapter 2 of the *Foundations*: "I think how necessary it is if monasteries of nuns are founded, that there be men who follow the same rule."

17. = Angel de Salazar.

18. May 3, 1579 to Mary of St Joseph.

19. July 22, 1579 to Mary of St Joseph.

20. February 1, 1580 to Mary of St Joseph.

21. December 21, 1579 to Nicholas Doria.

22. *Ibid.*

23. = Delegates of the Provincial.

24. February 27, 1581 to Gratian.

25. October 26, 1581 to Gratian.

26. March 2, 1577 to Mary of St Joseph.

27. February 1581 to Gratian.

28. December 18, 1579 to Gratian.

29. July 1577 to Gaspar de Villanueva.

30. April 17, 1578 to Gaspar de Villanueva.

31. =The Confessor of Seville.

32. Public opinion in Seville was very critical and the Carmel there had disturbed the Inquisition.

33. April 9, 1577 to Mary of St Joseph.

34. November 1576 to Gratian.

35. December 7, 1576 to Mary of St Joseph.

36. November 21, 1580 to Mary of St Joseph.

37. February 1581 to Gratian.

38. End of 1580 to Gratian. EDITOR'S NOTE: Peers dates the letter containing this passage as "About October 1580," p. 777.

39. October 21, 1576 to Ambrosius Mariano.

40. Jerome Gratian's autobiographical work, "The Peregrination of Anastasius," gives the sad story of the *beata* Joan Calancha who entered the Carmel of Beas, where she stayed only a week. At Seville a nun went insane. See *Peregrinación de Anastasio* ed. Giovanni M. Bertini (Barcelona: Juan Flors, 1966), pp. 185–86. Coll. "Espirituales Españoles," A, 18.

41. May 3, 1579 to Mary of St Joseph.

42. October 1575 to Gratian.

43. =The insanity of a nun.

44. June 4, 1578 to Mary of St Joseph.

45. July 4, 1581 to Gratian.

46. End of 1580 to Gratian. See note 37, *supra.*

47. July 25, 1577 to Anne of St Albert.

48. July 1577 to Mary-Baptist. EDITOR'S NOTE: The dating given by Peers is somewhat different, i.e., "Late July 1577 (?)."

49. ". . . provided that the Mother Prioress is satisfied that he has the *virtues* and learning requisite . . ." Constitutions of Alcalá, No. 44, *Teresian Ideal*, p. 516.

50. December 21, 1579 to Nicholas Doria.

51. See Constitutions of Alcalá, No. 74, *Teresian Ideal*, p. 532.

52. See Mary of St Joseph, "Ramillete de Mirra, e Historia de sus persecuciones." *Libro de recreaciones, Ramillete de mirra, avisos, maximas y poesias,* ed. Silverio de Santa Teresa (Burgos: Tip. de "El Monte Carmelo," 1913), pp. 127–77.

53. May 3, 1579 to Mary of St Joseph.

54. July 22, 1579 to Mary of St Joseph.

55. January 1580 to Mary of St Joseph.

56. *Ibid.*

57. On Sister Beatrice.

58. July 4, 1580 to Mary of St Joseph.

59. May 3, 1579 to Mary of St Joseph.

60. June 4, 1578 to Mary of St Joseph.

61. "I don't much approve, I assure you, of the sisters of your monastery writing down what happens in their prayer . . . They can imagine many, many things . . . " March 28, 1578 to Mary of St Joseph.

62. March 2, 1577 to Mary of St Joseph.

63. *Ibid.*

64. June 4, 1578 to Mary of St Joseph.

65. October 23, 1576 to Gratian: "Still, sometimes this may be true, as may have been the case, for she is a very good person."

66. See, for example, the letter of November 2, 1576.

67. End of December 1578 to Gratian. EDITOR'S NOTE: Peers dates the letter containing this passage as "March 1578 (?)."

68. March 2, 1577 to Mary of St Joseph.

69. Most likely the *Way of Perfection*—February 10, 1577 to Lawrence de Cepeda.

70. November 2, 1576 to Mary-Baptist.

71. =Gratian.

72. March 2, 1578 to Gratian.

73. November 2, 1576 to Mary-Baptist.

74. February 10, 1577 to Lawrence de Cepeda.

75. June 1574 to Teutonius de Braganza.

76. July 3, 1574 to Teutonius de Braganza.

77. January 6, 1575 to Teutonius de Braganza.

78. August 7, 1580 to Teresita, her niece.

79. End of May 1574 to (Dominic) Bañez.

80. November 26, 1576 to Louis de Cepeda.

81. =Gratian.

82. October 5, 1576 to Gratian.

83. November 2, 1576 to Mary-Baptist.

84. For the following references see the letters to Lawrence de Cepeda dated January 17, February 10 and 27-28, 1577.

85. A piece of property she advised him to purchase.

86. She condemns all ostentation too, especially if it is inconsistent: "I don't approve of these young Discalced Carmelites with their mules and their saddles. As to making you go barefoot without sandles, I never even had that idea; you are too barefooted already . . . In my opinion, you would look strange barefooted and traveling on good mules." December 12, 1576 to Ambrosius Mariano.

87. Peter usually lived off the charity of Lawrence.

88. C, 2, 1, 9.

89. "We must not try to win over souls like bodies, by force of arms." January, 9 1577 to Gratian.

ST THERESE OF THE CHILD JESUS AND SPIRITUAL DIRECTION

Louis Gillet, O.C.D.

Father Louis is a member of the Southern French Province of Discalced Carmelites and devotes himself both to writing and to spiritual direction.

"**A** Saint Who had No Director: St Thérèse of the Child Jesus" is the real subject of this article, even though this differs slightly from the title above.

As we ask St Thérèse about spiritual direction, the query immediately leads to two other questions: (1) Did the saint have directors and what was her line of conduct in their regard? and (2) How did she proceed when the direction of the novices was entrusted to her? Direction received (passive); and direction given (active). Only the former aspect will concern us here.

I do not have a formal study to offer; I shall only investigate to what extent and according to what method St Thérèse had recourse to spiritual direction. In the three earlier articles an opportunity was offered to construct the theory of direction. Now I would like to show spiritual direction as lived, i.e., how the saint was directed in her approach to God. I will base this solely upon her writings, the process of canonization and on recent findings made available in the Centenary Editions of her works.[1]

81

As much as possible, I will let the facts speak for themselves, without trying to draw from them any general laws or absolute principles. Between the spiritual direction received by St Thérèse and that received by St Teresa of Avila there are numerous differences which forbid hasty generalizations.

Is it true that St Thérèse did not have spiritual directors? We are already well aware of the difference between her and St Teresa of Avila. It is not only two or three priests who claim the glory of having directed the great Reformer of Carmel. Three religious orders dispute this honor: the Jesuits, the Dominicans, and the Carmelites. Each order proudly points to several outstanding directors, some of them saints. There is nothing like this in the case of St Thérèse. Historians scarcely dare point out one or two confessors who had any influence upon her spiritual life. From the beginning spiritual poverty's note rings out, and we will hear it almost continuously until the end of this article.

This first surprise increases when we hear the saint state explicitly that Jesus alone was her Director. Sister Mary of the Trinity asked her: "Who then has taught you the Little Way?" "Jesus alone has taught me. No book, no theologian has instructed me," was her reply.[2] What interpretation is to be placed on this statement?

We do not have to define the term "spiritual director." We take the word in its accepted sense: a priest to whom one has recourse habitually, not simply for the purpose of receiving absolution, but to receive advice for the organization and the development of the spiritual life. Very frequently the term of spiritual director is confused with confessor.

The first question which presents itself is this: Who were the confessors of the saint, and what role did they play in her spiritual formation? St Thérèse approached confession regularly, like all Christians anxious about their progress in divine love. She manifests no inimitable originality on this point. She either received this sacrament every or every other week. Nothing more. Although certain vocal prayers such as the rosary, will become difficult for her, she never speaks of the difficulty she could have experienced in the avowal of her faults.

Pauline Martin was under the direction of Father Ducellier, assistant at the Cathedral of St Peter. She took little Thérèse to him in the summer of 1878 for her first confession.[3] The *Autobiography* has preserved the simple and enlightening story of this first meeting between Thérèse and the priesthood.[4] He remained her confessor until she entered the Benedictine Abbey in October, 1881.

Father Domin, chaplain of the Benedictine boarding school and confessor to the pupils, had much more to do with Thérèse. Until 1886 he heard her confession, he taught her catechism, and he preached the communion and the annual retreats.[5] When she was obliged to discontinue her studies and return home, Thérèse placed herself under the guidance of Father Lepelletier, curate at the Cathedral and confessor to Mr Martin. He directed her till her entrance into Carmel.[6] Her reference to him in her *Autobiography* was: "I'd taken as a rule of conduct to receive, without missing a single one, the communions my confessor permitted, allowing him to regulate the number and not asking." She made her confessions in the cloister to Father Youf who died a few days after her own death, October 7, 1897. She does not seem to have received any special support from him during her trials. She speaks of him on June 5, 1897: "Father Youf told me with reference to my temptations against the faith: 'Don't dwell on these, it's very dangerous.' This is hardly consoling to hear, but happily I'm not affected by it."[7]

The extraordinary confessors, Father Faucon and Father Baillon, heard her several times a year, but they did not consider themselves as particularly charged with the care of her soul.[8]

She could have spoken with other priests on the occasion of retreats and sermons at the Carmel. Father Pichon, S. J., gave a retreat there from May 20–28, 1888, a few weeks after Thérèse had entered. She would willingly have chosen him as her director, but he was transferred to Canada. He died on November 15, 1919, after having testified in the Process of Beatification, and without ever having talked with her again.[9]

In the following years, the retreats were preached by Father

Godfrey Madelaine, 1890, 1896; Father Alexis, 1891; Father Déodat, 1892; Father Lemonnier, 1893, 1894, 1895.[10]

What is striking in these historical recollections is the docility of the saint in submitting to circumstances in the choice of her confessor. She chooses the confessor of her older sister or her father, the one at the boarding school or at the Carmel. It would be a distortion of the real facts and of her personality to picture her as going from one confessor to another in search of an ideal guide.

With the same simplicity she had recourse to the priests who happened to be preaching the retreats. Is this a lack of personality? Indifference? Independence or pride? Would it not rather indicate a well developed spirit of faith? "When she had charge of the novices, . . . she never permitted them to criticize sermons or conferences. It was not that she thought all priests spoke equally well, but she could not bear for people to dwell on the shortcomings of their preaching. The same was true of the shortcomings of priests themselves: the spirit of faith did not allow these to be discussed, she said."[11]

She explains how she conducted herself in confession. "I took very little time over my confessions, and never said a word about my spiritual life."[12] She submitted for absolution the acts which appeared to her imperfect, but she never strayed into those wordy exposés which are generally the outcome of a deep examination of oneself. Mother Agnes adds: "At this time of her life (13-15 years of age) she saw clearly what God was asking of her. Beyond determining how often she could go to holy communion, she had nothing of consequence to discuss with her confessor."[13]

Among the priests who heard her confession, were there any who profoundly impressed the saint? Twice, she confided to Mother Agnes, she had experienced a very great joy. The first time, when she was fifteen and a half, her confessor, Father Pichon, told her that she had never offended God seriously. The second time, when making the retreat of 1891, Father Alexis told her that her imperfections, which stemmed from weakness, did not offend God.[14] These two priestly interventions appear later as providential liberations. They removed from her the fears and hesitations which could have curbed her ascent, but they are isolated acts which do not characterize what we customarily term spiritual direction.

She did make, however, a positive attempt to choose Father Pichon as her director. She wrote him before her First Communion recommending herself to his prayers. On this occasion she told him that soon she would enter Carmel and that he would be her director.[15] Was this step influenced by the example of her sisters? Pauline and Marie had Father Pichon as their director, and they made no secret of this in the family. In 1886 Marie, accompanied by her father, went to Calais and to Douvres to welcome Father Pichon on his return from America.[16] When her entrance into Carmel was fully decided, Thérèse wrote to him on October 23, 1887: "I thought that since you were taking spiritual care of my two sisters, you would be willing to take care of me."[17] She considers him her director from this day. At the conclusion of the meeting they had at the Carmel, he said to her: "My child, may Our Lord always be your superior and your novice master." When she recalled this statement seven years later, she said: "He was this in fact, and he was also 'my Director.' . . . my heart quickly turned to the Director of directors, and it was he who taught me that science hidden from the wise and prudent and revealed to *little ones*. The little flower transplanted to Mount Carmel was to expand under the shadow of the cross. The tears and blood of Jesus were to be her dew, and her sun was his adorable face . . . "[18] These last words force us to realize something which sheds light on our problem.

Of all the priests who attended to her spiritually from the age of fourteen to her death, Father Pichon is the only one to whom she gives the name of director, and the only one whom she mentions in her correspondence.[19]

After she entered the cloister she wrote him every month. In the months of July and August, 1897, she sent him a long letter in which she tells him all that God has done for her and what she thinks of his love and mercy. She submits to him also her hopes and her desires to do good after her death. "My entire soul was there," she was to confide.[20]

It would appear at first glance that the Jesuit was her director. However, he answers her letters only once a year.[21] Was he unable to do more? Did he consider more frequent answers useless? Did these yearly letters fulfill an important function? We know that he encouraged Thérèse in her vocation, that he delivered her from the fear of having lost baptismal innocence, and that he was a great support to her. May we believe that his influence was more decisive than that? Evidently not. Officially he was director of the saint. In reality, God did not permit him to direct her in the full sense of the word—whom he manifestly intended to form himself. Father Pichon realized what was essential in direction without burdening or bending the soul with an indelicate touch. On her side, Thérèse depended on him despite the distance and the silence, but her dependence was very light. She had recourse to him, but she went beyond him. This explanation teaches us new ideas on direction, broader ideas, more flexible, which do not tally with the current notion of spiritual direction.

In these slight references to Father Pichon, it would be inexact to read only a tendency in Thérèse to follow her sisters, or only a thoughtless imitation of what is done in the religious life. She was fully aware of the importance of direction. "Seeing innocent souls at such close range, I understood what a misfortune it was when they were not formed in their early years, when they are soft as wax upon which one can imprint either virtue or vice. . . . God has no need for anyone to carry out his work, I know, but just as he allows a clever gardener to raise rare and delicate plants, giving him the necessary knowledge for this while reserving to himself the care of making them fruitful, so Jesus wills to be helped in his divine cultivation of souls."[22] Direction is not something superfluous; it is not a spiritual luxury. It enters into the divine plan for all sanctification.

Thérèse did not merely give intellectual assent to this truth. She acted upon it. "I can affirm that the Servant of God took counsel," testified Father Pichon.[23] Although she was not always understood by her ordinary and extraordinary confessors, neverthless she submitted her thoughts to them and followed their advice without reservation.

She willingly consulted Father Baillon and said that he gave her good advice.[24] With reference to holy communion, she said that one should tell her confessor the attraction she experienced to receive her Lord.[25] When she composed the Act of Oblation, she desired that this act be judged by a priest. Father Lemonnier and his superior examined it, and she was reassured.[26]

With the advice of an enlightened director, she copied the *Credo* and carried it constantly on her person in a copy of the New Testament. She even desired to write it in her blood.[27] She did not allow herself to be habitually directed by her own inspirations. Although she was compliant with all providential designs, she sought counsel in order to obtain certitude. But what liberty and ease there was in these consultations! Although Father Pichon was officially her director, she spoke to other priests, presenting not only her daily problems, but even problems connected with the holiness for which she was striving.

At the age of twelve, during the retreat for solemn communion, she was assailed by scruples. It was above all on the eve of her confessions that these increased. Was not this spiritual difficulty something relevant to her confessor alone? She did not think so. She presented all her sins, all her wild thoughts, to her older sister, Marie. Her sister tells us: "I tried to cure her by telling her that I took her sins upon myself (they were not even imperfections) and by allowing her to confess only two or three of them, which I indicated to her myself."[28] Thérèse obeyed. "I spoke only to her of my scruples, and I was so obedient that my confessor never knew about my wretched malady. I told him just the number of sins, and not one more, that Marie had allowed me to confess. I could have passed for the least scrupulous of people in spite of being extremely so."[29] She did not hesitate to confide her faults to her sister. Is this the result of a childhood practice? Is it the effect of her early formation? In 1878 her mother wrote: "She is very lovable and frank; it's curious to see her running after me making her confession: 'Mamma, I pushed Céline once, I hit her once, but I won't do it again.' (It's like this for everything she does.)"[30] Here we have an instinct of purity allowing no peace until the one taking the place of God in her regard has heard the avowal of her faults.

She held the same attitude with regard to temptations which moralists would place on the borderline between confession and direction. On the eve of her profession, her vocation appeared to her as simply a dream, a chimera. The demon whispered to her that the Carmelite life was not for her, that she was misleading her superiors in advancing on a way to which she was not called. The darkness became so dense that she was convinced of only one thing: having no vocation, she must return to the world. What was to be done in such a case? She decided to reveal the matter without delay to the novice mistress. Upon hearing it, she laughed at the idea, and reassured Thérèse completely. This act of humility put the devil to flight "since he had perhaps thought that I would not dare admit my temptation. My doubts left me completely as soon as I finished speaking; nevertheless, to make my act of humility even more perfect, I still wished to confide my strange temptation to our Mother Prioress, who simply laughed at me."[31] In these two episodes, can we not admit that the success achieved was more or less an approbation of her mode of acting, which was at the same time simple and bold?

Her freedom is evident in another manner. Except during the period of her scruples, which lasted a little more than a year, her mind is restful and quiet. She was certainly not one to consult ceaselessly. During Mother Agnes' term of office as prioress, she did not go to her for the monthly spiritual direction.[32] In the various acts of her religious life, among the decisions to be made, she will choose with an infallible certainty. She will ask only when doubt persists after personal reflection. When she is in possession of light, she will keep silent. The case of her vocation is typical. Ordinarily, it is concern over one's vocation that gives rise to the necessity of direction. Would we not be inclined to judge severely the adult who would enter the religious life without having received the approbation of a spiritual director? Did Thérèse foresee this eventuality? Mother Agnes stated at the process: "The question of her becoming a nun was so simple that she never even dreamt of looking on it as a problem that needed the enlightenment of a director. She had known what she wanted since she was ten."[33] She did not deem it necessary to talk the matter over with Father Lepelletier, who was her confessor. When he read in the *Univers* the account of the audience with Leo XIII, in the course of which a young girl of fifteen asked the Holy Father for permission to enter Carmel, he immediately surmised it was Thérèse Martin, and he went to ask an explanation from Sister Agnes of Jesus. This independence of direction is not an indication of imprudence and pride. Enlightened by an inspiration which left no doubt, she has a perfect right not to seek from human teachers what our Lord has taught her directly. "I was in darkness and secure," sings John of the Cross.[34]

Without having had a spiritual director in the strict sense of the term, St Thérèse did not want to advance alone during her life. While safeguarding her liberty, she consulted others every time her conscience demanded it. She would have been willing to make herself known and she attempted to do so. This aspect of passive direction is not the least important, nor is it the least difficult. We are moving deeper into our study. She felt something beyond the conceptual, the conscious, and she experienced an extreme difficulty in explaining herself. "Psychology has brought to light, in a region deeper than that of the concept, phenomena of understanding which prepare and direct the formation of the concept. These are, for example, outlines which were totally unperceived for a long time because philosophers saw only the manageable results of the mind, that is, concepts, and because they were not looking at the rules which preside over the elaboration and the usage of these concepts. Revault d'Allormes has already untangled in part the mechanism of the schematization, a mechanism which will elaborate types of judgments and reasonings that are more lived than thought. Now, outlines are situated midway between the concept and deep thought. The solution of a problem, the central idea of an article to be written, or of a conference to be given, really develop within the orientation indicated by outlines, but, in themselves, they have their link in the mind at a deeper level. The concept is totally superficial, it is our work already practically detached from ourselves, it is ours rather than ourselves; the outline is more ours, for it is identified with our activity; creative thought itself is less ours than it is ourselves."[35]

What modern philosophy states regarding knowledge must be extended to the whole person. Beyond what our understanding discovers about what we are is a somewhat dark region which we can explore thanks to an intelligent reflection, thanks to the sciences which are forming and gaining ground each day. Beyond, in more mysterious depths, there is hidden what philosophers call the "spiritual center" of the being. Is it possible to reach it in order to dissociate it and to make a synthesis of it conformable to our own concepts, as was done recently with regard to the material center of the atom? This is a fascinating problem the solution of which is of great interest to those involved in spiritual direction. Direction is carried out in relationship to the person. Well carried out, it presupposes that the person is grasped in his depths and in his totality.

These brief remarks present only a natural understanding of man. See how the drama becomes complicated when we wish to reach man in his concrete totality: to what constitutes us in our human nature, God adds his supernatural gifts which the specifically human sciences are incapable of grasping directly. This divine life which the Christian receives is not a logical entity, neither is it an abstraction; neither is it the same among all God's children. It is personalized: this ultimate perfection of the supernatural gifts is as impenetrable as what philosophers call the "spiritual center," and this in such a way that our psychological investigations come up against not two mysteries simply juxtaposed within us, but a mystery all the more obscure because the gift of God is received in the "spiritual center" where it is placed in a living way, making one with this spiritual center and increasing its impenetrability.

St Thérèse had not taken a course in philosophy. What we learn with difficulty listening to human teachers, she saw in a higher light. "One feels it is absolutely necessary to forget one's likings, one's personal conceptions, and to guide souls along the road which Jesus has traced for them."[36] This road is already established by God in the nature of the individual and in the graces granted. "I saw first of all that all souls have very much the same struggles to fight, but they differ so much from each other in other aspects that I have no trouble in understanding what Father Pichon was saying: 'There are really more differences among souls than there are among faces.' "[37] In these last words she states the experience of St John of the Cross: "God leads each one along different paths so that hardly one spirit will be found like another in even half its method of procedure."[38]

She discovered great depths in her character. We can readily understand why she deplored her inability to express what she felt and to make herself known as much as she desired. To an aunt she wrote: "I wish I could make you read my heart, but there are some things that cannot be expressed in words."[39] And to Céline: "I wish my heart and all it contains could tell you what it thinks of you. Some things cannot be written. The heart alone understands."[40]

She approves the wisdom of her older sister: "I find you are very right to maintain silence, and it is only to please you that I write these lines. I feel how powerless I am to express in human language the secrets of heaven, and after writing page upon page I find that I have not yet begun."[41] Even with Mother Agnes she experiences the same difficulty in expressing herself. "If you only knew how long I would talk if words could express what I think, or rather what I feel."[42] We could say that the entire extent of her conscious being, already at peace, is tempered by her according to its real value and that it no longer arrests her attention. She goes straight beyond it to the mystery of life and of grace which lies at the heart of her existence. She actually feels those depths. Her letters are revealing in this respect. Some teach us nothing about herself; others expose her natural richness, especially her tenderness towards her own. God's gifts in her show up only in an indirect light which acquaintance alone can grasp.

Understanding that she must first make herself known if she is to be directed, she made an attempt to lead her guides to the mystery of her personality. Did she succeed? When asking Father Pichon to take her under his direction, she wrote: "I wish I could make myself known to you, but I am not like my sisters. I cannot express in a letter all that I feel. I believe, Father, that in spite of all this, you will understand me. When you come to Lisieux, I hope to see you at Carmel in order to open my heart to you. God has granted me a great grace. For a long time I have desired to enter Carmel. I believe that the moment has arrived. Papa wants me to enter at Christmas. How good Jesus is to take me at such an early age! My uncle thinks me too young, but yesterday he said that he wants to do the will of God. I just returned from Carmel, where my sisters told me that I could write you and tell you what was taking place in my heart. You see that I have done this."[43] Those last words are delightful. She states simply that she has acquitted herself of her intention to make herself known. But what has she revealed? The fact that she cannot state what she feels! Much later, February 16, 1891, Father Pichon answered a letter she had written: "I understand the silence of your soul. I see the remote recesses of your heart. I can read and reread the thought you do not express."[44]

The little saint always experienced this difficulty in expressing herself. And she experienced it when it was a duty for her to consult the mistress of novices and her prioress. "Far from hiding my dispositions from my superiors, I always tried to be an open book to them. Our novice mistress was *really a saint*, the finished product of the first Carmelites. I was with her all day long since she taught me how to work. Her kindness towards me was limitless and still my soul did not expand under her direction. It was only with great effort that I was able to take direction, for I had never become accustomed to speaking about my soul and I didn't know how to express what was going on within it."[45] "I am continually ill at ease with Mother Prioress. I cannot tell her what is in my soul. When I go to her for direction, I leave without joy."[46]

Was she more at ease confiding to those who attracted her? She confided in the venerable foundress, Mother Geneviève of St Teresa, from the very beginning of her postulancy. But the foundress was astounded at the boldness of her thoughts, and she disconcerted Thérèse by certain reflections. The venerable Mother even deemed it necessary to advise Sister Agnes to watch over her little sister to safeguard her against the illusions of an exaggerated confidence in God. We are not surprised, therefore, at this remark of the saint: "When the opportunity presented itself of opening my soul, I was so little understood that I said to God as St John of the Cross: 'Don't send me any more messengers who don't know how to say what I want to hear.'"[47]

It was to Mother Agnes that Thérèse preferred to make her childhood confidences. Beginning the *Autobiography*, she wrote: "A mother's heart understands her child even when it can but stammer, and so I'm sure of being understood by you, who formed my heart, offering it up to Jesus!"[48] And in a letter of May 30, 1897, a few months before her death: "Don't be troubled if your little daughter seems to have hidden anything from you. I say 'seems' because you know very well that, if she has hidden just a little corner of the envelope (she referred to her body as the envelope, and called her soul the letter), she has never hidden one single line of the letter. Who knows this little letter better than you?"[49] Mother Agnes had seen deeply into her sister, and, knowing her, was she not led to direct her more profoundly?

Did she pass by her own, unknown to them? And if so, did the direction she receive touch only certain free actions always removed from her inner self? Didn't she receive superficial and fragmented direction? Was she deprived of profound and complete direction?

Mother Agnes stated at the process: "Trust in God had become her special characteristic. She felt attracted to this in early childhood, and I had done all in my power to develop this bent in her. She once told me that she had been struck from childhood by this verse from the Book of Job: 'Even if he were to kill me, I would continue to hope in him.'"[50] Isn't this real direction? Without losing herself in analyzing the situation or focusing on secondary aspects Thérèse speaks to her older sister of her confidence in God. There is nothing artificial in this candid outpouring by which she reveals—perhaps unawares—the depths of her soul. Did Pauline realize the importance of her sister's words? Under the influence of the Holy Spirit, she encourages her sister to develop this confidence. This deserves our attention. It was not Mother Agnes who instilled this confidence in Thérèse; she simply facilitated its growth. She had not created her little sister. She respected her individuality and God's grace, and she fostered their development.

Mother Agnes continues: "After her entry into Carmel, Thérèse felt the need to submit the spiritual way to which she felt drawn to the opinion of an enlightened spiritual director. Hers was a combination of desire for the peaks of sanctity and a powerful attraction towards a childlike trust in and complete surrender to our Lord's kindness and love."[51] These lines clearly show us the permanence and the evolution of the grace proper to the saint.

Until she entered the cloister, Mother Agnes' approval was sufficient. Now that she has seized, in all its vehemence, the force which was guiding her towards the heights, and her weakness which appeared to oppose this attraction, she asked herself whether she was not mistaken. Only a priest could judge if she was on the right way or suffering delusions. She will experience no peace till the priestly word has settled the question. Everything is at stake. It is no longer a question of an action to perform, but the deep meaning of her entire life must be settled.

"It was God's will that she should find great difficulty in making her sentiments understood, and it was years before she found the director she was looking for."[52] Father Pichon scarcely hears her and then departs for Canada. He writes her rarely. In his talk with her, he had given her great encouragement by assuring her that she had never lost baptismal innocence. He does not seem to have passed judgment on her basic problem. Father Blino happens to be at the monastery and the saint tries to explain her great desires: "I want to love God as much as St Teresa!" "What pride and what presumption," answers the austere religious. "Limit yourself to correcting your faults."[53] Thérèse conducts herself admirably during these years of waiting. She does not become discouraged nor panic; neither does she move heaven and earth to meet the right director. In spite of these repeated misunderstandings, she remains calm, inflexibly certain. She accepts humbly the reproaches leveled at her supposed presumption.

This peaceful humility finally obtains the needed enlightenment. Father Alexis comes to preach at the monastery in 1891.
The retreats had been very difficult for the saint. She prepares this
year for the retreat with a very fervent novena. She foresees great
suffering. Is it not being said of the retreat master that he is better
at converting sinners than helping souls to advance? Once more
she surmounts her fears and makes the attempt: "I had hardly
entered the confessional when I felt my soul expand. After
speaking only a few words, I *was understood* in a marvelous way
and my soul was like a book in which this priest read better than I
did myself. He launched me full sail upon the waves of *confidence and love* which so strongly attracted me, but upon which I
dared not advance. He told me that *my faults caused God no pain,
and that holding as he did God's place*, he was telling me *in his
name* that God was very much pleased with me. Oh! how happy I
was to hear those consoling words!"[54]

The hand of God is visible in this fact. From a human
standpoint, Thérèse should have kept silent. Was not the secret of
her soul too delicate to reveal to this priest who specialized in the
conquest of sinners? The saint did not give ear to these human
promptings. Childhood convictions told her that the priest would
talk in the name of God.[55] With a fear born of former misunderstandings, she speaks to him of her confidence and love. Can she
cast herself on a confidence without bounds while she still offends
God? "Your sins cause God no pain! You will never have enough
confidence in the divine mercy!" It is God who speaks. The priest
is telling her only what she has already foreseen.

In August, 1890 [*sic*], she had written Mother Agnes: "It seems
to me that Jesus can easily grant me the grace of offending him no
more, or of committing only those faults which don't offend him,
but serve to humiliate me and render love more strong."[56] From
this retreat onward, says Mother Agnes, Thérèse surrendered
herself entirely to confidence in God and she searched the
Scriptures for an approbation of her boldness. She repeated the
words of St John of the Cross: "One obtains from God as much as
one hopes for."[57]

Did Father Alexis visualize the consequences of his words to
Thérèse? Did he realize that he had actually fathomed the depths

of the soul of this little Carmelite who had revealed her spiritual ambitions so timidly? We state explicitly that spiritual direction does not necessarily presuppose in the director a knowledge of the depths of the soul he reaches, nor the import of the words he pronounces. The efficacy of direction comes from God himself, and that efficacy can give power to sacerdotal words without the priest even perceiving it.

The director is nothing but an instrument in the hands of God. St John of the Cross teaches: "These directors should reflect that they themselves are not the chief agent, guide and mover of souls in this matter, but that the principal guide is the Holy Spirit, who is never neglectful of souls, and that they are the instruments for directing them to perfection through faith and the law of God, according to the spirit God gives each one."[58] His role is not the same as that of the teacher of the human sciences. A professor is appointed to teach philosophy, literature, mathematics, etc., which reveal only the conclusions of reason. It does happen that a director has recourse to certain precedents: learns how to pray, to discern what is sinful, to choose a certain mortification. We would say that this is horizontal direction. It is useful, and it bears fruit, but it is not sufficient in itself. We must join to it vertical direction, which takes into consideration the grace proper to the one being directed. A delicate work! Even to suppose that the continual advancements of psychology permit us to delve more deeply into the mystery of the individual, there still remains a sphere which will escape scientific explanation. The director will never penetrate that sphere except with the light which God alone can dispense. This work does not stop at the integral knowledge of the one he is directing. It is necessary that his word be efficacious; it must be light and force. It will have this power only if it is penetrated by the divine motion, in such a way that the action of the director is nothing but an instrument the effect of which belongs principally to God.

St Thérèse has sensed it. She has marked the limits of what we call direction in a few very exact statements. She wrote to Mother Agnes: "Are you not the one who taught me to know and love Jesus?"[59] And to her older sister Marie: "are you not the angel who has led me and guided me on the road of exile until my

entrance into Carmel?"[60] St John of the Cross speaks no differently: "Let directors be content with disposing them for this
according to evangelical perfection, which lies in nakedness and
emptiness of sense and spirit; and let them not desire to go any
further than this in building since that function belongs only to
the Father of lights from whom descends every good and perfect
gift" (Jas 1:17).[61]

This presence and this invisible action of God which the saint
experienced when she took counsel explains her attitude toward
direction. When she was sick, her novices asked her: "Give us
some advice about spiritual direction. How must we go about it?"
She replied, "With great simplicity, but without relying too
much on help which might prove inadequate when you come to
make use of it. You would soon find yourselves forced to say, like
the spouse in the *Song of Songs*: 'The guards have taken away my
cloak, they have wounded me; it was only by getting a little
beyond them that I found my Beloved' (5:7; 3:4). If you ask the
guards humbly and without being overdependent where your
Beloved is, they will tell you. But, more often than not, you will
find Jesus only after you have left all creatures behind."[62] These
counsels are nothing but the outcome of her own experience. She
expressed her own conduct with regard to Father Pichon. She
enunciated a principle which modern psychology has brought to
light: To give oneself to God, one must have a spiritual director,
but the gift will not be entire till the soul advances beyond the
director, without ceasing to be directed.

Several important traits characterize the passive direction of St
Thérèse. She wished to be guided; to be instructed; from the dawn
of reason when she learned the Our Father and Hail Mary at the
knees of her mother, until her last day when she begged her
Mother Prioress to teach her how to die, she remained always
docile to the divine lessons.

What answers must be given to this determined will? If, during
her childhood and youth, counsel was not lacking, from the very
beginning of her religious life it was rare. However, it never failed
her. Little by little human direction receded in favor of direction
from the Holy Spirit.

Finally, we admire the liberty and the purity of the saint in her direction. God did not permit his "little queen" to be compromised by a director. She herself had too sharp a sense to attach herself in an exaggerated manner to the instrument which God had supplied. This attachment would have been a screen between her soul and the light from on high.

In this masterpiece, the soul of little Thérèse, we can affirm that God was particularly jealous. Without rejecting human instruments, whom he associates in all sanctification, he had willed that her direction be transmitted by men who would not measure the grandeur of the role they enjoyed. He had willed that his direction would be seen more clearly than in the lives of other saints where human instruments are more apparent.

St Thérèse of the Child Jesus did not have a director in the strict sense of the word. She was directed, and for her are verified the words of the Book of Deuteronomy, which the Church has chosen for the Introductory Antiphon of her Mass: "He led her about and taught her, and he kept her as the apple of his eye. As the eagle he spread his wings and has taken her on his shoulder. The Lord alone was her leader."[63]

She can sing with St John of the Cross: "I had no other light or guide than the one that burned in my heart."[64] (Trans. J. Clarke)

NOTES

1. EDITOR'S NOTE: In order to mark the centenary of St Thérèse's birth in 1973 a team of scholars was established to compile definitive critical editions of the saint's works. The team has had free access to the monastery archives in Lisieux for all their work, and it has produced several erudite volumes on which several I.C.S. translations have been based and from whose work future translations will be derived. See *Story of a Soul* (Washington: ICS Publications, 1976), p. xvii, hereinafter referred to as "S", and *St Thrèse of Lisieux: Her Last Conversations* (Washington: ICS Publications, 1977), p. 7, hereinafter referred to as "LC". Both these I.C.S. editions were translated by a member of the I.C.S., Fr. John Clarke OCD, who also has translated this article.

2. Procès Apostolique, *Proces de Beatification et Canonisation de Sainte Therèse de l'Enfant-Jesus et de la Sainte-Face,* II (Rome: Teresianum, 1976), p. 480. Cited hereinafter as "Process."

3. See "Biographical Guide for Proper Names, 'Ducellier,'" LC, pp. 298-99.

4. S, pp. 40-41.

5. See "Dictionnaire des noms propres, 'Domin,'" Sainte Thérèse de l'Enfant-Jésus et de la Sainte-Face, *Correspondance Générale*, II (Paris: Cerf-Desclée de Brouwer, 1973), p. 1200 and S, pp. 75–90. Cited hereinafter as "*Correspondance*."

6. See Dictionnaire des noms propres, "Lepelletier," *Correspondance* II, p. 1205 and S, pp. 104–05.

7. LC, p. 58. See Biographical Guide for Proper Names, "Youf," LC, p. 309.

8. See Dictionnaire des noms propres, "Baillon," *Correspondance* II, p. 1198 and Biographical Guide for Proper Names, "Faucon," LC, p. 299.

9. See Biographical Guide for Proper Names, "Pichon," LC, p. 306.

10. See Dictionnaire des noms propres, *Correspondance* II: p. 1198 for Fr Alexis (Prou); p. 1200 for Fr Déodat (de Basly); pp. 1204–05 for Fr (Armand-Constant) Lemonnier; and p. 1205 for Fr (Godfrey) Madelaine.

11. Mother Agnes (Pauline) Martin, "Testimony for Beatification Process," *St Thérèse of Lisieux by Those Who Knew Her: Testimonies from the Process of Beatification* trans. and ed. Christopher O'Mahoney (Huntington, Ind.: Our Sunday Visitor Inc., 1976), p. 38. EDITOR'S NOTE: This work is an edited translation of excerpts from the canonization processes cited in Note 2, *supra*. Cited hereinafter as "OSV".

12. OSV, p. 52. EDITOR'S NOTE: The French original has "*sentiments intérieurs*" for the term "spiritual life" rendered by O'Mahoney.

13. *Ibid.*

14. S., p. 174.

15. EDITOR'S NOTE: This letter, along with all the letters received by Fr Pichon, is no longer extant. A draft copy of one does exist, however—see notes 17 and 43, *infra*. Some idea of what Thérèse wrote can be had from the text of Fr Pichon's reply dated May 6, 1884, *Correspondance* I, p. 172.

16. See Thérèse's own remarks about this in a letter to Marie dated October 2, 1886, *Correspondance* I, pp. 211–12.

17. *Correspondance* I, p. 254. A draft of this letter was conserved: it is dated as October 23 (?), 1887.

18. S, pp. 150 and 151–52.

19. See *Correspondance* I, pp. 452–54 for letter of January 23–25, 1889; pp. 459–60 for letter of February 28, 1889 and *passim* for quotations of Fr Pichon's sayings by Thérèse.

20. This letter is not extant.

21. S, p. 151.

22. S, p. 113.

23. Procès Apostolique, *Process* II, p. 114.

24. Fr Baillon became extraordinary confessor of the monastery in 1892. See *Correspondance* II, note e, p. 678.

25. OSV, p. 52.

26. Mother Agnes (Pauline) Martin, OSV, p. 46.

27. See French edition of LC, *J'entre dans la vie: Derniers entretiens* (Paris: Cerf-DDB, 1972), photographic reproduction between pp. 80 and 81.

28. Sr Marie (Martin) of the Sacred Heart, "Testimony," OSV, p. 88.

29. *Ibid.*

30. S, p. 22.

31. S, p. 166.

32. See Ch. 12 of the old version of her life *Histoire d'une âme* (Lisieux: Office Central de Lisieux, 1924), p. 224. This chapter was a posthumous addition to Thérèse's own texts.

33. OSV, p. 52.

34. Dark Night of the Soul Poem, st. 2, I.C.S. ed., p. 295.

35. Gaston Rabeau, *Le jugement d'existence* (Paris: J. Vrin, 1938), p. 202.

36. S, p. 238.

37. S, p. 239.

38. F, 3, 59.

39. November 14, 1887 to Madame (Céline) Guerin, *Correspondance* I, p. 285.

40. April 27 (?), 1889 to Céline Martin, *Correspondance* I, p. 481.

41. S, p. 189.

42. September 3, 1890 to Sister Agnes (Pauline) Martin, *Correspondance* I, p. 567.

43. October 23 (?), 1887, *Correspondance* I, p. 254.

44. February 16, 1891 to Thérèse, *Correspondance* II, pp. 632-33.

45. S, p. 151. Underlining in original. The novice mistress at the time was Sr Mary (de Chaumontel) of the Angels. See Biographical Guide for Proper Names, LC, p. 304.

46. January 8, 1889 to Sr Agnes (Pauline) Martin, *Correspondance* I, p. 441.

47. Sr Mary of the Trinity, *Process* II, p. 480. See St John of the Cross, C, 6, 6-7.

48. S, p. 15.

49. May 30, 1897, *Correspondance* II, p. 994.

50. Mother Agnes (Pauline), OSV, p. 42.

51. Mother Agnes (Pauline), OSV, p. 52.

52. *Ibid.*

53. See note h to May 19-20, 1890 letter from Thérèse to Céline, *Correspondance* I, pp. 533-34.

54. S, pp. 173-74. Underlining in original.

55. S, p. 40.

56. This letter is now dated September 3, 1890. See *Correspondance* I, p. 567.

57. Mother Agnes (Pauline), OSV, p. 43. See St John of the Cross, N, 2, 21, 8.

58. F, 3, 46. EDITOR'S NOTE: See the article of Lucien-Marie Florent, *supra.*

59. January 21, 1894 to Mother Agnes, *Correspondance* II, p. 744.

60. September 2-3, 1890 to Sr Marie (Martin) of the Sacred Heart, *Correspondance* I, p. 566.

61. F, 3, 47.

62. Sr Geneviève (Celine) Martin, "Testimony," OSV, p. 134.

63. Dt 32:10-12.

64. Dark Night of the Soul Poem, st. 3, I.C.S. ed., p. 295.

MISCELLANY

THE TIMELINESS OF LISIEUX

Hans Urs von Balthasar

Father von Balthasar needs no introduction to our reading audience. The eminent Swiss theologian gave the present text in the form of a conference for the 1973 centenary celebrations of Saint Thérèse in Notre Dame Cathedral (because the crowd in attendance was too large to be accomodated in the auditorium of Paris' Institut Catholique).

S he has already been studied so much, and so well, this young 24-year-old woman who left us scarcely more than a little book, some letters and a few words! But the more attention we give her, the broader are the horizons that open up. Doubtless that is characteristic of great saints: they live in God's infinite world, and his eternity manifests itself in their temporal life. Nevertheless, the contours of the finite world do not grow indistinct. In the heavenly Jerusalem each great vocation occupies a well-determined place, distant from others, but not unrelated to them. Like the stars, they form constellations. With the art of celestial geometry spoken of by Claudel, we can measure the relationships between Thérèse of Lisieux and John of the Cross, Teresa of Avila, Joan of Arc, John the Evangelist, Augustine and Thomas Aquinas. Important in such calculations are the divine missions, which determine the *form*, to which correspond as *matter* the natural dispositions of the person: Simon, son of Jonah, thus lends himself as matter to the form of Peter.

What was the religious atmosphere of Les Buissonets? That is at most a question of matter, and we are well aware of the liberty

103

Thérèse took regarding it in subordinating it to her own vocation. For the great artist, all matter (even if imperfect) is like a
welcome ultimate disposition: it is as necessary to him as Christian Bach was to Mozart, or the Italian tales to Shakespeare, or the
Spanish romance to Corneille. But no matter, however well
prepared it may be, will enable us to suspect the inspired form
that is to come forth from it. Consequently psychologists and
psychoanalysts waste their time with Thérèse, as do physicians
who launch into conjectures about the illness of her early years.

In contrast to all these attempts to approach her on the
material level, we see the perfect lucidity of the Theresian form, of
that mission developed to the fullness of a luminous and transparent clarity. What Thérèse says of Mary: "Who could ever have
invented the Blessed Virgin?"[1] can be said of all great vocations,
when the one called has responded as well as possible to the
vocation. There is a rightness about them which bears witness to
itself; those who do not perceive this are to be pitied.

The great saints are surely signs that the Holy Spirit sets up
through the course of history to show the Church the right road,
both doctrinal and practical, which she would have trouble
finding and following without them. Yet, from the human point
of view, they are often unwelcome, inopportune signs, guides
who are followed imperfectly or too late (after their death). Are
not canonizations frequently a means by which the Church
relegates the appeals of the Spirit to the archives? Jean-Marie
Vianney was, without the shadow of a doubt, a living and clear
appeal to restore the practice and the theology of personal
penance: what have we done about it? Lourdes showed just as
clearly that the Immaculate Conception is not a marginal reality
of Catholic theology, but that it is situated at the very heart of
"the spouse without stain or wrinkle." Newman was set up as a
beacon signaling that in ecumenical matters, whatever the sacrifice involved, it was necessary to move beyond the stage of the
"via media," to which we are returning today. Charles de Foucauld was a totally inopportune index finger pointing toward the
desert, the indicator of a gratuitous contemplation, without
regard for immediate results, but having a profound fruitfulness

for the Church. When did so many Catholic professors, preoccupied with sociology, ever perceive these signs? And when have *we* followed them? The saints have little chance among us. *We know better than they.* In many cases, even those of Ars and of Lisieux, we *exempt ourselves by claiming* that these messages have had their time, and that we can, in all tranquility, raise our eyes toward new stars.

We go even further: the aristocratic quality of the saints becomes suspect to us. Is it not a democratic Church of the laity that must today seek its way in this secularized world? Don't the saints have a great advantage in the sense that they can jump right into the middle of the circle which most human beings—and with reason—can only approach painfully from the outside? Aren't the saints too naive when, giving little attention to exegetical problems, they take the word of Scripture at its face value? Don't they propose an overly artificial light, when we should rather, to be honest, be groping along in the night in which we are today in solidarity with all of skeptical and atheistic humanity? But let us not deceive ourselves! When Paul claimed to be all things to all men, it was certainly not to be a skeptic with the skeptics, nor an atheist with the atheists. What benefit would that have been for the skeptics and the atheists? It was only from the burning center of Christian love that he was able to draw enough strength to shine in all directions and to make the light penetrate the darkest corners. An apostolic work can only be the fruit of the gift of self, without reserve or qualification. The aristocratic character of the saints consists in their being unique, and, as unique, inimitable. But God gives them this singularity only to enlighten a countless multitude. Who is more inimitable than the stigmatized Francis, and what family in the whole world is more vast than his? Who is more inimitable than Mary, but who would not want to take shelter under her mantle? Who is more inimitable than Christ, who nonetheless offers himself to us, commands us to imitate him. Thérèse recognized this paradox, and she found the way to make her exceptional love a road accessible to all "little souls." She wanted for herself only what could be adapted to her whole spiritual family. She deemphasizes the difference between what is unique and what is imitable; we might even say that (in a new and disconcerting manner) she emphasizes what love has that is specifically *divine* in the midst of a specifically *human* reality, and that she has consequently enabled theology and anthropology to interpenetrate each other. That is what we would like to demonstrate by surveying three themes in her work which prove its timeliness.

(1) The perfectly natural unity of *love of God* and *love of neighbor*. The love of God is lived in so radical a manner that the love of neighbor seems to have no place within it. But, for Thérèse, the real proof of the Christian authenticity of our love for God is precisely our love for our neighbor, and thus she resolves practically a problem which *theoretically appears insoluble*.

(2) The paradoxical unity between *childhood* and *passion*— "of the Child Jesus and of the Holy Face." This unity, too, is so nonarbitrary that it stands out against a theological background which provides its whole foundation.

(3) Her theology of *hope*, which, existentially, permits her to *dare* everything with God, because she is, existentially, ready to risk all in this adventure—even to the loss of all personal orientation.

These three themes are, of course, not the only aspects of Theresian theology, but by means of them we hope to show at least that this theology is *authentic* and of an extreme importance to us.

Before approaching these points in detail, however, I would like to make a few more general remarks in order to better situate this profoundly Catholic thought.

Thérèse's thought always proceeds from that *central point*, from which alone Christian truth can manifest itself to the intellect and pass into practice. In this regard, the somewhat petty religion of those she lived with provides her with a completely adapted material and foundation.

(1) Thérèse presupposed *indisputably* that the *articles of faith*, based on the Bible and proposed by the Church, are the expres-

sion of divine truth as communicated to us. In this she simply follows the principle of St Thomas Aquinas: "The profane sciences do not argue with a view to proving their principles; they rely upon them and, from there, argue to demonstrate such and such propositions within the science. Likewise sacred science does not claim, by means of argumentation, to prove its own principles, which are the articles of faith: it receives them and, from there, establishes its theses."[2] The real presence of Christ in the Eucharist, the virginal maternity of Mary, the Catholic Church as mystical communion of saints and as visible society, hierarchically organized, with Leo XIII at the head, the efficacy of prayer and of personal sacrifice, but also love of family and of all nature created by God the Father, joyful aspiration to the promised eternal life, all that and many other things as well are, for Thérèse, not the occasion of investigations and uneasy questions, but a completely secure point of departure.

The fact that, in her last moments, Thérèse participated in the doubts and the denials of the atheists is quite another matter. This was an ultimate effect of her willingness, as a Carmelite, to sit at the table of sinners and "taste the bitterness" with them;[3] "I wanted to drink this chalice to the dregs."[4] *Because she* first *believed*, she could then enter into the obscurity of faith.

(2) Her faith is precisely a faith which bathes in the *current of life and of love circulating between Christ and the Church*. There is no other place where one can objectively perceive God's revelation. It is only in the connection between the faith of the primitive Church and the life of Jesus (which this faith renders intelligible), it is only in the word of Scripture inspired by the Spirit (which poses and supposes such a connection) that one has access to and participates in the world of divine revelation. In the final analysis, it is the unbreakable connection between Mary and her Son. Thérèse shows Pauline "the picture of the holy Virgin nursing the little Jesus: "Only that is good milk; you must tell Dr de Cornière that."[5] Thérèse knows her place: "I want to be a daughter of the Church."[6] "Yes, I have found my place in the Church, in the heart of the Church, my Mother, I will be love," for "I understood that the Church had a Heart, and that this

Heart was burning with Love."[7] This love is nothing other than that response, so perfect in Mary, to the love of God in Jesus Christ: Thérèse "wants to be *fascinated* by Your divine glance, [she] wants to become the *prey* of Your Love . . . [of the] burning Abyss of this Love."[8]

(3) This is to say that, for Thérèse, *the multitude* of the articles of faith *is totally reduced* to this flow of life which is its beginning, its direction and its goal, and that precisely this reduction renders them fully luminous. To attain the perfection of love, none of the articles of faith is superfluous. The Canticle of Canticles, which, for John of the Cross and for the whole theological tradition of the Church, constituted a kind of secret sanctuary, is also for Thérèse a center of her spirituality. She said to her sister Marie that she would like to have commented on it.

These preliminary remarks are aimed solely at pointing out the *considerable advance* of the saints in the area of theology. Their point of departure is where so many auxiliary sciences, at the limit of their capacity, end up. They are not useless, to be sure, and several of them, like exegesis, can shed great light upon the essence of love, provided at least that they are resolved to make the leap of faith, which is the precondition for all understanding of Scripture and theology's point of departure. What delays there are, however, and how much *lost effort* when one neglects this *theology of the saints* as a rule for an authentic interpretation of revelation! This is interpretation translated into existence and into prayer, and, if God wills, likewise into speculative thought. The inspired accuracy with which the *least speculative saints* insist upon certain aspects of the Christian life can have unpredictable effects on the living theology of the Church. Consider the *Rule* of St Benedict, the *Testament* of St Francis of Assisi, the *Exercises* of St Ignatius. Like these writings and others, the life and words of Thérèse draw from their own rightness an ever new strength to guide us.

Finally, her theology is essentially a theology of the *Holy Spirit*. Thérèse is the child of the Father, the spouse of the Son only within this ecclesial, sacramental and more especially monastic universe in which she moved and reflected. It is not historic revelation, but its reverberation in the Christian life, *the way of salvation*, which absorbs her attention. All the structures of the Church, including the sacraments, interest her only from this point of view. Thus the *"little way*," the "little doctrine" actually takes the central place. Thérèse presupposes dogma and includes it, but she lives—like Fra Angelico—by contemplating a lived Christian existence. Her doctrine is wisdom in the biblical sense of the term. It is significant that, in the terrible sufferings of her last days, Thérèse definitely knew by experience the *truth of her doctrine*: "I really feel now that what I've said and written is true about everything."[9] This truth is not an abstract logic, but a value existentially experienced. It is the Christian art of loving. This is what we will understand as we survey the three themes for our consideration.

LOVE OF GOD AND OF NEIGHBOR

Here we start with the famous problem of the Christian dimensions, of the vertical and the horizontal. The solution should not be sought in some kind of vague compromise juxtaposing these two dimensions: God on one side, the world on the other. There is, first of all, the immense religious passion for God as "the *All*," according to the expression in Ecclesiasticus (43:27), the All and the Unique One whom we must love with *all* our heart, with all our soul and with all our strength (Deut. 6:4 ff). Thus we have the *aporia*, which is not simply Thérèse's creation but that of the Bible: how to authentically love our human brother, who, far from being the all, seems to be only an insignificant thing, while our whole heart already belongs to God? Nowhere does Thérèse take explicit note of this *aporia*. What is clear is that she wants to love God alone: "I felt the desire of loving only God, of finding my joy only in him."[10] We find this at the beginning of her book. And, at the end: "You know, O my God, I have never desired anything but to *love* You, . . . Your Love has gone before me, and it has grown with me, and now it is an abyss whose depths I cannot fathom. Love attracts love, and, my Jesus, my love leaps towards Yours, it would like to fill the abyss which attracts it, but alas! it is not even like a drop of dew lost in the ocean! For me to love You as You love me, I would have to borrow Your own Love, and then only would I be at rest."[11] "All created being, which is nothing, makes way for the Uncreated, who is reality."[12] If such passages and many others attest that, from experience, Thérèse knows God as the All of love (to the extent that in the final analysis the soul can love him only by virtue of the divine love itself), she was never tainted by the pantheistic idea that upon entering into God mankind could lose its personality. And if her first letters speak continually of the passing of time and of the desire for eternity, if the little girl, toddling along with her hand in her father's hand, sees her name written in the stars, "then desiring to look no longer upon this dull earth . . . I threw back my head,"[13] she dreams nonetheless of the reunion of her whole family in heaven; and, what is more important, she learns, in the irresistible approach of eternity, to know the value of the *earthly moment*: "The day will come when the shadows will disappear, then, there will remain for me only joy, rapture . . . Let us profit from our unique moment of suffering, let us see only each instant. One instant is a treasure."[14] To what can we attribute her about-face from the futility of time and of all earthly things to the recognition of the value of the *"now,"* of *"today"* to which Thérèse devotes a whole poem?

The fact is that this about-face originates *in God himself*: Christians know his love only as a result of his abasement into history, because of his concern for us and his intervention on our behalf. We must therefore admit this mystery: Although God is All, he nevertheless permits us to be something, he confirms us in our own identity and loves us as we are. But there is more: in his abasement (*abasement*, the word recurs three times in a single page of Manuscript A 2v-3),[15] in his "folly of the cross," the love of the suffering God becomes fruitful and redemptive, it lends us the form, the measure and the strength to imitate him. That is why the love between Thérèse and God does not remain a closed dialogue, but, from the beginning, as soon as the ideal of Carmel has awakened within her (before Pauline's entrance), it has become a dialogue in which the whole world has its place. And the more her love for God grows pure and perfect, the more it becomes fruitful for the world, with a fruitfulness such as God appreciates: "Just as a torrent, throwing itself with impetuosity into the ocean, drags after it everything it encounters in its passage, in the same way, O Jesus, the soul who plunges into the shoreless ocean of Your Love, draws with her all the treasures she possesses. Lord, You know it, I have no other treasures than the souls it has pleased You to unite to mine."[16] And we shall see that Thérèse is not thinking, like the Jansenists, of a limited number of souls. In the famous passages in which she discovers her mission in the heart of the Church (the mission of love), from the beginning she gives an *apostolic* meaning to this love: "I would be a missionary, not for a few years only but from the beginning of creation until the consummation of the ages."[17] Thérèse cannot appease this thirst for souls by great works, but by the only thing that is possible to her, the gift of self in suffering, which is expressed in the image that recurs like an obsession: that of the shedding flower, with petal after petal torn from the calyx and thrown away carelessly—"Let nobody be occupied with me, let me be . . . trampled underfoot, forgotten,"[18] until nothing remains of what was a flower except its perfume.

All that could appear farfetched, like the feverish dreams of a consumptive, yet it is the mark or seal of a delicate and sober art of love of neighbor, highly refined. As if Thérèse had nothing else to do but wear herself out inventing ways of showing a face full of cordial and effective love to such and such a disagreeable, contrary, jealous, hurtful, insufferable sister. In the second part of her last manuscript to the prioress, from whom she had much to suffer right up to the end, she explains to her delicately and not without some slyness, but in reference to the Eucharistic Sacrifice of Jesus, how she learned to penetrate ever more deeply into the subtleties of love of neighbor and of enemies, in the spirit of poverty and of obedience, and how, despite all the vexations, she kept a loving attitude: "I take care to appear happy and especially *to be so.*"[19] In the education of her novices she knew how simultaneously to teach her doctrine of inexorable forgetfulness of self—that is the "little way"—and to deepen it within herself.

The Christian unity of love of God and of neighbor is profoundly *theological*: it is situated in the imitation of the Son who does only his Father's will. This will is to present the Son (and, in him, God in his entirety) to the world. The perfectly harmonious and undistorted figure of little Thérèse shows that this theological mystery is by no means absurd.

She provides us with the image of first-class Christian humanism. She detests all solemnity, even among the saints. She distrusts all exceptional phenomena to which "little souls" cannot aspire. We know the passages in which she resolutely opposes certain attitudes of the great Teresa and sometimes even of St John of the Cross, thus freeing Carmel from the burden of a sort of obligation to mysticism. She resists to the end the dreadful desire of her sisters to canonize her during her lifetime: "We used to say that she was patient, that she was holy, that she was beautiful."[20] Her reply: "I feel a keen joy not only when others find me imperfect, but especially when I feel so myself." Or: "When I think we are taking care of a little saint!" Her reply: "Well, so much the better! However, I would want God to say it."[21] She puts everything back in its proper place with an imperturbable humor that causes those present, who are eager for edification, to burst out laughing.

All her natural talents attained a sublime development. In the course of her few years, her intellect never ceased growing. She can, thanks be to God, apply to herself the words of the Psalmist: "I have had understanding above old men, because I have sought your will."[22] She brings to bear upon the other nuns, on her novices, and even on her prioress, a penetrating gaze which nothing escapes, but which judges everything from the viewpoint of love: both infinitely indulgent and inexorably concerned for God. Her *will* is of iron, she does not indulge herself in anything, everything counts. After her hemoptysis, she continues to work hard, and complains of nothing. When dying, she still holds a glass tremblingly for hours because her infirmarian has fallen asleep. But I would like to stress especially the extraordinary, brilliant and perfectly healthy ardor of her *imagination*. Though her poetry remains, as to form, a prisoner of the taste of her time—where, after all, would she have learned the language of

Péguy or of Claudel?—her mind is a bubbling spring of the most pertinent, the most original and the most unforgettable images which, I am not afraid to say, render her the equal of the two great Reformers of Carmel in poetic power. Let us not limit ourselves to the images of flowers, clouds, rain, dew, sun, the little drop of water that is lost in the ocean.[23] There are also the brand new comparisons of the toy, the little ball of no value that can be thrown on the ground, kicked, pierced, left in a corner or even pressed to one's heart.[24] There is the obscure grain of sand trampled under the feet of passersby.[25] There are the symbols of grace: the steps of the staircase too high for the little foot of the child, whom the mother then lifts up;[26] the elevator, that new invention in the homes of the rich, which Thérèse proceeds to appropriate for herself;[27] the physician who removes the stone from the path of his son;[28] the donkey of La Fontaine carrying the relics to which Thérèse compares herself;[29] the lottery ticket;[30] the little paintbrush;[31] there is that new form of suffering: the pinpricks,[32] the half-extinguished wick from which the candles are lighted and which finally lights up the universe.[33] There will also be the whole special imagery of suffering to which we will return later. All that is Theresian humanism: *Gratia elevat et perficit naturam, etiamsi perficiendo destruit illam* (Grace elevates and perfects nature, even though in doing so it annihilates it.)

CHILDHOOD AND PASSION

Thérèse took as her motto the two extreme moments of Jesus' life. In the light of these two extremes, the mystery of the God-man unfolds before her eyes. Together they manifest the same fundamental attitude of the Son with regard to the Father and with regard to mankind: nakedness, abandonment, vulnerability. Thérèse secretly wanted the name "of the Child Jesus" and she received it without having asked for it. She gave precise and detailed explanations of what she understands by "being a child": "It is to recognize our nothingness, to expect everything from God . . . it is to be disquieted about nothing, and not to be set on gaining our living . . . it is not attributing to oneself the virtues that one practices. . . . Finally, it is not to become discouraged over one's faults . . .''[34] On the whole, it is the mystery of total abandonment to God, without self-preoccupation, to God by whom one knows oneself to be loved infinitely, as the child is loved by his father. It is evident that such an ideal of pure and confident self-renunciation is possible only for a Christian, in the mystery of the eternal Son of God become a human child. And it is only by reason of the absolute confidence of the Son in his Father that the Father can propose the passion to the Son. All the gifts of the Father, even the most painful, the most cruel, the most inconceivable, are good, because a father can give only benefits to his child. In short, if the redemption of humanity is possible, it is solely because the Son of God remains always the Child of the Father. Thérèse recognized very clearly the unity that binds childhood and passion. Speaking of Isaiah 53, she can thus say: "These words . . . have made the whole foundation of my devotion . . .''[35] In her "Dream of the Child Jesus," childhood and passion are reflected in each other. The child sees in a dream the instruments of his martyrdom, "his child's face . . . he sees disfigured, bleeding! . . . unrecognizable! Jesus is well aware that all will abandon him, yet the divine Infant smiles at this bleeding face.''[36] The child is the eternal subject, the passion is a temporal attribute which is superadded to him: it is understood from childhood, and not inversely.

To be a child, for Thérèse, is to combine a limitless and fully confident *availability* with the certitude of being able *to formulate all one's desires*. In the child, the identification of docility and ingenuousness is the perfect symbol of the Trinitarian mystery of the relationships between Jesus and his Father in the Spirit. Thérèse cannot bear anyone's having "respect" for God.[37] She wants to live with God as familiarly as the Son with his Father. This presupposes that one accepts everything from God, like a child. She does not want God to handle her carefully. "Tell him," she says to Marie, "never to put himself out on my account.''[38] Thus, on the one hand, she shows an indifference pushed to the extreme: "I don't want to die more than to live; that is, if I had the choice, I would prefer to die. But since it's God who makes the choice for me, I prefer what he wills.''[39] She says the same thing in a thousand ways: "Yes, my God, I want it all!"[40] "I would choose nothing."[41] She asks Marie to arrange it so that she will not cough so much so as not to wake Céline, "but I added: If you don't do it, I'll love you even more."[42] Finally: "God made me always desire what he wanted to give me."[43] With regard to indifference, she arrives at the point where God "doesn't know what to do with me."[44] *But she knows very well how to deal with him*: "It's in this way that I've taken God in."[45]

At this moment the relationship reverses itself: the other side of childhood is limitless *confidence*. There is hardly a word that appears more often with Thérèse than *boldness*: "Confident to the point of boldness in his goodness as Father";[46] "daring desire . . . bold confidence."[47] "Is this rashness? No, for a long time You have allowed me to be bold with You."[48] Joining the two aspects, she speaks of "bold abandonment," of her "rash abandonment."[49] This dialectic which, viewed through the image of childhood, appears quite simple, truly disappears in the abyss of the Trinitarian mystery: the total abandonment of the Son to the will of the Father is identified with the will of the Son always granted by the Father (Jn 11:42; 17:24).

Having arrived at this theological summit, we cannot avoid speaking of certain *dangers* which threatened Thérèse and momentarily blurred her clarity of vision, without however compromising it definitively. Her ideal of childhood demanded total candor, free of any preoccupation with self, about *the* extraordinary character of her election. A first mishap occurred when, at the age of ten, she was cured by the smile of a statue of the Virgin and knew rightly that she ought not to speak of this grace. "Ah! I thought . . . never will I tell anyone for my *happiness would then disappear*."[50] But her sisters had already guessed something and gave her no peace until she yielded. Then everything was messed up at the parlor of Carmel: Thérèse was placed by her entourage on the pedestal of one miraculously cured. Without its being her fault, she lost part of her naive spontaneity. The second fault had more serious consequences. Father Pichon declared in the confessional, with great solemnity: "You have never committed a single mortal sin."[51] But from all Thérèse's declarations (in particular in her poems that treat of the rivalry between the lily and the rose or of the love of innocent souls and of sinful souls), it is clearly evident that Thérèse understood this declaration as affirming that she had *never sinned*. Nowhere does she make mention of the idea of venial sin. Whereas Mother Agnes, in the *Novissima Verba*, wrote: "One could believe that it is because I have been preserved from *mortal sin* that I have such great confidence. . . ,"[52] the yellow notebook, the green notebooks and the Ordinary Process read: "One could believe that it is because I have *not sinned* that I have such great confidence."[53] From this would arise difficulties that were almost insurmountable, but finally were surmounted when it was a question of sitting at the table of sinners, of confessing common sin in the indistinct communion of saints. We have already spoken of the third danger: that of being canonized by her sisters while still alive. She is almost totally beyond the reach of this danger; she was beyond such temptations. She replies simply with a superior humor. But even in that there is still expressed her constant need to esteem herself, to be preoccupied with herself, a permanent trait which will stay with her to the end and perhaps deprived her of the possibility of being led by God into the real dark night. On the day of her death, in the midst of her agony, she can still affirm: "Yes, I have understood humility of heart. . . . It seems to me I'm humble."[54] How strange it is also, this need she has to leave her reflection: "Why are you looking so intently at the bottom of the chalice?" "Because my reflection is there; when I was sacristan, I used to love doing this. I was happy to say to myself: My features are reflected in the place where the Blood of Jesus rested . . . How many times, too, have I thought that at Rome, my face was reproduced in the eyes of the Holy Father."[55]

THEOLOGY OF HOPE

If the theology of childhood and that of the passion are timely for us because we would like to *eliminate* them from the image of Jesus we make for ourselves, the theology of hope in Thérèse is timely because it *corrects* our own aspirations. For her, the theology of hope does not proceed from the need to change the present state of the world; nor is it the *lukewarm* expectation that all will end well between mankind and God. For Thérèse, it is the logical consequence of her rash boldness which cannot be maintained apart from an absolute availability to do the will of God in all things, however painful and demanding that may be. "My folly is to hope."[56] Thérèse hopes for sinners, she hopes boldly for *all* sinners, *to the extent* that she is ready to substitute herself for sinners, to *pay* for them. The expansion of the horizon of her hope is proportionate to the growth of her ecclesial availability, it is, properly speaking, the hope of the Church as being Immaculate, and it is only by reason of the communion of saints that it is a hope in which *all* are authorized to share. "My hopes," says Thérèse, "touch upon the infinite."[57]

In the official theology of the West, since Augustine at the latest, unlimited hope finds itself shackled by the certitude that a certain number of people will be damned, and, in a still more disastrous way, by the doctrine of a double predestination erected into a system. But it is significant that, from the Middle Ages up to the modern epoch, a whole series of women saints have silently protested against this masculine theology, and, being strong in their heartfelt boldness and having a direct access to the mystery of salvation, they have expressed a boundless hope. Limiting ourselves to the greatest names, let us mention Hildegarde, Gertrude, Mechthilde of Hackeborn, Mechthilde of Magdeburg, Lady Julian of Norwich, Catherine of Siena, to whom could doubtless be added Catherine of Genoa, Marie of the Incarnation and even Madame Guyon. But the theology of women has never been taken seriously nor integrated by the establishment. Nevertheless, after the message of Lisieux, thought must finally be given to this in the current reconstruction of dogmatic theology. Obviously Thérèse—like those who preceded her—was not able to plumb the depths of the problem of damnation and God's justice; that was not a part of her mission. But in a great heartfelt outburst, she discovered that God's love cannot be limited to his justice (this is an idea that we find already in St Anselm, who, in this case, draws upon Augustine): "His Justice . . . seems to me clothed in *love*."[58] Moreover, it is God's *love*, unrecognized by sinners, which is forgotten by most Christians, even by priests and religious; it is *this love* that most needs consolation. Thus, on the Feast of the Trinity in 1895, Thérèse offered herself as a holocaust to the merciful love of God. In explanation of the "victimation," here is what Thérèse says: ". . . believe in the truth of my words: we never have too much confidence in the good God, so powerful and so merciful! We obtain from him as much as we hope for! . . ."[59] Thérèse is also familiar with the words of the Lord to St Mechthilde: "I tell you in truth, it is a great joy for me when people expect great things from me. However great may be their faith and their boldness, I will overwhelm them far beyond their deserts. In fact, it is impossible that they not receive what they have believed and hoped to receive from my power and from my mercy."[60] "My excuse," says Thérèse, "is that I am a child, children do not reflect upon the extent of their words," and finally she is "the child of the Church, since she is Your spouse."[61] How then do royal parents fulfill the desires of their child? Is not such hope *blind*? Thérèse is prepared to say so: "It is blind hope that I have in his mercy."[62] She also adds to her list the expression of St Paul: "I never ceased hoping against all hope."[63]

It is indispensable that we situate this hope properly; exactly where Thérèse encounters Jesus: in his childhood and in his passion, that is to say, in the total vulnerability of divine love, outraged and forgotten, that one can find only in the stripping of one's own heart. Such is the Carmelite vocation: to be present at the point of encounter between the sinful world and the suffering love of God. Drawing inspiration from a verse of Isaiah 53, Thérèse writes: "I too wanted to be without luster, without beauty, alone to tread the wine in the press, unknown by every creature."[64] Then the weak child becomes the strong virgin, the sister of that Joan of Arc whom she loved so much and whose death by fire she wanted to share, and the fire did not spare her. In her boldness, Thérèse draws upon herself the divine anger: "In order that Love be fully satisfied, it is necessary that It lower Itself, and that It lower Itself to nothingness and transform this nothingness into *fire*."[65] We know in what manner God took her at her word by withdrawing from her the light and the joy of faith, hope and love. If she is consumed slowly, inexorably, in this frightful passion, whose cruelty is revealed to us by the new documents, this is because she is *paying* for her bold hope. She resolved "not to rise from this table filled with bitterness . . . before the day that You have appointed."[66] Again we have a flood of images: she is walking in an underground passageway, poorly lighted, not knowing whether she is advancing.[67] She is Tom Thumb sowing his treasures;[68] the child abandoned at the railway station, the trains come and go but none of them carries her away;[69] Robinson Crusoe on his island, who waits for a ship that never appears;[70] the bird with a cord tied to its foot;[71] someone offers her a cake, but as soon as she tries to take it, a hand withdraws it;[72] she is chained in a prison.[73] The beacon that indicated the port of heaven disappears.[74] A wall rises to the heavens and hides the stars.[75] A piece of cloth is stretched over the frame, but nobody comes to embroider it.[76] And finally the splendid image, which includes all that she has said about grace: "It reminds me of a greased pole; I've made more than one slip, then, all of a sudden there I am at the top!"[77] In all these obscurities did she lose hope? She lost the strength of it, the impetus to give it to others, to her constantly increasing family.

Thérèse certainly seems to be the most joyful saint. She shows us how marvelous and poignant it is to live in intimacy with God. And she is afraid of nothing. She belies Christopher Fry's comedy "The Lady's Not for Burning." Yes, the Lady wants to burn. She plays with the fire. She loves the adventure. She is absolutely antibourgeois. *We* have made Christianity a complicated, morose, obsolete affair. We are old, God is eternally young, he needs youth which radiates his temperament and his humor.

Lisieux has in no way lost its timeliness.

Let me conclude with a remark from a foreigner. For the Catholic world, France has been the land of great saints. That is her Christian genius. Is she well aware of this today? Why regale us endlessly with commentaries on Hegel and Feuerbach, Marx, Nietzsche and Freud, with whom we have nothing in common? It is already 60 years since Péguy chided the Sorbonne for being Kantian and sociological. "We must renounce this fine High German speech," he said. Quite so: we have received Charles de Foucauld, Madeleine Delbrêl, Henri de Lubac and so many others. But we are insatiable beggars: may France continue to give us the alms of Catholic Sanctity! (Trans. C. Latimer)

NOTES

1. LC, p. 177.
2. *Summa Theologica*, Ia Iae, p. 8.
3. S, p. 215.
4. S, p. 218.
5. LC, p. 84.
6. S, p. 253.
7. S, p. 194.
8. S, p. 200.
9. LC, p. 200.
10. S, p. 79.
11. S, p. 256.
12. Letter of September 7, 1890 to Sr Marie (Martin) of the Sacred Heart, *Correspondance* I, p. 574.
13. S, p. 43.
14. Letter of April 26, 1889 to Céline (Martin), *Correspondance* I, 478.
15. See S, 14-15.
16. S, p. 54.
17. S, p. 193.
18. S, p. 275.
19. S, p. 228.
20. See LC, p. 180.
21. LC, p. 181.
22. S, p. 209.
23. S, p. 77.
24. S, p. 136.
25. S, p. 207. See also S, p. 275.
26. S, p. 207.
27. *Ibid.*
28. S, p. 84.
29. S, p. 234.
30. LC, p. 51.
31. S, p. 235.
32. Letter of March 15, 1889 to Céline (Martin), *Correspondance* I, p. 473.
33. LC, p. 99.
34. LC, pp. 138-89.
35. LC, p. 135.
36. Letter of January 21, 1894 to Mother Agnes (Pauline), *Correspondance* II, p. 744.

37. LC, p. 74.

38. LC, p. 63.

39. LC, pp. 50-51.

40. LC, p. 203.

41. LC, p. 190.

42. LC, p. 149.

43. LC, p. 94.

44. LC, p. 75.

45. LC, p. 182.

46. *Novissima Verba*, 3.8.ba (Lisieux: Office Central de Lisieux, 1927), p. 113.

47. S, p. 72.

48. S, p. 255.

49. S, pp. 198 and 199.

50. S, p. 66.

51. S, p. 149.

52. See LC, p. 73, No. 4.

53. LC, p. 89.

54. LC, p. 205.

55. LC, p. 192.

56. S, p. 200.

57. S, p. 192.

58. S, p. 180.

59. See old version of her life *Histoire d'une âme* (Lisieux: Office Central de Lisieux, 1940 ed.), p. 246.

60. See Ida Görres, *The Hidden Face* (New York: Pantheon, 1959), p. 279.

61. S, p. 224.

62. Letter of September 17, 1896 to Sr Marie (Martin) of the Sacred Heart, *Correspondance* II, p. 895.

63. S, p. 136.

64. *Novissima Verba*, p. 119.

65. S, p. 195.

66. S, p. 212.

67. S, p. 212 and Letter of August 30-31, 1890 to Sr Agnes (Pauline), *Correspondance* I, p. 557.

68. S, p. 23 and LC, p. 180.

69. LC, p. 62.

70. LC, p. 136.

71. LC, p. 133.

72. LC, p. 47.

73. LC, p. 144.

74. LC, p. 65.

75. S, p. 214.

76. LC, p. 64.

77. LC, p. 80.

THE HISTORICAL SETTING OF ST TERESA'S LIFE

Teófanes Egido, O.C.D.

Father Teófanes Egido is a professor of history at the State University of Valladolid, Spain, the city blessed by the presence of the fourth foundation of St. Teresa.

INTRODUCTION[1]

There has been an evident lack of proportion in the study of St Teresa; much has been written about her spiritual life, resulting in an extensive bibliography primarily on mystical and doctrinal themes. These are always inspiring, but run the risk of presenting a saint without real contacts with her times, with their concrete problems, and with the special place of a woman fully integrated into her society (or in opposition to it).[2] To detach her from the historical conditions of sixteenth century Spain, from the particular circumstances of the Church in which she lived, can ultimately obscure her supernatural experience and her ecclesial work of reform; on the other hand, attention to her human qualities is an increasingly indispensible condition for understanding her total work, and even more essential for the comprehension of her writings.

Very evident and understandable conditions have influenced classical historiography of St Teresa. But especially since the saint lived during one of the most thoroughly examined periods of Spanish history (although some aspects still remain obscure), today's historian cannot easily avoid the reproach that Teresian writers have not yet freed themselves from basic presuppositions of the past, now anachronistic, depriving the saint of a thorough and adequate treatment.

A review of the Teresian bibliography, necessarily brief, brings us to the following conclusions: The baroque biographies of Yepes and Ribera, in spite of their insights, do not satisfy present demands, which require other answers to the problems raised by Teresa's writings.[3] Strangely enough, the polemical overtones and contexts which conditioned the Carmelite sources, the "Chronicles" of Jerónimo de San José, and even more those of Francisco de Santa María,[4] reappear today in essays as current as those of Donázar and Moriones,[5] although with the guilty parties reversed; whereas before Gratian was charged with side-tracking the Teresian charism, now Doria bears the blame. Fortunately, the initial efforts of Mir[6] are being completed by Efrén de la Madre de Dios and Steggink, in a work as ambitious and valuable as it is partially unfinished,[7] and by the concrete contributions of Isaías Rodríguez, Enrique Llamas, Maroto, and Dobhan, which cast new light on aspects indispensable for understanding Teresa.[8]

For such reasons, the attempt to place the Teresian work in its real historical context requires setting aside in good part the views offered up till now. For our part, in particular, we will focus more intensely on the new aspects and conclusions proceeding from perspectives which are more general and—except in the cases just mentioned—far removed from the intracarmelite polemic, the perspectives offered by such authors as Domínguez Ortiz, Márquez Villanueva, Homero Seris, Américo Castro, Sánchez Albornoz, Gutiérrez Nieto, and so on. With the indirect illumination they provide, and with a review of the partially unexplored primary sources, we will attempt to present the least deficient picture possible of some of the essential factors for the comprehension of the Teresian writings.

THE TIMES AND MILIEU OF SAINT TERESA

This long-standing, almost antiseptic, treatment is all the more surprising because St Teresa's work bursts upon the scene as a document of the first order, as valuable as it is barely explored, for tracing the real history of that Spain which witnessed, with astonishment or indifference, her shining steps. Accustomed to contemplating her in her mystical isolation, we frequently forget that the "Madre" did not turn her back on her own times. Totally immersed in them, she not only reveals the popularity of the Inquisition,[9] but even transmits very personal views on matters which, at least in appearance, had little to do with her immediate concerns: her dissatisfaction with the process of Portugal's annexation;[10] suspected rebellions of the "moriscos" of Seviſle;[11] the failure of Phillip II's military policy against the Protestants;[12] premonitions of difficulties from the imminent religious wars in France;[13] the "Italian situation";[14] or the spiraling inflation which ruined many, enriched a few, and forced her to increase enormously the economic provisions for the survival and security of her monasteries,[15] etc.; without mentioning for the moment problems of the social order, admirably examined in the frank and lively comments of an exceptional eyewitness.

Nevertheless, it is not the intention of our study to focus on the investigation of these historical problems. Hoping to assist the understanding of Teresa's writings, we prefer that our own pages set hers in their historical framework, in their milieu, in the actual concerns which explain or motivate them, though admittedly it is difficult to avoid being charmed by the lively portrait drawn from her works.

The Teresian Milieu

St Teresa spent her whole life in Castile. Only once did she leave Castile proper when, half-deceived by her adored Father Gratian, she made the foundation in Seville. She did it reluctantly, and in a masterful chapter [of the *Book of Foundations*] left her own record of the ill-fated journey, of the heat so different from that of her homeland, of the fevers, the roads, and the inns.[16]

Furthermore, fortune did not smile on the early history of this foundation, which, through unforeseen circumstances, found itself involved in obscure Inquisitorial processes and subject to pressures which went against the independent style of the "Madre."[17]

She did not hide her distaste for Andalusia, and the Teresian custom of passing over shortcomings in silence is resoundingly broken when she judges the Andalusians "a strange and deceitful people,"[18] above all deceitful, and so little in accord with the frank character of this typically Castilian woman, who hated duplicity. "This place fully deserves its reputation."[19] "These are not my kind of people here,"[20] she finally says, and, with the greatest candor, "I don't get along with the people of Andalusia."[21]

The absence of Andalusia from the Madre's program of foundations[22] has other understandable causes besides her personal experience and the opinion then current in Castile about the Andalusian religious atmosphere.[23] The licence from the superior general to extend her Discalced reform was limited to Castile;[24] outside of the permitted region, therefore, any new house would raise immediate jurisdictional problems, as happened in the curious case of Beas, and in that of Seville itself.

Given her spirit of obedience, and taking into account the limitations initially imposed on her by her General, it would be senseless to continue inquiring into the motives behind her admitted preference for the Castilian region. Nevertheless, there are other reasons which explain the rapid spread of reformed monasteries throughout Castile. A glance at the map of these foundations shows that they coincide with the Castilian urban centers, with a definite imbalance in favor of Old Castile. This raises the question of what caused her resistance to founding in rural areas (even those of Castile itself) and her disappointment at the impossibility of making a foundation in Madrid.

Such a preference is not at all mysterious. Old Castile (and the New Castile familiar to the saint) was the most urbanized Spanish kingdom, the richest in population, resources, and money. Modern demographic and economic studies only confirm, with ever more reliable data, the indisputible, showy, and for today disconcerting Castilian superiority.[25] Heavily populated cities meant security for her nuns and ready alms; if the cities were rich, so much the better, for Teresa was well aware that the possibility of living in poverty was based on the apparent paradox of being located in centers of wealth.

Because of this, the Teresian reform among the nuns was substantially an urban phenomenon. Because she was removed from the rural world, perhaps through old tendencies of her "judeoconverso"[26] heritage, population centers dependent on agrarian activities never entered into her original plans. When, due to circumstances beyond her control, she had to relent, she made no effort to hide her reluctance, just as she did not hide her disappointment with the miserable little site of Duruelo, as too poor a cradle for the first stammers of the brilliant reform she envisioned among the friars.[27]

Nor was she really original in this matter. The geographical distribution of the religious clergy, in contrast to the more reasonable distribution of the secular clergy, coincided with the centers of greatest urban density. The cartographic studies of Molinié-Bertrand and the analyses of complementary sources by Felipe Ruiz only confirm the Teresian effort to settle in places where religious orders traditionally (and materially?) accumulated, in accord with the attraction exercised by large populations.[28]

In the Introduction to the *Book of Foundations* another fundamental explanation for such preferences can be noticed: communication. The role that the road played in the activity of the Mother Foundress is well-known, obsessed as she was by her journeys, always foreseeing crude resting places, and condemned in her old age to interminable travel. Villuga's *Index of Roads*, widely used during those years, reaffirms that the saint's travels corresponded with the least difficult (though still hazardous), most frequented network of roads drawn across her Castile.

Thus, alongside the prescriptions of obedience, but more basic (if that were possible), weighty demographic, social, and economic conditions supported the Castilianism of the Madre. The outlying districts, distant, less densely populated, and in economic decline, do not appear in the pages of St Teresa, who was as unfamiliar as other Castilians with those regions, which they considered "strange."[29]

The Age and Its Problems

This Castilianism was a determining element of Teresa's mentality, activity, and many of her reactions, so much so that it is impossible to imagine her reform having been born in any other kingdom of the Iberian Peninsula. Its origins must be placed in opulent Castile, "the intellectual and spiritual capital of Spain,"[30] as Chaunu says, in a time of astonishing expansion, and specifically in the two decades between 1560 and 1580, the best in its history;[31] yet the root cause of its profound poverty was already hidden deep within. St Teresa intensely experienced this Castile, with which she felt identified, whose splendor explains her fortunes and whose miseries she had to suffer in her flesh and spirit.

Thus, Teresa's life—lengthy considering the conditions and life-expectancy in the 16th century—unfolded at a unique time. Born in 1515 (shortly before the arrival of Carlos I with his glorious but ominous heritage) and dying in 1582 (when the policies of Philip II were already rigidly defined), she was a witness, silent or outspoken, of radical changes and postures, more radical than a simple, distant glance leads one to suspect. The magnitude of this theme requires a necessary restriction to the episodes which most directly affected St Teresa, and which are essential to a more adequate understanding of her writings, where such events are dimly or clearly reflected.

Her life coincided with far-reaching changes in the political and economic orientation of Castile; from the peninsular concerns of another time, from the recently attained (though only apparent) religious unity, and from the Mediterranean orientation of the Catholic Monarchs [Ferdinand & Isabella], it passed to the enormous European commitments which arrived with Carlos and his multi-territorial legacy.[32] Later she had to undergo the transition from a Castile open to the whole world during the

Emperor's first years, to the progressive withdrawal which would harden into the isolation ("tibetización") of Philip II, excellently studied by Gutiérrez Nieto.[33] During her adolescence in Avila and first years at the Encarnación, Teresa was perhaps unaware of this brilliant Castile, with its openness, Erasmism, and initial crises. Because of the complete lack of writings relative to this period it has left no mark on her pages. The reaction after the 1540's, the radicalization of Philip II, resulted in closed and anti-Reformationist positions, as justly (though perhaps anachronistically) condemned as they were fruitful. For Teresa in particular they had surprising effects.

The campaigns of the Inquisition, the expansion of the "Indices of Forbidden Books," deprived her of the authentic wellsprings of her spirit. This fact explains partially, if not totally, the phenomenon of her delayed mystical development. The *Index* of the Inquisitor Valdés (1559) robbed her of books in the vernacular which constituted her spiritual nourishment. Since she was always a friend of books—an unusual thing in a woman of her time—the measure overtook her at a critical moment, and her words convey with the utmost candor the great change occasioned by the definitive self-isolation of Castile:

> When they forbade the reading of many books in the vernacular, I felt that prohibition very much because reading some of them was an enjoyment for me, and I could no longer do so since only the Latin editions were allowed. The Lord said to me: "Don't be sad, for I shall give you a living book." I was unable to understand why this was said to me, since I had not yet experienced any visions. Afterward, within only a few days, I understood very clearly, because I received so much to think about and such recollection in the presence of what I saw, and the Lord showed so much love for me by teaching me in many ways, that I had very little or almost no need for books. His Majesty had become the true book in which I saw the truths.[34]

Castile, closed to Europe, open to heaven, with its iron-fisted police system to intercept every outside ideological intrusion which might smell of heresy,[35] with the Holy Office of the

Inquisition (as popular as it was feared) to smother possible internal outbreaks: this situation explains the significance of Teresa's work, which was originally linked less with Trent than with strong reformist currents prior even to Luther.[36] Protestantism might have been the initial motive for undertaking the Reform, as the protagonist herself testifies in vigorous pages of her *Life* and the *Way of Perfection*. Yet historically one ought not to forget the double element of old Hispanic reformism and that particular "counter-reformism" rooted on the one hand in the failure of Charles V's diplomatic and military policy, and on the other in the climate created in Spain between 1559 and 1562. During these years, Castile was shaken by news of Inquisitorial processes and autos-de-fe, while the powerful establishment mobilized its whole propaganda machine to arouse public opinion against the French Calvinist "iconoclasts."[37]

Teresa, without understanding these matters too clearly—who did then?—confused the confessional groups, called the French Huguenots "Lutherans," and mounted her reform with the warlike imagery of soldiers, lieutenants, captains, battles, and medieval castles, something inexplicable in any other time or place not experiencing the adventure and singular commitment of the Castilian "crusade." She was driven to spread her "dovecotes" by her desire to compensate for the churches destroyed by those "Lutherans"; in each episode of the *Foundations* one senses her conviction that she is engaged in a singular combat for the "Peace of the Counter-Reformation."

The Novelty of the Teresian Reform

The novelty of her reform, nevertheless, cannot be seen exclusively as the product of a violent, armed offensive, but rather as a reformist approach to prayer forged basically from favorable elements and from tensions which appear more acute the deeper we probe. The spiritual atmosphere of Castile, long viewed as a model of unity, could not have been more radically divided. The supporters of the decrees of Trent found themselves in irreconcilable conflict with the more rigorous projects of the "Prudent King" (let us note that the masculine branch of the Teresian reform knew how to take advantage of the propitious opposition of the monarch to the directives of the Curia).[38]

In more intimate circles, the currents of spirituality did not (always) run in the same direction. The Teresian writings, which alternate between unconcern and apprehension about the "difficult times" in which they were conceived, clearly reveal the sometimes tragic opposition. The hostility between well- or poorly-defined groups was apparently justified by the wave of "illuminism" which hit certain sectors predisposed by Spanish traditions, by erosion from foreign trends, by the undeniable influence of Erasmus, and later of Lutheranism.[39] The reigning climate of suspicion identified Lutheranism, illuminism, recollection, and mysticism without any great effort to distinguish them from one another. Moreover, given the combination of "orantes" [pray-ers], women, and Jewish ancestry, we can understand the real battle which Madre Teresa—with these three counts against her—had to wage so that her "spiritual" orientation not be denounced by the zealous watchdogs of the faith, and so that she might transmit a reform made up of communities of pray-ers ["orantes"].

With the formidable instrument of the Inquisition made to their measure and always at hand, the cenacles of "espirituales" [spirituals, i.e. those interested in contemplative prayer] found themselves unarmed, abandoned, and always on the verge of being branded as heretics[40] in the face of the attack of the "theologians," armed with all their crushing apparatus and unresponsive to the desire for a personal, experimental encounter with God even more daring than Protestantism's.

This is the key to that liberating sigh of the Madre at the moment of her death: "In the end I die a daughter of the Church."[41] Without taking this into account it is impossible to have any idea of the meaning of her reform, conceived precisely in a meeting of "spirituals,"[42] nor of her struggle for the recognition of a woman's right to the prayer of recollection.[43] And although she made use of them only when it suited her, the primitive nucleus of her autobiography is nothing else than an account intended to convince the "letrados" [literally "learned," the term was commonly used at the time to refer to scholastic theologians] that her experiences and her spirit were not of the devil. Moreover, her insistence on the value of the "letrados," her easy congeniality toward them, the fruitful friendship which joined her with some of them, appear to us as tactical maneuvers adopted to allay suspicions, since Madre Teresa, "spiritual," woman, descendant of "judeoconversos," had more in common with the contrary party. The really strange thing is that, given the unfavorable climate, she did not encounter even more opposition in a Castile so violently polarized.

The general program—a praying counterreformation—strongly tied to a historical motive and a function of ecclesial needs, was embellished with a number of features which were almost all explainable in terms of the trauma which her life in the Encarnación had caused her. Instead of an enormous monastery the Madre erected small houses; the evident social inequality and economic differences were erased with absolute equality, with the rejection of titles, and by the most stringent sharing of material goods; the frequent trips outside the cloister—a form of disguised beggary—would be another of the Teresian obsessions, solved by the more Tridentine cloister; the overflowing number of nuns, many starving, would be reduced to 13 or 20 so that they might live less concerned about eating and more attentive to God, thanks to the anticipated alms, or to dowries and secure revenues.

Thus a new style of the Carmelite life was born praying, happy, and without the tensions or the social resentments which, as Steggink has revealed, did exist in the Encarnación.[44]

The radical division in the spiritual world turned sharper and more intransigent in the social order. Today we are discovering that beneath—or above—the classical molds in the Castilian social structure (estates, castes, classes, or all of them together),[45] there existed a more rancorous division between the dominant sectors of "Old Christians" and the oppressed descendants of the "judeoconversos." In which of these two groups do we locate St Teresa? The question is suggestive, fruitful, and rather new.

THE LINEAGE OF SAINT TERESA

Certainly a title of this kind at the beginning of a contemporary Spanish history calls to mind out-dated forms, bordering on
the most fanciful genealogical erudition. Nevertheless, in the
Castilian atmosphere of the sixteenth century (in which Teresa
lived) and the beginning of the seventeenth (in which her biographies took shape), genealogy had become a universal and significant obsession.[46] The difference between descent from ancestors of
uncontaminated blood and descent from Jewish or mixed [i.e.
Moorish] ancestors produced an enormous gap which affected not
only well-known, vital attitudes, but also served as the precondition for the social integration of some, or in the case of others,
enforced the feeling and reality of social marginalization through
an impenetrable "invisible frontier," enclosing them in an environment where they lived together, longing for release,[47] in a
historical prolongation of the old ghettos.

In current historical investigation of the "judeoconverso"
minorities, the case of Doña Teresa de Ahumada is one of the best
understood, contributing to the clarification of the real situation
of a group of undoubted significance in that radicalized society,
in such a way that her family history can be considered a model of
so many others, less well-known, who suffered the same vicissi-
tudes.

What do we find in the lineage of St Teresa? To put the
question another way: was the ancestry of Doña Teresa de
Ahumada pure, wholly comprised of "Old Christians," or on the
contrary was there among her direct ancestors some Jew, "judeoconverso," or "reconciliado" [i.e., someone formally "reconciled"
to the Church after conviction for having returned to the practices
of their former religion]? Much depends on the answer. If her
lineage was pure, Teresa belonged to the Spanish group which
was untainted, triumphant, in the majority and with plenty of
opportunities and rights; if any drop of Jewish blood ran through
her veins—mixed Moorish ancestry was more exceptional—she
belonged to the other group, numerous and powerful, but mar-
ginalized. The terrible "statutes of Purity of Blood" ["Estatutos

de limpieza de sangre''] had just thrown the "judeoconversos" into a vulnerable position, by excluding them from the majority of religious orders, from the military, from higher education, from holding offices and benefices, and leaving them exposed to suspicion and denunciation. In response, such exclusions would finally lead to the adoption of postures of despair or hostility toward the structure forged by such social attitudes, hostility which in the course of time (according to the radical Américo Castro) would develop into a peculiar anarchism, and which, more immediately, as in the case of Teresa, would explain the retreat into the intimate fortress of mystical experience.

Saint Teresa's Response

It must be said that, despite one of the most understandable and deep-rooted obsessions of her time, Madre Teresa was so little bothered with the preoccupation with lineage that she wanted to tear it up by the root in her monasteries, in further defiance of the customs of the epoch. Whether or not this was because of a special policy of not wanting to reveal secrets of caste, naturally or supernaturally rising above principles acceptable to others, it is certain that in the whole extent of her writings one cannot find a single allusion to the purity of her origins nor to the nobility that her family obtained long ago through "letters of pedigree."

During her whole life and with all of the persons with whom she dealt, she who laughed at social "honor" kept a more than suspicious silence. The innumerable witnesses of her processes of beatification and canonization could never produce a personal testimony of the Madre in which she asserted the human purity of her ancestry. Those examined were content to insist monotonously that they "had heard" about this from others; all that they had heard from the mouth of the saint—as one of many testified—was "that she gave great thanks to the Lord our God that she had been raised by good Christian parents."[48]

Nor did the beloved and intimate confidant Gratian come to suspect the tragic truth which the Madre was guarding. He declares his own conviction [of her purity of blood] and in one of his minor writings relates an explicit though indirect occurrence whose significance has not escaped discerning observers. In a dialogue—a literary device—with Ana de San Bartolomé, he marvels at the simplicity with which the nurse-companion of the saint confides to him the humble lineage of her parents, laborers of modest means. The response to Gratian—from the perspective of 1613—is extremely valuable:

> You have told me of your lineage more readily than the blessed Madre Teresa de Jesús. When I had inquired in Avila into the lineage of the Ahumadas and Cepedas, from whom she was descended, and who were among the most noble families of that city, she became very angry with me because of what I was doing, saying that it was enough for her to be a daughter of the Church; and that it grieved her more to have committed a venial sin than if she had been descended from the vilest and lowest peasants ["villanos"] and Jewish converts in the whole world.[49]

This unique confession is the most unambiguous that we have about her lineage. Her reaction to Gratian's inquiry leaves one with the suspicion that she knew the truth. At any rate it implies a protest very typical of her style against the oppressive but popular obsession of those Castilians, and connects perfectly, as we will see, with the tremendous irony scattered throughout all her writings against honor understood in this manner. In light of this, hypotheses such as the following seem absurd: "St Teresa esteemed highly, as did everyone, having been born of noble parents; from her earliest childhood she would hear in her house interminable praise of her noble background."[50]

The Falsification of the Teresian Genealogy

St Teresa's secrecy and silence were broken dramatically and with the greatest simplicity some ten years after her death by an unrestrained chorus of voices. Witnesses for the processes and the first biographies traced a bright lineage in keeping with the aristocratic ["hidalgo"] mentality which saw her in its own image, with purity of blood as an unquestioned presupposition. This finally produced a falsification so complete and habitual that it would not have become known to history had it not concerned such an exceptional person.

The Misrepresentations of the Processes

The unconscious and well-intentioned falsification has already attained its completion in the series of witnesses who gave their depositions in St Teresa's canonical processes. The detailed analysis of such a source on this point, which has still not been submitted to rigorous methodological treatment, would be worth the effort. A reading of the data relating to this important dimension of Madre Teresa's life yields the following conclusions.[51]

Among the 141 depositions in the first process, which took place during the final years of Philip II's reign, 54 avoid the subject of ancestry, something particularly odd given the universal preoccupations of that milieu, and all the more significant since among these 54 are found all of Teresa's relatives and all of the witnesses from Avila (with the exception, of course, of Julian of Avila's favorable testimony). In spite of everything, in the years immediately following Teresa's death, the undeniable majority of those questioned affirm that the saint's parents were "noble and important people," "well-known nobility," etc. What does this mean?

Given the likelihood that by 1590 a long process of assimilation had already solidified into its logical and familiar final stage, the responses turn out to be colorless and conventional, since they are replies to the first question of the investigation: "Who were her parents and was she baptized?"[52] Most of the witnesses merely prove Teresa's baptism *a fortiori* by affirming that her parents were of noble blood, since, as they expressly state, it was inconceivable to the mentality dominant at the end of the 16th Century that noble parents would not, of necessity, baptize their daughter.

In the second place—and the phenomenon is more noticeable in the monasteries of Discalced nuns—all the signs indicate that a prior agreement was reached before the time of the deposition; the majority testified using identical expressions, and with a very suspicious unanimity.[53] The model which dictates such responses is undoubtedly stereotyped.

On the other hand, everyone without notable exception makes a clear distinction: when they speak of the saint directly, they swear by their statements, but when they refer to the social status of her parents, they take refuge in the formulas "I have heard it said," "It is well-known," etc., without ever claiming that they knew this directly from Teresa, thus continuing the circumspection which predominates in her writings.

In any case, the majority opinion regarding her nobility signifies nothing; everyone was aware that there was no strict, nor even general, correspondence between degrees of nobility ["hidalguía, nobleza, Grandeza"][54] and purity of blood, just as the *Tizón de la Nobleza* [*The Blight of the Nobility*] and the *Libros verdes*, amid rude outcries, tried to prove.[55] Those who had ancestors who were too questionable could count on many recourses to have themselves declared nobility.

On account of this, and to allay all suspicion, it was necessary to claim that the progenitors of the Madre were "Old Christians." Doing so constituted an innocent, unintentional, yet complete falsehood. And so four of the 141 witnesses classified Teresa's parents as "Old Christians": Fr Bañez, Fr. Yanguas, the Duchess of Alba and Don Juan Muñoz Ortega—that is to say, two Dominicans, an aristocrat, and a deputy magistrate of Segovia, members of the four groups excessively concerned about the Statutes of Purity of Blood.[56]

In the processes of canonization—during the final stage of 1609-1610—the interrogation now formulated the mandatory question differently. Among so many official witnesses—many of whom did not know the Blessed Madre Teresa personally—it is not surprising that the majority affirm the nobility of Don Alonso de Cepeda with tiresome uniformity, accommodating themselves to the questionnaire ["rótulo"], which employed the following terms: "ex nobilibus Alphonso de Cepeda et D. Beatrice de Ahumada, legitimis, christianis coniugibus nata . . . , baptizata" ["born of the noble Alonso de Cepeda and Beatriz de Ahumada, legitimate and Christian spouses . . . baptised"].[57]

But the most noteworthy thing is that what before was exceptional becomes universal, above all in Avila, where previously there had been an eloquent silence. Of the 49 official witnesses, 16 accepted the formulation of the questionnaire (that is to say, they tacitly assented to the nobility of the parents), 17 repeat in their response the opinion suggested by the questionnaire, and 15—this is new—affirm their social status as "Old Christians" with all that this implies. The most common thing—with words again too similar to be spontaneous—is to bring forward the powerful argument of the "voice of the people and the knowledge of the city," meaning, as the Magistrate and so many more say, "they were well-known nobles, free of all Jewish and Moorish background." A good percentage extended this honorable title to the grandparents, or said expressly that "the Holy Madre Teresa de Jesús and her ancestors are well-known nobles and Old Christians, free from any kinship or stain of Moors or Jews or any other sect condemned or punished by the Holy Office."[58]

The processes of this last phase confirm something highly questionable about those circumstances: honor, public opinion, concretized in purity from any trace of the conquered castes (to which the Madre was apparently indifferent), was projected onto her by those Spaniards who could not conceive that a saint might have contacts, however remote, with the Jewish convert stock, or with the Moors, recently expelled in those days after gigantic campaigns mobilizing the public opinion reflected in these testimonies.[59]

The Inertia of the Biographers

The falsifications of the processes became firmly established in the biographies of St Teresa. Since this series of works was begun in the midst of the geneological furor, the obligation to avoid the very least association of a hero with Moors and Jews—especially with Jews—was taken for granted. Today we know in part the misrepresentations to which such figures as Luis Vives, Nebrija, Suárez, Cota, Fernández de Oviedo, José de Anchieta, Hernando de Talavera, etc., were subjected. The same thing happened with Teresa: not only was the sanctity of the heroine at stake, but also the honor of her order.

Although he does not deal directly with the issue in his *Life of St Teresa*, Fr Yepes indicated in other places his conviction regarding the antiquity of the Teresian lineage.[60] Fr Ribera, basing himself on a false letter of pedigree, states the enduring thesis: "she was born of noble lineage on both sides."[61] We do not know what the first official chronicler of the Reform, the unfortunate Fr Quiroga, thought about this. However, in spite of his modern vision of the science of history,[62] Fr Jerónimo Ezquerra de San José, in his *History of the Discalced Carmel* (Madrid, 1637) affirms the premise that "no one denies that human nobility is like an enamel of virtue, a stimulus to do the good, an incentive to aspire always to the better,"[63] etc. Then afterwards he sets down an interminable list of forebears, each more illustrious than the last, until we find ourselves with a Teresian ancestry linked to families of the Reconquest, with those who fought against the enemies of Christianity in the old enclaves of Leon or among the most ancient restorers of Avila.

The raw materials of Fr Ezquerra's work, suppressed by his superiors, were used freely and shamelessly by his successor, Francisco de Santa Maria. The family tree is enriched, St Teresa becomes related by marriage to the Pulgars, and—thanks to the ingenuity of the new official chronicler—Fr Francisco de Santa Maria (Pulgar) becomes a satisfied nephew of the Saint, through the paternal line.[64] In the middle of the seventeenth century, Fr Antonio de la Madre de Dios, after a well-organized investigation sorting through many papers and gathering information, offered a luxurious genealogical tree relying on the Cepeda's old patents of nobility, jealously guarded by the saint's nephews in Osuna. It now seemed that the pure, absolutely pure lineage of Teresa de Ahumada was forever established.[65]

And thus everything remained, ready to be repeated by learned historians at the beginning of the twentieth century, preferably by aristocrats,[66] or by Discalced Carmelites, convinced—and what Spaniard wasn't after the *Cortes* of Cadiz?[67]—that their Madre was the authentic representative of the dominant "Spanish race,"[68] or who reacted, like any "Old Christian," in the style of Silverio de Santa Teresa, the driving force behind Teresian studies. He summed up the whole current of traditional opinion with what was at that time a natural and indisputable claim: "St Teresa was descended from pure blood; in other words, in her ancestry there were neither Moors nor Jews."[69]

A Sensational Discovery

These illusions dissolved dramatically in 1946, when Américo Castro sounded the alarm. His master work, written in exile, goes beyond the fine, elementary introduction to the phenomenon of Teresian mysticism reflected in his essay *Teresa la Santa*,[70] and confronts the personal mystical experience of Teresa, its peculiar expression. His analysis of the Teresian "I" and her intimate confession relates them less to belated European influences than to the life and structure of a Spanish minority with eastern roots and caste (character): namely, the "New Christians." This intuition, quite undeveloped and without immediate impact, opened up new avenues for understanding Teresa Sanchez, as Castro insists on calling her.[71]

Oddly enough, despite his famous acumen and his historical knowledge—rather imperfect, to tell the truth—he had not learned that an industrious scholar had discovered the documentary key to his hypothesis two years previously. Among a group of lawsuits, Alonso Cortés happened to find a suit of the Cepedas, in which, alongside the testimony supporting the family, that of the opposing party revealed the half-suspected truth: that Teresa's father and grandfather were of Jewish extraction, and had been "reconciled" by the Toledan Inquisition and had done public penance during the grace-period of 1485.[72]

The suit is apparently one of those involving the residents of some place, who were harrassed by taxes, and the recalcitrant *hidalgos*, to force the latter to help alleviate the overwhelming burden, something from which they were exempted by their ambiguous social status [of nobility]. In this case it concerns the apportionment of the emergency tax imposed by the new and impoverished King, Carlos I, in 1519. The Council of Majalbálago (Avila) did not want to exempt the brothers Francisco Alvarez de Cepeda and Alonso, Pedro, and Ruy Sanchez de Cepeda, of doubtful nobility, from paying the required 100 maravedís. The case went to the Court of Appeal ["Audiencia"] in Valladolid.[73]

The witness of the litigants, undoubtedly bribed, insisted on the well-known "hidalguía" of the Sánchez de Cepeda family. On the other hand, the Council's witnesses, those from Avila, brought cruel and repetitive accusations about the status of Juan Sanchez of Toledo and his sons as "converso and reconciliado." The details allow no room for doubt. Any suspicion that this could all be the result of a pre-arranged plot—always possible, in fact—disappears when one takes into account that among these witnesses against the family are a brother-in-law and nephew of Juan Sanchez himself. If that weren't enough, a notarized statement of the Holy Office of the Inquisition, brought from Toledo, resolves in complete detail, and in an authoritative and unquestionable manner, the already half-solved mystery:

> I, Francisco Perez, secretary and notary public by the apostolic and royal authority, and confidential notary of the Holy Office of the Inquisition of the city and archdiocese of Toledo and its environs, certify that in the books and registers of this Holy Office it appears and is recorded that on the twenty-second day of the month of June, in the year 1485, Joán [i.e., Juan] de Toledo, merchant, son of Alonso Sanchez, inhabitants of Toledo in the district of Santa Leocadia, gave, presented, and swore to a confession before the then lord inquisitors, in which he said and confessed that he had done and committed many serious crimes and delicts of heresy and apostasy against our holy Catholic faith. Likewise a large number of persons listed and recorded by districts appear in a book, among the other books and records of this secret office, entitled *Index of Persons Reconciled in the City and Archdiocese of Toledo*, among which said names contained in said book is listed, in the parish of Santa Leocadia, Joán de Toledo, merchant, son of Alonso Sanchez. Furthermore, I certify that it does not appear nor is found in the said books, registers, and records of this said Holy Office that the bachelor Fernando de Santa Catalina, son of said Juan de Toledo, has been reconciled. . . . Dated in the said city of Toledo, the nineteenth day of the month of July of 1520, and I have signed with my customary signature in testimony to the truth.[74]

This discovery was reported during a very active decade for Spanish historiography; there is nothing unusual, therefore, about the silence with which it was greeted. Alonso Cortés himself, in the face of the unexpected discovery, did not know whether to be incredulous or to minimize its significance.[75] Besides, the problem of the *judeoconversos* was not as thoroughly investigated as it is now, nor did it exercise the fascination it does in our own time. It was necessary to wait until the 1950's before the fruitful consequences of this piece of information, which at first glance appeared to be of merely academic interest, could be appreciated to their full extent.

For the time being, when the discovery came belatedly to the attention of Américo Castro, it provided him with a wonderful opportunity to proclaim the accuracy of his previous intuition, although this required some fancy footwork which was not entirely honest.[76] In any case, what was needed was a rigorous contribution which would incorporate the new data in an illuminating work. The opportunity came in the biography of St Teresa, published as an introduction to the *Book of Her Life* by Fr Efrén de la Madre de Dios in 1951,[77] which attempted in part to integrate Teresa into the complex milieu in which she lived.

In spite of the positive and truly original elements in its historical treatment, local scholars were upset with the thesis that Teresa might not have been born in Avila;[78] official historians were disturbed by something of greater consequence. As Domínguez Ortiz says, not without reason, Efrén, influenced by prevailing opinions and in order to save the "honor" of the Saint's grandfather, "had recourse to an absurd hypothesis"[79]: that Juan Sanchez, the brilliant merchant and "Old Christian," because of inevitable contacts with Jews and "the destructive atmosphere of those days . . . , apostasized from his religion."[80] "As if it were possible and likely," responds Américo Castro with undisguised annoyance, "that, when so many Jews were being converted to Christianity by means of tortures and massacres, a Toledan named Sanchez, at the end of the 15th century, would have had himself secretly circumcised."[81]

It follows from what has been said that the professional historians were the ones responsible for illuminating the rich personality and significance of Teresa with the new data on her status as a *judeoconversa*. Thanks to their objective stance—of which the Discalced Carmelites still cannot exactly boast—

Domínguez Ortiz has been able to situate the figure of St Teresa within the complex world of the *judeoconversos* of 16th century Spain; he has put into a rigorously historical form that which in Américo Castro is constructed out of intuitions on a scaffolding of literary elements.[82] Seris has retraced the Teresian lineage more accurately and realistically, without giving way to the fantastic constructions of the past.[83] Although some of the conclusions of Marquez Villanueva may seem extreme, he has offered an enviable synthesis of the social attitudes and inherent conflicts in the life and the writings of Teresa,[84] while the scholarly elaborations óf Gomez-Menor provide indispensable documentation which links the familial world of the saint with the economic and social preoccupations of her *judeoconversa* heritage.[85]

The Cepedas, A Typical Judeoconverso Family

Thus, during the Toledan grace-period in the year 1485 (a space of time granted to the "Judaizers" so that they might turn themselves in and receive favorable treatment), the grandfather and future father of Doña Teresa (Sanchez) de Cepeda—two generations at the same time—were reconciled and did public penance.

Obligatory processions in which they wore the *sambenito*,[86] the sign of their condemnation preserved in the respective parish, and the memory of the witnesses, all joined to brand the New Christians as "confesos" [i.e., converted Jews]. In addition, those who did this penance were disqualified from holding any desirable municipal offices, and from undertaking a number of activities which, given their hereditary dedication to business, seemed vital.[87] And perhaps most painful of all, the "marranos" [lit., "pigs," a nickname given the *judeoconversos* at that time], set in an antagonistic social milieu, had to face a world of not always silent hostilities, of polite opposition, and of social isolation. This created a suffocating atmosphere for them, in which they were torn by the double desire both to prove the authenticity of their religious beliefs and to erase the stigma, today recognized as unjust, but perfectly normal to the Old Christians of that era.

Teresa's family boldly engaged in this battle. She would inherit a social position which, though not without certain shadows, was to all appearances already clear, shaped in the struggle and success of previous generations. In this sense, her documented family history can serve as a valid historical model of the path followed by so many *judeoconverso* clans of her time in their desire, first of all to erase the stain [of Jewish blood], and ultimately to obtain full social integration. We believe it will be useful to follow, however briefly, the rough course of this particular voyage.

If Cantera's suspicions are correct, the cautious Juan Sanchez of Toledo must have achieved legal rehabilitation some ten years after his reconciliation, by making use of the opportunities offered by the needs of the royal exchequer which always benefitted from speculating on the situation of the converts.[88]

The second objective was to erase all tell-tale signs of his background. There was nothing better for recently converted Jews than to escape from the place where they might be exposed. Teresa's grandfather, with his "reconciled" sons, emigrated from Toledo on a date which is uncertain, but for motives which would be easy to ascertain even if the attorney in the aforementioned lawsuit had not already stated them, after having brought the inquisitorial proceedings of Toledo to light: "For which reason he left there and came to live in the said city of Avila, in the occupation of a merchant, as he was previously."[89]

Later developments center on the struggle to hide his real status. Succeeding at this was a privilege reserved to wealthy Jews, who were the exception, despite so many myths to the contrary. But Juan Sanchez was among the privileged, and it must not have cost him too much to provide himself (perhaps around the year 1500) with a certificate of *hidalguía* from the Audiencia of Ciudad Real,[90] reaffirmed by those obtained twenty years later by his sons.[91] Evidently they could count on bribed witnesses, with complicity which involved not only the litigants, but also the public prosecutor, the judges (this time from Valladolid), and the whole central Administration, now determined to consider as "hidalgos" those who some thirty years before had been "reconciled" by the Inquisition and had done public penance.

The certificate of *hidalguía* did not fool the public, too much on guard against such subterfuges. It is clear that "hidalgos" constituted in this way were objects of hatred, directed against those nobles "of five or six thousand *reales*," as the Alcalde of Zalamea calls them, who could buy a document, but not blood, from the king.[92] But the document could be wielded like a weapon, enlivening the private and public history of so many families in Hapsburg Spain; it served to resolve official disputes,[93] to justify privileged status and exemption from direct taxation. And besides the fiscal advantages, those blessed with certificates of *hidalguía* could participate in the *alcalde de hidalgos'* lottery in their respective parishes for positions on the city council, as did the Cepedas henceforth.[94]

Once the legal requirement was satisfied, they began the difficult struggle for social acceptance. The general "bourgeoise" eagerness for assimilation into the nobility, although it might begin with this lowest and unspectacular step of *hidalguía*, is well known to historians of the sixteenth century. Without considering the various financial matters involved, the aims and achievements manifest the determination to erase the past by the most helpful means: that of marriage with nobles, in defiance of careful legislation and the fury unleashed against those daring to mix their tainted blood with the good lineages.[95] This is what happened with the Cepedas (and with thousands of families in their situation): "because they are married to daughters of *hijos-dalgo* and have the favor of the magistrates they have been and continue to be counted as *hidalgos*."[96]

The most difficult step had been accomplished, but at these levels one had to resort to every means possible to maintain the reputation and honor which compensated for such efforts. It was necessary to bury, as it were, indiscreet reminders. For this nothing was more important than dropping the tell-tale patronyms. Who knew in the third generation that the real family name of the Cepeda y Ahumada was Sanchez, whose *sambenito* hung in the parish of Santa Leocadia, and who was aware of the real Toledan (not Avilan) origins of Madre Teresa's family?

The enviable opportunity to go to the "Indies" [i.e., America] opened up the chance for *conversos* to destroy the memory of suspicious origins, to receive new titles, and to display deceptive but legitimate coats of arms. There it was possible to consolidate more inconspicuously the honor acquired by so many frauds, and the title "Don," so much haggled over in the mother country, was not so hard to obtain in the new territories. The Conquest ["conquista"] of the New World provided access to military commands; the Inquisition, which was slow in making its presence felt in those lands, did not appear (to be) as impassioned, leaving the converts a liberty of movement inconceivable in the kingdoms of the Iberian peninsula.[97] Success and the passage of time would ensure that upon return—whenever that might be—remote accusations would be forgotten.

Legally, *conversos* were forbidden any presence in a land whose discovery had been financed in large part by people of their lineage. Nevertheless, and in spite of so many legal restrictions, it is beyond dispute that "there were many, very many *conversos* who went to America,"[98] attracted by the lure of such generous opportunities for prestige and monetary gain.

While this is not the most suitable place to review the various means utilized by the outcasts to outwit the complex legal system,[99] it is clear that among the camouflages available, going to the Indies proved most helpful for Teresa's family. Leaving aside the fate of "Don" Alonso's daughters, of the child who did not survive [sic],[100] of the son who fell in battle in Africa [Juan de Cepeda, Teresa's half-brother] and the one who died as a youth among the Dominicans [Juan de Ahumada], the remaining brothers of Teresa all undertook the Indian venture.[101] The majority of them died there in rash military campaigns passionately denounced by Fernández de Oviedo.[102] In the end only two returned. One [Pedro de Ahumada] passed his life in hardship in the rank of *hidalgo* and at the same time a pauper.[103] The other, Lorenzo, enjoyed the fortune of a colonial officer, using the silver of the Americas to help his beloved sister's enterprise of the foundations, and investing his money in the acquisition of property and honor, in the creation of an entailed estate [*mayorazgo*],[104] and in transactions not particularly profitable in the short run, but which got one of his sons [Francisco] married into no less prestigious a line than that of the Albuquerque e Infantado, to the unconcealed delight of Madre Teresa.[105]

When a great-nephew of the saint received the coveted uniform of the Military Order of St James in the first part of the 17th century,[106] the full cycle of a model history of struggle and rejection was completed. In just a few generations they had relentlessly climbed the steps for the *judeoconverso* lines, as described by Caro Baroja on the basis of the general pattern observed in successful cases: "transformation by means of letters or certificates of simple *hidalguía*, transformation by means of permission to go to the Indies, transformation by obtaining offices and honors of higher quality, transformation by entering the military orders."[107]

The Lifestyle of A Judeoconverso Family

The process of integration, contrived by means of falsifications, ultimately transfigured the original lifestyle of these families, and their bourgeoise extraction continues fading away as a result of so much denial, until it solidifies into an environment similar to that of the dominant sectors, ruled in their turn by the obsession with nobility (hidalguism).

St Teresa's father was born and raised in a household which had nothing to do with the lifestyle of the nobility, and much—everything, in fact—to do with that of merchants and businessmen, immersed in economic activities in keeping with their *judeoconverso* status, and especially strong in Toledo, where this powerful and well-known bourgeoisie, "made up in large part by the mercantile class of mixed blood," dominated the life of the city.[108]

Don Juan, the patriarch of the family and the saint's grandfather, was a merchant dealing in fine cloths, perhaps one of the businesses most favored by the opportunities of nascent capitalism, and he probably profited from the opportunities offered to those of his "race" by Henry IV.[109] Having moved to Avila for the reasons already indicated, he set himself up there as a dealer in fine silk ["trapero"], a business which his sons carried on "in a rich store of cloths and fine silks."[110] The "reconciliation" [i.e.,

the Toledan Inquisitorial process and public penance] apparently did not affect excessively the upward march of his fortune,
furthered by other interests which were as profitable as they were
essential in his world: the collection of rents from tenant farmers
["arrendamientos de pan"] and financial administration for the
rich archbishopric of Toledo and the sees of Salamanca and
Plasencia.[111] His sons, at least initially, tried to round out the
family business from their location in Avila; "in the said city they
have had and continue to have rent-revenues, the *tercias reales* as
well as votive offerings and other incomes, and are trying and
have tried to be landlords and merchants, and from this have lived
and continue to do so in said city."[112]

The case of the Cepedas, advancing upward by wealth, punished by the Inquisition nevertheless breaks the classical pattern
by maintaining at one and the same time very suspicious and
"servile" occupations together with the habits, lifestyle, and
reputation of *hidalgos*, as is solemnly attested by numerous
witnesses. These never tire of repeating that "they are very
honored and wealthy men, and behave and have behaved very
decently, and have kept and continue to keep horses, and are
themselves well-dressed and of elegant speech"; that "all of them
live as gentlemen and worthy men"; that "they were associating
with gentlemen ["caballeros"] and important persons ["hombres
hijosdalgo"] of the city and kept apart from the commoners,
living very decently as *hijosdalgo* in their households, which were
very rich."[113]

These noble-bourgeoise, who called into question the overly
rigid social stratifications, had to put up a front before groups as
unequal as those of the Government and the stoutest of the
"simple commoners."[114] It was not difficult to deceive the first,
since it had turned into the most willing of accomplices. But
popular opinion, on the other hand, was much less merciful with
the parvenu than is usually supposed. The harassment to which
the *judeoconverso hidalgos* were subjected is reflected perfectly in
the letters of St Teresa, and one must first of all understand the
simple yet powerful economic motive behind it: the flight to
privileged levels of society had the consequence of heaping the

progressively mounting burden of taxes, assessments, and services onto an ever decreasing number of taxpayers.

Social resentment would take care of the rest. And in this way, Teresa's family, like innumerable other Castilian families, found themselves faced with the unavoidable choice between *hidalguismo*, with all its consequences, or continuing to follow the activities appropriate to their heritage. The public, in contrast to the simplistic and surprisingly anachronistic point of view of Brenan, and of a certain commentator from outside the historical field,[115] was more merciless than the official establishment, and its harassment determined the final fate of these groups, anxious for the social acceptance which was refused them (which the public haggled over) and which only became accessible at the cost of abandoning the true source of their wealth. The choice, whenever possible, was always for identification with the *hidalgos*. This was the case with the family circle of the Cepedas within which Teresa was raised.

The grandfather, merchant and *hidalgo*, was more merchant than *hidalgo*. His sons—as we have seen—at first followed in his footsteps as merchants, landlords, and *hidalgos*; but by 1519—and clearly in 1523—they boast almost solely of their nobility.[116] Teresa's father, as demanded by his social standing, and contrary to the notion that *judeoconverso* predispositions were unchangeable, spent half of his wealth on property. Without as broad a monetary base as was needed, the noble lifestyle could not cope with the alarming inflation which was unleashed just at that time and which did not spare him. He had to mortgage his estate, found it necessary to liquidate his first wife's dowry, after that of Doña Beatriz, and he was embroiled in endless debts until finally, at Christmas of 1543, he died completely ruined, pursued by a swarm of creditors. His sons, to the deep sorrow of Teresa, took the lead in an embarassing spectacle, treating the will as worthless rubbish, and suing for "the ordinary wardrobe of the said Doña Catalina [del Peso, Don Alonso's first wife] and half of the common bedding, because he had married a second time," and Doña Maria, the daughter by the first marriage, was entitled to a piece of the two-part bed.[117]

The conclusion of this stage of the family's development was the usual one, already noted. The brothers of the saint who had not already done so set out for the Indies to search for new, but not bourgeoise, opportunities. Hidalguism was a universal and decisive factor in the social and economic dynamics of Castile at that time, and the struggle for the conquest of honor offered access to this condition by honorable means, but not without a certain monetary element involved.

THE SOCIAL PROTEST OF SAINT TERESA

Teresa's social attitudes, though basic for the understanding of her writings, are often overlooked (when not unintentionally misrepresented) by classical Teresian historiography; fortunately, however, they have been brought to light in recent years. Anyone casually reviewing the biographies—though not her own account of her life ["Relación de su vida"]—might conclude at first glance that the Madre assented to the principles of the society in which she lived and took a keen interest. With the cooperation of the monarch, and under his protection, she made a series of foundations, thanks to the patronage of eminent aristocrats, with whom she maintained sometimes intense relations through her letters. Coming from an *hidalgo* family, she seems to have contracted the sentiments and perceptions related to the principal factor in the collective social judgment of worth: "la honra" [honor].

Nevertheless, an impartial reading reveals to us that her writings, with denunciations ranging from the subtle to the transparent, must be added to the most insistent protests of the victims of the "establishment" of her day, and of its highest values. St Teresa aligns herself with the caustic and anguished denunciations which abound in "La Celestina," "El Lazarillo de Tormes," "Guzmán de Alfarache," and so many other less prudent non-conformists in that Castile,[118] chained to socio-moral systems which were designed for the benefit of the dominant caste, or, more probably, handed down unchanged from the time of the Reconquest.[119]

The Teresian Preoccupation With "la Negra Honra" [*Black Honor*]

Today, undoubtedly, we are hardly able to begin to grasp something like honor, which was the very soul of social behavior in Castile in the second half of the sixteenth century. Our historical frameworks, slumbering in categories which scarcely transcend materialism, need to free themselves from their stupor to convince us that there was a long period in which honor (call it that, or prestige, or reputation, or what you will), was a fundamental factor in politics, social position, and vital attitudes. In attempting to penetrate the constants (operative) in the Spaniards of the past, the historian Bennassar, an observer of the authentic reality of Spain, could record as a basic principle that "if there were one passion capable of defining the behavior of the Spanish people, it would be that of honor."[120]

Travellers who visited Spain in the sixteenth century, those who visited it at any time during the "Old Regime", could find no words to explain to their compatriots their perplexity before the insane Castilian exaltation of a quality which they considered trivial.[121] Basically, they had good reason for their surprise, given the considerable transformation which honor and its influence had undergone down through the centuries.

Originating perhaps in the medieval period and considered as the epitome and code of knightly virtues, in its concept and application, was converted into the ideological tool of the feudal system, along with valor, loyalty, and fidelity. The Spanish Reconquest was an exceptional ally in exploiting such virtues, and despite the changing political situation, inertia turned something positive, like this passion, to the benefit of the monarchical, aristocratic society. In the sixteenth century, when the grandiose justification for it had disappeared, the concern with honor crystalized into two basic dimensions: sexual (decorum, publicly acknowledged virginity in the unmarried woman, fidelity in the married) which affected women exclusively; and hereditary (absence of ancestors of Jewish or Moorish blood, a pure ancestry), with a direct impact on men. A loss of "honor" in the first sense might be forgiven, but there was no possibility, at least in theory, of repairing a breach of "honor" in the second sense.

The most peculiar feature of the Spanish situation, and the thing which made no sense to foreign visitors, was the substantial social importance which honor enjoyed by the time of St Teresa. It was not merely a personal matter, but something with which society (the "others") showed its agreement by unanimous consent. Thus, of the two basic components of honor—personal character and public reputation—the second predominated over the first to the point of making it disappear altogether. The Spaniard became a slave of "others," depending in the most sensitive areas of his personality on public opinion, on what "they" would say. Speaking for honorable Spaniards, Lope de Vega translates into verse the same old idea which already runs through "Las Partidas": "Honor is something due to another,/ no man is honored by himself,/ since honor is in the other, not in oneself," etc.[122]

Thus the attribute acquired an almost exclusive social importance, but was so fragile that any shot might bring it down, even more so when the connotations of dishonor spread to a whole gamut of occupations, from intellectual and commercial pursuits to the lowliest mean and servile labor. Simple envy, jealousy, or spite found a thousand opportunities for secretly nursing old social resentments and economic interests, and causing with impunity the "social death" of individuals and families, who were automatically banished to the numerous group of outcasts.

This is not the most appropriate place to insist on the dire consequences for its own intellectual and economic future which such an attitude would have in this Spain of the "pure-blooded," nor on the tragic situation in which the "New Christians" found themselves. Américo Castro—whose radical views must be significantly modified in the light of the findings of such be nafide historians as Sánchez Albornoz, Domínguez Ortiz, Eugenio Asensio, Gutiérrez Nieto, etc.—has traced with unparalleled vividness the tragedy caused by honor so understood, lived, and—we ourselves would say—exploited.[123]

St Teresa, belonging to the most vulnerable class or social

group, suffered in all its severity this violent tragedy, from which Felipe II profited in a consciously pursued policy.[124] Therefore, to attempt to understand her writings in depth without taking the importance of this problem into account would constitute an absurd enterprise. Situated in a time permeated by such a universal preoccupation, Teresa in her writings was genuinely obsessed with honor, which stands out everywhere, and in the most unexpected passages. A linguistic study would yield the conclusion that the cumulative burden of this experience became one of the constant structural elements of her entire literary work, and that the author was another of the many Spaniards who, like Janus with his two faces, kept watch to protect all sides from the easy attacks on an unprotected reputation.

The general problem in the first of its aspects, the sexual, appeared at the early age in which Teresa opened up to social feelings. When she remembers her sentimental relationship with her cousin, the narrator hastens to stress the risk such an occurrence presented to the family reputation, "through the complete loss of my 'honor' ["honra"] and the suspicions of my father."[125] There is no need here to relive the ephemeral flirtation, or to deal with the question of making an anachronistic moral evaluation of it (an issue over which so much ink has been spilled), her conviction (along with those who counseled her) that it might have been excused since it "was in view of a possible marriage,"[126] and her father's natural solution of closing her up in a convent school to ward off the danger; what matters is the strength which Teresa ascribes to the motive for her actions at a time when the supernatural stimulus was subordinated to the social one of honor, "which brought me torment in everything I did."[127]

Such an experience was not just an adolescent episode. Later, when she was already a religious at the Encarnación, the mentality of that little half-monastic, half-hidalgo world accentuated her feelings. Doña Teresa de Ahumada confesses that in spite of her inclination toward "everything about religious life," she was not disposed "to suffer anything that seemed to be scorn,"[128] and that the destitute condition of the monastery was one of the factors which restrained her commitment to God during that period of tension between prayer and inappropriate friendships, or conversations in the parlor with benefactors of the convent. The turning point, (which came) when Doña Teresa was a mature woman in her forties, was the liberation resulting from her definitive "conversion"; but her autobiographical account reveals that the continuation of such visits had been due to the nuns' intimations that by these conversations with the brilliant Avilan gentleman "I was not losing my honor but rather that it was increasing."[129]

Her vision(s) of the stern Christ, of the large toad, and of hell determined the radical change in the long process of the spiritual life of Doña Teresa, and in her evaluation of social approval.

The evolution with respect to the other aspect of honor, that of purity of lineage, is not as clear in the socio-spiritual dynamics of Teresa's life. There are too many secrets hidden in *judeoconverso* families to look for concrete indications in a language which, when dealing with the problem, does so with obscure allusions or relies on cryptic expressions which defy every attempt at clarification. One thing is certain: we do not know when she would have found out, or when she might have been told, the fatal secret, but St Teresa was aware of the tragic note which "darkened" her origins and her family traditions. Her grandfather's money, the certificates of nobility, the *hidalgo* lifestyle—if these managed in the long run to erase the stain, and to hide it from outsiders for a while, they did not manage to deceive the most intimate circles in Avila.

In fact, her fellow citizens forgave nothing. When Lorenzo de Cepeda had recently returned from the Indies, his sister tried to convince him of the inappropriateness of using the "Don" which was granted to the Spanish colonist-pensioners. Her preoccupation with such advice is as significant as the series of arguments she uses in Seville to convince him. But in Avila Lorenzo found himself without his sister and in the company of his headstrong brother-in-law, Juan de Ovalle, who forced him to return to his old tricks. Avilan society reacted, and the Madre is very explicit about this matter: "really no other form of address is being used in Avila now, which is disgraceful. Just because it has to do with them, it has affected me very deeply," as she confided to a niece.[130]

Her immediate reaction to Ovalle's decision to become involved in contracts (an occupation associated with the "New
Christians"),[131] her loud protest when it came to her attention
that the incautious Gratian was stirring up people's memories in
Avila to bring to light the illustrious background of his beloved
Madre,[132] her insistence that the success of her reform was due to
the hand of God, since "it cannot have been because I was of
illustrious descent that he did me this honor," [133] etc., confirm the
conviction of Seris, Américo Castro, and Márquez Villanueva that
Teresa knew her real social status.

One who understands this well need not look for arcane
expressions in her works. Whenever the Teresian writings bring
on the scene any of the many personages who crossed her life's
path, the Madre, with exquisite delicacy, hastens to introduce the
figure with a note about his (or her) famous lineage and honored
position. But the reader is astonished at the opening pages of the
Book of Her Life ["Relación de su vida"]: not one allusion to the
"Old Christian" background of her forebears, presented simply as
"virtuous and God-fearing" people.[134] This is the best evidence of
a tremendous honesty in the face of the great campaigns of
deliberate concealment which characterized her day.

Her awareness of a "stained" lineage decisively affected the
Teresian conception of the world and of life, knowing as she did
that the mark prohibited her from associating herself with the
Old Christian criteria and immersed her in the private and public
drama of her *judeoconverso* class, torn between anxiety for social
acceptance and the anguish of rejection. Her expressions of pain
reveal corresponding attitudes of bitterness which, though they
did not result in as clear a literary expression or social protest as
some would have wished,[135] can nevertheless find their explanation in this intimate feeling of being an outcast.

Sublimation of Social Principles

A strong, violent protest shapes Teresa's attitude towards the
social presuppositions of her day. If her censures are always
surrounded by spontaneous humor, and, taken in themselves, are
a bit mischievous, the absence of resentment places Teresa's good-

natured satire far from the bitter attacks of the other literary genre, also proceeding largely—if not totally—from the *judeoconverso* environment.

Teresa's attitude in this matter is quite clear. The Eternal Lord's easy acceptance of spiritual boldness shatters the seriousness of the exalted of this world who are unable to smile at the minute details of a complex etiquette. The liveliness of chapter 37 of her *Life* obviates the need for comment on the ridiculous lengths to which courtesy had been taken in a society so complicated by minor points of honor; "the world is such that we would have to have longer lives—if some part of our lives is going to be spent in serving God—to learn all the nice points and new rules and practices of etiquette." The inescapable contrast between the permanent (God) and the passing (such worldly vanity) is clearly expressed, and always appears whenever the saint broaches the subject. No less clear is the utterance of her genuine sigh of relief—she who previously was always honor-conscious—at the definitive break of enclosing herself in San José and giving up the foolish expressions of courtesy which had brought her to such a pass "that when I entered this monastery of St Joseph I still didn't know how to live."[136]

Freedom from such conventions based on human respect and opinion explains the absolute liberty with which St Teresa destroys the keynote of *la honra* with her best weapon: irony. The brief dialog she held with the first Discalced friar, Fr [Anthony of Jesus] Heredia, when she surprised him sweeping the entrance to the chapel [at Duruelo], is very well-known; but perhaps we have not reflected sufficiently on the underlying destructive element in the foundress's sly question ("What is this, my Father? What has become of your honor?") and the friar's response ("I curse the time I had any"), reported with real pleasure by the narrator.[137] In a delightful passage where she describes the strange life of the first Sevillian novice [Beatriz de la Madre de Dios], this contrast emerges prominently: the tormented existence of the young lady destined for an honorable marriage into a comfortable life and the sharp contrast with the joy of the nun attracted to humble labor ("so that we had a hard time getting the broom away from her").

The happy transformation is explained with an exclamation full of implications: "What the love of God was able to do when she was no longer concerned with her own honor!", and the effect of such a liberation could not be more positive: "She was so content that she grew quite fat."[138]

After all, this is no more than an indication. In open opposition to Américo Castro's position, historians continue to make clear that not all the artifice surrounding the supreme principle of honor, insofar as it is related to lineage, has a purely racial significance. Other profound interests relating to class, and therefore more connected with wealth than with ancestry, were also operative in the somewhat conventional and quite rigid stratification—the explanation of which is debatable—between the "pure" and the "tainted". This underlying reality, indicative of the intense and silent struggle, stirred in Teresa's mind and is translated into pages which undermine the highest images of social status. Her own family history—the exalted prestige in her grandfather's household, her father's economic privation so that he might maintain the external splendor of his rank—enabled her to pronounce judgment on what has been called "the disruptive role of money"[139].

Teresa declared to the four winds that the idea of honor not sustained by money or estate is a bald-faced lie: "It would be a wonder if any poor person were honored in the world." She is aware that "In fact, here below people in paying honor don't take into account the persons themselves, however much these persons may deserve the honor, but their wealth."[140]

The Teresian writings must be seen from this point of view as eloquent monuments of the disillusionment of her times. Her criticisms, which could be multiplied in innumerable quotations,[141] constitute the best corrective to simplistic or excessively one-dimensional presentations which are unconcerned with connecting to material interests such constant and vigorous reactions then in Castile.

Only by taking this as a point of departure can one understand the real severity, unusual in her style, with which she lashes out against the wretchedness of *la honra*. We have already noted how her long stay in the Encarnación traumatized her in many ways. Teresa reacted strongly to the division between the well-to-do *doñas*, living comfortably in their private apartments, with their servants or maybe even with their slaves, with extensive resources, and those who were physically starving.[142] As a foundress she gave concrete expression to this reaction in her monastery of San José and in those which followed it.

All this justifies and situates historically that supreme disdain shown, whenever possible, for "points of honor", for "*la negra honra*", which she came to call "the boreworm", the dissonant note, "the chain which no file can break", etc. etc. Her social background and her prior religious experience will be the elements which help shape in all its magnitude her fearless struggle to destroy this tremendous "concern" which destroys efforts toward perfection.[143] And as a corrective, this fight constitutes in good part the framework upon which she built her interpretation of her reform as well as her conception and experience of perfection, maintained by a feeling of profound humility. "Trampling these points of honor underfoot"[144] is a prerequisite for entering onto the path of perfection, she writes, "because the soul's profit and what the world calls honor can never go together."[145]

Nevertheless, she is aware of how deeply rooted *la honra* is in her milieu, and so her string of serious and humorous attacks on the core of its existence is not directed so much at destroying it in the world (an undertaking doomed to failure) as to sublimating it in the few who might enlist in her "Way": in a word, it is [not] a matter of abandoning universal principles but of supplanting false with true honor.[146] Given her dualistic vision, she opposed to the world's opinion—which preoccupied her so much at the beginning, and was the mainstay of human honor—the only one which matters, God's. All her allusions to "artificial displays," "fleets of trifles," "of mud,"[147] are in contrast to God, "who honors us, whose own honor was in being humbled." Hence, intimacy with him entails contemptuous and bitter attacks: "never pay attention in like matters to the opinion of the crowd."[148]

The *Way of Perfection*, the programmatic writing of her
reform, has this liberation as its mainstay and is the greatest
joyful proclamation of the nature of true honor: "to lose a
thousand honors for You."[149] Pride in earthly ancestors is re-
placed by glorious descent from the Virgin or Carmel's forebears;
money-based honor by the honor of poverty; titles and surnames
by titles of religious profession [of Jesus, of the Cross, etc.]; there
is not the slightest chance of introducing the discriminatory
Statutes of Purity of Blood, etc. On the other hand, she does not
hesitate to denounce with a certain harshness infiltrations, those
honors that the devil invents in monasteries,[150] such as seniorities,
titles of "Reverend" in address,[151] and all the many other details
which manifested a willingness to transfer attachments to human
honor into the religious life.[152]

In reality, Teresa, who majestically despises that which was
most prized by her society, sets herself up as an untiring combat-
ant for the honor of her Spouse, so mistreated by the Lutherans,
as she repeats unceasingly throughout her *Foundations*.[153]

Saint Teresa's Social Attitudes

Although Teresa's position in opposition to *la honra* is clear,
her behavior towards the different social classes does not appear
free from contradictions, which can be explained sometimes by
the saint's realism, other times by the prejudices of her class.

In the book of the *Foundations* and in the evidence of her
correspondence, we have seen—and we will insist on this more
later—the Madre's resistance to founding reformed houses in
rural areas. Undoubtedly the fundamental motive at work in this
refusal is the economic demands of her foundational program,
but the essentially urban tradition of the *judeoconversos* may also
be involved. América Castro has tried to show how the peasant
came to represent the final stronghold of declining honor and
purity of lineage;[154] given this viewpoint, we can understand
Teresa's direct oral allusion to "the vilest and lowest peasants and
Jewish converts in the whole world". Without necessarily accepting this as completely authentic—perhaps the exact wording is
due more to Gratian's reporting that to the saint—or accepting

Castro's comments without reservation, his exegesis may have a basis in reality: "We would expect," he says, "a gentler qualification in a person of such charity and so detached from worldly vanity. But precisely because of her *converso* status, she disliked the peasant because he was free from the stain that mortified her, and the Jewish convert who was a reflection of her own disgrace."[155]

Possibly Don Américo's imagination need not have resorted to such lofty extra-historical speculations. The peasant held no interest for Teresa and as a result is totally missing from her writings.[156]

At the opposite extreme, it is a different matter with the aristocracy. It is enough to review her correspondence to be convinced that she mixed as an equal with the most powerful nobility of the time: the duke and duchess of Alba, the princess of Eboli, Doña María de Mendoza, Doña Luisa de la Cerda, the Marquesa de Villena, Doña María de Acuña, etc., etc., are only some of the figures in the gallery of highly placed persons who parade through her life and her writings.[157]

Her relations with the "elite" of the social register are, nevertheless, uneven. The unconditional—though not submissive—friendship of the widow of the brilliant Secretario Cobos, and the unquestionable generosity of Doña Beatriz de Beaumont, contrast strongly with the stinginess of Doña Luisa, who abandoned her during the bitter days in Toledo, with the erratic attitude of the Duchess of Alba, the neurasthenic Doña Ana de Mendoza or the scheming María de Acuña. One detects in all these ladies (and it is only natural given the demands of their times) the desire to use the famous nun as a showpiece, and as a sign of social prestige for those who sponsored the foundations.

The Madre's response, which includes her constant and unwavering gratitude, is not without its practical outlook, and she tries to take advantage of worldly vanity (almost always feminine) for her work with a freedom very much her own. In this way Eboli and Alba (the two rival "Parties" at the court) could be desirable allies to sway the royal will, in case—as actually happened—the king's intervention should be needed. The spectacular and drastic break with the neurotic Doña Ana is only too well known,[158] as are the unfortunate events which caused the resentment of the princess of Eboli. Teresa originally owed little to the Duke and Duchess of Alba for the foundation in their town; but then along came Doña Juana de Ahumada, with her husband and children, in need of recommendations,[159] attained but dearly paid for by the duchess's caprices. The unreliability of Doña Luisa de la Cerda did not manage to destroy their deep friendship, but the machinations of María de Acuña forced a decisive estrangement. With the rest she maintained more or less cordial relations, as circumstances dictated, but almost never was either party disinterested.

Undoubtedly in this analysis of St Teresa's social attitudes it is more revealing to study her general attitude toward the aristocracy than her personal relationships. It is a shame that her thinking should be set down only after she had already trampled the world under her feet, depriving us of the possibility of following an evolution which would certainly be very interesting in so perceptive an observer. By the time her opinion can be studied it is already clearly marked by hostility toward the aristocratic character and manners. The account of her first contact with noble circles during her first sojourn in the La Cerda mansion (Toledo, 1562) is enlivened by sharp observations which range from humor to disenchantment with the myth of the *Grandeza*, characterized simply as "a lie". Her conclusions could not have been more radical: "I saw how little should be our esteem for the status of nobility", and "I totally abhorred every desire to become a lady of the nobility."[160]

At the other extreme of her lifespan, a year before her death, she had to deal with the spectacular desertion of Doña Casilda de Padilla, whose vocation she describes so delightfully while speaking of the foundation at Valladolid. The event again provokes reflections that tend to excuse the defection. She does not blame "the poor girl who is the biggest loser," and her searching analysis penetrates the whole economic manipulation undertaken by the fickle elder daughter and by the Jesuits interested in diverting the inheritance toward a college of the Society; but at the center of everything lies the conviction that "His Majesty must not want us to be honored among the lords of the earth,'' ending with the crystal-clear exclamation, "May he deliver me from these lords who do whatever they want and are so "capricious.''[161]

Between these two events Teresa's life and work were marked with complications and very explicit criticisms which confirm her coolness toward or frank rejection of aristocratic style. In any case, it repelled her to have to deal with a social class so taken up with conventions. Her biographers hasten to relate with a certain merriment her boldness with certain ladies of the Court in 1569,[162] comparable only to her outstanding courage with the princess of Eboli, quite understandable in one who was disgusted by "so much lordship and fuss.''[163]

Chapter 10 of the *Foundations* is a masterful and forcefully drawn portrait of the contrast between the natural behavior of Casilda de Padilla, still almost a child, and her siblings on the one hand, and on the other the satiric observations, no less bitter for being delicately expressed, launched forcefully against the fundamental tenets of the *Grandeza*: enhancement of family estate, and, in this case, in the claim to the governorship of Castile. The writer cannot find adequate words to castigate the blindness of the aristocracy: "where parents think their honor consists in not forgetting the dunghill of this world's goods.''[164] Teresa had no sympathy for "advantageous" marriages, the most normal arrangement at that time, family pressures and so many worldly forces. Thus she expresses herself once again with unaccustomed harshness: "Oh illustrious people, for the love of God open your eyes. See that the true knights of Jesus Christ and the princes of His Church, St Peter and St Paul, did not follow the road you follow! Do you think a new road must be built for you? Don't believe it.''[165]

The sarcasm of her language is a faithful reflection of a practical attitude. Although exceptions can be found, it is very clear that she did not like members of the higher nobility in her convents. The childish daring of Casilda deceived her, and the extravagances of the princess of Eboli taught and scarred her. Only thus can the battle she undertook with the benefactress

Doña Elena de Quiroga be understood. In repeatedly denying her entrance, she resolutely weighed the desire not to anger her uncle, the Inquisitor General, and not to fail in the then hoped for foundation of Madrid; but even more important was her deeply-rooted aversion to risking the absolute equality found in her monasteries.[166]

At the center of this feeling about the aristocracy one finds the same opinions as in the question of honor. Her social protest is balanced by sublimation and by the contradiction existing between the Castilian social structure and the divine, so totally unlike. The true Lord revealed to her the profound foolishness of an earthly social system of which she herself was a victim, because he "isn't like those we have as lords here on earth, all of whose lordship consists in artificial displays."[167] The nobility's obses- s.on with ancestry—and blood counts here as much as wealth—is a "hell" that the foundress wishes to see destroyed in her houses, where "she who is of more noble birth should speak less of her parentage; all must be equal." She finds good arguments for such a reversal of the social order by the spiritual one, although they are taken from the legends of the *Flos sanctorum*: "O college of Christ, where St Peter, being a fisherman, had more authority— and the Lord wanted it so—than St Bartholomew, who was a king's son!"[168] The social pattern of which Teresa dreamed has few similarities with that which she was forced to endure: hers was a nobility which has "little to do with temporal goods" and is based on the radical exchange in virtue of which "the rich are the slaves and you are the masters."[169]

In the delightful—and daring—commentary on the verse of the Song of Songs: "your breasts are better than wine", the implicit comparison which underlies all her works springs up in the contemptuous remark: "Let worldly people worry about their lordships, riches, delights, honors, and food, for even if a person were able to enjoy all these things without the accompanying trials—which is impossible—he would not attain in a thousand years the happiness that in one moment is enjoyed by a soul brought here by the Lord."[170]

Lest things be distorted, we believe that Teresa's contempt for "the lowliness of things of the world" is primarily a response to a supernatural impulse. But it cannot be denied that the power of her language finds its best channel for expression in the pain and discouragement produced by her personal experience as a "New Christian."[171]

Her aversion toward the aristocracy changes into pity, actually a bit scornful, when the saint alludes to the enormous class of *hidalgos*, with their burden of honor and without the financial means with which to maintain their costly prestige. This lower nobility which lived poorly, trapped between penury and the demands of their position, was beaten by the combination. Taking refuge in a grand idleness, because of their meager revenues and the lack of enthusiasm they tended to show for menial labor, they were one of the outstanding objects of the satire of the time.

Madre Teresa's voice joins the chorus over which Lazarillo de Tormes rightly presides. With a few brief strokes she paints for us—she who might have witnessed in part this same family drama at the death of her father—the passion of this class of impoverished nobility. When she portrays with unequaled mastery Doña Teresa Laiz, foundress of Alba de Tormes, and refers with a certain surprise to the fact that she had to reside in the miserable village of Tordillos, she makes the astute observation: "It is very sad that, because of so much vanity in the world, people prefer to tolerate the lack of instruction in the solitude of those places, and many other things which are a means of enlightening the soul, rather than to lose a single point of so-called honor."[172]

If it were not known from other historical sources, the data in these words would suffice to deduce the general state of those in situations similar to that of Teresa de Laiz. This is so common that when Teresa sets out to emphasize the holy stoicism of an exemplary nun of Valladolid [Beatriz de la Encarnación] she finds no better metaphor for her constant equanimity than one referring to that class: "she resembled one of those highly honored persons who, although starving, would rather die than let anyone know they were hungry."[173]

Pity for the starving *hidalgo* and alienation from—if not

outright rejection of—the reality and manners of the aristocracy
alternate with an admitted sympathy towards merchants, doctors,
bankers, secretaries, middle-rank ecclesiastics, accountants, those
whom she does not hesitate on occasion to present as "my
friends."[174] They are precisely the ones who best understand her
work, the authentic and unconditional benefactors, and those
who almost always get her out of the many difficulties she had to
face and which we can study in the book of the *Foundations*.

Today there is no doubt that these bourgeois constituted the
most active element of the mass of Spanish *judeoconversos*.[175]
The closeness and the sympathetic treatment of this group which
is found in her pages is not, therefore, a pure coincidence, a
certain casual attraction; rather, it is the result of knowing that
she is moving in her own environment, and that she can do so
with that naturalness and freedom which the other classes do not
permit. Márquez Villanueva, an astute observer of these facts, has
rightly insisted on her "predilection for that social milieu of the
solid bourgeoisie, a social group of which the saint herself was
the most outstanding example."[176]

The Problem of the Judeoconversos

From what has been said, we can conclude that two fundamental factors have contributed to conceal the deep traces that her
judeoconverso ancestry might have left on her human attitudes:
the typical tendency of her caste to cover up its origin in every way
possible until finally it was completely hidden; and the isolated
hagiographic biographies, which were imprisoned in prejudices
that were once understandable but are inexplicable today. Hence
the need for an exegetical endeavor, which is indispensable for an
adequate understanding of many of her pages.

One must begin with the fact that lineage, the most perceptible
discriminating mark of honor, and subsequent social discrimination, had solidified by this point in Teresa's time into a climate
pregnant with tensions and special interests. The legion of those
fighting for the destruction of such barriers does not seem
numerous, but it is bold. Teresa is found among the determined
militants who favor the eradication of something which required

all possible prudence even when merely alluding to it, given the risk of being maliciously identified with illuminism and other heresies [177] and given the conviction that this called into question the supreme principle of the established social order.

What has been said should suffice to convince us that Madre Teresa proceeds with the loftiest contempt for such a social order. The principle, "I have always esteemed virtue more than lineage," [178] contains a revolutionary basic axiom ahead of its time, virtuously subversive, which is difficult to appreciate today. The saint on many occasions repeats something which would become universal in the eighteenth century from other perspectives, and the direct reference to the *judeoconversos* and to the burning issue of the purity of blood is hidden from no one.

More than once society placed her in the dilemma of choosing between the two extremes, and one must think that in critical circumstances her innate inclination toward the social class of her own extraction placed her in difficult situations, in which "proper" (Old Christian) society reacted against the liberties of the Madre. The splendid chapter dedicated to the foundation in Burgos must be read in this light. [179]

In Burgos opposition to merchants of *confeso* origin was alive in all its harshness. [180] Moreover, it is no secret that the principal aid the foundress received came from the bourgeoisie, working in professions proper to their caste (administrators, doctors), nor that the lay supporter of the foundation, Catalina de Tolosa, must be suspected of bearing the same mark. When the narrator [Teresa] is expounding the tenacious resistance of Doña Catalina in the face of interminable difficulties which sprang up at every turn, it is not surprising to find the unexpected exclamation relative to her unbreakable spirit: "How much more courage for doing great things do servants of God have than do those of noble lineage who fail to serve him." Her immediate attempt to cover up this spontaneous accusation [181] only confirms the suspicion that she has spoken the truth.

It is in Toledo that Teresa's feelings and her profound convictions are put to the test, this time without any kind of amelioration. Moreover, the saint, contrary to her custom, does not use a special argot to mask the true nature of the problem, which past historiography has attributed principally to a disagreement between the Council and the ecclesiastical governor, and also to the fastidious character of Diego Ortiz, the executor.[182] The suspicious insinuation of Ribera, "someone secretly influenced the governor against her,"[183] is clearly illuminated by the woman who was both chronicler and victim of the events: "During the days when I was dealing with Alonso Alvarez about the foundation, it seemed wrong to many people, who told me so, because they did not consider them [the family of benefactors] to be illustrious or *caballeros*, although very good, as I have said, and that in a place like Toledo I ought not lack any advantage."[184]

The ecclesiastical license was obtained after the energetic chapter of faults with which the foundress courageously castigated the astonished governor. Nevertheless, permission was granted with an extraordinary condition: that the monastery be founded in poverty. This clause undid the plans of the foundress, determined as she was not to lose the troublesome but substantial legacy; therefore, she decided on the middle course of giving the large chapel to the *judeoconverso* merchants, "and they could have no part in anything to do with the monastery." This fiction served little purpose; to have a chapel for burial was a sign of prestige and an enviable means desired by the *raza* to seal social acceptance and to erase their *confeso* background.[185] Hence we can see that the one seeking the right in opposition to the Ramirez family was an "important person", that is, of pure lineage. This is one more case, then, of the radical hostility between the two castes, well studied by historians of the Statutes of Purity of Blood, which had its center of focus in the city of Toledo.[186] We need to recognize the gravity and implacability which marked this hostility in order to understand the real context of the saint's unaccustomed perplexity "in the face of so many opinions" and in the face of "all the tales with which they went to the Governor."[187]

The question became so critical that the Madre's hesitant attitude before powerful pressures merited for her a "serious rebuke" of divine origin for having paid attention to the innuendos.[188] The text of the harsh and angry message from God, just as the saint heard it, has been preserved, related by her with graphic intensity which needs no comment:

> While I was at the monastery in Toledo, some were advising me that I shouldn't give a burying place to anyone who had not belonged to the nobility. The Lord said to me: "You will grow very foolish, daughter, if you look at the world's laws. Fix your eyes on me, poor and despised by the world. Will the great ones of the world, perhaps, be great before me? Or are you to be esteemed for lineage or for virtue?"[189]

The action of the winter of 1569–1570 amounted to a challenge to the nobility. The immediate history of the house confirmed the correctness of the decision to grant the desired burial place to someone "who was not of the nobility";[190] in the long run the challenge will reveal a decided will to dispense with prejudices of this sort, led by the conviction of "how unimportant these lineages and social classes will be before the judgment seat of God."[191]

If the timing and the serious intervention from on high confirmed her in a manner of proceeding which was in keeping with her disposition in her "external affairs," Teresa's attitude as far as her Reform was concerned remained constant and unbroken. There is no doubt that the original direction of her first steps and the foundation of San José in Avila are surrounded by nuns whose surnames clearly manifest their ancestry.[192] In her *Constitutions* there is not the least hint of discrimination. The conditions for admission of novices center around an examination of their aptitude for prayer, their desire for perfection and "contempt for the world";[193] we already know where Teresa's interest in such contempt originates. The same principle of contempt for lineage runs consistently and eloquently through the whole length of the *Way of Perfection*.

All this means that the primitive reform during the time of the saint—and the same was true of the Constitutions of the Discalced friars—did not accept the Statutes of Purity of Blood. It is another contrast with the mentality of the regular orders of her time, with the masculine branch of the Calced Carmelites itself,[194] and even with the feminine branch, whose *Constitutions* became harder as a result of the proviso of 1566 which prohibited the entry of anyone descended from Moors or Jews.[195]

The silence of her works—there are no explicit texts of the saint regarding this issue—is in contrast with her realistic and unprejudiced attitude. It is not necessary to delve into surnames indicating contaminated lineage or erudite genealogies; it is the nurse-secretary of Madre Teresa, Ana de San Bartolomé, who on an appropriate occasion, tells us of the Teresian practice. When the Discalced Carmelite nuns had been transplanted to France and Belgium, the post-foundational tensions accompanied the two protagonists, Ana de San Bartolomé and Ana de Jesús; because of their very different dispositions, a confrontation was not long in coming. Carmelite historians have focused only on specific differences, missing the more fundamental one, intensely lived out in a setting far removed from Castilian preoccupations with caste. Ana de Jesús, who reacts as an Old Christian (let us not forget St Teresa's repeated criticisms of her on this point),[196] instinctively carried this heartfelt Spanish conflict with her and quite naturally equates the Calvinists of the new environment with Moors and Jews.

The conflict became so intense that Ana de San Bartolomé came to say of her rival: "If God has not given the Madre [Ana de Jesús] that spirit of charity with these souls, Your Graces must not be ruled by that." But the most important thing in the duel is that of all the arguments for admitting the ex-Calvinist novice passionately proposed by the simple nurse, the weightiest reason is the memory of St Teresa's way of acting toward the descendants of *judeoconversos*:

> I know that before the saint died some of those who are called Israelites were received and that they have been received afterwards as well. If in Spain in the time of our holy foundress this was done for the good of those who asked with proper intentions, why has it not been done in France with even more reason? (. . .) The Madre [Ana de Jesús] says that she must not receive any nun who might be

related to heretics and this is a pretext for leaving; because if she could not do so she would not have come here where all are related to heretics. Receiving them is the right thing to do to fulfill the obligation of our Rule and Constitutions, as was the spirit of our Holy Mother."[197]

All this took place in 1605, and it is interesting to note that among the reasons given is that "here [in France] there is no need to fear anyone except God," revealing the freedom from such prejudices and pressures as were operative in the oppressive climate of Spain, and which finally, as in the case of the Society of Jesus, did not spare the Teresian reform.

In fact, fifteen years after the death of the Foundress, with the stability of the new order now assured, the friars plunged headlong into the abyss which St Teresa had always feared: the Spanish Chapter of 1597 in the *Constitutions* formulated in that assembly, confirmed the vigorous Statute of Purity of Blood with all the rigor and gravity attached to it. The doors were hermetically sealed to "applicants of Jewish or Moorish ancestry, without exception, and those descended from *confesos* or *penitenciados* unto the fourth generation inclusive."[198]

The masculine branch of Carmel, in a rupture more profound than many internal disputes which obsessed historians of the order, shattered the then "quixotic" idea of a *judeoconversa* [Teresa] to create a refuge where charity, humility and equality might oppose the tremendous discrimination of her Spain, which was more radicalized than we can imagine. (Trans. M. Dodd and S. Payne)

NOTES

1. TRANSLATORS' INTRODUCTORY NOTE: The present translation, begun over a year ago as a labor of love, turned out to be more of a labor than anticipated by the translating team (Michael Dodd and Steven Payne). However, we have been persuaded to publish what we have completed thus far, since Egido's article contains a wealth of information which should be of great interest to Teresian scholars and is not yet available to the English-speaking reader. To effect our translation as accurately as possible, we have consulted several experts on the meaning of some doubtful passages; the defects which remain may be ascribed primarily to our limited knowledge of Spanish social and political history.

Egido's quotations from St Teresa are generally taken from the E.D.E. edition of her works, i.e., from Santa Teresa de Jesus, *Obras Completas* (Madrid: Editorial de Espiritualidad, 1976). Thus, in references to the saint's correspondence, Egido first lists the date and heading, followed by the number of the letter in the E.D.E. edition, as well as the number of the paragraph from which a particular quote is taken. We have preserved this numbering for the sake of anyone who might wish to consult the original Spanish.

Unless otherwise noted, we have tried whenever possible to use quotations from currently available I.C.S. translations in *The Collected Works of St Teresa of Avila* trans. Kieran Kavanaugh and Otilio Rodriquez, vols 1 & 2 (Washington: ICS Publications, 1976 & 1980). All other translations of the saint's words are our own. The numbering of chapters and paragraphs in the E.D.E. and I.C.S. editions is generally the same.

Finally, we have added several translators' notes, both to clarify certain obscurities in the text, and also to point out which of the secondary works cited are available in English translation.

2. One may contrast this with the abundant literature produced on the occasion of her proclamation as a Doctor of the Church. See Simeón de la Sagrada Familia, *Bibliografia del doctorado teresiano*, (Rome, 1971).

3. Francisco de Ribera, *La vida de la Madre Teresa de Jesús*, (Salamanca, 1590); Diego de Yepes, *Vida, virtudes y milagros de la Bienaventurada Virgen Teresa de Jesús* (Zaragosa, 1606).

4. Jerónimo de San José, *Historia del Carmen Descalzo* (Madrid, 1637); Francisco de Santa María, *Reforma de Nuestra Senora del Carmen de la primitiva observancia hecha por Santa Teresa de Jesús*, vol. 1 (Madrid, 1644).

5. Anselmo Donazar Zamora, *Principio y fin de una Reforma, Una revolución religiosa en tiempos de Felipe II* (Bogotá, 1968); Ildefonso Moriones, *Ana de Jesús y la herencia teresiana: ¿Humanismo cristiano o rigor primitivo?* (Rome, 1968), popularized in *El carisma teresiano: Estudio sobre sus orígenes* (Rome, 1972). TRANSLATORS' NOTE: The last mentioned work is available in English as *The Teresian Charism: A Study of the Origins*, trans. Christopher O'Mahony, OCD (Rome: Teresianum, 1972).

6. Miguel Mir, *Santa Teresa de Jesús: Su vida, su espíritu, sus fundaciones*, 2 vols. (Madrid, 1912).

7. Real progress was made in *Tiempo y Vida*, by Efrén de la Madre de Dios, placed at the beginning of the first volume of *Obras de Santa Teresa* (Madrid, 1951), and here cited as *Tiempo y Vida* I. This study was completed and partly corrected in the work done in collaboration with Otger Steggink, *Tiempo y vida de Santa Teresa* (Madrid, 1968), the most serious and complete work of its type. This latter volume (cited as *Tiempo y vida*) incorporates that which is directly related to Teresa in Otger Steggink, *La reforma del Carmelo español: La visita del General Rubeo y su encuentro con Santa Teresa 1566-1567* (Rome, 1965), part of which is repeated once again in *Experiencia y realismo en Santa Teresa y en San Juan de la Cruz* (Madrid: Editorial de Espiritualidad, 1974).

8. Daniel de Pablo Maroto, *Dinámica de la oración: Acercamiento del orante moderno a Santa Teresa de Jesús* (Madrid: Editorial de Espiritualidad, 1973); Isaías Rodríguez, *Santa Teresa de Jesús en la espiritualidad española* (Madrid, 1972); Enrique Llamas Martínez, *Santa Teresa de Jesús y la Inquisición española* (Madrid, 1972). The thesis of Ulrich Dobhan, "Teresa von Avila: Welt, Gott, Mensch," (Würzburg, 1976), has successfully placed Teresa's anthropology in its

exact historical context. TRANSLATORS' NOTE: Dobhan's thesis has been published as *Gott-Mensch-Welt in der Sicht Teresas von Avila* (Frankfurt am Main: Peter Lang, 1978).

9. L, 33, 5. Compare the interpretation of Henry Kamen, *La Inquisición española* (Barcelona, 1972), pp. 110–111, which would need to be complemented with the humor of the allusions in the *Vejamen* 1 and 4. TRANSLATORS' NOTE: Kamen's book was originally published in English as *The Spanish Inquisition* (New York: New American Library, 1966). The *Vejamen* is known in English as "Judgment Given by St Teresa Upon Various Writings on the Words 'Seek Thyself in Me'."

10. With keen insight she laments the death of the king of Portugal, shows herself to be a pacifist, and even tries to get Don Teutonio de Braganza to act as a mediator in the imminent conflict; see the Letter to Gratian, August 19, 1578, 2, and the Letter to Don Teutonio de Braganza, July 22, 1579. TRANSLATORS' NOTE: Don Teutonio de Braganza belonged to a branch of the Portuguese royal family and became Archbishop of Evora, Portugal; his nephew was one of the claimants to the Portuguese throne after the death of Cardinal King Henrique.

11. Letter to María de San José, July 4, 1580, 14. She is interested in knowing the truth of the rumor about this Moorish uprising circulating throughout Castile.

12. W, 1.

13. Letter to Don Teutonio de Braganza, June 1574, 66, 5.

14. Letter to Doña Inés Nieto, October 31, 1575, 4.

15. Undated fragment, perhaps from the end of 1579, listed as Letter #439 in Santa Teresa de Jesús, *Obras Completas*, 2d ed. (Madrid: Editorial de Espiritualidad, 1976).

16. F, 23. Beas, far removed from the center of Teresian activities, was another foundation made by mistake. This mountain village was attached to the civil Chancellery of Castile but under the ecclesiastical jurisdiction of Andalusia, a fact unknown to the Madre who, had she realized it at the time, would "in no way" have agreed to make the foundation (F, 24, 2). She never tires of maintaining that Beas is not in Andalusia (Letter to María Bautista, September 1574, 64, 3), a sentiment shared by the town's inhabitants. See Efrén J.M. Montalva (Efrén de la Madre de Dios), *Beas y Santa Teresa* (Madrid: Editorial de Espiritualidad, 1975), containing the topographical report ordered by Felipe II in 1575, pp. 139–55.

17. See Enrique Llamas, *Santa Teresa de Jesús y la Inquisición española* and the correspondence of 1576.

18. Letter to Padre Rubeo, June 18, 1575, 6; Letter to María de San José, September 9, 1576.

19. Letter to María Bautista, April 29, 1576.

20. *Ibid.*, 12.

21. Letter to P. Rubeo, January 1576 (91, 14); Letter to Diego Ortiz, December 26, 1575, 3.

22. "I desire that they take few houses in Andalusia" (Letter to Gratian, March 23–24, 1581, 4), she writes in reference to the Discalced. The foundation of Granada did not fall within the saint's program; for this reason she relegated it to Ana de Jesús.

23. In the letter to P. Rubeo already cited (n. 10) she tells him "the friars of Castile seem very good to me, now that I see the ones here." Authentic data which

confirms the saint's appraisal can be found in Steggink, *La reforma*, pp. 181ff.

24. O. Steggink, *op. cit.*, pp. 414–15.

25. Alvaro Castillo, "Population et richesse en Castille durant la seconde moitié du XVIe siècle," in *Annales. ESC* (1965) 719–33; Nöel Salomon, *La vida rural castellano en tiempos de Felipe II* (Barcelona, 1973).

26. TRANSLATORS' NOTE: The word "judeoconverso" refers to the Jews who were forced to convert to Christianity in order to avoid expulsion from Spain, and to their descendants. Since this is a technical term for which there is no simple English equivalent, we will generally leave it untranslated.

27. F, 13–14.

28. Felipe Ruiz Martín, "Demografía eclesiástica hasta el siglo XIX," in *Diccionario de historia Eclesiástica de España*, 2, 683–733; Annie Molinié-Bertrand, "Le clergé dans le Royaume de Castille à la fin du XVIe siècle: Approche cartographique," in *Revue d'Histoire économique et sociale* 51 (1973) 6ff; cf. Antonio Domínguez Ortíz, *El Antiguo Régimen: Los Reyes Católicos y los Austrias* (Madrid, 1973), pp. 118-21.

29. It doesn't bother her very much to get rid of the foundation in Pamplona: Letter to Catalina de Cristo, September 15-17, 1582, 4.

30. Pierre Chaunu, *L'Espagne de Charles Quint*, Vol. I (Paris, 1973), p. 307.

31. Pierre Vilar, "Le temps des hidalgos," in *L'Espagne au temps de Philippe II* (Paris, 1965), p. 32; Felipe Ruiz Martín, *Lettres marchandes entre Florence et Medina del Campo* (Paris, 1965), p. XL.

32. From the immense bibliography dealing with this period of Spanish history, cf. the work of the specialist Manuel Fernández Alvarez, *La España de Carlos V* (Madrid, 1966); this book is volume XVIII of *Historia de España* under the direction of Menéndez Pidal.

33. J. Ignacio Gutiérrez Nieto, "La discriminación de los conversos y la tibetización de Castilla por Felipe II", off-print from *Revista de la Universidad de Madrid*, IV (1973).

34. L 26, 5. The censors of *The Way of Perfection* show us indirectly the real intention which moved Teresa to criticize sharply such a prohibition of spiritual books. She writes: "Hold fast, daughters, for they cannot take from you the Our Father and the Hail Mary"; "and when books are taken away from us, this book cannot be taken away, for it comes from the mouth of Truth Itself, Who cannot err" (W [Escorial Codex], 36, 4; 73, 4). The censor is not far off when he notes in the margin: "It seems here that she is reprimanding the Inquisitors who prohibited books on prayer." (TRANSLATORS' NOTE: In the Kavanaugh/Rodriguez translation of the *Way*, the two quotations from St Teresa are to be found in chapter 21, paragraph 8, and in chapter 42, paragraph 5; the censor's remark appears in footnote 8 of chapter 21.) So certain was this that in the second redaction, elaborated and destined not only for the narrow circle of San José in Avila, the saint suppressed these passages. To understand the sense of these changes, see the Introduction to the *Way* by Daniel de Pablo Maroto in *Introducción a la lectura de Santa Teresa* (Madrid: Editorial de Espiritualidad, 1978), pp. 269-310.

35. To understand this vigilance as well as the abuses, see Kamen, *op. cit.*, and the interesting data of Enrique Llamas, "Documentos inquisitoriales con referencia a le economía del Principado de Cataluña (1574-1577), existentes en el British Museum de Londres." in *Cuadernos de historia económica de Cataluña* 7 (1972):255-70; Celo de la Inquisición por la pureza de la fe en el siglo XVI:

Documentos mss. sobre libros y folletos, en el British Museum (1574-1592)," in *Studium Legionense* 14 (1973):9-48.

36. Melquiades Andrés Martín, *Reforma española y reforma luterana: Afinidades y diferencias a la luz de los místicos españoles (1517-1536)* (Madrid, 1975).

37. See the analysis of this aspect by Daniel de Pablo Maroto in "Introducción al *Camino de perfección,*" chap. 2,2, in *Introducción a la lectura de Santa Teresa,* pp. 282-84. The study of the spiritual movement of recollection ["recogimiento"], analyzed in M. Andrés Martín, *Los recogidos* (Madrid, 1976), also casts light on this phenomenon.

38. This is treated, perhaps with some exaggeration, by Steggink, *La reforma,* pp. 69ff, 438ff.

39. These Spanish phenomena, so distorted by former generalizations, are being set in proper perspective by historical investigation. See the fundamental work of Antonio Márquez, *Los alumbrados* (Madrid, 1972), with the suitable corrections of M. Andrés, *Nueva visión de los alumbrados de 1525* (Madrid, 1973); Idem, *El misterio de los alumbrados de Toledo, desvelado por sus contemporáneos* (Burgos, 1976).

40. Melquiades Andrés, "El movimiento de los 'espirituales' en España en el siglo XVI," in *Salmanticensis* 22 (1975):333-48.

41. Efrén-Steggink, *Tiempo y Vida,* p. 761.

42. L, 32.

43. Daniel de Pablo Maroto, in *Dinámica de la oración,* pp. 83ff., devotes a brilliant chapter to this problem: "La polémica oracionista del siglo XVI y la reacción de Santa Teresa."

44. Steggink, *Experiencia y realismo,* chap. 1.

45. This is carefully explained in J. Ignacio Gutiérrez Nieto, "La estructura castizo-estamental de la sociedad castellana del siglo XVI," in *Hispania* 33 (1973):519-63.

46. See Américo Castro, *La edad conflictiva,* 3d ed. (Madrid, 1972), ch. 2.

47. Antonio Domínguez Ortiz, *Los judeoconversos en España y América* (Madrid, 1971), p. 219; Eloy Benito Ruano, "Del problema judío al problema judeoconverso," in *Simposio Toledo Judaico* (Toledo 20-22 abril 1972), II, [Toledo, n.d.], pp. 7-28. TRANSLATORS' NOTE: Here the text contains a form of "desvivirse," a verb used by some contemporary Spanish historians to refer to the "desire to 'unlive' the past, to escape," the "process of denial of one's own life." See Américo Castro, *The Spaniards: An Introduction to Their History* (Berkeley: University of California Press, 1971), pp. 146-47.

48. *Procesos,* 2, 122 (cf. note 51 below).

49. Jerónimo Gracián de la Madre de Dios, *Espíritu y revelaciones y manera de proceder de la Madre Ana de San Bartolomé, examinado por el P., su confesor,* ed. Silverio de Santa Teresa, *Biblioteca Mística Carmelitana* (henceforth, *BMC*), vol. 17 (Burgos, 1933), p. 259.

50. Efrén de la Madre de Dios, *Tiempo y Vida* I, p. 160. Later we will see how the author corrected this first point of view, which does not diminish the indisputable value of his work.

51. The original Processes have been edited by Silverio de Santa Teresa, *BMC,* vols. 18-20 (Burgos, 1934-1935). This edition contains lacunae and errors which demand a broader effort to present such necessary documentation in a critical form.

52. *Procesos* 1, 2.

53. See the answers of the nuns in Madrid (*Procesos* 1, 290-355), and in Segovia (Ibid., 1, 421ff.). The coincidence is even greater in the remissorial processes "in specie" [i.e., the later official inquiry of the Apostolic Process into the *specific* virtues and miracles of Teresa], 2, 194-201, to mention only one of many instances.

54. TRANSLATORS' NOTE: The terms used here refer to different levels of the Spanish social hierarchy. "At the top of the scale came the *Grandes de España*," a very limited group "drawn from the oldest families of Castile and Aragon," according to J. H. Elliott. These were the possessors of *Grandeza*, who "enjoyed the special distinction of being allowed to remain covered in the presence of the King, and of being addressed by him as *primos*, or cousins." At the other extreme were the *hidalgos* (or *hijosdalgo*), aristocrats of the lowest rank who nevertheless were exempted from taxation, could claim the honorary title *Don*, and were eligible for various civil and ecclesiastical positions closed to those of mixed blood. However, as Egido explains, those with money could become officially *hidalgos* by purchasing certificates of *hidalguía*, as many *conversos* did. The *caballeros* ("knights" or "gentlemen") also belonged to the lower ranks; in fact, since the terms *caballero* and *hidalgo* are sometimes used interchangeably, we have not tried to distinguish them carefully in this translation.

Between the two extremes of the social scale were various other divisions of *nobleza* ("nobility"); this latter term seems to have a more fluid meaning, which need not concern us here. Egido's point is simply that, in reality, there were individuals of mixed ancestry at every level of the social hierarchy. For further information on the composition of the Spanish aristocracy, see John H. Elliott, *Imperial Spain: 1469-1716*, (New York: Penguin Books, 1978), pp. 110-18.

55. Concerning the *Tizón de la nobleza* and *Libros verdes*, significant though poorly-made attempts to demonstrate the mixed bloodlines of the most elevated families of Castile and Aragon, cf. Julio Caro Baroja, *Los judíos en la España moderna y contemporánea*, vol. II (Madrid, 1962), pp. 253ff. In the Appendix of volume III (287ff) he transcribes one of the innumerable copies of the first of these invectives.

56. *Procesos* 1, 6 (The amplification of Bañez is curious: "And he has also heard it said that the said Madre Teresa de Jesús had a brother who was a Hieronymite, by which it was understood that she was an Old Christian"); 239, 244.

57. Biblioteca Nacional de Madrid, Mss. 12.036, fol. 6r.

58. *Procesos* 2, 206, 387, 412; 248, 254, 598; 278, etc.

59. Precisely at this time the mobilization of public opinion had reached its high point in preparation for the expulsion of the *moriscos*. Cf. Joan Reglá, *Estudios sobre los moriscos*, 3d ed. (Barcelona, 1974), p. 48.

60. In the *Procesos* (1, 276), he testifies as follows about the ancestors of the saint, that she was "of such an ancient and well-known line, that the present Marqués de las Navas, in speaking of the said Madre with this witness, declared that her family line was more ancient than that of the parents and grandparents of the said marqués."

61. *Vida de la Madre Teresa de Jesús*, cited from the 1602 Madrid edition, p. 40.

62. Menéndez Pelayo's evaluation of P. Ezquerra's *El genio de la historia* is well-known. Cf. the judgment of Professor Solano Costa in the "Prólogo" to the edition of this work completed by Higinio de Santa Teresa, (Vitoria, 1957).

63. Cited and accepted by P. Silverio de Santa Teresa, *Historia del Carmen Descalzo* (henceforth, *HCD*), vol. 10, (Burgos, 1942), p. 300.

64. *Reforma de los Descalzos*, I, pp. 14-17.

65. This exceptional document—the existence of which we learned of from Jacinto Pascual—dates from 1646, and has the long title *Traslado auténtico de la ejecutoria de nobleza de los padres de Nra. Gloriosa Me. Sancta Teresa de Jesús, cuyo original está en Osuna en poder del capitán D. Josef de Cepeda, Alcalde ordinario de aquella villa en el estado de los caballeros hijosdalgo. Y juntamente el árbol genealógico de la Sancta y algunos apuntamientos sacados de testamentos y escrituras auténticas, de las cuales se coligen los deudos de la Sancta que van en el árbol y otros* ["An authentic copy of the letters patent of nobility of the parents of Our Glorious Mother Saint Teresa of Jesus, the original copy being in Osuna in the possession of Captain D. Josef de Cepeda, First Magistrate of that town for the estate of *caballeros hijosdalgo*. And including the genealogical tree of the Saint and some remarks taken from wills and authentic writings from which are ascertained the relatives of the Saint to be found in this family tree and in others"]. Conventual Archives of the Discalced Carmelite Fathers in Avila, Miscel., lib. 1.

66. Francisco Fernández de Betencourt, "Los parientes de Santa Teresa", in *Boletín de la Real Academia de la Historia* 58 (1911):216-223; Marqués de Ciadoncha, "Los Cepedas, linaje de Santa Teresa, Ensayo genealógico, *ibid.* 99 (1931):607-52. See also the works of the excellent Teresian scholar Bernardino de Melgar, *Ibid.* 67 (1915):358-66; 381-82.

67. TRANSLATORS' NOTE: The *Cortes* of Cádiz declared St Teresa the Patroness of the whole Spanish domain on June 28, 1812. See Silverio de Santa Teresa, *Saint Teresa of Jesus (1515-1582)* (London: Sand & Co., 1947), p. 164 and *HCD*, VIII, pp. 817-22.

68. As the most significant example, cf. the curious four volume work *La Santa de la raza* (Madrid, 1929-1935), by P. Gabriel de Jesús, otherwise without great historical value.

69. *HCD* I, 22.

70. *Teresa la Santa*, (Madrid, 1929). Castro re-edited this work (Barcelona, 1972) and, as always in his revisions of previous books, made numerous modifications.

71. Américo Castro, *España en su historia (Cristianos, moros y judíos,)* (Buenos Aires, 1948). TRANSLATORS' NOTE: This appeared in English translation as *The Structure of Spanish History*, trans. Edmund L. King, (Princeton, N.J., 1954). The change of viewpoint, in this case, is explained in the full introduction placed before the second edition of *Teresa la Santa* mentioned above. Cf. the detailed study of this evolution in our article, "La novedad teresiana de Américo Castro" in *Revista de Espiritualidad* 32 (1973):82-94.

72. Narciso Alonso Cortés, "Pleitos de los Cepeda", in *Boletín de la Real Academia Española* 25 (1946):85-110.

73. The lawsuit in question is found in the Archives of the Royal Chancellery of Valladolid, Hall of the Hijosdalgo, leg. 45, no. 5, from which Alonso Cortés transcribed it. The researcher will find to his unpleasant surprise that it has completely disappeared.

74. Pleito, ed. Alonso Cortés, p. 90.

75. *Loc. cit.*, p. 101, where it can be seen that Alonso Cortés resists believing in the significance of his find.

76. *La realidad historica de España* (title of the 2d and following editions of

España en su historia), (Mexico, 1954), p. 156. Eugenio Asensio reproaches him for his dishonest claim, in "La peculiaridad literaria de los conversos", in *Anuario de estudios medievales* 4 (1967):337.

77. See note 7 of this article.

78. Ferreol Hernández, *Santa Teresa de Avila* (Avila, 1952).

79. *Los judeoconversos*, p. 205.

80. *Tiempo y Vida* I, p. 170.

81. Américo Castro, *La edad conflictiva*, p. 101. It should be noted that the most outstanding Teresian scholar, Efrén de la Madre de Dios, whose importance in the historical treatment of St Teresa cannot be doubted, admitted in the later revision that the saint's grandfather was a *judeoconverso*; but he made matters worse when he tried to justify his first position. *Tiempo y Vida*, p. 4. In *Santa Teresa por dentro* (Madrid: Editorial de Espiritualidad, 1973), pp. 18–19, he is more explicit.

82. A. Domínguez Ortiz, *Los judeoconversos*, where he synthesizes previous works.

83. Homero Seris, "Nueva genealogía de Santa Teresa", in *Nueva Revista de Filologia Hispanica* 10 (1956):365–84.

84. Francisco Márquez Villanueva, "Santa Teresa y el linaje", in *Espiritualidad y literatura en el siglo XVI* (Madrid-Barcelona, 1968), pp. 139–205.

85. José Gómez-Menor, *El linaje familiar de Santa Teresa y de San Juan de la Cruz* (Toledo, 1970); *Cristianos nuevos y mercaderes de Toledo* (Toledo, 1970).

86. TRANSLATORS' NOTE: One recent author describes the *sambenito* as "a yellow tunic with large green crosses at back and front, which was later hung up in the culprit's parish church with an inscription recording his name and offences." See Stephen Clissold, *St Teresa of Avila* (London: Sheldon Press, 1979), p. 4.

87. See the list of forbidden offices in *Nueva Recop.*, Book 8, sect. 2, decrees 1–2. They even "encountered difficulties in acting as primary school teachers." A. Domínguez Ortiz, *op. cit.*, pp. 149, 223. Cf. F Márquez Villanueva, "Conversos y cargos concejiles en el siglo XV", in *Revista de Archivos, Bibliotecas y Museos* 63/2 (1957):503–40.

88. Francisco Cantera, Pilar León Tello, *Judaizantes del arzobispado de Toledo habilitados por la Inquisición en 1495–1497* (Madrid, 1969).

89. *Pleito*, p. 87.

90. We have not found this document, which is presumed by Mir, Fernández de Betencourt, Silverio, Efrén. See *Tiempo y Vida* I, p. 172.

91. This is to be found in the Archives of the Royal Chancellery of Valladolid, Secc. Reales Ejecutorias, Leg. 365-1. A photograph of the family document is in the Archivo Silveriano, Burgos. This document is what constitutes the fundamental argument for the work cited in note 19 above. These "purchases" of rulings by *conversos* was an official business which, if not very profitable, was at least well-managed by the Exchequer of Carlos V. See Ramón Carande, *Carlos V y sus banqueros*, III, pp. 422ff.

92. BAE edition, 12, 70.

93. Julio Caro Baroja, *op. cit.*, II, pp. 304–32.

94. *Procesos*, II, 278.

95. Julio Caro Baroja, *op. cit.*, II. pp. 258, 262.

96. *Pleito*, p. 94; H. Seris, *loc. cit.*, p. 373.

97. See Pierre Chaunu, "Inquisition et vie quotidienne dans l'Amérique espagnole au XVIIe siècle", in *Annales ESC*, (1956):228–36.

98. Julio Caro Baroja, *op. cit.*, II, p. 336.

99. A. Domínguez Ortiz, *op. cit.*, pp. 130–31.

100. TRANSLATORS' NOTE: There seems to be an error here. *Tiempo y Vida* indicates that Teresa had two sisters and nine brothers. Egido's text seems to suggest that there was a tenth brother who died in childhood, but we can find no record of this.

101. Manuel María Polit, *La familia de Santa Teresa en América* (Friburgo Br., 1905). For information on the fate of the saint's brothers, see *Tiempo y Vida*, pp. 36–41.

102. See the fury with which this abusive historian attacks the noble pretensions of the Cepedas in the Indies in *Quincuagenes de la nobleza de España*, Edic. V. de la Fuente, vol. 1 (Madrid, 1880), p. 491.

103. Pleito, p. 107.

104. TRANSLATORS' NOTE: "Mayorazgo" is a technical term for a traditional Spanish "institution designed to prevent the dispersion of a family's property by making it indivisible, inalienable, and hereditary in a certain line of descendants"; see Bartolomé Bennassar, *The Spanish Character* (Berkeley: University of California Press 1979), p. 276.

105. Letter to Lorenzo de Cepeda, December 28, 1580, 6–8. Also to the same, December 15, 1581, 1–2. Note that although this social preoccupation might not have concerned her much, she is interested in the promotion of her relatives.

106. H. Seris, *loc. cit.*, p. 375.

107. *Ibid.*, pp. 329–30.

108. J. C. Gómez-Menor, "La sociedad conversa toledana en la primera mitad del siglo XVI", in *Symposio* II, pp. 51–63. To understand the economic and social environment of the class to which St Teresa's grandfather belonged, see Eloy Benito Ruano, *Toledo en el siglo XV* (Madrid, 1961).

109. "Look what sort of man is this, who I will have you know was secretary of the king, Don Enrique," said a clerk at the shop in Avila to Mateo Julián, who wanted news of the absent merchant. Pleito, p. 92.

110. Pleito, pp. 91, 92, 93, 98.

111. *Ibid.*, pp. 92–98.

112. *Ibid.*, p. 94. TRANSLATORS' NOTE: The Spanish text is somewhat obscure. According to our research, Charles V instituted the *tercias reales*, a tax of one-third of all the funds collected by the Church in Castile, including votive-offerings, to raise additional revenues for the Spanish Crown. In Teresa's day, individuals with money generally invested in rent-properties and government bonds, the annuities on the latter coming from taxes. The implication here seems to be that the Cepedas, though exempted from taxation themselves by the certificate of *hidalguia*, earned part of their living, either directly or indirectly, from rent and tax-collection. For further background on the question of taxation in sixteenth century Spain, see Elliott, *Imperial Spain: 1469–1716*, pp. 199–207.

113. *Ibid.*, pp. 93, 94, 98.

114. TRANSLATORS' NOTE: The "pecheros" were the commoners who, in contrast to the nobility, were subject to taxation. Hence, the term may also be translated as "tax-payers."

115. Gerald Brenan, *San Juan de la Cruz*, (Barcelona, 1974), in an excursus dedicated to the Jewish ancestry of St Teresa, pp. 111ff builds up increasingly unhistorical evaluations of this problem, which he does not understand in any depth. The oversimplification has been taken to its ultimate conclusion in J. M. González Ruiz's reflections on Brenan's work in *Sábado Gráfico*, no. 931, April 5, 1975. TRANSLATORS' NOTE: For the English version of the Brenan passage, see Gerald Brenan, *Saint John of the Cross: His Life and Poetry*, with a translation of his poetry by Lynda Nicholson (Cambridge: Cambridge University Press, 1973), pp. 91-95.

116. On this date they obtained the certificate mentioned in note 91 above.

117. Concerning this final tragedy, see *Tiempo y Vida*, I, pp. 429-30.

118. Américo Castro, *La edad conflictiva*, p. 45.

119. As Claudio Sánchez Albornoz proves in opposition to Américo Castro in *España, un enigma historico*, 2 vols. (Buenos Aires, 1962).

120. Bartolomé Bennassar, *L'homme espagnol: Attitudes et mentalités de XVIe au XIXe siècle* (Paris, 1975), p. 167. Marcelin Defourneaux also includes this passion—along with the Catholic faith—among the two essential elements of the Spanish spirit: *La vie quotidienne en Espagne au siècle d'Or* (Paris, 1964), p. 36. TRANSLATORS' NOTE: Both works are available in English. See Bartolomé Bennassar, *The Spanish Character*, p. 213; and Marcelin Defourneaux, *Daily Life in Spain in the Golden Age* (Stanford, Cal.: Stanford University Press, 1971), p. 35.

121. See the excellent examples in J. García Mercadal's collection, *Viajes de extranjeros por España y Portugal*, 2 vols. (Madrid, 1959).

122. The verses of the *Comendadores de Córdoba* are actually less vigorous than the words of the *Partidas*, Lib. II, Tit. 13, 1.4.

123. See the corrections to Américo Castro in the studies cited in note 139.

124. See the previously cited article by J. I. Gutiérrez Nieto. TRANSLATORS' NOTE: We assume the author is referring to the article mentioned in note 33 of the first section of this article.

125. L, 2,6. TRANSLATORS' NOTE: The translation here is our own.

126. L, 2.9.

127. L, 2,5.

128. L, 5,1.

129. L, 7,7. Possibly the person in question was the propertied Don Francisco de Guzmán of the *judeoconverso* family of the Bracamonte. See the data relevant to this identification and to the person himself in José Vicente Rodríguez, "Cinco cartas inéditas de San Juan de Avila", *Revista de Espiritualidad* 34 (1975):369.

130. Letter to María Bautista, April 29, 1576, 11. See the complaint about Juan de Ovalle's defiant attitude in the same letter.

131. Letter to Doña Juana de Ahumada, December, 1569, 5: "I do not like these contracts my brother [i.e., her brother-in-law, Doña Juana's husband] speaks of."

132. See note 49.

133. F, 27, 12.

134. L, 1.1. Note that the saint emphasizes her father's love of reading, something highly suspicious in a society which was partly at odds with these inclinations.

135. A Domínguez Ortiz, *Los judeoconversos*, pp. 215-217, and Eugenio Asensio. "La peculiaridad literaria", p. 337, have nuanced these partially coinciding expressions in *judeoconverso* literature with greater historical rigor than Castro.

136. L, 37, 9.

137. F, 14, 6.

138. F, 26, 12-13.

139. J. I. Gutiérrez Nieto, "La estructura castizo-estamental", *passim*. Eugenio Asensio, from another angle, has corrected the too disembodied and non-historical vision of Américo Castro, by penetrating the economic scope of the Statutes [of Purity of Blood] in "Notas sobre la historiografía de Américo Castro (Con motivo de un articulo de A. A. Sicroff)", *Anuario de estudios medievales* 8 (1973):349-92.

140. W, 2,6; 22,4.

141. To give only a few examples, see *Meditations on the Song of Songs*: "the poor are never much honored"; W (E), 20, 1; L, 20, 27, etc.

142. Steggink's work, *La reforma*, reveals with precision the lamentable situation in this regard at the Encarnación. Maroto emphasizes it in the Introduction to the *Way, Introducción a la lectura de Santa Teresa*, pp. 286-87.

143. L, 31, 20-21; W, 12, 7. TRANSLATORS' NOTE: The translation here is our own.

144. L, 4,7; 21,9. TRANSLATORS' NOTE: The translation here is our own.

145. W, 36, 3.

146. TRANSLATORS' NOTE: The word "not" does not appear in the Spanish text, but seems necessary to convey the meaning of the sentence.

147. L, 37, 5-6.

148. W, 21, 10; 36, 5. TRANSLATORS' NOTE: The translation of W, 36, 5 is our own.

149. W, 3, 7.

150. W, 36,4.

151. She complains about this to Ana de Jesús, who was hardly in agreement with the Madre on these points, in a letter, May 30, 1582, 10.

152. On the surface St Teresa always had this concern; so much so that, in the grace of her spiritual marriage, when God shows her the dowry of a nail, he expresses himself like any knight before his spouse: "From now on not only will you look after My honor as being the honor of your Creator, King, and God, but you will look after it as My true bride. My honor is yours, and yours Mine." *Spiritual Testimonies*, 31. This took place around September, 1572. TRANSLATORS' NOTE: According to Kavanaugh-Rodriquez, the account is dated November 18, 1572. It appears as number 25 in *Obras Completas* (Madrid: EDE, 1976).

153. A more detailed study of this dimension is found in our Introduction to the *Foundations, Introducción a la lectura de Santa Teresa*, pp. 241-68.

154. *La edad conflictiva*, pp. 175ff, the chapter entitled "El labriego como último refugio contra la ofensiva de la opinion."

155. *Op. cit.*, p. 202.

156. The documentation set forth by Salvador de la Vírgen del Carmen (*Teresa de Jesús*, vol. 1, pp. 349-353) to accentuate Teresa's good relations with the "country folk" proves just the opposite of what the author intends.

157. P. Salvador de la Vírgen del Carmen, *Teresa de Jesús*, 2 vols., (Vitoria, 1968), has carefully presented the gallery of all the personages and classes with whom St Teresa dealt; nonetheless, we cannot agree with many of his views.

158. *Tiempo y Vida*, pp. 498ff.

159. See one such letter of recommendation, written to Inés Nieto, October 31, 1575, 1.

160. L, 34, 4-5.

161. Letter to Gratian, September 17, 1581.

162. Francisco de Santa María, *Reforma*, I, lib. I, cap. 2; *Tiempo y Vida*, p. 363.

163. Letter to María Bautista, July 18 [or 16], 1574, 5.

164. F, 10, 9.

165. F, 10, 11.

166. See the constant denials of entry to Cardinal Quiroga's niece in letters to Don Gaspar de Quiroga, June 16, 1581; Don Dionisio Ruiz de la Peña, July 8, 1581, 1–2; to the same, September 13, 1581, 2, etc. In this instance, as in other rare cases, she had to yield, which demonstrates the flexibility the Madre maintained while seeking never to compromise the future of her reform.

167. L, 37, 5.

168. W, 27, 6.

169. *Meditations on the Song of Songs*, 2, 9.

170. *Ibid.*, 4, 7.

171. Many Teresian passages must be read in this context. Even close aristocratic friends like Doña Luísa de la Cerda and Doña María de Mendoza could find in her letters recommendations which were daring and offensive to their way of life: "You know that you must lose some of your formality with me and gain humility." [Letter to Doña Luísa, November 2, 1568] "Oh, if you had as much control over your interior affairs as you do over externals!" [Letter to Doña María, March, 1569] Finally, let us note that Teresa's behavior is not free from certain contradictions. She, who has trampled the world beneath her feet, does not hide the delight which seizes her when her brother Lorenzo acquires the property of La Serna; he should not worry that the transaction was not as profitable as a possible investment of the money gained in America in rent property, because with the acquisition "you have given something more to your sons than property, that is, honor" (Letter to Don Lorenzo de Cepeda, January 2, 1577, 10). What happened with La Serna can be compared with her satisfaction at the marriage of her nephew Francisco with Doña Orofrisia de Mendoza, who "is related to the loftiest families of Spain", "first cousin of the Duke of Albuquerque's mother" and—this is important—"possible heiress to the estate" (Letters to Don Lorenzo de Cepeda, December 15, 1581, 1; December 28, 1580, 5–8).

172. F, 20, 2.

173. F, 12, 6. Compare this with the criticisms expressed by the social historians of this epoch. Cf. especially those noted by Annie Molinié-Bertrand, "Les 'hidalgos' dans le Royaume de Castile à la fin du XVIe siècle: Approche cartographique", in *Revue d'Histoire économique et sociale* 52 (1974):68–69.

174. F, 15, 6.

175. See the pertinent data in J. Gómez Menor, *Cristianos nuevos y mercaderes de Toledo*, already cited.

176. "Santa Teresa y el linaje", pp. 163–164. Teresa's thoughts on the classes on the margin of society are not as clear. How can we avoid relating to her *judeoconverso* origin the fact that until 1562 she felt no "natural compassion" for the poor? The account of the reception of this grace is a complete confession. (*Cuentas de conciencia*, 2,6). (TRANSLATORS' NOTE: In Kavanaugh-Rodriguez, this appears as *Spiritual Testimony* No. 2, 4, dated 1562 from Toledo.) The poor, as such, are absent from her undertaking. When, as in Toledo, she runs across the helpful Andrada, she took advantage of his services, but not without first having expressed her prejudice against the ragged youth (F, 15, 6-9). Slaves

are a different matter. While insisting on the real exception of her father, who, in spite of the universal practice, never agreed to have them as domestic servants because of the demands of charity (or because of scarcity of money?), she immediately reveals (L, 1) that the custom of slavery had demographic, social and economic importance not only in the Court but also in the center of Castile (See Manuel Fernández Alvarez, *La sociedad española del Renacimiento*, Salamanca, 1970, p. 187, which should be corrected in the light of the Teresian data). The most interesting point is to see how she does not hesitate to admit slaves (*negrillas*) into her ranks, though it be as lay sisters and at the cost of dispensing them from the demands of the regular observance. We call attention to the eloquent facts and their expression in letters to María de San José, June 28, 1577 and July 11, 1577. Naturally this happened in Seville, the main slave center of Spain at that time. See Antonio Domínguez Ortiz, *Orto y ocaso de Sevilla* (Seville, 1974), pp. 101-05.

177. See the confusing milieu in which it is necessary to disentangle other allusions of the period, mistrust and reticence which threatened the different parties, in A. Sicroff, *Les controverses des statuts de "pureté" de sang* (Paris, 1960), p. 187. Good documentation of these denunciations can be found in the appendix of A. Dominguez Ortiz, *La clase social de los conversos judios en Castilla en la Edad Moderna* (Madrid, 1955).

178. F, 15, 15.

179. F, 32.

180. Márquez Villanueva, *loc. cit.*, p. 158, cites the bitter and expressive satire of this time and place: "Diálogo entre Laín Calvo y Nuño Rasura".

181. F, 31, 30. Immediately after having let slip this unintentional accusation, she makes the marginal note: "although she lacked nothing as regards purity of lineage, her background being very *hidalgo*".

182. TRANSLATORS' NOTE: The complications which arose in the erection of the house in Toledo should be studied in F, 15. At the time, the Archbishop, Bartolomé de Carranza, was imprisoned by the Inquisition. Meanwhile a special ecclesiastical governor, Don Gómez Tello Girón, and a council for the administration of the archbishop's possessions, were in charge of the archdiocese. Teresa was making the foundation on the basis of a bequest by Martin Ramirez, who had left the execution of his will in this regard to his brother Alonso Alvarez. Alvarez, however, virtually handed over this task to his son-in-law, Diego Ortiz, and the latter placed so many conditions on the transaction that Teresa was forced to look elsewhere for help.

183. *Vida*, II, 13 [Ribera's biography of Teresa].

184. F, 15, 15.

185. See Márquez Villanueva, p. 144, where there is a penetrating study of this problem.

186. A Sicroff, *op. cit.*, devotes considerable space to the Toledan history, the most significant and violent in this regard. See also A. Domínguez Ortiz, *Los judeoconversos*, pp. 89ff.

187. See the Toledan problem in all its dimensions and background in the cited works of Eloy Benito Ruano and José Gómez Menor.

188. She says in F, 15, 16: "Our Lord desired to give me light on this matter, and thus he told me once how little this affair of lineage and status will matter before the judgment seat of God; and he rebuked me sharply for having given heed to those who were speaking to me about this thing which was of no concern to those of us who have already rejected the world."

189. *Spiritual Testimonies*, 5.

190. F, 15, 17.

191. F, 15, 16.

192. See the detailed history in the monumental and well-informed unpublished work of Lucinio del Santísimo, *Historia de San José de Avila*, T. II.

193. *Constitutions*, 21.

194. O. Steggink, *op. cit.*, p. 205, records the complaint of some friar against the excessive liberality of the superior in admitting "many descended from Jews, and it happens that when such as these present themselves for entrance into other religious orders, they are accustomed to tell them ironically: 'Go to the Carmelites'."

195. "In receiving girls be careful that they be not of parents of ill-repute, nor of Jewish or Moorish blood, nor illegitimate, but of praiseworthy parentage". *Institutiones et ordinationes observandae a R. Magistris, Patribus, et Fratribus Carmelitis provintiae Beticae* (Seville, 1566), p. 37. The section cited deals with *sanctimoniales*. This document must have been among those of the first Discalced Carmelites, and P. Andrés de la Encarnación's conjecture that the saint might have raised an opinion concerning these conditions (*Memorias historiales*, BN, Mss. 13.483, nos. 202, 205), does not seem very reliable. At least there is no trace of it in the Teresian legislation.

196. The chroniclers have preserved an anecdote which, if true, quite eloquently shows the differences which existed in this regard between the Madres Teresa and Ana de Jesús. Madre Ana announced to the saint that a noble [*caballero*] relative of hers [Ana's] wanted to see her; the saint related this sarcastically to P. Baltasar Alvarez who was present at the time: "Has Your Reverence heard what Ana de Jesús has come up with? That a noble relative of hers is here, just so we might realize that she has noble relatives. As if these things mattered to religious, especially among the Discalced Carmelites!" Mentioned in *Tiempo y Vida*, p. 488.

197. The novice Louise d'Abra, a convert from Calvinism, was to be an important element in the initial history of the Teresian Carmel in France. The conflict is simply and vividly narrated in the letters of Blessed Ana de San Bartolomé to Cardinal Berulle and to a Spanish Carmelite friar, *Lettres et écrits spirituels de la Bienhereuse Anne de Saint Barthélemy*, ed. Pierre Serouet (Bruges, 1964), pp. 33, 37-38, 39, 40. In an unpublished little work, composed towards the end of her life, she returns to this theme which she always considered essential (fol. 47-49). For the whole context of the polemic we refer the reader to Julian Urquiza, *La Beata Ana de San Bartolomé y la transmisión del espíritu teresiano*, (Rome, 1977).

198. The entire ordinance is worth knowing: "Let the novices when they enter the order give information about the purity of their ancestry so that in the investigation, following the questions of the *Motu Proprio* of Sixtus V, a specific question be put as to whether the candidate is of Jewish or Moorish descent at all or if he have any ancestors up to the fourth generation inclusive who were *confesos* or *penitenciados*. When the novice has given this information, let him be advised in secret before taking the habit that should anything contrary to this testimony be discovered, the order is free to expel him, and that his profession will be null and void, because the order does not accept it. And let him be advised of the same in the final examination prior to profession." (The same is demanded in Portugal and Mexico.) *Constitutiones del Capítulo de Madrid, 1597*, in Fortunatus a Iesu et Beda a SS. Trinitate, *Constitutiones Carmelitarum Discalceatorum 1597-1600* (Rome, 1968), p. 613.

BUDDHISM AND THE NADA OF ST JOHN OF THE CROSS

Anthony Haglof, O.C.D.

Father Anthony Haglof has published articles in Spiritual Life, *the quarterly publication of the Discalced Carmelites of the Washington Province. He now lives at "The Common," a retreat center—house of prayer in New Hampshire.*

In *The Living Flame of Love* St John of the Cross makes a comparison between physical objects on the surface of the earth, which gravitate toward the center of the earth, and the human soul, which is also separated from its gravitational center, its resting place when no obstacles are in its way. For the soul this center is God: "The center of the soul is God."[1] The significance of this statement lies in the fact that John of the Cross is not here making any comparison or analogy, as by saying that the center of the soul is like God, has certain similarities to God, or is created in God's image. Instead, he says that the center of the soul *is* God. Surprising as this seems to many of us, reflection makes it clear that it is only because there is something of God's nature in us that there is any possibility of revelation, divine communication with mankind, to begin with; yet, "God's nature" is no entity that can be divided up and parcelled out. Where any of it is, there is all of it, the life of God in its entirety. The purpose of revelation is to abolish those elements at the surface of our being which obscure this God-life within us, in order that it might become more and more manifest. "He must increase, and I must decrease" (Jn 3:30).

As the soul, entering more deeply into itself, approaches its center, the boundary distinction between itself and God becomes more and more tenuous, for the soul is discarding all the egoistic accoutrements which hinder the realization of its true life in God. The term "God," of course, does not refer to any limited or definable entity, and we may therefore speak of progressively deeper centers in God which are likewise progressively deeper centers in the soul, through which it must pass in order to attain its deepest center. According to St John of the Cross, there are as many different centers in the soul as there are degrees of love possible, with love considered the essence of the divine nature itself, the magnetic or gravitational force continuously drawing the soul toward its deepest center. Once it has attained this center it is totally immersed in God and lives the life of God purely, simply, without intermediary.

It follows that the soul, too, is not anything that can be described in enclosing terms or strictly defined, since it grows out of God, in a real sense, and can only be adequately defined in terms of the depths of its roots. We cannot track down the nature of the soul short of God himself, since it is of its nature in process, an "openness" to the life of God which has no stable identity short of this life. St Augustine spoke of creation as so many seeds planted by God, each to flower according to God's own purpose and design, just like Christ's parable which compares our human lives to seeds thrown into the ground and destined to become something other than themselves, a "something" which, says St Paul, creation awaits on tiptoe. As finite and historically conditioned beings we look forward to this fully-grown state as future, call it "heaven," the "coming of the kingdom," "return to paradise," "parousia," but these are only so many symbols for the life of God which is in us in its entirety right now, however hidden or obscured by our superficial (historical) "selves." "Good," says one famous medieval spiritual writer, "does not have to come into the soul, for It is already there, albeit unrecognized."[2] This loss of perception is what the mythologies of most religions refer to as a "Fall"—from a primeval paradise, or from Oneness, Bliss, Grace, to which we are called to return. Plato, interestingly, held that our present existence in the body is punishment for some wrong committed in the past, an intuition variously confirmed by many later philosophers and mystics, for example the Catholic Ruysbroeck: "God is our Superessence; in him we were One before our creation."[3]

The soul, then, is oriented back toward the same fullness from which it has emerged, or in another manner of speaking, destined to grow back into God. Now, this can only happen to the degree that the soul senses its alienation from God, its True Self according to many Hindu mystics, and is thus motivated to actualize its unlimited potential by focussing its attention on God. And since God transcends the world of objects and things, of phenomena and separate beings, even "spiritual" beings (God is not *a* being but rather the inconceivable Ground of all beings), such focusing of attention can take place only by way of faith. This accounts for the centrality of faith in the writings of St John of the Cross, whose teaching is concerned precisely with this union, or "re-union," with God. Just about every paragraph of the second Book of *The Ascent of Mount Carmel,* as thorough a treatise on the true meaning of faith as has been written in the Christian tradition, is concerned with faith as the only proportional means of union with God, since only faith proposes God to us as he is: infinite, beyond all conception and imagination. What happens in genuine faith—not to be confused with a shoddy and far more common "belief" as in certain propositions or verbal statements of faith—is that the self-imposed limitations and constrictions of the mind, considered here as pilot of the soul, are eroded. Human consciousness becomes more and more proportioned to the infinite consciousness of God, or better, expands into and participates in the "superconsciousness" of God. This is the import of the many passages in *The Spiritual Canticle* where John of the Cross says that, as the soul approaches union, it appears to be God, receives all the properties of God, obtains all the possessions of God, lives the very life of God, etc. The soul is now entering into its deepest center, and the conceptual distinction between God and the soul which from an observer's viewpoint can never disappear, has in fact begun to retreat to unity at the level of experience; whence the oft-used term "union." One Hindu interpreter for the West describes the process in the following terms:

> In the final stage of *samadhi* (Hindu term for "union") the conscious division and separation of the self from the divine being, the object from the subject, which is the normal condition of unregenerate humanity, is broken down. The individual totally surrenders to the object of his worship, and in surrendering is totally absorbed by it. He becomes what he beholds.[4]

In beholding God beyond the forms, figures and concepts of sense and intellect, that is to say, in faith, the soul becomes transformed into God.

It is in this context that we can best understand the basic concepts of Buddhism in their relation to the *nada* (nothing) of St John of the Cross.

THE THREE FUNDAMENTAL TRUTHS OF EXISTENCE ACCORDING TO BUDDHISM

Anatta / *No-self*

We recognize that the soul is not a stable, mechanical unity but an ever-flowing process of readjustment and integration, a constantly new and changing way of existing.[5] From this flows the most basic of the *three fundamental truths of existence* according to Buddhism, known in the language of the original Buddhist scriptures (Pali) as *anatta*. *Anatta* is variously translated as "no self," "no ego," "no I," even "no soul," but what it means is no stable, isolated and eternally enduring entity that can properly be called mine. In other words, what at present I might consider to be my private, hard-core, separate personality is more fragile than I ordinarily admit. It cannot be hooked, cornered, or in any way captured because it exists in a state of constant flux. To think that there is any permanent and unchanging substance which is my own private property is pride and arrogance but, even worse, an illusion. If such a static substance of my own did or could in fact

exist it would have no possibility of change, growth, development, and would remain forever just as it is, in hell (which is a
static and unbending state of mind). It is true that ordinarily each
of us has a solid self-concept of precisely who we are and what
differentiates us from other people. But we can understand that
this concept has no absolute value because it is composed of
entirely relative, fortuitous and transitory factors, e.g., who my
parents were, what my education has been, where I have been, the
people I have encountered and their influence on me, etc. These
and other factors have gone into the construction of my present
self-concept, but it is quite conceivable that they could have been
different, in which case "my" self-concept would be different; and
whatever this concept is now or in twenty years (if I respond to
new people and influences), it will be altered, and so what I
experience to be "the real me," my self or soul, will be different.
Of course, we can always step back from "our selves" at any given
moment and admire them, or hate them, fondle them, pamper
them, defend them against all attacks (real or projected) from the
enemy, etc. In fact most of us spend a substantial part of our lives
doing this, though in the end we shall see it to be nothing more
than looking back after having put our hand to the plow, toying
with dead memories instead of tending to Reality in the now.

One of the better known discourses of the Buddha is the second
discourse after his so-called enlightenment, called, "On the Non-
Existence of a Separate Self," in which he says,

> The body cannot be a separate self, for it tends to destruction.
> The sensations and feelings cannot be a separate self, for they
> likewise are passing. So also with perceptions and predispositions.
> Thoughts cannot be a separate self, for they have no staying power,
> like lightning they break up in a moment. All that which is born
> and formed (i.e., brought forth into existence and therefore histori-
> cally conditioned) is transitory and liable to change. Therefore it
> cannot be said of it, This is mine, This am I, This is my self.[6]

Buddha does not conclude from this, however, as many of his
Western interpreters have believed, that there is therefore ultimately just nothing, no stability to be found anywhere. For in
another well-known passage he says:

> If there were not that which is not-born, not-become, not-made, not-compounded, there would be no escape from that which is born, become, made compounded. But there is that which is not-born, not-become, not-made, not-compounded. Therefore an escape from the born, become, made, compounded, is known.[7]

The Buddha claims to have discovered this escape upon his enlightenment, after which he set out to teach it for a period of forty-five years until his death. Now Buddhists do not use the term "God," at least as people in the West understand it, because the Buddhist approach to Reality is existentialist, even "practical," and so little concerned with philosophical speculations. The Buddhist mind has little understanding of, or often where there is understanding, little patience with metaphysical abstractions. For it experience is everything and words and concepts are cheap, all the more as they refer to cosmic or transcendental realities of which we have no direct experience. However, this reference by the Buddha to that which is unborn, unbecome, unmade and uncompounded is totally commensurate with the Scholastic concept of God as completely simple, absolute, eternal being. This is one significant piece of evidence that Buddhism is concerned with the same religious realities as Christianity, found more specifically in the Christian apophatic mystics, among whom we have St John of the Cross.

Buddha's insistence on the truth of no-self, then, is a purely practical measure, intended to warn us against resting in or relying upon any false ideas of a self. Our inborn and all but irresistible tendency is to become the slave of some self-image or other, fashioned extraneously from our world-experience of people, things, events, ideas; and this image, by definition something short of Reality, brings us out of our True Being, rooted in God, by way of false identification. Thus it is that those who have attained the end of the spiritual pilgrimage unanimously stress the impotence of any self-concept and the importance of overlooking this in faith. Two remarks of St Teresa sound apropos in this regard: "We must turn from self toward God . . . If we never rise above the slough of our own miseries, we do ourselves a great disservice;"[8] and ". . . let us leave our reason and our fears in his hands and forget the weakness of our own nature, which is apt to cause us so much trouble."[9] When John of the Cross says that virtue does not consist in experiences or good works, but in the desire to be forgotten and held in contempt, he is saying essentially that the primary obstacle to a genuinely spiritual life is this over-refined and over-regarded sense of a stable self. And when he speaks of elevating the memory, by means of hope, above every natural prop—form, figure, fantasy, thought, concept, idea—this includes the particular form and concept of the self, which at any given moment is only a memory anyway, somewhat like the illusory circle of fire made by a whirling torch. He writes pertinently:

> Of all these forms and manners of knowledge, the soul must strip and void itself, so that there may be left in it no kind of impression of knowledge, nor trace of anything whatsoever, but rather the soul must remain barren and bare, as if these forms had never passed through it, and in total oblivion and suspension. And this cannot happen unless the memory be annihilated as to *all* its forms, if it is to be united with God.[10]

This memory purification, rightly understood, is of the essence of the ascetical doctrine of John of the Cross which, like the Buddha's teaching, should be seen as practical and positive, though it must appear negative to those who live in whatever degree of servitude to cut-and-dried ego idols and the innumerable images which sustain them. The latter, however, cannot contradict the ageless wisdom we are here investigating, confirmed as well by the empirical findings of modern psychology that the progressive reduction of all drives, greed, ambition is part of the normal personality growth pattern and the attainment of "personal" satisfaction, the only way of release from the confinement of false identification. Many are the degrees of disidentification that correspond, as we have seen, with what John of the Cross calls the progressively deeper centers of the soul which represent the degrees of liberation into the life of God.

In dealing with the teachings of John of the Cross and Buddhism we are concerned with the higher states of disidentification, attained to by perhaps few members of the human race at any given time, in which all identification of the True Self with any object, concept, body, feeling, thought, image, or idea whatsoever has ceased, and the soul has realized its identity with the Ground of its being, that which we call God. Yoga philosophy, out of which Buddhism grew, explains identification thus:

> I AM represents the pure awareness of self-existence and is therefore the experience of the pure consciousness of the One Being. When this consciousness becomes involved in matter . . . the knowledge of its real nature is lost and the I AM changes into "I am this," where "this" can be the subtlest vehicle through which it is working, or the grossest, namely the body.[11]

Dukkha / Malaise

This process of identification connects us to the *second fundamental truth of existence* according to Buddhism, one which is also the first of Buddhism's *Four Noble Truths* (hence its centrality in the Buddhist schema): *dukkha,* or suffering. Once we have become aware of ourselves as separate and apparently independent beings we simultaneously feel a certain inadequacy, since anything "on its own" or cut off from the One Source of Life is necessarily inadequate. As a result we automatically desire any number of things which will fulfill us or remedy this inadequacy. If it could be argued that these desires have a tutorial role to play in the unfoldment of the possibilities latent within every individual, from the top of Mount Carmel it could perhaps be just as convincingly countered that every desire—not excluding the desire for God himself insofar as this is outward- and upward-directed according to certain human preconceptions *about* God— is a meandering path that comes to a dead-end. It is for this reason that John of the Cross spends the entire first book of the *Ascent* explaining how desires are the root of all evil, since they proportion the soul, of unbounded capacity, to that which is infinitely unworthy of it. The *Third Noble Truth* of Buddhism is the necessity of extinguishing all desires in order to attain to the highest and most integrated state of existence, *nirvana.* For the plain truth is that all things belonging to conditional existence, including the "things" of the mind, are just as transitory as our separate selves and so can never fulfill us. "Form," according to the Buddhist scriptures, "is as holes and cracks, bubbles and smoke. Its origin and extinction exist jointly."[12] The Psalmist of the Old Testament had the same vision when he said, "All nations are as naught before you"; and St Augustine in his *Confessions* affirms: "I beheld these others beneath you, and saw that they neither altogether are, nor altogether are not. An existence they have, because they are from you; and yet no existence, because they are not what you are. For only that really is that remains unchangeably."[13] Thus, to grasp at the forms which, according to Buddhist teaching, arise simultaneously with human existence (with the fall of man from Paradise or "Oneness") can only be the cause of inevitable pain; hence we face the fundamental truth of *dukkha.*

Dukkha is a difficult concept to translate into English. It does not refer to the extremes of suffering or grief, but rather to a general malaise or uneasiness which undergirds the whole human condition. It is what one poet called the "sad, still music of humanity," often pervading the lives even of those who at any given time appear to be contented and happy, since human happiness is frequently accompanied by a myopic view of the world which fails to take account of its ultimately unsatisfying and transitory nature. Madame de Rieux, the French author, came close to the meaning of *dukkha* when she said that there is in all men and women an impediment to happiness, namely, weariness of what they have and a desire for what they have not. On the other hand, however, *dukkha* does not just mean that all life is suffering, or that life is essentially suffering, for Buddhist teaching is no more fundamentally pessimistic than the teachings of Christ or John of the Cross, both of whose messages can be thus maligned by isolating certain passages from their total context. What it means is that life as the vast majority of the human race lives it is accompanied by the disappointment and frustration which result from attempting the impossible: fulfillment from things, events, people, the realm of phenomena (called by the Buddhists *samsara*) which comes and goes, affording some passing satisfaction, but which still leaves us with a feeling that something is missing. This "something missing" is what Madame de Rieux was talking about, the cause of a certain frustration, and this frustration is *dukkha.*

Anicca / Change

Dukkha, then, arises from seeking stability in the midst of flux, which leads us into the *third fundamental truth of existence* according to Buddhism—so closely bound up with the first two that we may here pass over it briefly—*anicca,* or change. All around us we see people and things coming into existence, remaining for a while, growing, decaying, and dying. This "wheel of birth and death," so called by the Buddhists, is the most fundamental and pitiless law of all existence. The apparent slowness of the process from our human perspective is what deludes us into thinking that we can find any stability whatever in it, and leads us to think in terms of persons and things rather than processes and events. But as the seed becomes the seedling and the egg becomes the fledgling, the little boy becomes the youth becomes the old man, and where throughout these processes is any stable, unchanging entity to be found? Answer the Buddhist scriptures, "What was is not, nor will it be; what will be was not and is not; what is was not and will not be."

THE WORLD OF THE MIND AND THE VIA NEGATIVA

We have seen that when Buddhism speaks of the futility of seeking stability in the midst of flux, it means not only the flux of the outer world but also of our inner worlds, that which includes all the diversified mental activities which specify man as man. Because these mental worlds keep pace with the total process of humankind's evolution, and so represent a higher degree of being or reality than that which belongs to the outer phenomenal world, we tend to be unaware that they can only represent, or symbolize, the highest Reality, and so must finally be experienced as just as relative and passing as the realm of material phenomena. It is obvious enough that the world of thing-forms offers no satisfaction of the kind we aspire to, but it remains less obvious that the mental worlds to which we turn for compensation are ultimately just as transient and unfulfilling. We flee to ideas, abstractions, and images to relieve us from the *dukkha* which is our unavoidable experience in the changing world, in somewhat the same way as the Jews fled to Yahweh to protect them from their enemies. But Yahweh turned out to be fickle, much more exalted and unpredictable than the Jews had projected, meaning, of course, that their original conception of him was a misconception, as all human conceptions of the divine are fated to be.

It was for this reason that God's original revelation of himself to the Jewish people, through Moses, was designed to discredit conception. When Moses insists that God give himself a name so that the Hebrews would believe him when he told them he had held converse with someone who promised to help them out, the name God reluctantly gives, as a concession to human weakness, is really not a "name" at all in the proper sense (though it was the best God could do without distorting the truth!). In Hebrew the "name" is not a noun but a verb form (originally, *EHEYEH*), literally meaning "I AM BEING," or "I AM EXISTING," with emphasis on the continuousness or the dynamism of the act of being or existing. It was as if God said, with a little impatience, "All right, tell them that I AM BEING sent you," which contented Moses and his people for a while, as at least it seems to be some kind of name. But what it really means is, "My name is nameless." Only idols can have names, because idols are things. But I, the living God, am not a thing, or any other kind of being properly speaking, and therefore cannot have a name.

God, as we have said, is not *a* being as creatures are beings, each with its own proper name for distinguishing it from other beings. He is rather the Ground of all beings, Existence itself. If the "discussion" between God and Moses had been at a more philosophical level, God might have said, "My name is just TO BE—don't add anything else!" Nonetheless, because Moses had apparently held converse with someone who plays favorites, someone with whims, plans, and desires like the rest of us, only

with more wherewithal to actualize them, this was a harder
commandment to obey than all the later Sinai commandments
put together. The later Jewish custom of avoiding utterance of
the "Holy" (totally "Other") name of YAHWEH (derivative of
EHEYEH) has its roots in this initial revelation, but in actuality
the Jews made this "wholly Other" God into their tribal protec-
tor, who naturally did not come through on every occasion just as
they projected and would have liked. Our own images of God
lead us astray just as inevitably; that is the reason why John of the
Cross stresses the necessity of approaching God by the faith
which, he says, completely darkens the mind as regards God, and
not according to any understanding or conception we can have of
him, whether it come by thought, reason, symbol or vision.
"Hence while the intellect is understanding, it is not approaching
God but withdrawing from him."[14] Moses Maimonedes, the great
Jewish theologian of the twelfth century, said the same thing:
"Every time you establish by proof the negation of a thing in
regard to God, you become more perfect, while with every
assertion or concept you follow your own imagination and recede
from the true knowledge of God."[15]

Either of these statements might serve as a charter statement of
the so called *via negativa*, the apophatic tradition or negative
approach to God, where we find both the Buddhist scriptures and
the works of St John of the Cross. It is commonly considered a
"mystical" approach to God, but absolutely speaking the word
"mystical" is irrelevant here, as there is only one approach to the
Ultimate Reality of God and, as John of the Cross says, it
precludes mental activity as a proportionate means for union
with God because God infinitely surpasses the most exalted
thought man can have of him. The clear and distinct knowledge
of God which anyone might pretend to have is necessarily a
projection from sense knowledge he already has, according to the
Scholastic axiom that there is nothing more in the mind than has
already been absorbed through the senses. But the senses, of
course, are geared for interaction with the phenomenal realm of
samsara, and so provide no means of access to God other than
symbolic. We can make innumerable statements *about* God in the
form of myth, poetry and symbol, and most scriptural descrip-

tions of God fall into one of these categories. Thus, God is a mighty warrior who tramples nations under his feet, the great ruler over all the earth, a glorious king seated on his throne, a just judge, a merciful and loving father, a consuming fire, etc. At a recent East-West ecumenical dialogue a Christian saw fit at one juncture to remind his fellow Christians that they were speaking too anthropomorphically of God, whereupon a Buddhist spoke up to say that even idol-making has its place, since it is all the easier then to smash one with others. The famous Sufi mystic Rumi lyricized for all seekers of the Infinite when he wrote:

> I am a painter, a maker of pictures.
> Every moment I shape a beauteous form,
> And then in Thy presence I melt them all away.
> I call upon a hundred phantoms and indue them with Spirit;
> When I behold Thy presence I cast them in the fire.

Symbols are helpful for guiding the soul toward union with God, but they can just as easily be obstacles, to the degree that their symbolic value is not appreciated, since all symbols merge in the pure and simple Reality of God in a manner transcending thought and imagination. For this reason God is approachable only by faith. In its initial stages religion is ordinarily anthropomorphic. God is conceived of as whatever type of magnified man, and this notion has some truth in it, though it is a truth which must be purified, and in the process of purification one begins to enter upon the *via negativa.* Most informed or educated persons are at some point on this *via,* even if the majority are not able to explicitate their experience in any other than general or superficial terms and even though—as we have said—few reach the stage of the mystics we are concerned with here. A commentator on Dionysius the Areopagite, the most famous Christian interpreter of the *via negativa,* describes it in the following manner:

> The contemplative life is one of concentration, in which one moves from external things into the obscure depths of the soul, casting away the separate elements and forms which he draws from his environment into the center of his personal spirit. Having

sucked the nourishment from the various fruits growing in their different proper zones around the Stream of Life, he assimilates these vitalizing elements into his own tissues (finding different foods suitable to his advancing strength), and throws the rind away as no longer needed. The rejection of the husk in which the nourishing fruit had grown is called by Dionysius the *via negativa*.[16]

In the *Spiritual Canticle* John of the Cross speaks of the truths of religion as presented by doctrines, dogmas, creeds, vocal prayers and reasoning as the mere rind of a piece of fruit.[17] The fruit, which is the actual reality of the life of God infused into us, even in the here and now, is what we are after, and when this has been attained the rind no longer serves any purpose.

This area of the *via negativa* is precisely where John of the Cross accompanied by the spiritual heights of the whole Christian tradition has so much in common not only with Buddhism but with most of the other great Eastern religious traditions as well. In Zen (the essence of Buddhism), in the Yoga tradition of Hinduism, and in the Chinese Taoist tradition the concept of detachment (or, better, emptiness) is central, since it is only in emptiness that anything new can happen, and the real purpose of religion is to enable us to grow by opening ourselves to the perpetual newness of the life of God within us. Just as, according to Taoism, words can be written only on an empty page, water poured only into an empty glass or flow only through an empty pipe, or light come only through an empty window, so the Word of God can come to ripen only in an empty soul. This is the reason Buddhist philosophy and John of the Cross seem to concentrate so much on negation, while they are in fact talking about the only true liberation, from entanglement in the mind as well as in the world. They propose no idea of what is to fill the mind's void because the idea would exclude the fact, in much the same way as a picture of the sun painted on a window pane would shut out the true sun's light. This is the meaning of John of the Cross's numerous assertions that "no form, figure, image, or idea, whether heavenly or earthly, natural or supernatural, that can be grasped by the memory is God or even like to him."[18] By hope,

operating inseparably with faith and love, we absorb the life of
God not according to any preconception, which would be impossible anyway, but directly, as it exists in its elusive and
unimaginable reality. The medieval philosopher Nicholas of
Cusa said in his treatise *Of Learned Ignorance*: "I was led in the
highest learning that is ignorance to grasp the incomprehensible,
not by way of comprehension, but by transcending those perennial truths that can be recalled by reason."[19]

NIRVANA AND UNION WITH GOD

The culmination of the *via negativa* is the state which John of
the Cross refers to as "union" and Buddhism *nirvana*. According
to the latter, all things come from One Essence and are destined
by the same One Law to return to that Essence. The return is
called *nirvana*. Says the Buddha, "When one understands thoroughly the three truths (*anatta, dukkha, anicca*), that all things
are of one essence, and when he lives this understanding, then is
he released unto *nirvana*."[20] *Nirvana* is an existential term,
concerned with a transformed state of being. Literally it means
"to be extinguished," as of a fire. Another of Buddha's well-
known sermons is his "Fire Sermon," in which he says that all
things in phenomenal existence are on fire, on fire with the
flames of sensations, mind-impressions, desires, anger, delusion,
all of which lead to the further flames of grief, despair, misery, old
age, and lamentation. In Yoga philosophy these come from what
are called *klesas* or "roots of pain," the most fundamental of
which are *asmita*, sense of a separate self, and its offspring *avidya*,
ignorance. The aim of yoga as a discipline is to eliminate these
altogether. *Nirvana* is the cessation of all the waves and churn-
ings and circlings of the mind which come from the *klesas*, a state
of total peace. At a more scientific or philosophical level, Buddhism holds that everything which is brought into separate
existence contains within itself the inherent necessity of dissolu-
tion. The Buddha said that he proclaimed the causes of separate-
ness and how those causes cease to be. Their cessation is *Nirvana*.
Hence the *Four Noble Truths of Buddhism*, as distinguished

from the *three fundamental truths of existence* discussed above, in a nutshell are *dukkha*, the cause of *dukkha* (desire), the removal of *dukkha* by the removal of desire, and the eight-fold path for overcoming desire and attaining *Nirvana*.

It is understandable from the foregoing why *nirvana* has most often been interpreted in the West as a state of nothingness—the extinction of life, love, or whatever meaning Christ came to bring into our lives. Such impressions, however, have been the portion only of those who know nothing more of Buddhism than a few sentences of superficial and distorted hearsay. For just as the *via negativa* is really affirmative, the only way to the truth of what is, so *nirvana* is nothing negative but simply the recognition of that same truth: desires, grasping, clinging and the little self which they fabricate separate us from our True Being in which we are all One, and therefore feel a natural joy, love and compassion for all fellow beings. The Buddhist scriptures are full of quotations to the effect that *nirvana* and the detachment leading to it are not the lack of feeling and indifference of nothingness but a state of supreme joy and peace: "He who dwells in an empty abode, whose soul is full of peace, enjoys superhuman felicity, gazing solely on the Truth;"[21] "Happy indeed are those who live without hatred, greed and ignorance";[22] "Happy are we who call nothing our own; feeding on joy we live like shining gods."[23] Frequently Buddha himself refers to *nirvana* as the supreme happiness: "The *tathagata* (one who has arrived at ultimate Truth) lives in the pure land of eternal bliss even now while in the body, and he preaches the law of religion unto the whole world, so that thou and thy brethren may attain the same peace and happiness."[24] And so, Buddha is known as the All-Compassionate One: having attained to the truth of existence and realized his solidarity with all "deluded beings," he spontaneously desires to lead others to that same end. Elsewhere one of Buddha's disciples asks him, "Lord, if there be no thoughts, no mind activity, no *atman* (self), how can there be Immortality?" and Buddha replies, "Thinking is gone but thought continues; reasoning ceases but knowledge remains."[25] We can best understand this state of thought perduring without thinking in the light of the Christian concept of the

Word, the One Word which, according to St John of the Cross God spoke at the beginning of creation, his first and last Word. As with all words we may consider this one as rooted in a Thought, which is, however, beyond the comprehension of the meager human mind, or in Buddhist terminology "pure like space" and so beyond imagining, only defiled by human attempts to think about it. Thinking at best can only compare, select, and evaluate in terms of an ever-receding ideal. The dogmas and systems of philosophy it creates, whatever tentative or symbolic value they might have, all too easily imprison the mind until, in a Zen phrase, it mopes like a monkey in an empty cage, ignorant of the Word, its own intrinsically pure nature. *Nirvana* begins to arise spontaneously, in earnest faith, when the impossibility of touching Reality by means of the thinking mind has been thoroughly understood.

It is significant for our comparative study that Buddha defines *nirvana* in the same way as St Thomas defines the beatific vision, wherein, says he, *ratio*, the thinking, reasoning, calculating aspect of the mind, ceases, but in which *intellectus*, a simple, intuitive understanding of the truth, absorbed in a simple gaze, remains. Like the beatific vision, *nirvana* should be understood as the outcome of a series of progressive intuitions that Life precedes all of its forms (I AM WHO AM) and therefore defeats every direct attempt to grasp it. It arises from the growing existential acknowledgment that man's optimal state of consciousness is one of detachment, which alone can be one of total obedience to his cosmic duty. To those still within the thraldom of *asmita* and *avidya* (i.e., the great majority of us) it will necessarily appear to be negation of one kind or another, but in fact it is the power of creation which comes with realizing the vanity of clutching at clouds, the necessity of losing one's life in order to find it. Finally, it is freedom, unimpeded by the self-frustration and consequent self-limitation inherent in all desire.

In Herman Hesse's crowning and Nobel Prize winning novel, *Magister Ludi*, the budding magister asks his own master if those who have strong desires, preferences, and aversions are not simply more intense natures, others less intense. Says the master,

That seems to be true, and yet it is not. To be capable of everything and do justice to everything, one certainly does not need less spiritual force and élan and warmth but more. What you call intensity is not spiritual force, but friction between the soul and the outside world. This is passion, and where passion dominates, that does not signify the presence of greater desire and ambition, but rather the misdirection of these qualities toward an isolated and false goal, with a consequent tension and sultriness in the atmosphere. Those who direct the maximum force of their desires toward the center, toward true being, toward perfection, seem quieter than the passionate souls because the flame of their fervor cannot always be seen. But I assure you, they are nevertheless burning with subdued fires.[26]

These subdued fires are what John of the Cross calls living flames of love, which lift the soul above the separation effected by desire back to Oneness with God and all-embracing compassion with everything that exists. He who wishes to follow the saints must then give up all thoughts of "I" and "mine," but this cannot make him poorer; for what he destroys are the walls that kept him imprisoned, and what he gains is an experience of infinite relationship, according to which every individual is essentially connected with all that exists, and thus embraces the world in his own soul, sharing its deepest experiences. Again St Thomas, in whose works we find corroborated the most exalted truths of the spiritual life, certainly discerned the grounds for such a relationship when he said that the soul of man is, in a certain way peculiar to itself, all-embracing.[27] Humankind is unconsciously conditioned by society to believe that the purpose of the ego is restrictive rather than expanding, and so comes to use it as a dam to hold back wider perceptions of reality. To open the sluice gates, he feels, would be to lose everything he has gained, but here is his fundamental delusion; for everything short of True Being must be lost in any case, and as A. F. Bentley puts it:

Let no quibble of skepticism be raised over this question of the existence of the individual. Should he find reason for holding that he does not exist in the sense indicated, there can in fact be no derogation from the reality of what does exist. On the contrary, there will be increased recognition of reality. For the individual can be banished only by showing a plus of existence, not by alleging a minus. If the individual falls it will be because the real life of man, when it is widely enough investigated, proves too rich for him, not because it proves too poverty-stricken.[28]

Mankind loses no more in surrendering what it thinks of as its "self" than an electrical power generating plant loses when a light bulb burns out.

The classical accounts of "mystic" enlightenment from all religious traditions emphasize the experience of Unity here described which, as it is approached, reverses the development of the sensuousness, fullness of detail and vivacity of image associated with primitive thought concerning the divine, as well as of abstract mental activity. With this reversal there arises a de-differentiation or merging of all boundaries which hitherto had specified the finite "I" as separate from its object world. By concentration on God in faith the soul is transformed into God, and thus partakes of the absolute knowledge that is founded on an identity of the mind which knows with the object which is known. The Eastern traditions emphasize that this identity is a primeval identity, the soul's original and only true identity even while it labors under the contrary impressions of yours and mine, ego and God, soul and flesh, "old man" and "new man." "To such an extent are we admitted and absorbed into Something that is one, simple, divine, illimitable," says the Catholic Tauler, "that we seem no longer distinguishable from it."[29] John of the Cross refers to this state quite exhaustively in theological terms and symbols which, he is acutely aware, are finally only words, and so worlds removed from the actual experience:

> God vitally transforms the soul into himself, all its faculties, appetites, movements, are changed to divine. . . . The union wrought between the two natures in this state is such that both appear to be God. . . . In glory and appearance the soul seems to be God and God seems to be the soul. . . . In the union of glory the soul's intellect will be God's intellect, her will his, and her love his love. . . . The soul breathes in the same spiration of love that the Father breathes in the Son and the Son in the Father, which is the Holy Spirit. . . . The soul becomes deiform and God through

participation. . . . Souls possess the same goods through participation that the Son possesses through nature. As a result they are truly gods by participation, equals and companions of God.[30]

Other mystics, both East and West, have described this absorption as the realization of a vaster self than that to which we are accustomed. Whoever considers the above passages will understand that this vaster self is only another term for the indescribable foundation of our being which words cannot approach, but which we call God.

NOTES

1. F, 1, 12.

2. *The Theologia Germanica of Martin Luther* trans. and ed. Bengt Hoffman (New York: Paulist Press, 1989), p. 70. Coll. "The Classics of Western Spirituality."

3. Quoted by Aldous Huxley, *The Perennial Philosophy* (New York: Harper and Row, 1970), p. 31.

4. Sri Radhakrishnan, *Eastern Religions and Western Thought* (London: O.U.P., 1969), p. 50.

5. It is important to recall in this context that existence means, literally, "to stand forth" from the ground of being and therefore, as even St Thomas Aquinas and Dionysius the Areopagite point out, it cannot properly speaking be applied to God, who *is* the ground of being. It is applied to God by way of analogy.

6. Ananda K. Coomaraswamy, *Buddha and the Gospel of Buddhism* (New York: Harper and Row, 1964), pp. 40, 41.

7. Rune E. A. Johansson, *The Psychology of Nirvana* (New York: Doubleday, 1969), p. 47.

8. St Teresa, C, 1, 2, 10.

9. C, 3, 2, 8.

10. St John of the Cross, A, 3, 2, 4 (= p. 227 Peer's ed.). See also A, 3, 9.

11. Claudio Naranjo and Robert Ornstein, *The Psychology of Meditation* (New York: Viking, 1971), p. 78.

12. Henry Clarke Warren trans. and ed., *Buddhism* (New York: Atheneum Press, 1970), p. 185.

13. *Confessions*, Bk. 7, ch. 7 and Bk. 11, ch. 4.

14. F, 3, 48.

15. Moses Maimonides, *The Guide for the Perplexed* (London: Pardes, 1904), p. 75.

16. Clarence Edwin Rolt trans., *Dionysius the Areopagite on the Divine Names and The Mystical Theology* (London: Macmillan, 1966), p. 25.

17. C, 12, 4.

18. A, 3, 11, 1.

19. Quoted from Frederick Crosfield Happold, *Mysticism* (Baltimore: Penguin, 1971), p. 42.

20. Johansson, *Psychology of Nirvana*, ch. 14.

21. Coomaraswamy, *Gospel of Buddhism*, p. 178.

22. Lama Anagarika Govinda, *The Psychological Attitude of Early Buddhist Philosophy* (London: Rider, 1969), p. 61.

23. *The Dhammapada*, 199 and 200.

24. Paul Carus, *The Gospel of Buddha according to Old Records* (Chicago: Open Court Pub. Co., 1915), p. 174.

25. Carus, *Gospel of Buddha*, p. 154.

26. Herman Hesse, *Magister Ludi (The Glass Bead Game)*, (New York: Bantam, 1969), p. 69.

27. *Summa Theologica*, Ia Iae, q. 1, 16 ad 3.

28. Arthur Fisher Bentley, *Inquiry into Inquiries* (Boston: Beacon, 1954), p. 4.

29. Augustin Poulain, *The Graces of Interior Prayer: A Treatise on Mystical Prayer* (St Louis: Herder Co., 1950), p. 272.

30. C, 21, 4; 22, 4; 32, 1; 38, 3; 39, 3, 4, 6.

POVERTY AND PRAYER IN ST JOHN OF THE CROSS

Camillus-Paul D'Souza, O.C.D.

Father Camillus-Paul is an Indian Carmelite who did his theological studies in Rome. More recently he has taught philosophy to seminarians in his native country.

Poverty is scarcely a univocal concept. It is something that sometimes refers to the state of having nothing. It is thought of as having no value; or even as the very opposite of value. Some people regard poverty as a sin. And some rich people find this sin quite unforgivable.

Is it then surprising that theologians have to do a bit of wrestling in order to thrust poverty on to their audiences as value and virtue and beatitude? Let us not blame theologians for this assault on our society. It is the Gospel that is responsible for this insight. "Blessed are the poor, theirs is the kingdom of heaven" (Lk 6:20). This is an idea that runs through the pages of the New Testament, and through the ages of Christendom. Christ has proclaimed once and for all that whatever the lack of value in poverty as such, it holds an unsuspected treasure for those who consider it in Christian perspective. This treasure has been variously explored by the Fathers of the Church and by the founders of religious orders and congregations, as well as others. Although Christ himself assured us that we would always have the poor with us, he did intend that poverty of spirit in the rich should move them to alleviate the actual misery in which the poor wallow. But certainly the kingdom of God is more than the combating of poverty on the socio-economic level. St Francis experienced the beatitude of poverty. Not only did he not combat poverty; he surrendered himself to "her." (So much depends on perspectives. It was more than a question of a lover seeing Helen's beauty in a brow of Egypt.) St Teresa of Jesus associated poverty with greater evangelical perfection re-inforcing intercession on behalf of the Church.[1]

Our purpose here is to attempt an analysis of what St. John of the Cross meant by, and saw in, poverty. Without losing ourselves in unnecessary details, we may find it not too difficult to establish the main lines of his scheme in which the "kingdom of heaven" giving sense to poverty is interior union with God. Poverty of spirit confers—as has already been mentioned—socio-economic benefits; and St John of the Cross is quite aware of this. These benefits he throws into relief by first recounting the ills produced by inordinate attachment to temporal goods. Such attachment easily deflects people from true discernment. Everyone knows how much the administration of justice is hampered by bribery and corruption, not only in backward countries like India, but also in advanced nations like America. Against this sort of love for gifts, St John of the Cross cites Isaiah the prophet: "They all love gifts and allow themselves to be carried away by retributions, and they do not judge the orphan and the widow's cause does not come to them and their attention".[2]

Poverty of spirit as regards temporal goods is recommended by David who warns us "that even though riches abound, we must not set our hearts upon them".[3] Such detachment is to be sought not only because of spiritual motives, but also because of the temporal advantages it promises. "By dismissing joy over temporal goods he is not only delivered from the pestiferous kinds of harm we mentioned . . . but in addition he acquires the virtue of liberality. Liberality is one of God's principal attributes and can in no way coexist with covetousness,"[4] especially with the convetousness of one who "has made for himself gods out of money and temporal goods."[5]

Temporal goods are riches, and riches—the holy Mystical

Doctor perceived as Marx would perceive and insist three centuries later—are the economic basis of society. He says: "By temporal goods we mean riches, status, position and other dignities, and children, relatives, marriages, etc."[6]

This type of good things he distinguishes from "natural goods," the expression he uses to refer to "beauty, grace, elegance, bodily constitution, and all other corporal endowments; also in the soul, good intelligence, discretion and other talents. . . ."[7] He requires that poverty of spirit be exercised not only with regard to temporal goods but also with regard to these "natural goods." Detachment from "natural good" paves the way to humility and "general charity towards one's neighbor."[8]

The Mystical Doctor, as is obvious, is not unmindful of his neighbor. He never loses sight of the beneficial implications *of one's* poverty of spirit for *the other*. His primary concern in promoting poverty of spirit is—as we shall presently see—prayer and union with God. But it is worthwhile to remind ourselves that his mysticism, far from ignoring his fellows or even neglecting other human beings, derives its basic inspiration from the glad tidings that were preached first to the poor.[9] A detail that evinces St John's analytical ability in this respect is provided in his treatment of what he terms "sensory goods"—those apprehensible to the senses of sight, hearing, taste, smell, and touch and to the interior faculty of discursive imagination.[10] When speaking of too much attachment to sweet perfumes and too inordinate rejoicing in the "good" things of this sense, he says: "Joy in sweet fragrance foments disgust for the poor, which is contrary to Christ's doctrine, aversion for servants. . . ."[11] From all this we gather, in the first place, that whereas most of us are inclined to conceive poverty of spirit as detachment from temporal goods, the Doctor of Carmel regards it as detachment from and withdrawal of one's heart from temporal as well as natural and sensory goods. Of course there is no adequate and exclusive distinction between "temporal," "natural" and "sensory". They are mutually inclusive, or at least may occasionally be so. For the practical purposes of the spiritual director in St John of the Cross, the distinction comes in convenient and handy. Poverty of spirit is going to be extended by him to other spheres as well. He has surely under-stood that the "sensory" is natural to mankind; and what is "natural" is, to a large extent, merely temporal. Nonetheless, this is not the "temporal," the privation of which *we* associate with poverty.

The charism of St John of the Cross allows him no more than glimpses of the beneficial effects of poverty of spirit on one's neighbor, in general, and on one's needy neighbor, in particular. The Spirit thrusts him in a different direction; and that thrust colors his entire vision, including his concept of the poverty that is proclaimed blessed because of its claim to the kingdom of God. He seems rather to be so fascinated and allured by the kingdom, that the good things of the world and of creatures scarcely have a claim to be considered good. "Now all the goodness of creatures in the world compared with the infinite goodness of God, can be called evil, since nothing is good, save God only" (Lk. 18,19).[12] Could this conviction have affected St. John's attitudes toward his neighbor in general and to the poor in particular, to the extent of tempting him to regard poverty as a fortune rather than a misfortune? "All the wealth and glory of creation is utter poverty and misery in the Lord's sight. The person who loves and possesses these things is completely poor and miserable before God and will be unable to attain the richness and glory of the state of transformation in God; the miserable and poor is ex-tremely distant from the supremely rich and glorious."[13] The whole thrust of St John's charism is towards this transformation in God. This is what constitutes, in his understanding, the ultimate finality of the interior and inherent dynamic of Chris-tian and especially religious existence. This he identifies with the peaks of the life of prayer.

It is from this lofty standpoint that he makes his estimate of temporal, natural, sensory and other created goods . . . and finds them wanting. Not that created things are evil in themselves; he himself assures us that "since the things of the world cannot enter the soul, they are not in themselves an encumbrance or harm to it. . . ."[14]

This type of reasoning is in line with the Gospel assertion that it is not what enters a man that defiles him, but rather that which proceeds from within his heart.[15] ". . . . it is the will and appetite dwelling within that causes the damage."[16] Since the things of the world outside ourselves cannot harm us unless they enter, or rather their desire enters and dwells within us, our task must be to void our wills of inordinate desire for and attachment to them. Applying this principle to "sensory goods," we learn that the sensory perceptions of hearing, sight, smell, taste and touch, being unavoidable, do no harm to a person who keeps himself unattached to their impressions. The same holds good for "temporal goods." "Man should not be joyous over riches, neither when he possesses them, nor when his brother possesses them, unless God is served through them."[17] Thus David, though manifestly rich was actually poor, because "his will was not fixed on riches."[18] On the other hand, had he been really poor, without his *will* being so, there would have been no true poverty, because "the appetite of his soul would have been rich and full." The poverty, then that has relevance for St. John of the Cross, is the emptying of the soul, and especially the will of all disorderly affection for temporal goods, and also—as has been mentioned—for "natural" and "sensory goods."

That the mystical theologian intends to rid the person of *disordered* attachment to these and other "goods," is evident from his own statements. Proceeding quite methodically in his analysis of the "goods" in which the will can rejoice, he divides the object of this joy into: temporal, natural, sensory, moral, supernatural and spiritual.[19] We are already acquainted with the first three categories. "Moral goods" are the virtues and the habits in so far as they are moral; for example, the practice of the works of mercy, or, urbanity and good manners.[20] "Supernatural goods" are the gifts and graces of God that exceed our natural faculties: the *"gratiae gratis datae."* Such are the gifts of prophecy, the working of miracles, the power of healing, the gift of tongues, etc.[21] Spiritual goods are "all those that are an aid and motivating force in turning the soul to divine things, and to converse with God, as well as a help in God's communication to the soul.[22] Far from being restricted to temporal goods, poverty of spirit is extended through all the categories enumerated. This poverty, however, is not something absolute, unconditional and unqualified. Its application differs from category to category. There are some general criteria for its application. For one thing, sight must never be lost of the purpose and end to which the author of the *Ascent of Mt Carmel* is leading the soul: namely, transformation in God through divine union. In order to attain to this, the soul must keep *all* its love for God. Hence, St John treats of the aforementioned goods, "in their proper order, *regulating the will according to reason,* lest it fail to concentrate the vigor of its joy upon God, because of the hindrance these goods may occasion."[23]

This general principle leads to another: "the will should rejoice only in what is for the honor and glory of God, and the greatest honor we can give him is to serve him according to evangelical perfection: anything unincluded in such service is without value to man."[24]

The heights of prayer, for St John of the Cross are, as we have seen, the state of transformation in God and the graces that accompany that transformation. But what are the lowlands? Which is the path that will lead us to the heights? The answer of St John of the Cross is simple. To reach the consummation of love, he makes love the starting point. For a treatise on the "active night" and denudation of the will with the aim of educating it, "I have found no more appropriate passage than the one in Chapter 6 of Deuteronomy, where Moses commands: 'You shall love the Lord your God with all your heart, and with all your soul, and with all your strength' (Dt. 6:5). This passage contains all that a spiritual man must do, and all that I must teach him here, if he is to reach God by union of the will through charity. In it man receives the command to employ all the faculties, appetites, operations and emotions of his soul in God, so that he may avoid the use of his ability and strength for anything else."[25] This is the first and the greatest commandment, together with St John's very reasonable understanding of it. And since the first commandment is intended for everyone, what the mystical doctor teaches here about the "active" night, is intended, likewise, for all good Christians. All Christians are expected to start off on the "ascent of Mt Carmel," and to strive and strain for its peaks as hard as they can. There is no chance that they will ever succeed by their own efforts to attain to infused contemplation, as there is no hope that they will ever manage to purify their wills entirely by their own endeavors. The active night extends through sense to spirit, as is easily perceived from the list of categories of "goods" in which the will can rejoice, but from which it should withdraw its joy, in order to keep its strength for God. "As we outlined for the sense faculties, a method of emptying the sense faculties of desire for their objects, . . . so for this spiritual night we will present, with the Divine help, a method of emptying and purifying the spiritual faculties of all that is not God."[26] In the first book of the *Ascent*, St John has already the mortification of the senses, desires and appetites dealt with. In the second, he leads the intellect to the emptiness and void wrought by the theologal virtue of faith. In the third, he leads the memory and the will to the emptiness and privation induced in them by hope and charity. ". . . these three virtues place a soul in darkness and emptiness in respect to all things."[27] The "darkness" refers to the night; the "emptiness," obviously, to poverty. We find "poverty" associated also with the passive nights of sense and spirit, which are more effective in refining the soul than the soul's own efforts. What the passive night of sense does is purge the one who undergoes it of self-esteem, making him acutely conscious of his wretchedness and misery.[28] When one is thus brought low, one better understands the respect that is due to God, who as the psalms tell us "raises the poor from the dunghill."[29] Moreover the soul is cured, to a great extent of its spiritual avarice, as well as of its spiritual lust and gluttony and other "spiritual" vices.[30] This sensitive purgation serves more for the accomodation of the senses to the spirit than for the union of the spirit with God, and the emptiness and poverty to which it reduces the person, is not yet sufficient. In the night of the spirit, "God divests the faculties, affections and senses, both spiritual and sensory, interior and exterior. He leaves the intellect in darkness, the will in aridity, the memory in emptiness, and the affections in supreme affliction, bitterness and anguish. . . ."[31] This contemplative purgation is the same or about the same as nakedness and poverty of spirit.[32] One of the afflictions caused by the lofty state of prayer called dark contemplation is that it "makes the soul feel within itself . . . its own intimate poverty and misery. . . . The soul experiences an emptiness and poverty . . ." [33] which place it in a strange void.

Hence, poverty is an idea that, for St John of the Cross, has little to do with the lack of things—whether they have or have not temporal or economic value. Poverty has reference rather to the interior dispositions of the soul—its affections, desires and appetites. This "poverty of spirit" has perceptible effects and consequences in the dealings one has with one's neighbor and in the social domain. But St John's prevailing and overwhelming preoccupation is the relevance of poverty in the life of prayer. Far from restricting the notion of poverty to the temporal sphere, and to detachment from temporal goods, he extends it to detachment from natural and sensory goods as well. He requires reasonable detachment even from moral and spiritual values in accordance with Gospel demands.

The whole spectrum of values, from economic values to moral and spiritual ones are thus included within the range of this all-embracing poverty, and may be termed its object. And as for the subject that is to be stripped and reduced to poverty, it is the senses: the faculties and appetites of the soul, namely, the memory, the intellect and especially the will.

Poverty, therefore, is the same as spiritual nakedness, detachment, emptying, darkening and mortifying of all the tendencies in the soul that constitute an obstacle to transformation in God through union. Poverty of spirit then, is a term almost equivalent to "dark night." The degree of one's poverty is directly proportionate to the degree of one's prayer. The term includes the whole of asceticism preparatory to the mystical experience. Over and above that it includes also the contemplative or mystical purification. The active attainment of this poverty depends to a large extent on the individual's co-operation with grace, constantly inviting him to love God with all his heart, with all his soul, with all his mind and with all his strength.

NOTES

1. See St Teresa of Avila, W, chs. 1 and 2 passim.
2. A, 3, 19, 6.
3. A, 3, 20, 1.
4. A, 3, 20, 2.
5. A, 3, 19, 8.
6. A, 3, 18, 1.
7. A, 3, 21, 1.
8. A, 3, 23, 1.
9. Mt 11:6.
10. A, 3, 24, 1.
11. A, 3, 25, 4.
12. A, 1, 4, 4.
13. A, 1, 4, 7.
14. A, 1, 3, 4.
15. Mt 15:19-20.
16. A, 1, 3, 4.
17. A, 3, 18, 3.
18. A, 1, 3, 4.
19. A, 3, 17.
20. A, 3, 27, 1.
21. A, 3, 30, 1.
22. A, 3, 33, 2.
23. A, 3, 17, 2.
24. *Ibid.*
25. A, 3, 16, 1.
26. A, 2, 6, 6.
27. A, 2, 4, 4.
28. N, 1, 12, 2.
29. N, 1, 12, 3.
30. N, 1, 13.
31. N, 2, 3, 3.
32. N, 2, 4, 1.
33. N, 2, 6, 4.

THE FIRST PRINCIPLE OF CHRISTIAN MYSTICISM

David Granfield, O.S.B.

Father David Granfield is a Benedictine actively engaged in a spirituality seminar of the Catholic Theological Society of America. He teaches law at Catholic University of America.

INTRODUCTION

A life of prayer, directed as it is to union with God, needs a sound principle which will integrate theory as well as practice. Now a principle is a beginning, a starting point from which being or knowledge proceeds; both aspects, the existential and the cognitive, are operative in mystical theology which seeks both the means and the meaning of this divine union. Fortunately, in the Discourse after the Last Supper, Jesus formulated just such a twofold principle.

> He that has my commandments and keeps them, he it is that loves me; and he that loves me will be loved by my Father and I will love him and manifest myself to him (Jn 14:21).[1]

This principle with a promise—obedience leads to presence—coordinates law and love and light. Law sets up the norm, love fulfills it, and light results. When asked for clarification, Jesus repeats the principle, rephrasing it slightly but without changing it substantially; for the abiding presence of the Revealer and the

213

Revealed, Jesus and his Father, form the core of the manifestation.

> Judas, not the Iscariot, said to him, "Lord how is it that you will manifest yourself to us and not to the world?" Jesus answered and said to him, "If anyone loves me, he will keep my word, and my Father will love him and we will come to him and make our abode with him (Jn 14:22–23).

Transcending national and sectarian boundaries, Jesus issues an invitation to everyone, but imposes the law of love as the condition of vision. For he will manifest himself only to those who keep his word, his commandments—the two are synonymous. Unfortunately, the world will not experience this manifestation, because, not believing in him, it does not do his will. Nevertheless, Jesus does not dispel the world's unbelief by an overwhelming theophany. He has given to the world all that is necessary. If it is to realize this promised manifestation, it must do so the only way possible, by faith operating through love.

What I propose here is to examine the implications of the words of Jesus: "I will manifest myself to him." I will look at three areas: first, the Johannine context, focusing on the indwelling of the Paraclete, the Spirit of Jesus, and its effects as experienced by believers; second, the mystical interpretation given by the two Carmelite Doctors of the Church, St Teresa of Avila and St John of the Cross; and, third, the resolution of difficulties, harmonizing the mystical interpretation with the modern exegetical understanding of the text. Together, these three considerations will help us appreciate the richness of this promised manifestation.

THE JOHANNINE CONTEXT

The Discourse after the Last Supper reveals the full dimensions of the promise of Jesus to manifest himself to those who love him. This manifestation is essentially the experience of oneness which results in the soul from the effects of the indwelling Paraclete, the Spirit of Jesus. In this section, we will consider four observations about this Johannine revelation: first, the basis is the indwelling of the Paraclete; second, love, peace, and joy are the effects of this indwelling; third, together these effects give the experience of oneness; and, fourth, this unitive experience is the promised manifestation of the presence of Jesus.

The indwelling of the Paraclete enables Jesus, though he is with the Father, to be present to his disciples. The biblical testimony is straightforward. In the post-resurrectional interim, at least between the Ascension and the Parousia, Jesus is not bodily or physically present to the believers. Jesus, however, has sent to them the Paraclete, that is, the Holy Spirit as his personal presence. The promise of Jesus is thus fulfilled through the indwelling of this Paraclete. Raymond Brown summarizes the scriptural evidence thus:

> The one whom Jesus calls "another Paraclete" is another Jesus. Since the Paraclete can come only when Jesus departs, the Paraclete is the presence of Jesus when Jesus is absent. Jesus' promise to dwell within his disciples is fulfilled in the Paraclete. It is no accident that the first passage containing Jesus' promise of the Paraclete (xiv 16–17) is followed immediately by the verse which says, "I am coming back to you."[2]

The effects of the indwelling, the peace and the joy and the love they come from, show how personal and intense this presence can be. And certainly, whether or not we call it mystical, it is a peak religious experience. Let us look, then, at three perceptible effects of the indwelling of the Paraclete: love, joy, and peace.

The experience of love is the root of the other two effects, but the Johannine emphasis on love as a keeping of the commandments—its truest test—should not make us think of love only as a legalistic fulfillment of duty. Fundamentally, love is a personal response to goodness. As envisaged in the Last Discourse, both loving and being loved are rich experiences to which the words, "Abide in my love"(Jn 15:9), invite us. It is a call to the kind of experience that St Paul described to the Ephesians when he prayed that the Spirit might inwardly strengthen the believers, "that Christ may dwell in your hearts by faith, that being rooted and founded in love, you may be able to comprehend with all the saints, what is the breadth and length and height and depth, to know also the love of Christ which surpasses all understanding, that you may be filled unto the fullness of God" (Eph 3:17-19).

The experience of peace, the fruition of love, is the most obvious characteristic of mystical contemplation. For here growth in prayer is marked by a gradual pacifying of the faculties, beginning with the will in the appropriately named prayer of quiet. It is not surprising, therefore, that Jesus, after promising to manifest himself to those who love him, would say a few verses later, "Peace I leave with you, my peace I give unto you, not as the world gives do I give you peace. Let not your heart be troubled, nor let it be afraid" (Jn 14:27). Two chapters farther along, he adds, "These things I have spoken to you that you may have peace" (Jn 16:33). This promised peace, which comes from the indwelling Paraclete, elevates, directs, and intensifies the believer's power to love. That is why it is called a peace which the world cannot give, for it rises from the depths of the love that is poured forth by the Spirit.

The experience of joy becomes gradually but intermittently more intense as love deepens and prayer progresses. Although many trials, persecutions, and dark nights may be the plight of the believer, he is assured, "Your sorrow will be turned into joy" (Jn 16:20). And this will be "a joy that no one can take from you" (Jn 16:22). Moreover, it is the fruit of prayer, "Ask and you shall receive that your joy may be full" (Jn 16:24). What must we do, on our part, to achieve this abundant joy?

> As the Father has loved me, so have I loved you. Remain on in my love. And you will remain in my love if you keep my commandments, just as I have kept my Father's commandments and remain in his love. I have said this to you that my joy may be yours and your joy may be fulfilled (Jn 15:9-11).

Together the effects of love, peace, and joy lead to the experience of oneness. Each is a subjective sharing in the life of Jesus and through them we become aware of his presence. He tells us, as we have seen, "Remain on in *my love,*" for *"my peace* I give you," that *"my joy* may be yours." But why does he share these experiences with his followers?

> That they may be one, just as you Father in me and I in you, that they may be in us. Thus the world may believe that you have sent me. I have even given to them the glory which you have given to me, that they may be one, just as we are one, I in them and you in me, that they may be brought to completion as one (Jn 17:21-23).

This passage establishes the mutual indwelling of the Father and the Son through the Spirit as the model and the source of the unity of Christians. So complete is this primary unity that those who see Jesus see the Father. To bring the believer into this unity is the work of the Paraclete, the Spirit of Jesus. By means of the indwelling of the Paraclete, the faith which operates through love brings the believer to an awareness of his union with the Father and the Son. This process, culminating in experiential unity, begins with foundational unity; for only if the branches are part of the vine can they bear fruit. The Spirit of Jesus must dwell within us before he will, in response to our love, manifest himself.

This unitive experience is the promised manifestation— "completion as one." The intimate awareness of divine union that the indwelling Paraclete works in the believer brings to a climax Jesus' self-revelation on earth. Conscious presence is the substance of the promise. For Jesus promises the believer a light, a knowing, a revelation. Before saying explicitly that he will manifest himself, Jesus clearly prepares the way for a true understanding of what the promise means. He speaks of another Paraclete, the Spirit of Truth whom the Father will send: "You do recognize him since he remains with you and is in you" (Jn 14:17). Jesus tells his disciples that he will go away, but will return, and that, although the world will not see him any more, "You will *see* me because I have life and you will have life" (Jn 14:19). This thought, he elaborates, in the next verse, "In that day, you will recognize that I am in the Father and you are in me and I in you" (Jn 14:20).

Only after indicating the cognitive quality of the new experience, did Jesus promise that if anyone loves him, "I will manifest myself to him" (Jn 14:21). He then explains what the indwelling Paraclete will do: "He will *teach* you everything and *remind* you of all that I told you" (Jn 14:26); and, as the Spirit of Truth, "He will *guide* you along the way of truth. . . . and will *declare* to you all the things to come" (Jn 16:31).

The Paraclete's mission is, therefore, to complete the mission of Jesus. Brown thus concludes: "Jesus bore God's name because he was the revelation of God to men; the Spirit is sent in Jesus' name because he unfolds the meaning of Jesus for men."[3] Bultmann expresses the same idea more succinctly: "The Spirit, like Jesus himself, is Revealer."[4] In short, Jesus removes himself from our physical presence so that, through his Spirit, he can communicate to us his divine presence and thus more perfectly reveal his Father. So perfect is this communication that the first disciples of Jesus have no advantage over those of the latter days in terms of their faith relationship. "For both," Bultmann notes, "he stands the same distance away."[5] And he quotes approvingly Kierkegaard's remark: "There is no disciple at second hand. The first and the last are essentially on the same plane."[6] Thus to all generations, Jesus will reveal himself, but only through the response of faith to the self-revelation of God.

Rudolph Schnackenburg clarifies the interplay between revelation and faith. "Revelation is self-disclosure on the part of God."[7] But this communication is mediated to man through the prophets and above all by the Son who is the culmination and "the final and perfect revealer."[8] In opposition to Bultmann's narrowly existential view that revelation is not enlightenment but a happening, he insists that John teaches that revelation includes both the fact that Jesus is sent as the revealer and the content or message of that revelation.[9] Faith, for Schnackenburg is both intellectual and existential—involving "a total personal commitment to God"[10] and not simply a naked intellectual assent. Moreover, he notes the dual character of revelation, something we considered earlier in contrasting the disciples and the world.

Divine revelation is, therefore, "manifest" insofar as God potentially reveals and makes accessible to every man both himself and the revelation of salvation. Yet in another sense, it remains "hidden" insofar as it is not actually accessible to all men but only to those who believe.[11]

So far, from our analysis of the Johannine context, we see that the promised manifestation of Jesus comes primarily from the indwelling Paraclete, the Spirit of Jesus, and secondarily from the love—poured forth in our hearts by the Spirit—which brings peace and joy culminating in the experience of oneness. The awareness of this indwelling constitutes the fulfilment of the promise that Jesus made to manifest himself to all who believe in him and keep his commandments. Our next task, then, is to discover how manifest this divine revelation can be to those who excel in that total response which is a loving faith. We will consider what light mystical experience sheds on the Johannine text and the intensity of the promised manifestation.

THE MYSTICAL INTERPRETATION

Two great Carmelite mystics, both Doctors of the Church, have commented briefly on the Johannine text. Their writings are abundantly empirical, though clearly grounded in Thomistic theology. Of the two, St Teresa of Avila is the more descriptive; St John of the Cross, the more abstract. We will consider first St Teresa as she reports her own experiences and then St John as he discusses, also using psychological data, the theoretical structure of Christian mysticism.

St Teresa, in all her writings, insists on the necessity of the law of love—conformity to the will of God. For her, love means essentially that the wills of lovers be in harmony. Without this loving harmony, prayer is sterile; but with it, lavishly fruitful. She sums up her theology of prayer thus:

> All that the beginner in prayer has to do—and you must not forget this, for it is very important—is to labor and be resolute and prepare himself with all possible diligence to bring his will into conformity with the will of God. As I shall say later, you may be quite sure that this comprises the very greatest perfection which

can be attained on the spiritual road. The more perfectly a person practices it, the more he will receive of the Lord and the greater the progress he will make on this road.[12]

What is this great spiritual attainment? For St Teresa, and for most Christian mystics, it is transformation in God. The year before her death, she wrote a spiritual testimony, a report to the Bishop of Osma, who had once been her confessor. By this time, she had already experienced the transforming union or spiritual marriage, as she usually called it. In treating of this consummate union and the concomitant intellectual vision of the Trinity, she refers to the Johannine promise of which her experiences are the fulfillment.

> The presence of the three Persons is so impossible to doubt that it seems one experiences what St John [14:23] says, that they will make their abode in the soul. God does this by grace but also by presence.[13]

This awareness of presence is not merely the fruit of an act of faith, nor does it bypass faith. For faith must last as long as life does. Rather it is illumined faith, an intensification of the faith experience through unifying love, peace, and joy. As indicative of this conative aspect, note how, as she describes this intimate presence at its very apogee, she is still sensitively preoccupied with conformity to God's will.

> The presence is almost continual, except when a lot of sickness weighs down on one. For it sometimes seems God wants one to suffer without interior consolation: but, never, even in the first stirrings, does the will turn from its desire that *God's will* be done in it. The surrender to the *will of God* is so powerful that the soul wants neither death nor life, unless for a short time when it longs to die and see God. But soon the presence of the three Persons is represented to it so forcefully that this presence provides a remedy for the pain caused by his absence, and there remains the desire to live if *he will* in order to serve him the more.[14]

St John of the Cross, in speaking of the Johannine text, complements the interpretation of St Teresa that the promise is fulfilled by mystical experience. For both, it is applied to the same kinds of experience, the transforming union and intellectual visions; and for both, it is part of a journey in faith, "which alone is the proximate and proportionate means whereby the soul is united to God."[15] Nevertheless, he does not eliminate the possibility of further light, although he insists that faith differs from it "as pure gold from the basest metal."[16] In this same context, he gives a summary statement to the effect that Christian mysticism is really illumined faith and he sketches out the process of that illumination.

> The Holy Spirit illumines the understanding which is recollected, and illumines it according to the manner of its recollection, and the understanding cannot find any other and greater recollection than in faith; and thus the Holy Spirit will illumine it in naught more than in faith. For the purer and the more refined in faith is the soul, the more it has of the infused charity of God; and the more charity it has, the more it is illumined and the more the gifts of the Holy Spirit are communicated to it, for charity is the cause and the means whereby they are communicated to it.[17]

The direct references that St John of the Cross makes to the Johannine text are found in two different works. In the first, *The Ascent of Mount Carmel*, he discusses the stages that lead to the transforming union. Of special interest to us is his treatment of intellectual visions, like St Teresa's vision of the Trinity which we mentioned earlier. The function that they have in the developing life of contemplation will clarify the meaning of the Gospel word, "manifest."

St John distinguishes intellectual visions from sensory and imaginative ones, from which he would have souls detach themselves, for they easily impede union with God. Intellectual visions, however, are a touch of divinity, an experience and taste of God, "a part of the union towards which we are directing the soul; to which end we are teaching it to detach and strip itself of all other apprehensions."[18] Moreover, only those who have reached the state of union can have this knowledge, "because it is itself that union."[19] It is significant for us that he explicitly refers this naked knowledge or intellectual vision of God to the promise of Jesus. In fact, he tells us how to work for this great grace.

And the means by which God will do this must be humility and
suffering for the love of God with resignation as regards all reward;
for these favors are not granted to the soul which still cherishes
attachments, inasmuch as they are granted through a very special
love of God toward the soul which loves him likewise with great
detachment. *It is to this that the Son of God referred in St John* [He
quotes in full Jn 14:21]. *Herein are included the kinds of knowledge and touches to which we are referring, which God manifests
to the soul that truly loves him.*[20]

The second source of St John's references to the Johannine text
is a book which deals with perfection within perfection, *The
Living Flame of Love*. Earlier, he had discussed at great length
the transforming union, now he even surpasses himself in the
depth and sublimity of his analysis. "For although in the stanzas
which we expounded above [in the *Spiritual Canticle*], we spoke
of the most perfect degree of perfection to which a man may attain
in this life, which is transformation in God, nevertheless these
stanzas [in the *Living Flame of Love*] treat of a love which is
even more complete and perfected within this same state of
transformation."[21] In this rarefied mystical context, the reference
in the Prologue to Jn 14:23 dramatically reveals the dimensions
Christ's promise has for St John of the Cross.

There is no reason for marvelling that God should grant such high
and rare favors to those on whom he bestows consolations. For if
we consider that he is God and that he bestows them as God, with
infinite love and goodness, it will not seem to us unreasonable. For
God said that the Father and the Son and the Holy Spirit would
come to him that loved him and make their abode in him, and this
would come to pass by his making him live and dwell in the Father
and the Son and the Holy Spirit, in the life of God, as the soul
explains in these stanzas.[22]

St John of the Cross made two redactions of the *Flame*; in both
the section quoted from the prologue is the same. But in the
second redaction, when commenting on the first stanza of his
poem, he repeats the substance of the prologue section with some
minor variations and one important addition concerning the

means to be used. That change is significant here, not because he speaks of purgation and charity as required for divine union—that is his standard teaching—but because he assumes that if these are perfected, the soul will then experience, specifically as a fulfillment of Christ's promise, the mystical glories that he writes about.

> And it must not be held incredible that in a faithful soul which has already been tried and proven in the fire of tribulations and trials, and found faithful in love, there should be fulfilled that which was promised by the Son of God—namely that, if any man love him, the Holy Spirit would come within him and would abide and dwell in him."[23]

To sum up what we have seen so far of the Carmelite interpretation of the Johannine text, we conclude that: (1) the promise of Christ issues a general invitation to the fullness of the mystical life; (2) the mystical life is necessarily illumined faith, the soul's experience of being united with God; and (3) this illumination depends of love which is characterized by perfect detachment from creatures and perfect conformity to the will of God.

THE RESOLUTION OF DIFFICULTIES

Despite the cogency of the Carmelite interpretation of the Johannine promise, some exegetes show a deep reluctance to admit any mystical dimension whatsoever. Even Raymond E. Brown, wide-ranging and balanced though he is, seems to share slightly in this anti-mystical bias. He is at pains to safeguard the fundamental meaning of the text from any facilely romantic or vaguely gnostic misunderstanding that the notion, mystical, might suggest. And yet, authentic Christian mysticism must be grounded in the New Testament, including the Gospel of John.

We will examine three caveat-propositions derived from Brown. A clear appreciation of them will sharpen our focus on the richness of the experience that Jesus has promised to those who love him and on the relationship of that promise to true mysticism. In general, we can agree with the wisdom of these warnings without, however, having to conclude that a mystical interpretation or application of the text is unjustified. By doing so, we will be able to see actually how harmoniously the Carmelite interpretation accords with the essential holdings of modern Catholic exegesis. The three propositions are: first, the promised manifestation is not reducible exclusively to a vertical relationship with God; second, the promised manifestation is not restricted to the mystic presence encountered by an ascetical elite; and, third, the promised manifestation is not equivalent to a direct gnostic vision of the Godhead. Let us now examine each proposition separately.

When Brown speaks of Johannine unity, he distinguishes two kinds: the horizontal which the believers have among themselves and the vertical which they have with the Father and the Son. Both kinds are, of course, effectuated through the presence of the Paraclete. Brown does insist; "Unity for John is not reducible to a mystical relationship with God."[24] But he does not reduce unity to the horizontal or communal level either. "The vertical dimension, apparent in the frequent statements about immanence in the Last Discourse . . . means that the unity is not simply human fellowship or the harmonious interaction of Christians."[25]

Certainly, Christian mystics, although they appear to emphasize the vertical relationship, are keenly aware of the horizontal prerequisites. No true mystic attains the desired union with Christ unless he shares in his love for the members of his Body. Thus, St Teresa, writing about the Fifth Mansion of *The Interior Castle*, where she discusses the prayer of simple union—wherein the intellect and the interior powers are made passive, the will having already been made so in the prayer of quiet —explains the necessity of both dimensions. First, she sets up the goal: "What do you suppose his will is, daughters? That we should be altogether perfect and one with him and the Father as in His Majesty's prayer [Jn 17:21-23]."[26] She then elaborates on the necessity for this twofold love for anyone who hopes to enter the Fifth Mansion and attain union.

The Lord asks only two things of us: love for His Majesty and love for our neighbor. It is for these two virtues that we must strive, and if we attain them perfectly we are doing his will and so shall be united with him. But, as I have said, how far are we from doing these two things in the way that we ought for a God who is so great! May His Majesty be pleased to give us grace so that we may deserve to reach this state, as it is in our power to do so if we wish.[27]

The recognition of the need to preserve the general coverage of the promise—that the manifestation will be made to *everyone* who believes in Jesus and loves him—sometimes leads to an anti-mystical imbalance. Thus, for example, in writing of the promised manifestation (Jn 14:21), Brown states that the passage is not "concerned with the presence of Jesus encountered by the mystics: the presence of Jesus is promised, not to an ascetical elite, but to Christians in general."[28]

Obviously, Brown's intent is not to exclude Christian mystics, but to include all Christian believers. And rightly so, granted the fulfillment of the requisite condition. But what is that? "The condition upon which the indwelling depends: keeping Jesus' commandments and thus loving him."[29] Those who have fulfilled this condition most profoundly and wholeheartedly can be expected to experience this indwelling most fully. There is no doubt in Brown's mind that John considers presence as proportionate to love. He states explicitly: "The presence of Jesus in the Christian stands in parallelism with the presence of love in the Christian."[30] He goes even further: "The indwelling and the recognition are coordinate. As Bengel put it, the lack of recognition rules out indwelling, while indwelling is the basis of recognition."[31] A mystic, like St John of the Cross, would readily subscribe to such language. His own formulation is unequivocal.

God communicates himself most to that soul that has progressed farthest in love; namely, that has its will in the closest conformity with the will of God. And the soul that has attained complete conformity and likeness of will is totally united and transformed in God supernaturally.[32]

A concern over the syncretic character of much current spirituality and a lingering fear of gnostic tendencies in general, has prompted a cautious approach to "mystic" interpretations of St John. Thus, when Brown speaks of that great text, "That they may know you, the one true God, and Jesus Christ, the one whom you sent" (Jn 17:3), he calls it "the most 'gnostic' statement in the Bible."[33] But he hastens to distinguish it from Gnosticism, "for it is rooted in a historic event in a way in which gnostic thought is not."[34] He explains further, "Here 'know' means to be in a vital and intimate relationship with the Father and Jesus, and such a relationship comes through faith in Jesus and hearing his words."[35] Then he focuses on a point that is crucial for us: "John never suggests that this relationship can come through ecstatic contemplation of the divinity as in the *Hermetica*, nor through a mystic vision of God, as in the mysteries."[36] To grant Brown's conclusion, however, in no way rules out a Johannine mysticism; but it does require us to specify what this mysticism involves.

A common misunderstanding of Christian mystical experience is that it affords, after heroic purification, a direct vision of the Godhead. If so, the effects promised by Jesus—peace and joy and oneness—fall far short of this sublime gnosis, this face to face knowledge of God. But mystical experience and the beatific vision are not the same thing and St John does not confuse them. After contrasting Jesus with Moses, he says, "No one has ever seen God; it is God the only Son, ever at the Father's side, who has revealed him" (Jn 1:18).[37] In this connection, the Carmelite understanding of mystical experience proves fully in accord with Scripture. St Teresa states the principle simply: "The soul recognizes the presence of God by the effects which he produces in the soul, for it is by that means that His Majesty is pleased to make his presence felt."[38] She develops this important consideration:

> A kind of consciousness of the presence of God . . . is often experienced, excepially by those who have reached the Prayer of Union and the Prayer of Quiet. There we are on the point of beginning our prayer when we seem to know that he is hearing us by the spiritual feelings and effects of great love and faith of which we

become conscious, and also by the fresh resolutions which we make with such deep emotion. This favor comes from God: and he to whom it is granted should esteem it highly for it is a very lofty form of prayer. But it is not a vision.[39]

St Teresa applies this same principle when she speaks of spiritual marriage in the Seventh Mansion of *The Interior Castle*. She relates how her soul experiences "the greatest joy because Christ is now its life."[40] In order to assure herself of this special grace, she looks to the effects produced in her soul.

This, with the passage of time, becomes more evident through its effects; for the soul clearly understands by certain secret aspirations that it is endowed with life by God. Very often these aspirations are so vehement that what they teach cannot possibly be doubted; though they cannot be described, the soul experiences them very forcibly. One can only say that this feeling is produced at times by certain delectable words which, it seems, the soul cannot help uttering, such as, "O life of my life and sustenance that sustaineth me!" and things of that kind.[41].

St John of the Cross deals similarly with the possibility of a direct vision of incorporeal or spiritual substances—souls, angels, God. "Though these spiritual substances cannot be unclothed and seen clearly in this life by the intellect, they can nonetheless be felt in the substance of the soul by the most delightful touches and conjunctions."[42] So, fundamentally and essentially, mysticism is a faith experience, not vision. "This dark, loving knowledge, which is faith, serves as a means for the divine union in this life as does the light of glory for the clear vision of God in the next."[43] It is easy to see how far this view is from any claim to gnostic immediacy and how well it comports with the modalities of the Johannine promise.

In short, these three caveat-propositions which we have gathered together from Brown's discussion—warning us against a mysticism which is purely vertical, ascetically elitist, and presumptuously immediate—are not at variance with the Carmelite interpretation of the Johannine text, but rather, if understood fully, reinforce what is constitutive of all sound Christian mysticism.

CONCLUSION

Our focus has been on the promise of Jesus to whomever loves truly: "I will manifest myself to him." Both exegetes and mystics interpret the promised manifestation as a consciousness of union with Jesus through the indwelling of the Paraclete—the Holy Spirit acting as the personal presence of the absent Jesus.

This manifestation is not a direct vision of God but rather an intimate sense of union with him through the effects of love, joy and peace culminating in experience of oneness. St John's Gospel contains explicit pledges of these effects: the Carmelite Doctors use the Johannine texts to explain their own mystical experience and teaching. The highest mystical states, including the transforming union, are for them functions or fulfillments of this glorious promise.

It is not surprising that the first principle of Christian mysticism be found in St John's Gospel, which has been described as "the charter of mystics." For, as Brown observes, "The dominant interest in John is one of realized eschatology."[44] John, of course, also teaches an apocalyptic or future eschatology, but what is relevant for us is his emphasis on present actualizations: we already have eternal life; we now share in the glory which is to come; we experience through loving obedience the manifestation of Jesus himself.

Law and love and light, then, are progressive phases of the divine experience. This challenge of transcendence would clearly surpass our noblest efforts were it not for the promise and the presence of the Spirit of Jesus. Through the Paraclete, we can conform so perfectly to the will of God that—even in this life—we can receive a foretaste of that eternal Beauty which alone can quiet the restless surgings of our soul.

NOTES

1. The critical word, ἐμφανίσω, is translated variously but not conflictingly: Brown in the Anchor Bible and Knox use "reveal"; The Jerusalem Bible and the University of Chicago (Goodspeed) Bible use "show"; and the Douai-Rheims (Challoner) Bible uses "manifest." The latter reflects the Vulgate's "manifestabo" and was familiar to most of the mystics of the Latin Church, including St Teresa and St John of the Cross. Therefore, we will use the older translation for the text, John 14:21-23, but usually elsewhere we will follow the Anchor Bible translation by Raymond E. Brown, *The Gospel According to John*, (New York: Doubleday & Co., Inc., 1966 & 1970), Vols. 29 and 29A in "Anchor Bible" series.

2. Brown, p. 1141.

3. *Ibid.*, p. 653.

4. Rudolf Bultmann, *The Gospel of John*, trans. G. R. Beasley-Murray, (Philadelphia: The Westminster Press, 1971), p. 570.

5. *Ibid.*, p. 559. Cf. also the similar statement by Brown, p. 1142: "The later Christian is no further removed from the ministry of Jesus than was the earlier Christian, for the Paraclete dwells within him as he dwelt within the eyewitnesses. And by recalling and giving new meaning to what Jesus said, the Paraclete guides every generation in facing new situations; he declares the things to come (xvi 13)."

6. Bultmann, p. 559, n. 2 quoting from Kierkegaard, *Philosophical Fragments*, trans. David Swenson, (Oxford: Oxford University Press, 1936).

7. Rudolph Schnackenburg, *The Truth Will Make You Free*, trans. by R. Albrecht (New York: Herder and Herder, 1966), p. 94.

8. *Ibid.*, p. 99.

9. *Ibid.*, pp. 102-03.

10. *Ibid.*, p. 117. He refers to Vatican I, Session III, Chap. 3 (Denzinger 3008): "Since man is totally dependent upon God as upon his Creator and Lord, and since created reason is wholly subject to uncreated truth, we are bound to give to the revealing God, in faith, full obedience of intellect and will."

11. *Ibid.*, p. 113.

12. St Teresa, C, 2, 1, 8. (*The Complete Works of St Teresa*, trans. and ed. by E. Allison Peers).

13. *Spiritual Relations*, No. VI, Peers ed., p. 336 = Spiritual Testimony No. 9, I.C.S. ed., p. 365. EDITOR'S NOTE: The Alleluia Verse in the Carmelite Lectionary for the Mass of St Teresa on October 15 is this same passage from Jn 14:23. The obvious reason for its presence is the notion of indwelling and the current liturgical translation uses the word "dwelling-place," just as in the new I.C.S. ed. of *The Interior Castle*.

14. *Ibid.*

15. St John of the Cross, A, 2, 9, 1. (*The Complete Works of St John of the Cross*, trans. and ed. by E. Allison Peers).

16. A, 2, 29, 6.

17. *Ibid.*

18. A, 2, 26, 10.

19. A, 2, 26, 5.

20. A, 2, 26, 10.
21. F, Prologue, 3.
22. F, Prologue, 2.
23. F, 1, 15.
24. Brown, p. 776.
25. *Ibid.*
26. St Teresa, C, 5, 3, 7.
27. *Ibid.*
28. Brown, p. 646.
29. *Ibid.*
30. *Ibid.*, p. 781.
31. *Ibid.*, p. 639.
32. St John of the Cross, A, 2, 5, 4.
33. Brown, p. 507.
34. *Ibid.*, pp. 507–08.
35. *Ibid.*, p. 508.
36. *Ibid.*
37. See Brown's commentary on verse 18, pp. 17–18, 35–36. See also John 4:12 and 1 John 3:2.
38. St. Teresa, L, 27, 4.
39. *Ibid.*
40. C, 7, 2, 5.
41. *Ibid.*
42. St John of the Cross, A, 2, 24, 2. For this text and the next, I have used the more accurate translation of K. Kavanaugh and O. Rodriguez from *The Collected Works of St John of the* Cross, (Washington: ICS Publications, 1973).
43. *Ibid.*
44. Brown, p. 507.